UK & EUROPEAN
SHARE PRICE BEHAVIOUR:
THE EVIDENCE

UK & European Share Price Behaviour: The Evidence

Paul H Richards

Kogan Page, London
Nichols Publishing Company, New York

First published in Great Britain in 1979 by
Kogan Page Limited, 120 Pentonville Road, London N1
ISBN 0 85038 117 7

First published in the United States of America in 1979
by Nichols Publishing Company, PO Box 96, New York
NY 10024

Library of Congress Catalog No
78-24735
ISBN 0-89397-053-0

Printed in Great Britain by
Anchor Press, Tiptree, Essex

Acknowledgements

I should like to express my gratitude for permission to reproduce the following articles:

M G Kendall — 'The analysis of economic time series, Part 1: Prices', *Journal of the Royal Statistical Society,* Vol 116 (A), 1953

R A Brealey — 'The distribution and independence of successive rates of return from the British equity market', *Journal of Business Finance,* Vol 2, 1970, (Mercury House Business Publications Limited)

M M Dryden — 'Filter tests of UK share prices', *Applied Economics,* Vol 1, 1970, (Chapman & Hall Limited)

D H Girmes and D C Damant — 'Charts and the random walk', *The Investment Analyst,* No 41, 1975

J M Brew — 'The trustees' meeting - a city daydream', *The Investment Analyst,* No 28, 1970

R A Brealey — 'The impact of the market on British share prices', *The Investment Analyst,* No 24, 1969

S D Hodges and R A Brealey — 'Using the Sharpe model', *The Investment Analyst,* No 27, 1970

M A Firth — 'The performance of share recommendations made by investment analysts and the effects on market efficiency', *Journal of Business Finance,* Vol 4, 1972 (Mercury House Business Publications Limited)

M A Firth — 'An empirical investigation of the impact of the announcement of capitalisation issues on share prices', *Journal of Business Finance and Accounting,* Vol 4/1, 1977, (Basil Blackwell, Oxford)

M A Firth — 'The information content of large investment holdings', *Journal of Finance,* Vol XXX, No 5, 1975

R C Morris — 'Evidence of the impact of inflation accounting on share prices', *Accounting and Business Research,* spring 1975

A Saunders and P S Woodward ✕ 'Money supply and share prices: the evidence for the UK in the post-CCC period', *The Investment Analyst,* No 46, 1976

J M Samuels 'The performance of unit trusts', *The Bankers Magazine,* 1493, 1968, (BPC (Bankers Magazine) Limited)

T E Cranshaw 'Do new unit trusts perform better than old ones?' *The Investment Analyst,* No 26, 1970

J Dixon 'Composite measures of performance', summary thesis, Exeter University 1972

C W R Ward and A Saunders 'UK unit trust risk-return performance 1964-1974', *Journal of Business Finance and Accounting,* Vol 3/4, 1976, (Basil Blackwell, Oxford)

P Moles and B Taylor 'Unit trust risk-return performance', 1966-1975, *The Investment Analyst,* No 47, 1977

P H Richards 'Sharpe performance among pension funds?' *The Investment Analyst,* No 51, 1978

B H Solnik 'Note on the validity of the random walk for European stock prices', *Journal of Finance,* Vol XXVIII, No 5, 1973

J G McDonald 'French mutual fund performance: evaluation of internationally-diversified portfolios', *Journal of Finance,* Vol XXVIII, No 5, 1973

I should also like to thank Anthony Henfrey and Charles Ward for helpful comments and Sharon Rouse for her excellent typing.

Contents

Preface

Peter Baker, Managing Director, Schlesinger Investment Management Services Ltd.

I am delighted to write this preface to Paul Richards' book, which is an excellent and necessary addition to the literature on stock market efficiency. It sets out the implications for investment management on the basis that at least part of the market is efficiently priced. It is also a very valuable reference work given the format of introductory sections to each chapter followed by selected relevant articles.

It would be my hope that the debate which should be re-opened on publication will concentrate not so much on whether or not the market is fully efficient, but rather on what the implictions are for the investment industry if the market is in part efficient. The evidence is that the skill and expertise of the major investing institutions and their advisers, tend to make the major capitalisation stocks efficiently priced. (I am referring principally to the top 100 companies in the *Financial Times* actuaries all-share index which account for some two-thirds of the total capitalisation of the stocks comprising the all-share index).

The evidence, and indeed practical experience, suggests that it is not possible for any investor, institutional or otherwise, to out-perform the market index investing only in companies from the top 100 group. Given the fact that the major institutions have no real alternative to concentrating a major part of their UK portfolio in the top 100 group, does this not explain why the index is difficult to beat?

In his introduction Paul Richards refers to the 'important and indeed revolutionary implications for investment' arising from the concept of stock market efficiency. The main implication is that there is a powerful case for institutions to adopt a 'passive' investment approach to that 'core' of a portfolio likely to be invested in the top 100 companies, whilst pursuing an 'active' approach in 'recovery' stocks, small companies and the higher-yielding parts of the market within a properly diversified portfolio. Research resources could then be directed towards those parts of the market which appear to contain pricing inefficiencies. Unit trusts specialising in smaller companies and in 'recovery' - type securities have demonstrated good investment results relative to the index over statistically meaningful periods: this may represent evidence of some market inefficiency. As a rider to the concept of passive management, one obvious consequence is the cost of such management. In the US there is a differential management fee structure depending on whether passive or active management is pursued. Indeed the low management costs are one of the chief attractions of the index fund.

On the research front there is clearly a case for a change in the structure of brokers' research. At present the weight of investment research is towards the top 100 companies since these generate most business. Resources should be switched to those parts of the market which may be inefficiently priced, such as smaller market capitalisation stocks. The thinking stockbroker planning the possible future development of his business should certainly take these thoughts into consideration.

One development which can be confidently anticipated is the emergence of more stockbroker research relating to overall portfolio strategy rather than individual stock selection. There is nothing in the UK to match the outstanding work available on strategy in the US from, for example, Goldman Sachs, EF Hutton and Donaldson Lufkin and Jenrette.

The chapter on risk and performance (Chapter 2) should be required reading for all financial journalists whose duties include articles on the 'performance tables'. Such articles are consistently silent on the reality that risk and return are inter-related. Risk analysis and risk appraisal are in their infancy in the investment industry in the UK. The quality financial press has a responsibility to educate its readers on the facts that good 'performance', or high volatility, may just be a reflection of high risk and a poorly diversified portfolio. Professional investment managers have a responsibility not to persuade private individual investors to invest on the back of 'hot' performance, where such performance is attributable only to luck or high risk. Why are performance numbers which are not at all risk-adjusted given any credence in the UK? (As an aside I was delighted to see John Brew's classic article *The Trustees Meeting — A City Daydream* included in Chapter 2: if you missed it before, take the opportunity of reading it now.)

Paul Richards' book no doubt will find its way into the libraries of most institutions and stockbrokers. It is an important book dealing with a subject that the investment industry in the UK must face up to. Modern portfolio theory, of which market efficiency is but part, is not a passing fad. In the US, it has arrived in force with dramatic effects on the investment industry. Modern portfolio theory is largely in its infancy in terms of comprehension in the UK. It will develop here in due course and, in my view, with 'revolutionary' implications for the investment industry.

Introduction

The behaviour of commodity prices is a matter of concern for us all. Whether an aspiring Rockefeller or Bernie Cornfeld, or even a humble consumer of the end product, the market process by which commodity prices are determined impinges on everyone. It is not, therefore, surprising that much effort is and has been devoted to analysing this process, particularly with a view to producing price forecasts and thereby making profits. This book is primarily concerned with one type of commodity — European ordinary shares and in particular, those listed on the Stock Exchange (London), although much of the work and analysis set out here can be extended to and has obvious implications for other commodity markets such as the raw material commodity markets, the foreign exchange markets, and so on.

It is often suggested that investment is more of an art than a science, requiring 'flair' or 'imagination' or other intangible skills. This argument is sometimes invoked to explain successful results based on investment strategies which appear to lack any rationale: consider the examples of school investment teams, or the use of a pin, two methods which have sometimes been able to perform better than the professionals. However, the advent of computers has greatly facilitated the scientific analysis of share price behaviour. Consequently much work has been and is being undertaken to understand better this behaviour. The results of this work (often published in academic journals) have led to the formulation of the concept of 'efficiency' which has important and indeed revolutionary implications for investment. It is true that a theoretical justification for these results has been provided by Samuelson [1] based on the assumption of a perfect market. However, it is accepted that we live in a real and imperfect world and therefore throughout the book the emphasis is on what is observed and not what should be observed. 'Efficient Market Hypothesis' is thus an appropriate choice of name for this concept.

The nature of efficiency or the efficient market hypothesis can be explained quite easily. An efficient market is a place where the prices prevailing are the best available guide to the value or worth of the commodity being traded. Thus there is no better indicator of the value of a share than its current market price. The revolutionary nature of this concept lies in three major implications:

(i) Chartism (ie looking at historic prices) is a waste of time.
(ii) Much investment analysis has no economic value.
(iii) Professionally managed funds on average do no better and probably worse than a naïve policy of buy and hold.

As an explanation of the way the UK stockmarket works, the efficient market hypothesis is largely confirmed by the evidence. The reason for this is simple. The presence of many investors, analysts, stockbrokers etc in the market-place for shares ensures that competition is fierce and, as a result, share prices are generally right. That is to say, shares in general are neither cheap nor dear. In fact the stockmarket is quite a safe place because you are unlikely to pay too much for any particular share: equally, bargains will not come your way.

The ramifications of this discovery are considered in detail in the Conclusion. However it must be clear that if share prices are efficient, then a good deal of investment research is probably wasted. Indeed, the whole investment process is called into question. Should any time at all be devoted to investment analysis if share prices are efficient? Of course the answer is yes, for it is this type of activity which makes for efficiency. But the question which remains is whether there is too much investment research and whether the investment process, as it works at present, chokes off the excess?

Each of the three implications above follows from the three separate forms of the efficient market hypothesis and each form as it relates to the UK stockmarket is the subject of a chapter (Chapters 1, 3 and 4). Chapter 2 develops risk as the most important parameter in portfolio performance appraisal. A number of techniques are described which are used in later chapters. Chapter 5 is a review of the efficiency of European stockmarkets. This is not as comprehensive as the UK review but covers most of Europe.

Each chapter contains an introduction which reviews and analyses the UK research work relating to that topic. This is followed by a selection of the articles reviewed. The articles reproduced are chosen for their clarity and comprehensibility. Each introduction provides a synopsis and summary of the research literature while at the same time leaving much in the articles themselves into which the reader can delve.

CHAPTER 1

The Weak Form of the Efficient Market Hypothesis

The study of the behaviour of share prices has been greatly facilitated by the compilation of data on share prices in computerised data banks. Much work has been performed using these data banks, particularly in the US and as a result great advances have been made in portfolio science. Less work has been undertaken in the UK although a number of institutions, notably London and City Business Schools and a number of stockbrokers, have recently established data banks. Although perhaps lagging behind the US in this respect, the UK can claim to be one of the first in the field (Kendall's [2] work was published in 1953). One of the early conclusions of this work is that share prices appear to move randomly or unpredictably. That is to say, no pattern or logic could be observed in a series of share prices. This led initially to the formulation of the random walk theory and later, the efficient market hypothesis, as an explanation for the results of this research. The basic method on which the research is based is to determine whether profits can be made in the stockmarket by using the various techniques available — chartism, fundamental analysis and so on. It would appear (and this is the conclusion of the articles reproduced in this book) that in general one cannot do better than a simple policy of buying shares and holding them. In other words, the various valuation techniques do not help. One explanation of this phenomenon is that market prices are 'efficient' and that they already reflect the benefit of such valuation techniques. It is the competitive nature of the market, where prices are continuously under review from analysts and fund managers, which ensures that shares are efficiently priced.

As an explanation of share price behaviour, the random walk theory has encountered a certain amount of opposition. The suggestion that share prices fluctuate at random is taken to imply that prices are somehow without cause or that they are plucked out of the air and bear no relation to reality. Naturally, as a view of the way the stockmarket works this is regarded as ludicrous by even the least financially sophisticated. Indeed, further comparisons of the market-place to a fair game, (eg tossing a fair coin), have alienated the ideas even more. Of course the hypothesis is not saying this at all, rather it is saying the complete opposite. It is the high level of expertise of analysts and fund managers and the competition between them which ensures the efficient setting of prices and thereby the random nature of price changes.

Some further clarification may help. Efficient pricing implies that the market price of a share, at any moment in time, represents and discounts all that there is to know about that share. In other words, if a competent investment analyst were to go through all the available data relating to that particular company — accounts, industry data, economic statistics etc — and then make forecasts, and even if he were then to check these with other analysts, he is most likely to arrive at an estimate of the share price which is equal to the then market price. He would therefore conclude that the shares were neither undervalued nor overvalued. If an event occurs subsequently which alters the value of the firm and therefore the price of the shares, then such a change in the price must be random. Because if the change was not random this would mean that it could have been predicted, and if it could have been predicted then the effect on the share price would have already been discounted and no price change would have occurred.

Consider an example, a service company, consisting solely of £1,000 in liquid assets, treasury bills say, and having 1,000 shares in issue. In a simple world the share price will be £1. Now suppose the firm tenders for a contract which is worth £1,000. That is, if the firm gets the contract it will receive £1,000 in cash. Suppose further that there is competition for the contract and that our firm's chances of landing it are only 2/5ths (ie 2 out of 5). If the company announces it has a 40 per cent chance of securing a £1,000 contract, the share price would immediately rise to discount the value of this possibility. The value of the possibility is the mathematical expectation. This is simply the sum of the probabilities of each outcome multiplied by the value accruing to the firm under each outcome.

In our example, it is the following sum:

Two possible outcomes:

(i) Firm wins contract,
chances x value of outcome = 2/5ths x £1,000 = £400

(ii) Firm loses contract,
chances x value of outcome = 3/5ths x £0   = 0
Mathematical expectation   = **£400**

The value of the firm would rise to £1,400 to reflect the possibility of winning the contract. If the firm is successful and announces the winning of the contract the value of the firm will rise to £2,000 and the share price will rise to £2 per share to discount fully the value of the contract. If, on the other hand, the contract is awarded elsewhere our firm's share price will fall back to its original level of £1 reflecting no permanent change in the firm's value.

The three distinct states of the firm are set out below.

	Time = 1	Time = 2	Time = 3	
Announcement		Announce tender offer and chances of success	Announce success or	Announce failure
Value of firm	£1,000	£1,000 + 2/5ths x £1,000	£2,000	£1,000
Share Price	£1	£1.40	£2	£1

The change of share price between the second and third periods is a *random* movement. The analysis has shown that we cannot predict any more accurately the value of the firm prior to the award of the contract. The price movement between periods 2 and 3 is due entirely to chance. This does not mean that the firm placing the contract is behaving irrationally or indeed in a random fashion. Decisions on the placing of contracts are complex and involve the comparison of sometimes unquantifiable benefits (quality, delivery etc) and certainly an element of luck is bound to be involved.

Of course it can be argued that the example is somewhat artificial. No account has been taken of changes in the general market level. No doubt between periods 1 and 2, the pound will have fallen US five cents and between periods 2 and 3 government ministers will be

14

announcing cuts in public expenditure or an end to cuts or even both. These events will inevitably affect the general level of security prices. It is for this reason that it is often unwise to attribute share price movements to particular events. However, for the purposes of illustration, a somewhat ideal world (ie no politicians) is assumed, but this in no way invalidates the demonstration of the random process. Whatever product a firm is selling, demand for it will always be subject to a certain amount of uncertainty. It is this type of uncertainty from which the random nature of stock price changes derives.

The efficient market hypothesis can now be specified in a little more detail. The hypothesis suggests that investors, analysts and fund managers who operate in a competitive market are so expert at evaluating the worth of shares, that shares generally are fairly valued, being neither over-valued nor under-valued. Any subsequent adjustment to the share price must be random for the reasons given above. As a result, prices must follow a random walk. That is to say, each price change is random and is independent of the previous price change. But this is not to say that share prices are equally likely to go up as down. In our example the most likely (3/5ths chance) change of price between periods 2 and 3 is in fact downwards. However, the random walk hypothesis is perfectly consistent with a market which, as has been demonstrated over the longer term, has steadily risen.

As already mentioned, the hypothesis has been developed to explain various phenomena observed in studies of share price behaviour. These studies have important implications for all those concerned, however indirectly, with the stockmarket. For this reason it is useful to look briefly at the history of the development of the efficient market hypothesis.

History

Much of the empirical work on share price behaviour was performed during the 1960s following some work in the previous decade which had broken much new ground. However, one of the earliest studies was undertaken by Bachélier [3] in 1900. In his doctoral dissertation Bachélier set out for the first time a mathematical theory of speculative prices based on the proposition that share prices should have independent increments (ie today's price change should be independent of yesterday's). This theory was tested successfully against the French Government bond market over the period 1894-98. The most important principle he enunciated was that 'the mathematical expectation of the speculator is zero'. Equally, Bachélier is saying that the commodity market is a 'fair game'. This needs a little more explanation. Consider a fair roulette wheel without a zero and no other house bias. If you invest £1 in the 'odd numbers' consider what your mathematical expectation will be.

Two possible outcomes:

(i) Odd number comes up, win £1: probability x value of outcome	=	½ x £1	=	£0.50
(ii) Even number comes up, lose £1 stake: probability x value of outcome	=	½ x (–£1)	=	–£0.50
Mathematical expectation			=	**zero**

So having placed the bet, the expectation of the gambler is zero. Thus over a long period of time, and providing he can afford to continue playing, the gambler should come out even.

And so with commodity prices. In other words, providing the speculator can afford to continue playing (ie investing) in the long run he should come out even, making neither abnormal gains nor abnormal losses. Referring back to our example of the firm tendering for a contract, we can calculate the mathematical expectation of a shareholder buying at the end of period 2 at £1.40:

Two possible outcomes:

    (i) Firm wins contract, price rises to £2:
        (a profit of £0.60)
        probability x value of outcome   =   2/5ths x £0.60   =   24p

   (ii) Firm loses contract, price falls to £1:
        (a loss of £0.40)
        probability x value of outcome   =   3/5ths x (−£0.40) =   −24p

Mathematical expectation   =   **zero**

Once again the expectation is zero. Thus we can be as confident buying shares as when betting on a 'fair' roulette wheel. We know that in the long term we should come out even.

The next advance in the development of these ideas occurred somewhat by chance. A distinguished British statistician, Kendall [2], was investigating the behaviour of economic indicators over a period of time to determine whether long-term trends could be distinguished from short-term fluctuations. Kendall was trying to identify effects, similar to say trade cycles, in a series of weekly price data. Kendall used various series some of which were sector indices of share prices.

The conclusions of his work are worth quoting. 'In series of prices which are observed at fairly close intervals the random changes from one term to the next are so large as to swamp any systematic effect which may be present. The data behave almost like wandering series.'

Kendall was unable to discover any underlying trends and so could not derive any meaningful process which would help forecast future prices. Price movements appeared to be independent. Kendall concluded that, 'Investors can perhaps make money on the Stock Exchange, but not apparently by watching price movements and coming in on what looks like a good thing'.

Then, in 1959, two provocative papers were published in the US which triggered off a good deal of intensive cross-checking of the results. In the first, Roberts [4] was able to simulate the appearance of a chart of a market index by adding random numbers together. Starting with a number (445 in the diagram) he then added a random number to obtain the change on the first week, and a second random number to obtain the change in level between week 1 and week 2 and so on, thus obtaining a simulated chart of an index.

The power of this work is best illustrated diagrammatically. Figure 1a is a chart of the Dow Jones Industrial Average over a 52-week period. Below in Figure 1b, the simulated market level is charted. The similarity is striking. One can imagine a chartist expounding on the significance of the head and shoulders formation and whether or not a resistance level was being tested at week 43.

Roberts repeated this exercise for price movements, using random numbers again to generate price changes for the simulated index. Figure 2a records weekly changes in the Dow Jones Industrial Average during 1956 while below in Figure 2b, simulated changes in the index are plotted. Once again the simulated prices could pass for an actual series of

Figure 1a: Actual levels of stockmarket prices for 52 weeks

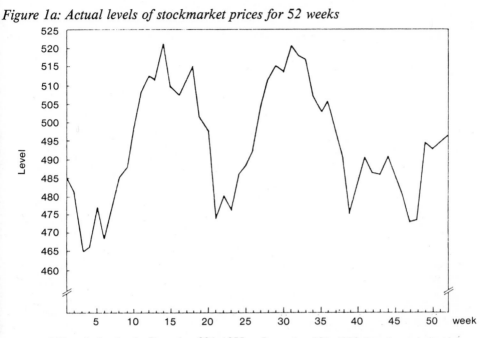

Friday closing levels, December 30th 1955 — December 28th 1956 Dow Jones Industrial Average

Figure 1b: Simulated levels of stockmarket prices

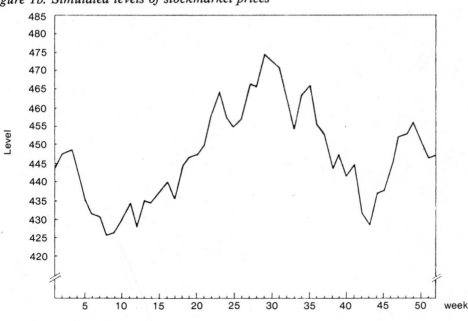

Source: Roberts, Stock Market Patterns, pp 5-6

Figure 2a: Actual changes in weekly stock prices for 52 weeks

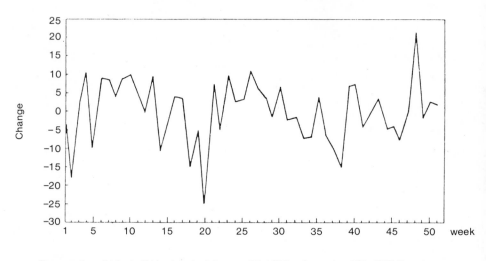

Changes from Friday to Friday (closing) January 6th 1956 — December 28th 1956, Dow Jones Industrial Average

Figure 2b: Simulated changes in weekly stock prices for 52 weeks

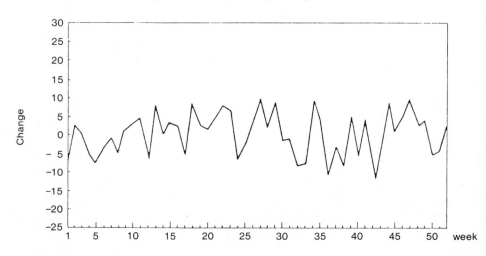

Source: Roberts, Stock Market Patterns, pp 5-6

price movements. No doubt a chartist could draw some sort of conclusion from the diagram as before.

However, this analogy helps to explain the nature of the random walk hypothesis. Each price change is independent of the previous change in the same way as random numbers are independent of each other. So, any chart of a share price over a period of time must look like a 'wandering series' to use Kendall's expression.

But this does not imply that the price change is in itself random. Price movements are merely reflections of changes in investors' expectations of returns. And these expectations are based on rational assessments which vary as events occur: for example, the winning of a contract in the earlier example. It is these events which occur at random and which therefore give rise to random share price movements. The role of the investor in this process is completely rational.

However, although strongly suggestive, this type of pictorial representation does not necessarily 'prove' that share prices follow a random walk. It certainly has a powerful impact, but it was left to other researchers to provide scientific evidence.

Osborne [5], a naval physicist, was one of those researchers. He scientifically analysed share prices to determine whether the price movements behaved according to the laws governing the movements of small particles in suspension — Brownian motion. Kendall had in fact already coined the expression 'economic Brownian motion'. His results were positive, implying that price changes are independent.

In the next decade in the US there was much intensive verification of these results using more extensive banks of data. These studies provide substantial support for the tentative conclusions of the early researchers. The explanation of the findings of this work is known as the *Efficient Market Hypothesis*. This is formulated in three distinct forms, the first of which is the subject of the rest of this chapter.

Weak Form Hypothesis

The weak form of the hypothesis is a restatement of the random walk model. The weak form states that historic price movements cannot be used to predict future price movements; or, as already stated, successive price movements are independent of (ie unrelated to) previous price movements. In other words, chartists who use historic price information to predict future-prices are basically wasting their time. Kendall provides the earliest evidence for this and his results warrant closer investigation.

Kendall [2]

In 1953, Kendall conducted a statistical investigation into the behaviour of commodity prices over a period of time to see if long-term trends could be distinguished from day to day fluctuations. He was seeking to identify any trends, such as trade cycles for example, which could be observed in the data. The investigation covered the period 1928-1938 and included mostly weekly data of 22 different commodity prices. Of these, 19 were the Institute and Faculty of Actuaries' indices of industrial share prices where each index represents a different industrial sector. The method of investigation used was to compare the change in each index over one week with the change over the previous week. To measure any relationship between last week's price movement and this week's (over the

10-year period), the correlation coefficient was calculated for each sector index. This coefficient is a statistical measure of the relationship between the two price changes and can take any value between +1 and −1. A coefficient of +1 would imply the highest degree of conformity between the two series and −1 would indicate the same degree of conformity although in a negative sense. A correlation coefficient of zero would imply that there is no detectable relationship between last week's price change and this week's; that is there is no correlation within the series (usually called serial correlation).

These computations produced virtually no evidence of serial correlation. The correlation coefficient for the Iron and Steel Index (series number 9) is 0.088, which is quite close to zero.

Kendall repeated this for a gap of two weeks: this week's price change was compared with what happened two weeks ago. In fact gaps up to 29 weeks were tested. No significant evidence of correlation was found; the correlation coefficients being close to zero, so close that he was forced to conclude,

'Such serial correlation as is present in these series is so weak as to dispose at once of any possibility of being able to use them for prediction',
and further that any success investors enjoy is due to:

'(a) chance;
(b) the fact that at certain times all prices rise together so that they cannot go wrong;
(c) having inside information so that they can anticipate a movement;
(d) their being able to act very quickly;
(e) their being able to operate on such a scale that profits are not expended in brokers' fees and stamp duties.

But it is unlikely that anything I say or demonstrate will destroy the illusion that the outside investor can make money by playing the markets, so let us leave him to his own devices.'

Kendall was clearly in no doubt about the results of his work. However, as hinted above, some 'weak' serial correlation was detected. The one-week comparison produced the largest coefficients throughout the series (although not the largest individual coefficient). The series with the highest measures of correlation were 'Investment Trusts', 'Total Distribution' and 'All Classes'. These have one thing in common. They are all indices containing a large number of components. Therefore by taking the market as a whole there may perhaps be some serial correlation. Looking at the other sectors, where a lesser degree of aggregation is involved, it may be significant that with only one exception, the coefficients are positive even though small. If there was no correlation whatsoever, then it would be more likely for positive and negative values to be evenly matched, as is the case with lags longer than one week. This might also suggest correlation, although weak.

This phenomenon has been confirmed by other researchers. At first glance it would seem that a system could be set up based on a policy of buying the market this week after it had just risen, and selling it if it had just fallen. However, there are a number of possible explanations for this effect and in fact profits cannot easily be made in this way. These are described later in the chapter.

One other interesting effect was observed. Of the other series tested, New York spot cotton prices (monthly) tested over a period of 125 years with a one-month gap exhibited significant correlation. Kendall suggested this to be a 'salutary warning against undue generalisation'. However, this effect has since been satisfactorily explained by Working [6]. Kendall used monthly cotton prices which were themselves averages of daily spot prices taken over the month. Working has shown that the use of averages can introduce correlation not present in the original series. He calculated that a monthly average of daily prices would generate a spurious correlation coefficient of 0.235. This accounts for the major part of the serial correlation detected. Had the effect been real rather than illusory, Kendall could conceivably have made a fortune in the New York cotton market. Perhaps this explains the gap between the end of the period covered by his data (1950) and the date of publication (1953).

Kendall was disappointed with his results, concluding that his only justification for publication was to spare another researcher the chore of repeating the computations and that more positive results would have to wait for better statistical techniques. Indeed, even in the discussion which followed the presentation of this paper, one of the participants inferred that the markets must be irrational. Of course, Kendall was mistaken, as was the participant. Kendall's results are extremely positive. He made the important discovery that historic price behaviour is no guide to future behaviour. The participant's inference is incorrect because if there was serial correlation he would infer the market to be rational, but if it were rational it would take note of the correlation and adjust prices until the correlation disappeared, but the market would then become irrational.

Brealey [7]

Brealey examined the behaviour of share prices in two different ways. Firstly he tested for serial correlation in the *Financial Times* actuaries' all-share index over the period 1962-68, using a lag of one day. Low positive correlation was observed, as Kendall had reported 17 years earlier. One improvement was made on this technique. The index is computed using price data obtained in the market. If these prices are not collected at exactly the same point in time, the index will take on some of the characteristics shown by prices averaged over a period of time. The spurious correlation in average monthly cotton prices (noted by Kendall) has already been explained by Working [6]. To avoid any such contamination in the data (likely in view of the large number of shares constituting the all-share index), Brealey constructed his own index comprising 29 of the shares in the FT 30-share index, taking the prices ruling at 2 pm exactly each day over a period of some 200 trading days (February to November, 1968). Using this, serial correlation was reduced although weak positive correlation was still noticeable. Over the same period, the all-share index had a correlation coefficient of 0.32 compared with 0.19 for the new index. Interpretation of this computation can only be tentative in view of the small number of observations (200). Over the longer period (1962-68) the all-share index showed a lower level of correlation (0.22) than observed in the 200 days (0.32). The results may simply be due to coincidence rather than to any fundamental cause.

The other method of analysis was quite different. Percentage price changes were calculated on a daily basis and the frequency of occurrence plotted.

The dotted line (technically a Normal distribution) indicates what should be observed (based purely on statistical considerations) if share price changes were perfectly random:

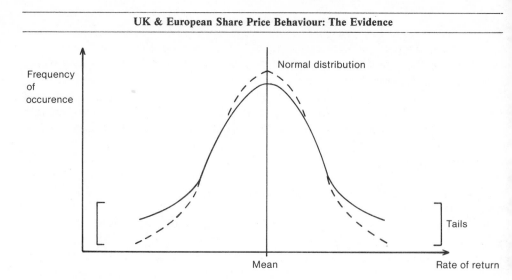

Frequency distribution of rates of return

the continuous line represents what is actually observed. Quite a good fit is apparent. Perhaps most interesting is the higher-than-expected frequency of small and large changes, which has also been found in the US. This effect, sometimes known as 'fat tails' may have some implications for the appropriateness of the statistical tests applied to series of share prices. Brealey pursued this point and in particular looked at behaviour on specific days of the Stock Exchange accounting period, noting that the extreme changes (represented by the 'fat tails') tended to occur at the beginning of the accounting period.

Brealey concluded that the weak serial correlation he observed was too small to be profitably exploited (because of expenses) and that such correlation did not seriously infringe the weak form of the hypothesis. It might be inferred from this comment that weak serial correlation is an infringement of the hypothesis although not serious. Only if we define the weak form of the hypothesis to be incompatible with any serial correlation, however weak, can Brealey's comment be appropriate. If such correlation cannot be profitably exploited, then for all practical purposes historic price information cannot be useful in the investment process. Since investment is undertaken in the real world and not in an 'ideal' world and costs (broker's commission etc) are involved, it is appropriate to redefine the weak form to take these factors into account. Thus weak correlation is not an infringement of the weak form unless it could be used to generate profits in excess of the associated expenses. Unless transaction costs are taken into account, weak correlation suggests only that the market is not perfect, which is hardly anything new. It is important therefore to make this distinction between the perfect market hypothesis (ie that the market is perfect) and the efficient market hypothesis. A test which proves only that the market is imperfect tells us nothing new and does not necessarily disprove the efficient market hypothesis.

Cunningham [8]
Cunningham, working on weekly data of the FT 30 share index (1935-69) and the Hoare Govett index (1965-71), also observed the persistence in price changes. But, of more

interest to the investor, he was able to formulate trading rules which he claimed 'should improve investment performance'. Specifically, he found that there was a 55 per cent probability of a rise in the FT index and a 45 per cent probability of a fall from week to week. Over the period covered, share prices went up more often than down. This is not inconsistent with the hypothesis. It must be the expectation of rational investors that share prices will rise. This is the only explanation for the existence of a reverse yield gap (ie the difference in yield between gilts and equities).

Given that a rise took place this week, the chances of a rise next week were found to be 57.4 per cent, greater than the average likelihood of a rise (55 per cent). Similarly, if the index had fallen this week, the chances of a further fall next week are 47.9 per cent - also above the average (45 per cent).

Week 1	Probability of a rise in week 2
Event: index rises	57.4%
Event: index falls	52.1%
Event: either index falls or rises	55.0%

Of course, knowing that a rise in the index is more likely to be followed by a further rise, than a fall is likely to be followed by a rise, does not of itself help the investor. He needs to know how much the rise is likely to be. Cunningham calculated this.

Interval	Average percentage change in the FT index following	
	either: a fall in the index	*or:* a rise in the index
1 week	− 0.05%	+ 0.18%
2 weeks	− 0.22%	+ 0.45%
3 weeks	− 0.22%	+ 0.55%
4 weeks	− 0.14%	+ 0.61%

Note that the signs of the changes are as expected. Rises are followed by rises and falls by falls. The rather small size of the rises indicates how weak this serial correlation effect is. The two-week interval appears to offer the best opportunity (showing a rise of 0.45 per cent, or 0.23 per cent per week) for the formulation of a trading rule. Cunningham suggests:

'When a sum becomes available for investment, find out whether the index is higher than it was 2 weeks ago. If the index is higher, invest immediately. If the index is lower than 2 weeks ago, postpone for 2 weeks the decision whether to invest this money and repeat the decision process then.

'By this method purchases should on average be about 0.25% cheaper, and in addition to this 0.25% gain there is the interest earned by cash available for investment when the decision to invest is postponed for 2 weeks and possibly for further 2-week periods. Assuming a 5% interest rate, the total interest accruing under the system described would amount to about 0.2% of all sums invested. Thus the total gain achieved by operating this system rather than a policy of immediate investment of available funds would be just under 0.5% of all sums invested.'

However, there is no easy road to riches. Kendall has already observed that serial correlation was more noticeable in the all-share index than in individual sector indices, and it may not therefore prove possible to invest in the all-share index (ie its constituents) to benefit from this rule. A simple buy and sell policy, using this rule, clearly would not generate enough profit to cover the transaction costs. As for improvements in timing, this trading rule looks plausible, but allowance must be made for periods of waiting until the method indicates a purchase and this will undoubtedly affect profitability. Ideally this suggestion should be tested on further data.

Trading Rules

Tests of trading rules can be used to examine the weak form of the hypothesis. These rules or systems generally operate on the basis of an investor watching price movements and buying or selling when he perceives a signal. The Cunningham 'system' generates buy signals each time the index has shown a rise over a two-week period. Other systems can be more sophisticated, although their objectives are simple: they all promise to generate fortunes overnight.

The 'Dow Theory', as it is known on Wall Street, is a simple chart system. When a share hits a peak and then falls back, it defines a resistance level. If, at a later point in time, the price approaches the resistance level and passes it, then the price will keep going up for a time to define a new resistance level. This breaking through a resistance level is the signal to buy. Similarly, a valley in the chart of the price defines a lower resistance level. Buy and sell signals are generated as follows:

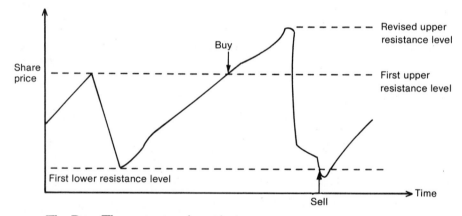

The Dow Theory system in action

The price-volume system, employed mainly in the US, states that when a share price moves up on large volume (ie of transactions) then there is an excess of buying interest and the stock will continue to move up. The converse applies for downward price movements.

The main problem with systems like these is that usually they are untested. No rational investor would adopt such a system and thereby incur heavy transaction costs without seeing some justification. This is where the validity of the system can be questioned, as testing is usually inadequate. Transaction costs are often ignored and tests are run on a very short time-scale of data: the data itself can often be the source of the system being tested. The following example demonstrates one of the more obvious traps the system followers fall into. The following table has two columns of prices. Each price is the closing price on Tuesday of each week. Consider column A. Examine the share price movements to see if a trading rule can be devised to make a profit over the period. Ignore transaction costs, the time value of money and opportunity costs and assume you can deal at closing prices.

Week Number	Column A	Column B
1	79p	139p
2	85p	139p
3	93p	135p
4	96p	120p
5	94p	118p
6	91p	129p
7	92p	129p
8	98p	124p
9	105p	118p
10	117p	116p
11	117p	122p
12	107p	130p
13	125p	135p
14	138p	135p
15	138p	131p

Doubtless the resourceful reader will be able to find several different rules. One system which works for column A (although it would be difficult to justify theoretically) is as follows:

If the closing price changes from an even to an odd number: BUY
If the closing price changes from an odd to an even number: SELL
Otherwise, if no change then no action.

This system could be called the 'Odd-Buy/Even-Sell' system. It generates profits as follows:

Week Number	Column A Price	Action	Profit
1	79p	BUY at 79p	
2	85p		
3	93p		
4	96p	SELL at 96p	+ 17p
5	94p		
6	91p	BUY at 91p	
7	92p	SELL at 92p	+ 1p
8	98p		
9	105p	BUY at 105p	
10	117p		
11	117p		
12	107p		
13	125p		
14	138p	SELL at 138p	+ 33p
15	138p		

The Odd-Buy/Even-Sell System

But before ringing your stockbroker, test the system on column B. Disaster — it does not work. The system only generates losses. What can be done? Perhaps devise a new system? Reversing decision rules of the Odd-Buy/Even-Sell system yields the following:

If the closing price changes from an even to an odd number: SELL
If the closing price changes from an odd to an even number: BUY
This would be called the Odd-Sell/Even-Buy system. The profits each system yields

on column B is given below.

Week Number	Column B Price	Odd-Buy/Even-Sell		Odd-Sell/Even-Buy	
		Action	Profit	Action	Profit
1	139p	BUY at 139p			
2	139p				
3	135p				
4	120p	SELL at 120p	− 19p	BUY at 120p	
5	118p				
6	129p	BUY at 129p		SELL at 129p	+ 9p
7	129p				
8	124p	SELL at 124p	− 5p	BUY at 124p	
9	118p				
10	116p				
11	122p				
12	130p				
13	135p			SELL at 135p	+ 11p
14	135p				
15	131p				

Odd-Buy/Even-Sell v Odd-Sell/Even-Buy

The new revised system generates profits. However, it can now be revealed that the column B prices are for the same share (Cavenham Ordinary 1975), as column A and that they represent the 15-week period following week 15 in column A. Thus the system formulated at the end of the first 15-week period would fail to work over the next period.

The lesson to learn here is that in any series of numbers, however long, a pattern can always be found which will produce profits. But this will not necessarily work in another series even if the other series relates to the same variable but is merely later in time. The fact that a system appears to work may unfortunately only be a temporary coincidence.

The example given does not prove that systems can or cannot work. It can only warn against the pitfalls of extrapolating from data on which the system does work to fresh data. If you think your system works you should first test it on a series of prices other than that series in which the system was discovered, and preferably over a long period of time. Allowance must also be made for transaction costs and a test portfolio should be constructed against which the performance of the system can be measured. If your system is still consistently successful on this basis then the author would be grateful for details (for inclusion in a later edition, of course). Most systems fail because of high transaction costs or because the market rises when the investor is in cash. Still maybe if you . . .

Dryden

Dryden has made four major contributions to the study of this topic. The first study [9] looked at aggregates of share prices, but in a novel way. The data comprised three sectors, 'All Shares', 'Industrials' and 'Mines'. Using daily FT closing prices and the change on the day, each data item was classified as either an 'increase', 'decrease', or 'no change'. Average figures for the total body of data were computed:

SECTOR	All Shares	Industrials	Mines
Average Proportions:			
Increasing	16%	17%	16%
Decreasing	17%	17%	15%
No change	67%	66%	69%
	100%	100%	100%

Thus, on average over the period studied, 67 per cent of shares showed no daily price change (as recorded by the FT). This does not imply that each of the 67 per cent of prices did not move during the day. Obviously a share can record 'no change' but still move up 50p and down 50p during the course of the day.

The method of analysis was to calculate the probabilities of a share starting out as either increase, decrease or no change and ending up in each of these categories. For the all shares group, Dryden calculated the following probabilities although the results for the other groups are similar:

% Probabilities		Day 1 Behaviour		
		Increase	Decrease	No Change
	Increase	59%	7%	8%
Day 2	Decrease	7%	64%	6%
Behaviour	No Change	34%	29%	86%
		100%	100%	100%

As is immediately apparent, there is a high probability for price changes to persist (ie for increases to be followed by increases and decreases to be followed by decreases) and for no change to be followed by no change. Thus he was able to conclude: 'There would, however, seem to be evidence of dependence among successive daily price change'. These results are what would be expected, but at best can only be regarded as a test of the perfect market hypothesis as is the second of Dryden's studies [10].

Dryden used information theory, which is really a branch of statistics or probability theory, to measure the accuracy of forecasts. Using the same data as before, the daily proportions of each category (increasing, decreasing and unchanged) were forecasted for the three sectors. The technique of forecasting was to use a weighted average of the proportions prevailing on preceding days. The weighting was required in order to attach more importance to those days nearest to the day for which the forecast was made. For the all-shares group the best rule took account of only two parameters, the proportion occuring on the previous day (p_{t-1}) and the long-term average proportion ($\bar{p}$), as follows:

$$\text{Forecast proportion, } p_t = 0.58\, p_{t-1} + 0.42 \times \bar{p}$$

This rule, and a number of others, were tested using the information theory technique. The results were compared with similar studies of the New York and Amsterdam stock exchanges. London appeared to exhibit more dependence of today's outcome on yesterday's, and generally, to behave more predictably. Acknowledging the fact that the analysis was performed on an aggregate basis (rather than an individual share basis) Dryden was unable to come to any firm conclusion as to the validity of the weak form hypothesis. However, his next study was more relevant.

Dryden [11] has examined the profitability of filter systems. A filter system works by triggering buy or sell decisions whenever the share price shows a movement in excess of the filter size. The principle involved is to use the fact that if there is serial correlation in the behaviour of share prices then a rise (fall) yesterday indicates an increased chance of a rise (fall) today. Thus a filter is chosen, say 5 per cent, to indicate that when yesterday's price rise (fall) was more than 5 per cent, a purchase (sale) should be made in order to capitalise on the expected further rise (fall). In this manner the profitability of a range of filter sizes, as applied to a number of different indices, was calculated.

This particular study is important in three respects.

(i) The profitability of the filter system was compared with what might be called a control system. Merely measuring the profitability *per se* of any system does not tell us whether that system is good or bad: it may be better to adopt a different system. For example, if we happen to test a system on a bull market, it is quite possible for that system to show profits but still be a bad system. Dryden compared the filter systems with a policy of 'buy and hold' applied to the index in question. In this way, due allowance is made for the market movement over the period. Also, it will be explained later in the book why this is a particularly appropriate choice of control system from a risk point of view. In addition, it is simple, with minimal administration and transaction expenses.

(ii) Transaction costs, although not explicitly taken into account, are discussed by Dryden and an approximate adjustment is suggested. The adjustments have been calculated for one set of Dryden's results:

Filter Size	0.1%	0.5%	1.0%	5.0%
Rates of Return (pa)				
'Filter System'	32.9%	20.2%	14.2%	2.2%
'Buy and Hold'	2.6%	2.6%	2.3%	–1.4%
Filter System after adjustment for trans-				
action costs (0.625%)	–17.1%	–0.2%	4.4%	1.0%
(2.00%)			–17.2%	–1.1%

FT actuaries 500 share index (daily observations, January 1963-April 1967)
(The cost adjustment is calculated by multiplying the average number of transactions per year by the cost and deducting this amount from the rate of return generated by the system).

It will be immediately apparent that the smaller filters produce the higher rates of return, but, because of the heavier incidence of transaction costs, produce the smallest net returns. At first glance, the two larger filters appear to generate profits in excess of the buy and hold rate. However Dryden's suggestion of average transaction costs of 0.625 per cent was intended for the smaller filters where the majority of transactions can be completed within the account, thus minimising the expenses. For the larger filters (ie 1.0 per cent and upwards) the average length of a transaction is longer than an account (14 days) and costs are therefore much higher, involving stamp duty and double broker's commission. This is allowed for in the second line of the adjustment. It will be noted that the 5 per cent filter still manages just to beat the control system.

(iii) Research work has largely been directed at the behaviour of indices. Although an aggregate index can reflect the nature of its component parts, as we have seen with the problem of averaging, indices can produce misleading results. Also, it is quite difficult to deal in an index as so many shares are involved.

Dryden recognised the advantages of analysing individual shares and included in his study Tesco Stores.

Filter Size	0.1%	0.5%	1.0%	5.0%
Rates of Return (pa)				
'Filter System long rate'	53.5%	55.3%	51.6%	−20.2%
'Buy and Hold'	13.8%	13.8%	13.8%	9.6%
'Filter System long rate' after cost adjustment				
(0.625%)	20.3%	22.8%	28.9%	−24.3%

(Tesco Stores, December 1962 - December 1964)

The 'long rate' is used here since even after transaction costs, it beats the buy and hold system. The 'long rate' is a simple variation of the filter system where sell decisions are triggered only after a buy decision: that is, short sales are excluded. Unfortunately the data covers only a short time-span. The best thing to do would be to test the filters on a different (hopefully longer) period of data to avoid the possibility of this result being just a temporary coincidence.

Dryden also calculated serial correlation coefficients for the three indices and noted, as would be expected, weak positive correlation. Overall, Dryden's method constitutes the first real attempt at testing the weak form of the efficient market hypothesis (as opposed to the perfect market hypothesis). As such, his results (with perhaps the exception of the Tesco Stores analysis) can be regarded as comfirmatory.

The fourth Dryden study [12] extended the individual share approach to 15 shares. The methods of analysis comprised those already used on indices:

(a) serial correlation,
(b) analysis of runs (see section on Kemp and Reid [13]),
(c) proportions showing increases, decreases or no change, and
(d) filter systems.

Dryden concluded: 'In general the statistical analysis carried out ... must be regarded as evidence in support of the random walk theory. Perhaps a slight qualification for evidence of dependence of a very short-run nature should be allowed — but a stronger case cannot be made'. The short-run dependence referred to was the comparatively high degree of serial correlation shown by some individual stocks for the smaller lags (1 and 2 days). A summary of these results is set out below.

Kemp and Reid [13]

Kemp and Reid extended tests for randomness in a sample of 50 shares. The method of analysis was to apply a number of sophisticated statistical tests. These tests were deliberately chosen to avoid possible conflict with the nature of the distribution of rates of return. Recall that Brealey [7] discovered some deviation (fat tails) in this distribution when compared with a normal distribution which might be expected on purely theoretical considerations.

Dryden's Results

Share/Stock	Serial correlation coefficients with lag 1 day	Rates of return averaged over 10 filters ranging from 0.2% to 4.0%	Buy and hold rate of return
Cater Ryder	0.07	10.7%	6.0%
Martins Bank	0.07	0.7%	22.7%
Midland Bank	0.24	12.4%	12.3%
Birmingham Small Arms	0.19	3.5%	19.4%
British Aluminium	0.05	12.3%	−6.9%
British Oxygen	0.05	6.4%	7.0%
Dunlop Rubber	−0.01	10.4%	17.1%
Illingworth Morris	0.01	23.7%	−4.1%
ICI	0.06	−0.5%	9.9%
Tesco Stores	0.14	7.9%	48.9%
Tube Investments	0.11	19.9%	8.7%
Turner and Newall	0.12	6.2%	3.4%
British Petroleum	0.08	−0.6%	8.7%
Burmah Oil	0.05	−6.6%	17.8%
Consols 2½% Undated	0.15	3.4%	3.7%

Data: Daily FT closing prices 1963/64

Notes:

(i)   The correlation coefficients are largely statistically insignificant and numerically small.

(ii) The filter rates of return (with the exception of British Aluminium, Illingworth Morris, Tube Investments and Turner & Newall) all perform worse than a buy and hold policy and this is before any allowance for transaction costs.

Mandelbrot[14] has suggested that this effect can be explained if rates of return belong to a different distribution (a Paretian distribution). If this is correct then certain statistical tests (parametric tests) would be inappropriate. By careful choice of test, the researchers neatly circumvented this problem. In fact the tests they used looked at the length and frequency of runs. Each daily price change is denoted by '+' for a price increase and '−' for a decrease. The price series is then written in the form:

Day	1	2	3	4	5	etc
Price	80p	82p	79p	76p	82p	etc
Symbol	+	−	+	−		etc

A run is a sequence of like signs (eg +++, −−) and the length of each run is simply the number of signs comprising that run (eg +++ and −−− both have length 3). The frequency of runs of different length was then compared with what would be expected from a purely random series. A typical comparison is provided by Lombard Banking:

	Number of Runs	
	Actual	Expected
Length 1	5	19.6
Length 2	11	8.4
Length 3 or more	8	3.0
Total	24	31.0

It is immediately apparent that there are fewer runs of length 1 and more runs of length 3 or more than would be expected. After testing for the statistical significance of this result, Kemp and Reid concluded that 'this series is significantly non-random'.

One problem was the situation where there was no change in the price. Should this be classified as a + or –? Kemp and Reid carried out tests after removing these data items from the series. This had the effect of reducing the proportion of their sample exhibiting non-randomness from 80 per cent to 50 per cent. Thus they felt justified in concluding that '. . . Share prices were conspicuously non-random over the period considered. This result, we feel, should be a caution to those who have been startled by the apparent finding of the randomness in share price movements in their studies'.

Of the results, which are summarised below, perhaps the most interesting is the discovery that the FT industrial index is random. This is in contrast to the earlier studies where aggregate indices generally exhibited weak positive correlation. However, the overall results can only be regarded as a test of the perfect market hypothesis but not the weak form hypothesis. No attempt is made to devise a system to make use of the non-randomness, nor to see whether sufficient profits could be generated to cover the transaction costs incurred. The problem still to be answered is whether there is sufficient non-randomness to infringe the real-world version of the hypothesis.

Girmes and Benjamin [15]

A statistical analysis was applied to 543 share prices (observed daily, October 1968 - April 1971). Two dates were chosen, say day 1 and day 10. A line is drawn between these points on the chart of the share price. The distribution of the number of intermediate prices lying above the line is then compared with what should be expected if the weak form hypothesis is true.

Of the shares tested, Girmes and Benjamin found: ' about 20 per cent . . . do not vary according to a random walk; about 20 per cent . . . seem to behave like a genuine random walk'; the balance, being neither one thing nor the other, were described as 'mixed'. However, the results can only prove that the market is not perfect. It can still be efficient or inefficient. Nevertheless, the study makes one important contribution. The efficiency of the market derives from the competitive nature of investing. Investment analysis and professional fund management ensure that prices are efficient. The large companies clearly get much attention since they nearly always feature in every portfolio. Smaller companies are less well researched and therefore there may be measurable inefficiencies. Girmes and Benjamin classified their results according to capital employed:

Capital Employed (1968)	Random	Mixed	Non-Random	Total
Under £10m	27(35%)	17(22%)	34(43%)	78(100%)
Between £10m and £100m	96(57%)	46(27%)	26(16%)	168(100%)
Over £100m	45(80%)	9(16%)	2(4%)	56(100%)
Total	168	72	62	302

The sample used here was reduced by the exclusion of financials (where size was difficult to measure) and preference shares which exhibited a high degree of non-randomness.

It will be immediately apparent that 'randomness' increases with capital employed. For companies having a capital employed in excess of £100m, market behaviour appears to be almost completely random and therefore a close approximation to perfect market behaviour. The implication is to look for degrees of efficiency and perhaps concentrate on the smaller, less well-researched companies.

Kemp and Reid: Summary of Results

Share/index	Whole Series	Series after removal of 'no changes'
Lombard Banking	NR	NR
Wagon Finance	NR	NR
Guinness	NR	R
Downing (GH)	NR	NR
Hills F	NR	R
Howarth	NR	NR
Mucklow	NR	R
Symes AE	NR	R
Henriques	NR	NR
Edinburgh Industrial Holdings	NR	R
Clarke Chapman	NR	R
Harland & Wolff	NR	R
Blaw Knox	NR	NR
Carrier Engineering	R	R
Edibrac	NR	NR
Greening (N)	NR	NR
Johnson Con.	NR	NR
Taylor Pallister	NR	NR
Brooke Bond Liebig 'B'	NR	R
British Syphon	NR	NR
Charrington, Gardner & Locket	R	NR
Cuthbert (RG)	NR	NR
Glaxo Group	R	R
Hensher 'A'	NR	NR
Hestair	NR	R
Inter City 'A'	NR	R
Nairn Williamson	NR	NR
Odex Racasan	NR	NR
Photo Me International	R	NR
British Leyland	R	R
Seddon Diesel	R	R
Brown Brothers	NR	R
Daily Mail and General Trust	R	R
Smith (WH) 'A'	NR	NR
Mill & Allen	NR	R
Hallmark Securities	NR	R
Land & House	NR	R
McKay Securities	NR	NR
Oddeninos	NR	R
Ropner Holdings	NR	NR
Lennards Deferred 'A'	NR	R
Lotus	NR	NR
Jute Industries Ordinary	NR	R
Uttley	NR	NR
Hanipha Ceylon	NR	NR
Lanka	NR	NR
Buffels	R	NR
Rand Selection Corporation	R	R
Nchanga	R	R
Metals Exploration	R	R
Malayan Tin Dredging	NR	NR
FT Industrial Ordinary Index	R	R
%Non-Random	**77%**	**50%**

Serial Correlation

There are a number of other tests for serial correlation: for example Griffiths [16] and Solnik [17] whose work on European stocks, which includes 40 UK companies, is covered in Chapter 5. Both studies observed low values of correlation, although Griffiths obtained a small negative value as did Guy [18], who explained that measurement error of prices could give rise to negative serial correlation. Suppose one monthly price was wrong, being too high. Then the preceding monthly rate of return would be increased and the succeeding monthly rate of return decreased. Thus a high rate would be succeeded by a low rate and would therefore give rise to negative serial correlation. If a price is too low, a low rate of return will be followed by a high rate which also induces negative correlation. Even though Guy used 10 years' data, measurement error cannot be eliminated.

Guy's study contains one other point of interest. Two groups were used: 50 major companies, and 49 random companies. As one might now expect, the major companies had correlation coefficients clustered tightly around zero whereas the companies chosen at random had larger coefficients.

Girmes and Damant [19]

Finally, having reviewed much evidence against the usefulness of historic prices, it is right to include the positive results of chart analysis. Girmes and Damant concede that little attempt has been made to measure the performance of chartists. However, they tested one typical chart system and obtained positive results. The system focused on one particular pattern, the well known head and shoulders top. This system generates a sell signal, when the price has outlined the pattern and dropped through the neckline.

Average profits of 13.5 per cent were made, although the individual figures varied widely. What is not clear is whether superior profits could be made to a simple buy and hold policy. Also, the data used was 'smoothed' to iron out short-term movements. Thus in practice it may not be possible to deal at prices which would generate the above-average profits figure. Also, it was not clear whether the short selling could be effected within the account. More development of the testing of this system is required before any conclusion can be reached.

The Analysis of Economic Time-Series—Part I: Prices

By M. G. Kendall

Division of Research Techniques, London School of Economics

(Read before the Royal Statistical Society, December 17th, 1952, Professor A. Bradford Hill, C.B.E., Ex-President, in the Chair)

Introduction and Summary

1. It has been customary to analyse an economic time-series by extracting from it a long-term movement, or trend, for separate study and then scrutinizing the residual portion for short-term oscillatory movements and random fluctuations. The assumption latent in this procedure is that the long-term and short-term movements are due to separate causal influences and therefore that the mathematical process of analysis corresponds more or less roughly to a real distinction of type in the generative system. When it began to appear that the classical method of analyzing stationary economic fluctuations into cycles and residual elements broke down, and that better accounts of such movements were given by autoregressive schemes in which the disturbance element played an integral part, it was an easy step to proceed one stage further, and to enquire whether the so-called trend in a series was in fact separable from the short-term movements, or whether it should be regarded as generated by a set of forces which also gave rise to the short-term movements.

2. The work described in the present paper sprang from this idea. It was necessary in the first place to find suitable material on which to test it and I give below particulars of 22 price-series, ranging from 486 terms at weekly intervals to 2,387 terms at weekly intervals, which were chosen for the purpose. I began to construct models and to fit them to these data and also to other series which are not mentioned in this paper; but before the work had gone very far it appeared that the pattern of events in the price series was much less systematic than is generally believed. This is perhaps the most significant part of the present paper. I shall not have space to deal with the corresponding phenomenon in production data, and shall mention only incidentally the problem of trend fitting.

3. Broadly speaking the results are these:

(a) In series of prices which are observed at fairly close intervals the random changes from one term to the next are so large as to swamp any systematic effect which may be present. The data behave almost like wandering series.

(b) It is therefore difficult to distinguish by statistical methods between a genuine wandering series and one wherein the systematic element is weak.

(c) Until some way has been found of circumventing this difficulty, trend fitting, and perhaps the fitting of any model, is a highly hazardous undertaking. It may be possible for an econometrician to test whether the data agree with a hypothesis suggested by prior analysis, but it may be impossible to discriminate between quite different hypotheses which all fit the data.

(d) There is experimental evidence and theoretical support for the belief that aggregative index numbers behave more systematically than their components. This *might* be due to the reduction of the random elements by averaging and the consequent emergence of systematic constituents; but it could equally well be due to chance. If it is, there will appear spurious time-correlations in aggregative series and the use of index-numbers in econometric work needs extensive reconsideration.

(e) An analysis of stock-exchange movements revealed little serial correlation within series and little lag correlation between series. Unless individual stocks behave differently from the average of similar stocks, there is no hope of being able to predict movements on the exchange for a week ahead without extraneous information.

The Data

4. For the purposes of this study I used 22 economic series as follows:

Actuaries' Index of Industrial Share Prices

	Period	Interval	Number of Terms
1. Banks and Discount Companies . . .	1928–1938	Week	486
2. Insurance Companies	,,	,,	,,
3. Investment Trusts	,,	,,	,,
4. Building Materials	,,	,,	,,
5. Coal	,,	,,	,,
6. Cotton	,,	,,	,,
7. Electric Light and Power . . .	,,	,,	,,
8. Gas	,,	,,	,,
9. Iron and Steel	,,	,,	,,
10. Oil	,,	,,	,,
11. Total Industrial Productive . . .	,,	,,	,,
12. Home Rails	,,	,,	,,
13. Shipping	,,	,,	,,
14. Stores and Catering	,,	,,	,,
15. Total Industrial Distributive . . .	,,	,,	,,
16. Breweries and Distilleries . . .	,,	,,	,,
17. Miscellaneous	,,	,,	,,
18. Total Industrial Miscellaneous . .	,,	,,	,,
19. Industrials (all classes combined) . .	,,	,,	,,
20. Basic cash wheat at Chicago in cents per bushel	Jan., 1883–Sept., 1934 (excluding 1915–1920 inclusive; one missing value interpolated for 10.3.1933)	,,	2,387
21. Monthly average of preceding series . .	Jan., 1883–Sept., 1934 (excluding 1915–1920)	Month	548
22. Spot cotton at New York in cents per pound .	Aug., 1816–Jan., 1951 (excluding 1861–1866 and 1914–20; one missing value for Oct., 1857, inserted as average of the two neighbouring months)	,,	1,446

Sources

For the actuaries' indices I am indebted to the Institute and Faculty of Actuaries who allowed me to extract the figures from the Institute's records.

Series 20 and 21 are taken from *Wheat Studies of the Food Research Institute*, vol. 11, No. 3, November, 1934 (Stanford University, California).

Series 22 is taken from *Statistics on Cotton and Related Data*, U.S. Department of Agriculture, Bureau of Agricultural Economics, Statistical Bulletin, No. 99, Washington, D.C., June, 1951.

5. The golden rule in publishing work on time-series is to give the original data. To do so in this case would have required about thirty pages of journal. I shall, however, be glad to make available copies of the series or the cards on which they have been punched. A good many of the secondary statistics are presented below but here also the working sheets are available to any responsible person who is interested. So far as possible I have not "edited" any of the series even where there was some case for making the attempt; but in some instances I have omitted war periods and should have been compelled to do so by the lack of data. All such omissions are indicated above.

Analysis of the Price Data

The Chicago Wheat Series (20 and 21)

6. Although the wheat-price series was not the first I examined it is useful to begin an expository account by considering it because it is a long series of prices wherein little or no element of aggrega-

tion enters. The Stanford Wheat Studies from which the data were taken give graphs of the series. They are unfortunately too long to reproduce on a page of this size.*

From the primary data the series of 2,379 first differences were constructed and a frequency distribution formed which is given as the marginal column in Table 1. It was here that the first fact of significance emerged, for the resulting distribution had nearly perfect symmetry and an appearance of approximate normality. The bivariate distribution of one difference against the next succeeding difference is even more illuminating. Table 1 is a condensed version and presents on the face of it an excellent picture of independence; on a regression diagram the two lines would almost coincide with the variate axes.

7. The decision to use first differences instead of the original series was not an arbitrary one. When a price is fixed on a free market both parties know what was the price of the previous transactions and use that price as a starting point for negotiation. It is the change, not the absolute value, which constitutes the fundamental element in the price determination. One can think of exceptions, perhaps, but for the commodities I am discussing they are not relevant.

8. At first sight the implications of these results are disturbing. If the series is homogeneous, it seems that the change in price from one week to the next is practically independent of the change from that week to the week after. This alone is enough to show that it is impossible to predict the price from week to week from the series itself. And if the series really is wandering, any systematic movements such as trends or cycles which may be "observed" in such series are illusory. The series looks like a "wandering" one, almost as if once a week the Demon of Chance drew a random number from a symmetrical population of fixed dispersion and added it to the current price to determine the next week's price. And this, we may recall, is not the behaviour in some small backwater market. The data derive from the Chicago wheat market over a period of fifty years during which at least two attempts were made to corner wheat, and one might have expected the wildest irregularities in the figures. To the statistician there,is some pleasure in the thought that the symmetrical distribution reared its graceful head undisturbed amid the uproar of the Chicago wheat-pit. The economist, I suspect, or at any rate the trade cyclist, will look for statistical snags before he is convinced of the absence of systematic movements. And he will be very right to do so.

9. One possible source of error is that, in treating as homogeneous a price-series extending from 1883 to 1934, we may be oversimplifying the hypotheses. The series was therefore divided into two sections covering the periods 1883–1914 and 1921–1934; and a bivariate distribution of first differences on the lines of Table 1 constructed for each. I omit the figures to save space, but the story told by each section was the same as for the series taken together.

There are seven widely outlying values in the whole series, and it did not seem to me to be sophisticating the data to omit them from the calculation of moments.† The following constants were computed from a more finely grouped distribution and are corrected by Sheppard's formulae for the grouping effect.

	Period 1883–1914	Period 1921–1934	Both Periods Together
μ_1'	0	0·0964	0·0289
μ_2	7·7576	22·7789	12·3294
μ_3	12·6787	34·5882	20·2709
μ_4	657·3073	2745·8873	1293·0607
β_1	0·344	0·101	0·219
β_2	10·856	5·292	8·506

The distributions are accordingly rather leptokurtic.

10. The general pattern of independence present in these data makes it very unlikely that there are large serial correlations present but to make sure they were worked out to the tenth order and are given in Table 2. For computing purposes it is easier to work out serial covariance

---

* The weekly series are, so far as possible, closing quotations on Fridays and are given to the nearest ⅛ cent. The monthly figures are averages of four or five weekly figures.

† Three values are due to a jump from September 21st to September 28th, 1888, of 53 cents and a recession the following week of 38 cents; four values are due to a similar movement in May, 1898.

TABLE 1

Frequency Distribution of Differences of Series 20, Difference between Weeks t *and* t + 1 *against Difference between Weeks* t + 1 *and* t + 2.

(Condensed to save space from original table for which the interval was one unit. Values falling on the border line of intervals were allotted ½ to each.)

Difference, t^{th} week less $(t+1)^{th}$ week; cents per bushel.	*Difference,* (t + 1)th *Week Less* (t + 2)th *Week; Cents per Bushel, Mid-point of Interval*																						
	−21	−19	−17	−15	−13	−11	−9	−7	−5	−3	−1	1	3	5	7	9	11	13	15	17	19	21	*Totals*
−17	—	—	—	—	—	—	—	—	—	—	½	—	—	—	—	—	—	—	—	—	—	—	½
−15	—	—	—	—	—	—	—	—	—	1	½	1	—	—	—	2¼	¼	—	—	—	—	—	5
−13	—	—	—	—	—	—	—	—	1	1	1	2	—	—	½	¾	¼	—	—	1	—	1	8½
−11	—	—	—	—	—	—	—	—	1½	—	½	½	2	1	—	—	1	1	—	—	—	—	7½
−9	—	—	—	1	—	—	—	2	2½	3	3½	4	2	3	2	—	—	—	1	—	—	—	24
−7	—	—	—	—	1	—	3	2½	3	4	10	8	5	2	6	1	—	1	—	—	1	—	47½
−5	—	—	—	1	1	1	5	5½	8½	9¼	23	28¾	16	8½	3½	1	2	—	—	—	—	—	114
−3	—	—	—	½	½	2	5	6½	16	28	64¼	91	27¼	12½	6½	—	1	—	—	1	—	1	263
−1	—	—	—	—	3	2½	4	12½	27½	86¾	232	236¾	78½	19	12½	1½	2	2	—	½	—	—	721
1	½	½	—	—	—	—	3½	10½	22	71	268½	207¼	82¼	29¾	6¼	3	1	—	1½	1	—	—	708½
3	—	—	—	—	—	—	1	5	13¾	30¾	82¼	89¼	47½	8¾	4¼	1½	½	—	—	—	—	—	284½
5	—	—	—	—	1	1	1½	3	7¾	16¼	18½	20½	11½	9	5	2	—	1	1	—	—	1	100
7	—	—	—	½	—	—	1	1	6	7½	11½	12½	6½	2½	—	1	—	—	—	—	—	—	50
9	—	—	—	½	1	—	—	1	2	2	1½	—	2½	1½	1½	2½	—	—	—	—	½	½	17
11	—	—	—	—	—	—	—	—	1	1	3½	—	½	1½	—	½	—	—	—	1	—	—	9
13	—	—	—	—	—	—	—	—	—	—	—	1	1	—	2	—	—	—	1	—	—	—	5
15	—	—	½	½	½	—	—	—	1	—	—	1	1	—	—	—	—	—	—	—	—	—	4½
17	—	—	—	—	½	—	—	—	1	—	—	3	—	—	—	—	—	—	—	—	—	—	4½
19	—	—	—	½	—	—	—	—	—	—	—	—	—	1	—	—	—	—	—	—	—	—	1½
21	—	—	—	½	—	1	—	—	—	1	—	1	—	—	—	—	—	—	—	—	—	—	3½
Totals	½	½	½	5	8½	7½	24	49½	114½	262½	721	707½	283½	100	50	17	8	5	4½	4½	1½	3½	2,379

Note.—There were also seven outlying pairs with values (−6·75, −53·0), (−53·0, 37·75), (37·75, −1·25), (−6·5, −30·75), (−30·75, 3·75), (−20·0. 53·0) and (53·0, 11·75). The last term of the series was taken with the first so that the total number of pairs is 2,386.

TABLE 2

Serial Correlations of First Differences of Wheat Prices (Series 20)

(Decimal points omitted)

Order of Correlation	Series 1883–1914 (n = 1,669)	Series 1921–1934 (n = 716)	Whole Series 1883–1934 (Omitting 1915–1920) (n = 2,385)
1 . . .	−078	−063	−071
2 . . .	+078	+051	+065
3 . . .	−000	+030	+014
4 . . .	−075	+042	−019
5 . . .	+007	−066	−028
6 . . .	−032	−071	−051
7 . . .	−016	−039	−027
8 . . .	−059	−064	−061
9 . . .	−047	+023	−014
10 . . .	−038	+034	−004
Large sample standard error . . .	0·025	0·038	0·020

for the primary series and to calculate those of the differences from formulae such as

$$\sum_{i=1}^{n-2} (x_{i+2} - x_{i+1})(x_{i+1} - x_i) = 2 \sum_{i=1}^{n-1} x_i x_{i+1} - \sum_{i=1}^{n} x_i^2 - \sum_{i=1}^{n-2} x_i x_{i+2}$$
$$+ x_1^2 + x_n^2 - x_1 x_2 - x_{n-1} x_n . \qquad (1)$$

For long series when end effects can be neglected this is for all practical purposes equivalent to

$$\tau_k = -\tfrac{1}{2} \Delta^2 \rho_{k-1}/(1 - \rho_1) \qquad . \qquad . \qquad . \qquad . \qquad . \qquad (2)$$

where τ represents the autocorrelations of first differences and ρ those of the primary series. In this case it was not much extra trouble to take end-effects into account and the serial correlations for the constituent series in Table 2 were calculated from the formula

$$r_k = \frac{\sum_{i=1}^{n-k-1} u_i u_{i+k} - \dfrac{1}{n-k-1} \sum_{i=1}^{n-k-1} u_i \sum_{i=k+1}^{n} u_i}{\left[\left\{ \sum_{i=1}^{n-k-1} u_i^2 - \dfrac{1}{n-k-1} \left(\sum_{i=1}^{n-k-1} \right)^2 \right\} \left\{ \sum_{i=k+1}^{n} u_i^2 - \dfrac{1}{n-k-1} \left(\sum_{i=k+1}^{n} u_i \right)^2 \right\} \right]^{\frac{1}{2}}} \qquad . \qquad (3)$$

where u_i is the difference $x_{i+1} - x_i$.

In calculating the serials for the two series together a weighted average was taken, the formula being

$$r_k = \frac{(n_1 - k - 1)c_1 + (n_2 - k - 1)c_2}{\{(n_1 - k - 1)v_{11} + (n_2 - k - 1)v_{21}\}^{\frac{1}{2}} \{(n_1 - k - 1)v_{12} + (n_2 - k - 1)v_{22}\}^{\frac{1}{2}}} \qquad . \qquad (4)$$

where n_1, n_2 are the number of terms, v_{11}, v_{21}, v_{12} and v_{22} refer to the variances of the first $n - k$ terms of the first and second series and the last $n - k$ terms of the first and second series respectively and c_1, c_2 are the covariances of the first and second series. Equation (4) has no very firm theoretical basis but it is obviously reasonable and will certainly not underestimate the magnitude of the serial correlations.

11. A comparison of the variances of the two parts of the series suggests that there has been an increase in variability since World War I. This is what one might perhaps have expected, but it is rather a nuisance from the point of view of analysis because it suggests that the series is not stationary. We have here an interesting and rather unusual case of a time-series for which the mean remains constant but the variance appears to be increasing. It is desirable to have a test of this type of departure from stationarity, distribution-free if possible. The problem is easy enough for a random series but not so easy for an autocorrelated series of unknown character, and as I do not require the test for present purposes I omit a discussion of the point.

12. A glance at Table 2 shows that the serial correlations are very small and, for most practical purposes, negligible. However, the first two serials are, in four cases out of six, more than three times their standard error as calculated from R. L. Anderson's formula

$$\text{var } r_k = \frac{n-1}{(n-2)^2} \qquad . \qquad . \qquad . \qquad . \qquad . \qquad (5)$$

There are several possible explanations of this effect. Anderson's formula is based on normality and constant variance in the series. From general experience one would not expect the sampling variance to be increased by departure from parent normality in the direction of leptokurtosis, the distribution being symmetrical and n large. Nor, as it seems to me, can we appeal to non-stationarity to account for the difference, because the discrepancies occur most markedly in the first part of the series. I proceed to consider two more practical possibilities, one that the primary series was rounded up (or down) systematically, the other that for hour-to-hour or day-to-day changes in price there were systematic variations which have been lost to view in the weekly figures.

13. Suppose that a series of values $x_1, \ldots x_n$ is systematically rounded up by amounts $\varepsilon_1, \ldots \varepsilon_n$, ε thus having a positive mean but being serially independent. We shall then have for the differences $u_i (= x_{i+1} + \varepsilon_{i+1} - x_i - \varepsilon_i)$, in long series

$$\text{corr } (u_i, u_{i+k}) = \frac{-\Delta^2 \rho_{k-1}}{2(1-\rho_1) + 2 \text{ var } \varepsilon/\text{var } x} \qquad k > 1$$

$$= \frac{-\Delta^2 \rho_{k-1} - \text{var } \varepsilon/\text{var } x}{2(1-\rho_1) + 2 \text{ var } \varepsilon/\text{var } x} \qquad k = 1 \qquad . \qquad . \qquad (6)$$

In our present case var x is of the order of 10 and (the series being given to the nearest $\frac{1}{8}$th) var $\varepsilon = \frac{1}{12}\left(\frac{1}{8}\right)^2 = 0 \cdot 0^2 13$. The effect of factors in var $\varepsilon/\text{var } x$, of the order of $0 \cdot 0^3 1$, in (6) is therefore quite insufficient to account for the observed size of the first serial. In any case it would not account for the sign of the second. Even if we suppose that the rounding off was alternately up and down, which would induce autocorrelation in the ε's, the magnitude of the effect would not be large enough to explain the observations.

14. Consider then the attenuation in serial relationship which may be caused by averaging over time-periods. Suppose a market is open from Monday to Friday, that any Monday may be regarded as following immediately on the preceding Friday and that the scheme of generation from day to day is a simple Markoff process

$$u_{t+1} = \alpha u_t + \varepsilon_{t+1} \qquad . \qquad . \qquad . \qquad . \qquad . \qquad (7)$$

It is fairly easy to show that the correlation between the average of the five daily prices in one week and the corresponding average in the succeeding week is given by

$$r = \frac{5\alpha^5 + 4(\alpha^6 + \alpha^4) + 3(\alpha^7 + \alpha^3) + 2(\alpha^8 + \alpha^2) + (\alpha^9 + \alpha)}{5 + 8\alpha + 6\alpha^2 + 4\alpha^3 + 2\alpha^4} \qquad . \qquad . \qquad (8)$$

For $\alpha = 0 \cdot 8$ $r = 0 \cdot 499$ and the correlation is reduced by 38 per cent. For $\alpha = 0 \cdot 5$ $r = 0 \cdot 178$ and the serial correlation between weekly averages is only a third of that between days. For $\alpha = 0 \cdot 1$ $r = \cdot 02$. Evidently the averaging over successive terms may obliterate some quite substantial serial correlation in prices. The weekly wheat figures were not, in fact, averages over the days of the week, but it is evident that the choice of one day in the week as the representative point will stilll further attenuate any day-to-day correlations.

A simple Markoff process would still not account for the negative sign of r_1 in Table 3 unless the correlation between successive days was negative, which seems unlikely but is not impossible owing to the tendency of a sensitive market to swing too far and to correct itself. I ought perhaps to mention that the possibility of "significant" serials appearing owing to very occasional exceptional values was dismissed after examination of the series at such values.

15. It may well be, then, that the observed serials, small as they are, have some significance. But evidently the systematic element is slight compared with the random component and a very precise technique is going to be necessary in order to extract it, unless we know what to look for.

Some of my colleagues have pointed out that the operation of first differences could easily reduce quite a large cyclical effect below the threshold of detectability. For example, if there were a ten-year cycle in the data, corresponding to about 500 terms of the series, the differencing of a sine wave of amplitude comparable in magnitude to that of the observed fluctuations would be to reduce the amplitude in the differenced series by a factor of about $2\pi/500$ but to double the variance of random effects. We cannot say, then, that the analysis has ruled out the existence of periodic terms. There may well be traces of a seasonal effect present. What we may fairly say, I think, is that we do not need to invoke them to explain the observations.

16. Series 21 is a derivative of Series 20, being a monthly average instead of a weekly one. A frequency distribution of first differences, which I omit to save space, tells much the same story as Series 20. For the moments I find, with Sheppard's corrections

	Whole Series	Omitting One Extreme Value at Each End
$\mu_1' =$	0·0776	0·0504
$\mu_2 =$	44·0256	34·8271
$\mu_3 =$	208·2139	6·4153
$\mu_4 =$	32,721·3887	6,914·5455

For the series on the right

$$\beta_1 = 0\cdot00151 \qquad \beta_2 = 5\cdot701$$

The distribution is nearer normality, as one might expect under the central limit effect. Some of the serial correlations are given in the reply to the discussion.

17. A comparison of the variances and fourth moments of Series 20 and 21 raises no reason to suspect their wandering nature. If $u_1, \ldots u_{4n}$ is a series of $4n$ weekly terms, the series of monthly terms is $\frac{1}{4}(u_1 + u_2 + u_3 + u_4)$, $\frac{1}{4}(u_5 + u_6 + u_7 + u_8)$, etc. For the differences of these typified by η, we have (means being approximately zero)

$$\text{var } \eta = \frac{1}{16(n-1)} \sum_{j=0}^{n-2} (u_{4j+1} + u_{4j+2} + u_{4j+3} + u_{4j+4} - u_{4j+5} - u_{4j+6} - u_{4j+7} - u_{4j+8})^2$$

or, for large n,

$$\text{var } \eta = \frac{1}{16n} \sum_{=0}^{n-2} \{(u_{4j+1} - u_{4j+2}) + 2(u_{4j+2} - u_{4j+3}) + 3(u_{4j+3} - u_{4j+4})$$
$$+ 4(u_{4j+4} - u_{4j+5}) + 3(u_{4j+5} - u_{4j+6}) + 2(u_{4j+6} - u_{4j+7})$$
$$+ (u_{4j+7} - u_{4j+8})\}^2.$$

If the differences of u, typified by ε, are independent we then have

$$\text{var } \eta = \frac{1}{16} \text{ var } \varepsilon\{1^2 + 2^2 + 3^2 + 4^2 + 3^2 + 2^2 + 1^2\}$$

$$= \frac{11}{4} \text{ var } \varepsilon \qquad \qquad \qquad (9)$$

The ratio of variances of the monthly to the weekly series is $34\cdot8271/12\cdot3294 = 2\cdot82$ against the theoretical value of $2\cdot75$. It may be shown similarly that $\kappa(\eta) = 113/64 \ \kappa(\varepsilon)$. For the whole series the ratio $\kappa_4(\eta)/\kappa_4(\varepsilon)$ is $3\cdot12$ and for the series omitting extreme values $2\cdot12$ against the theoretical value $1\cdot77$.

18. There seems nothing to be gained by taking averages of the monthly figures to obtain an annual figure. Under the central limit effect the resulting series would be nearly normal; and successive values would almost certainly be nearly independent.

19. In the past I have often wondered whether annual figures were much use in the study of economic phenomena, except of course in relation to intermittent variables like crop-yields. So much can happen in a year that one feels the underlying causational system to require examination under a finer structure than an annual interval. But if this wheat-series is any guide, it seems that what we gain by observing the phenomenon at short intervals is lost, or at any rate deeply obscured, by the stochastic discontinuity of the process. It may be that the motion is genuinely random and that what looks like a purposive movement over a long period is merely a kind of economic Brownian motion. But economists—and I cannot help sympathizing with them—will doubtless resist any such conclusion very strongly. We can at this point suggest only a few conclusions:

    (a) the interval of observation may be very important;

    (b) it seems a waste of time to try to isolate a trend in data such as these;

    (c) prediction in such a series, from internal behaviour alone, is subject to a wide margin of error and the best estimate of the change in price between now and next week is that there is no change.

British Industrial Share Prices (Series 1–19)

20. Series 1 to 19 are weekly index numbers based on 1930 = 100. (The price taken is that of Tuesday of each week, not an average of the week's quotations.) They are not all independently compiled, series 11 (Total industrial production) being an average of series 12–14, series 18 (Total industrial miscellaneous) being an average of series 16 and 17, and series 19 being an average of all classes. There are thus 15 independent series. During the period covered by the figures there were, I believe, some changes such as substitutions for quotations which dropped out. But this hardly affects my argument. Taken together, these are as complete and reliable a set of figures describing the inter-war movement of the U.K. industrial share market as one is likely to find.

21. The first 29 serial correlations were computed for each series and are given in Table 3. The method used was similar to that for series 20 except that corrections for means were omitted as being negligible and the variance of the whole series used in the denominator, the formula accordingly being

$$r_k = \frac{\dfrac{1}{n-k} \sum_{i=1}^{n-k} u_i\, u_{i+k}}{\dfrac{1}{n} \sum_{i=1}^{n} u_i^2} \qquad . \qquad . \qquad . \qquad . \qquad . \quad (10)$$

It may be shown that for these series this approximation can affect the third decimal place at the most, except perhaps for series 3. To resolve any doubt the serials were worked out exactly for this series and the exact values were found to differ from the approximate ones only in the fourth decimal place.

For some of the series a bivariate distribution on the lines of Table 1 was constructed. In some cases the general picture of independence was presented, but in others there were signs of dependence as reflected in the serial correlations. I have space to reproduce only one, that for Series 3, where the dependence seems to be the highest (Table 4).

22. Such serial correlation as is present in these series is so weak as to dispose at once of any possibility of being able to use them for prediction. The Stock Exchange, it would appear, has a memory lasting less than a week except perhaps for Investment Trusts (Series 3), Stores and Catering (Series 14) and all series together. It may be, of course, that series of *individual* share prices would behave differently; the point remains open for inquiry. But the aggregates are very slightly correlated and some of them are virtually wandering. Investors can, perhaps, make money on the Stock Exchange, but not, apparently by watching price-moments and coming in on what looks like a good thing. Such success as investors have seems to be due (a) to chance,

TABLE 3

Serial Correlations of Series 1–19, Lag 1 to 29

(Decimal points omitted)

Number of Series *(see Para. 4)*

Lag	1	2	3	4	5	6	7	8	9	10
1	058	052	301	125	148	087	181	096	088	−013
2	061	−016	356	−001	075	121	055	185	−055	045
3	014	082	158	−025	061	061	053	049	011	−024
4	−050	−019	164	−079	−056	015	−016	086	043	−022
5	−087	−082	066	−025	−055	−030	−084	−005	−015	044
6	−028	−093	−101	−034	−056	−125	−085	−022	−091	−034
7	−015	−006	−030	001	−054	−044	−092	−036	−076	−029
8	−011	−042	−042	−013	−001	−058	−055	001	−020	004
9	004	−025	−030	−041	−084	−118	−067	056	−022	005
10	015	008	−033	010	−063	−067	−012	027	−015	−044
11	045	−050	−013	−022	042	−037	064	025	007	052
12	002	000	−094	048	040	004	000	043	046	004
13	−014	037	−052	045	021	048	040	049	094	009
14	−017	004	009	008	−037	−056	081	067	−060	−025
15	−062	032	027	050	−006	062	047	046	−039	−019
16	030	006	008	118	076	015	039	049	069	002
17	072	079	109	030	068	153	041	119	076	043
18	097	049	086	045	030	070	018	028	−028	036
19	098	−016	080	−016	031	−017	−009	−055	−036	−015
20	−037	−077	020	−026	−046	072	−023	016	−033	037
21	009	060	031	074	−031	−078	−056	052	004	−021
22	−027	011	−056	044	−067	−094	−029	074	−023	076
23	−044	−151	−047	056	−004	−084	−029	−041	−091	−048
24	034	−005	−086	−023	−020	−017	−001	043	−049	017
25	104	017	031	069	−039	015	016	133	076	−009
26	021	080	−048	038	−001	−012	029	067	044	−032
27	000	004	011	−017	082	−046	094	044	032	−052
28	045	130	053	071	097	−011	036	036	040	087
29	−011	−040	050	−014	060	−014	033	037	061	031

Number of Series

Lag	11	12	13	14	15	16	17	18	19
1	195	010	053	230	237	034	200	177	234
2	061	−057	029	054	076	087	103	106	105
3	053	044	−044	018	054	003	053	058	066
4	−034	039	−014	001	−040	−056	−013	−044	−046
5	−051	−015	−034	−084	−062	067	−080	−044	−055
6	−102	−081	058	−146	−093	−002	−115	−079	−094
7	−072	018	−013	−144	−072	019	−104	−087	−093
8	−043	139	036	−057	−044	−114	004	−033	−041
9	−047	033	037	−038	165	−018	−003	−003	−008
10	−047	−044	021	042	021	035	012	−091	−023
11	−003	079	046	−006	013	085	−014	013	005
12	039	069	044	086	089	017	024	142	050
13	082	−009	−009	−047	−006	077	037	064	045
14	−029	−041	−107	004	−008	−036	−037	−029	−025
15	036	−129	096	067	018	−084	045	001	033
16	069	030	090	064	077	055	158	122	114
17	145	005	168	029	086	001	124	120	148
18	047	072	063	047	082	029	089	079	084
19	−010	013	042	−001	057	047	010	022	038
20	007	005	008	035	014	−078	−001	−045	−017
21	−018	−012	−030	090	043	041	009	031	008
22	−035	009	−027	032	013	064	−015	033	−006
23	−082	−056	022	−039	−082	−005	−053	−045	−070
24	−041	−032	−037	−034	−021	028	−008	−008	−028
25	051	036	−000	002	−001	058	−001	017	026
26	025	037	086	−038	−005	046	036	049	036
27	047	055	092	−032	052	−019	030	012	038
28	168	048	016	−037	007	023	072	063	075
29	−069	039	−054	−004	032	−014	018	001	014

TABLE 4

Bivariate Distribution of First Differences of Series 3, Difference between Weeks t *and* t + 1 *against Difference between Weeks* t + 1 *and* t + 2; *Units, One-tenth of a Point*

Difference t + 1th *Week Less* t + 2th *Week*

	< -12	-12, -11	-10, -9	-8, -7	-6, -5	-4, -3	-2, -1	0, 1	2, 3	4, 5	6, 7	8, 9	10, 11	≥ 12	Totals
< -12	5	2	4	5	1	2	—	—	1	—	—	—	—	1	21
-12, -11	4	1	1	—	3	1	3	—	—	—	—	—	—	—	13
-10, -9	1	2	2	—	2	2	4	—	—	1	—	1	—	—	15
-8, -7	3	2	—	4	4	5	4	—	1	—	1	—	—	1	25
-6, -5	4	3	2	4	7	11	9	3	1	1	—	—	—	1	46
-4, -3	1	2	2	6	7	17	13	14	2	—	1	1	—	—	66
-2, -1	1	1	1	2	9	19	14	18	5	5	2	2	1	1	81
0, 1	—	—	—	1	6	8	22	26	13	9	3	2	1	—	91
2, 3	—	—	2	1	1	—	5	15	9	4	3	3	—	1	44
4, 5	1	—	—	1	3	—	3	7	7	5	1	1	2	1	32
6, 7	—	—	—	—	2	1	—	3	1	2	—	2	1	2	14
8, 9	—	—	1	—	1	—	1	2	1	3	2	—	—	4	15
10, 11	—	—	—	—	—	—	1	2	2	1	—	1	—	1	8
≥ 12	—	—	—	—	—	—	1	1	1	1	—	2	3	1	14
Totals	21	13	15	25	46	66	81	91	44	32	14	15	8	14	485

(Left margin, rotated: Difference, t th week, less (t + 1)th week)

(b) to the fact that at certain times all prices rise together so that they can't go wrong, (c) to having inside information so that they can anticipate a movement, (d) to their being able to act very quickly, (e) to their being able to operate on such a scale that profits are not expended in brokers' fees and stamp duties. But it is unlikely that anything I say or demonstrate will destroy the illusion that the outside investor can make money by playing the markets, so let us leave him to his own devices.

23. There are several factors of these series of correlations requiring explanation.

(a) If we arrange them according to the magnitude of the first serial correlation, which seems a fair summary measure of internal correlation, we get the following order:

Series	3	Investment Trusts.
	15	Total Distribution.
	19	All classes.
	14	Stores, etc.
	17	Miscellaneous.
	11	Total Production.
	7	Electric Light.
	18	Total Miscellaneous.
	5	Coal.
	4	Building Materials.
	8	Gas.
	9	Iron and Steel.
	6	Cotton.
	1	Banks.
	13	Shipping.
	2	Insurance.
	16	Breweries.
	12	Home rails.
	10	Oil.

We can understand why this list should be headed by investment trusts, which are almost an aggregative index in themselves, and why it should be tailed by shipping, breweries, home-rails and oil. But it is not clear why banks and insurance companies come so low.

(b) Apart from investment trusts and stores, the series showing the greatest internal correlations are the aggregative series 11, 15, 18 and 19. We get greater serial correlation in the averages than in the constituent series, which at first sight seems absurd and in any case is very misleading. One possibility is that this effect is generated by the method of construction of the series, e.g., the use of geometric means, the substitution of new quotations and so on. With the help of Mr.

S. T. David and Mr. Haycocks I went into this explanation fairly thoroughly but it does not seem to account for the phenomenon. The use of geometric means could raise or lower the serial correlations but need not bias them upwards; substitution of new quotations is carried out only in December and its effect, even if systematic, would be so diluted in the correlation of weekly figures as not to explain the magnitude of the aggregation effects. A more likely explanation lay in the existence of lag correlations between the series and I revert to the point below in paragraph 28.

24. Whatever the reason, the existence of these serial correlations in averaged series is rather disturbing. If the effect is a general one, it means that we must be very chary of drawing inferences from series of index numbers of the aggregative type, which is most unfortunate because such series are, in many instances, all that the statistician or the economist has to work on. The so-called "cycles" appearing in such series may not be due to endogenous elements or structural features at all, but to the correlations between disturbances acting on the constituent parts of the aggregative series.

25. I am led to infer that wherever possible the econometrician must study individual series rather than aggregates, just as he must study closely neighbouring points of time rather than observations at long intervals. This may be part of the reason why attempts to fit simple models to a whole economy have usually failed. It is as though a physicist set out to investigate the properties of light without being able to isolate a pure colour and with a diffraction grating ruled at intervals of an inch apart. Such conclusions would apply to price data, or to any nundinal data where there is a rapid adjustment of forces in a fluid market. They may not apply with equal force to production data.

Cross-correlation of the Share-prices

26. To study the series further we have to examine the correlations between them. It is possible to pick out pairs from 19 individuals in 171 ways and even with modern computing facilities it was too laborious to work out a number of lag correlations for them all. I chose 28 pairs, taking those for which the analysis seemed likely to be most rewarding, as follows:

   (1, 4), (1, 5), (1, 6), (1, 9), (1, 12), (1, 13)
   (4, 5), (4, 6), (4, 8), (4, 12), (4, 13)
   (5, 6), (5, 8), (5, 9), (5, 12)
   (6, 8), (6, 9), (6, 11), (6, 12)
   (8, 11), (8, 18)
   (9, 11), (9, 12), (9, 13)
   (11, 12), (11, 13), (11, 18)
   (12, 13)

The numbers correspond to the series set out in section 4. The lags even worked out as far as the sixth each way, e.g., (1, 4) means that lag correlations were worked out between first differences of series 1 and 4 (Banks, etc., and Building Materials) for lags of -6 to 6, thirteen coefficients in all. The results are given in Table 5.

27. The main feature of this set of correlations is the smallness of the magnitudes for the lags. There are traces of correlation in some instances but, however real, they are very slight. Thus no series acts as a "leader" for the others. Not only is it impossible to predict a series from its own internal behaviour but it seems equally impossible to predict it from the behaviour of the other price series.

28. We can now revert to the aggregation effect mentioned in paragraph 23 and discuss it in simplified terms. Suppose we have a series of consecutive pairs of terms $(\varepsilon_1, \eta_1)(\varepsilon_2, \eta_2) \ldots$ (ε_n, η_n) with zero means. Consider the correlation of sums $E \equiv \sum_{i=1}^{n} \varepsilon_i$ and $F \equiv \sum_{i=1}^{n} \eta_i$. If the variance of ε_i and η_i is σ_i^2 we find

$$\text{corr}(E, F) = \frac{\sum_{i,j} \sigma_i \sigma_j \text{ corr}(\varepsilon_i \eta_j)}{\sum \sigma_i \sigma_j \text{ corr}(\varepsilon_i, \varepsilon_j)} \qquad i, j = 1 \ldots n \qquad . \qquad . \qquad (11)$$

TABLE 5

Lag Correlations of the Differences of Certain Pairs of Series from Series 1–19

Lag

Series	−6	−5	−4	−3	−2	−1	0	1	2	3	4	5	6
(1, 4)	−008	−066	−077	−021	036	028	414	100	015	008	023	−080	−125
(1, 5)	−060	−134	−137	−068	015	030	255	077	102	−011	015	011	−066
(1, 6)	−080	−037	−074	−087	019	029	228	126	163	010	062	−010	−118
(1, 9)	−023	−102	−139	−014	−027	−021	295	053	050	028	−020	027	−028
(1, 12)	−037	−023	−046	−029	017	−044	275	154	073	0003	−001	022	−118
(1, 13)	−033	−068	−060	−124	113	051	258	121	030	−015	004	−063	−070
(4, 5)	−064	−108	−102	002	034	070	425	200	035	052	−044	−019	016
(4, 6)	−059	−036	−047	−003	059	058	424	201	076	054	−027	−003	−089
(4, 8)	−037	−067	−015	−024	049	085	310	−002	023	030	006	−027	−046
(4, 12)	022	−071	−049	026	−009	−006	367	187	−006	059	031	018	−066
(4, 13)	048	−052	−033	054	046	111	320	096	019	002	−068	001	010
(5, 6)	−080	009	051	083	048	182	454	161	081	054	−043	−108	−134
(5, 8)	−013	−013	026	00001	044	009	272	004	025	035	−056	−042	007
(5, 9)	−075	−016	−065	070	013	096	661	226	033	024	015	−065	−053
(5, 12)	026	−014	−036	074	037	063	392	167	024	−013	025	−048	−072
(6, 8)	−040	−033	037	−004	064	024	194	014	−031	012	−003	032	−072
(6, 9)	−122	083	004	078	038	085	482	228	030	013	071	024	−115
(6, 11)	−127	−073	004	092	104	156	750	140	080	033	018	011	−124
(6, 12)	−095	−034	−031	110	014	089	368	194	−027	011	−024	033	−114
(8, 11)	−020	−049	−027	069	002	006	389	066	075	−002	023	−046	−030
(8, 18)	−033	−064	−032	055	−005	−046	399	079	125	002	010	−051	−028
(9, 11)	−087	−004	042	022	022	228	795	071	−032	033	−038	−060	−101
(9, 12)	−056	−025	041	039	008	016	469	110	−070	060	042	−048	−149
(9, 13)	007	−031	026	133	092	144	279	102	−037	047	−111	−029	−002
(11, 12)	−053	−035	−060	072	010	054	522	224	−024	059	036	−004	−120
(11, 13)	066	−076	038	082	042	199	407	140	041	011	−056	−067	021
(11, 18)	−051	−004	007	036	094	196	824	166	069	065	−108	−084	−101
(12, 13)	−039	−022	044	041	039	146	281	045	031	001	−085	−008	−031

Note.—Decimal points omitted. Lag counted as interval of first series after second, e.g., lag 2 for series (1, 4) is correlation of series 1 at time $t + 2$ and series 4 at time t.

or, if all the variances are equal,

$$\text{corr}(E, F) = \frac{\text{mean corr}(\varepsilon_i, \eta_j)}{\text{mean corr}(\varepsilon_i, \varepsilon_j)} \qquad . \qquad . \qquad . \qquad (12)$$

For my series I do not possess all the lag correlations but as an example of the kind of thing which may happen let us suppose that all the correlations $(\varepsilon_i, \varepsilon_j)$ have a mean value of $0 \cdot 4$ (this being about the mean of those values we have in Table 5) and that the mean correlation of (ε_i, η_j) is $0 \cdot 1$. Then we find

$$\text{corr}(E, F) = \frac{225 \, (0 \cdot 1)}{15 + 210 \, (0 \cdot 4)} = 0 \cdot 23$$

so that the first serial of the aggregate series is more than twice the mean serials of its constituents. It is a piece of good luck, I suppose, that the first serial of series 19 turns out to be $0 \cdot 234$.

29. The cross correlations of order zero suggest that there is a good deal of *simultaneous* sympathetic movement between the series; (simultaneous, that is, within the compass of a single week). They are more or less as one would expect but not always so big as a simple model of the economy would suggest. If we regard these random changes from week to week as due to exogenous elements, we must suppose that the elements are substantially different from one series to another, albeit not independent.

30. One could clearly take this analysis further, for instance by working out multiple regressions or attempting a component analysis to see whether there were any common factors. I have refrained from doing so at this stage for two reasons; one is that further experiments on other

45

price series and for different intervals of time are desirable before we refine the analysis; the other is that the existence of the aggregative effect would probably vitiate the findings and I think we shall have to go back to primary series before attempting to isolate components.

New York Cotton Prices

31. The New York spot cotton prices of series 22 are a salutary warning against undue generalization. They are monthly, not weekly, series and cover about 125 years. One might have expected them to behave like the wheat series, but they do not. Table 6 gives the serial correlations up to the sixteenth order. As there were obvious breaks in continuity during the

TABLE 6

Serial Correlations of Cotton Prices (*Series* 22)

(Decimal points omitted)

Order of Correlation	Period 1816–1860	Period 1868–1914	Period 1921–1950	Total Series (1816–1950)
1	346	393	227	313
2	096	046	−012	039
3	−049	−096	−027	−053
4	−045	−153	−172	−125
5	−075	−060	024	−032
6	−053	−075	095	−000
7	−013	−068	031	−010
8	015	−064	135	041
9	−037	−028	021	−012
10	001	071	122	068
11	029	088	−000	033
12	−051	080	−106	−038
13	−093	−006	024	−014
14	−143	032	047	012
15	−105	−011	025	016
16	−022	−050	042	008

American Civil War and during World War I, I have calculated the serials separately for the periods 1816–1860, 1868–1914 and 1921–1950.

The bivariate distributions of the type of Table 1 are regular, looking very much like a normal form, but the correlations are significant. We now find a pattern of behaviour rather like that of a simple Markoff series. The price-change from month t to month $t + 1$ is now clearly correlated with that from month $t + 1$ to month $t + 2$, but we do not require a memory of more than a month in the market to account for the serial correlation.

There are several possible explanations of this effect, although it is difficult to be sure whether any of them is the right one. Wheat is a commodity which is grown in both hemispheres and a continual supply on the market may keep the price more fluid than for cotton, a product of the northern hemisphere only. Moreover, crop forecasts are better for wheat than for cotton and there is a tendency for the latter to be underestimated at the beginning of the season; the slow improvement in estimates as the growing season proceeds might induce some correlation in the prices. The slower rate of progress of cotton through the manufacturing process may also have some effect. But whatever the reason, it seems that we are not entitled to generalize from one agricultural commodity to another and a systematic survey of the major raw materials of commerce is necessary before we can lay down any general rules.

First Experiments in Trend Fitting

32. The typical Yule autoregressive scheme which has been fitted to economic data with a certain amount of success may be written

$$\alpha u_{t+2} + \beta u_{t+1} + \gamma u_t = \varepsilon_{t+2} \qquad . \qquad . \qquad . \qquad . \qquad . \qquad (13)$$

It seems natural to generalize this by considering the case when the constants α are themselves slowly moving through time as the economy changes. I therefore examined the scheme

$$(\alpha_0 + \alpha_1 t + \alpha_2 t^2) u_{t+2} + (\beta_0 + \beta_1 t + \beta_2 t^2) u_{t+1} + (\gamma_0 + \gamma_1 + \gamma_2 t^2) u_t = \varepsilon_{t+2} \quad . \quad (14)$$

A second-order Yule scheme was chosen because general experience so far has indicated that nothing much is to be gained by taking higher orders into account; and second-degree polynomials were chosen because the general run of the series suggested that they would be sufficient and would keep the arithmetic within reasonable bounds. But a decision on these points is rather arbitrary and more extended schemes might be necessary in some cases. The fitting was carried out on the primary series not on the differences.

33. In equation (14), it will be noted, I have allowed the coefficient of u_{t+2} to vary with time. It would be more consonant with the idea of auto*regression* to take the coefficient as a constant, say unity. However, the more general expression has one advantage, namely that it allows for movements in the variance of the disturbance term ε, which may well vary in time, especially for price data. If the coefficients are small compared with the maximum observed value of t^2 equation (14) may be written

$$u_{t+2} + (\beta_0' + \beta_1' t + \beta_2' t^2) u_{t+1} + (\gamma_0' + \gamma_1' + \gamma_2' t^2) = (\delta_0 + \delta_1 + \delta_2 t^2) \varepsilon_{t+2} \quad . \quad (15)$$

which exhibits the scheme as an approximation to a generalized Yule process with trend in the variance of the disturbance.

34. It will also be noticed that (14) is not a stationary process. There is no reason why it should be. No economic system yet observed has been stationary over long periods. It is true that schemes of type (14) may be explosive, which all economic systems are not; but that only implies that in representing the slow movements by polynomials we are approximating to some non-explosive function, a familiar procedure to which no exception is taken in other fields of application.

35. I fitted a scheme of type (14) by least squares, that is to say, by minimising the square of the expression on the left for variations in the nine parameters. This leads to nine equations with coefficients of the type $\Sigma t^2 u_{t+2}^2$, $\Sigma t u_{t+1} u_{t+2}$, etc. They are troublesome to compute but there is no theoretical difficulty. For the experiment series 1, 6 and 8 (Banks, etc., Cotton and Gas) were taken. The following are the results. The origin in each case is at the 244th term so that t ranges from -243 to 242.

Series 1

$$(1 + 0 \cdot 0^2 1,279,208t - 0 \cdot 0^4 31,214t^2) u_{t+2} + (-1 \cdot 236,892,571 - 0 \cdot 0^2 2,127,249t$$
$$+ 0 \cdot 0^4 40,297t^2) u_{t+1} + (0 \cdot 236,578,860 + 0 \cdot 0^3,848,707t - 0 \cdot 0^5 9,021t^2) u_t = \varepsilon_{t+2} . \quad (16)$$

Series 6

$$(1 - 0 \cdot 0^2 3,435,032t + 0 \cdot 0^3,135,958t^2) u_{t+2} + (-0 \cdot 086,729,101 - 0 \cdot 0^4 95,266t$$
$$- 0 \cdot 0^4 54,730t^2) u_{t+1} + (-0 \cdot 921,767,317 + 0 \cdot 0^2 3,562,777t -- 0 \cdot 0^4 81,816t^2)$$
$$= \varepsilon_{t+2} \quad . \quad . \quad . \quad . \quad . \quad . \quad . \quad . \quad . \quad . \quad . \quad (17)$$

Series 8

$$(1 + 0 \cdot 0^2 1,273,056t - 0 \cdot 0^4 37,456t^2) u_{t+2} + (-1 \cdot 421,129,272 - 0 \cdot 0^2 2,055,170t$$
$$+ 0 \cdot 0^4 56,754t^2) u_{t+1} + (0 \cdot 422,070,596 + 0 \cdot 0^3 822,663t - 0 \cdot 0^4 19,549) u_t = \varepsilon_{t+2} \quad . \quad (18)$$

36. These equations were worked out before it had dawned on me that the parent series were behaving in a wandering way, and at that stage it was a surprise when Mr. K. H. Medin, working in my department, pointed out that there were identities in the coefficients. In fact, very approximately

$$\left. \begin{array}{c} \alpha_0 + \beta_0 + \gamma_0 = 0 \\[2mm] \alpha_1 + \beta_1 + \gamma_1 = 0 \\[2mm] \alpha_2 + \beta_2 + \gamma_2 = 0 \end{array} \right\} \quad . \quad . \quad . \quad . \quad . \quad (19)$$

For instance in (16)

$$1 - 1 \cdot 236,892,571 + 0 \cdot 236,578,860 = 0 \cdot 0^3313,911$$

and in (18)

$$- 0 \cdot 0^437,456 + 0 \cdot 0^156,754 - 0 \cdot 0^119,549 = - 0 \cdot 0^6251$$

It follows, of course, that we can write (12) as

$$(\alpha_0 + \alpha_1 t + \alpha_2 t^2)(u_{t+2} - u_{t+1}) - (\gamma_0 + \gamma_1 t + \gamma_2 t^2)(u_{t+1} - u_t) = \varepsilon_{t+2} \quad . \quad (20)$$

so that first differences obey a generalized Markoff scheme. The ratio

$$(\gamma_0 + \gamma_1 t + \gamma_2 t^2)/(\alpha_0 + \alpha_1 t + \alpha_2 t^2)$$

varies to some extent over the range of t; for Series 1 from about $0 \cdot 3$ at one extreme to $0 \cdot 2$ at the other, being about $0 \cdot 2$ over the middle range; for Series 6 from about $- 0 \cdot 7$ to $- 0 \cdot 5$, about minus unity over the middle range; for Series 8 about $0 \cdot 4$ over the middle range.

On the whole I regard this experiment as a failure. It seems asking too much of quadratic polynomials to expect them to give a good representation over series of 500 terms; and in any case it is doubtful whether the series are sufficiently systematic to react significantly to this kind of treatment. The only reason I refer to the trend-fitting problem at all at this stage is to call attention to its difficulty in the hope that others may be led to study it.

37. I am well aware that this paper raises more difficulties than it resolves. Most papers on time-series do. The results concerning the time-interval of observation, the aggregative-effects and trend-fitting seemed to me, however, to be important enough to justify publication, if only to prevent my fellow-workers from spending time on profitless inquiries. More positive results must await further exploration of individual series, not only of prices but of production, and attempts to improve available statistical techniques for analysing them.

Acknowledgments

38. The computations involved have been severe, particularly in connection with the lag correlations of series 1 to 19. I am indebted to Mrs. Joan Humphries and Miss Julia Grahame for a great deal of the work, which they carried out with zeal and gratifying cheerfulness. I am also indebted to Mr. E. C. Fieller and the National Physical Laboratory for allowing me to use the electronic A.C.E. in determining serial covariances. My colleagues in the Division of Research Techniques at the London School of Economics, particularly Mr. S. T. David and Mr. K. H. Medin, have been very helpful in exploring lines of inquiry, many of which are referred to only very briefly or are not mentioned at all, that had to be followed up to decide incidental points; and my colleagues among the economists have endured much in discussions about the econometric implications of the results.

The distribution and independence of successive rates of return from the British equity market

by Richard A. Brealey,*
Prudential Research Fellow,
London Graduate School of Business Studies

INTRODUCTION

This paper is concerned with two closely related topics. The first area of interest is the frequency distribution of rates of return from the British equity market. Such a subject is of prime interest to the statistician who is involved in the study of speculative markets. Statistical inference is almost impossible unless one can assume that the underlying process is stationary and many statistical techniques depend on the form of the distribution also being known. Yet this is not just a problem for the statistician, or rather, to be more accurate, we are all to some degree statisticians. Anyone who views the market behaviour in one period as a guide to the sort of behaviour that may occur in another period is automatically assuming a stationary system. The investor, who assumes that market movements over a series of months have the same characteristics as market changes over successive days, is acting as if the distribution is also stable. The individual, who judges his broker on the basis of his average record at predicting the course of the market, is beginning to make assumptions about the distribution of the mean, and the institution that contemplates the use of formal techniques of portfolio selection is probably behaving as if the distribution of market returns is normal.

Since a random series must tend to conform to one of a known family of distributions, the investigation of the nature of the frequency distribution almost inevitably leads to the consideration of the process that generates it. Again the subject is of concern to the statistician, for his task is considerably lightened if successive market changes are independent of each other. In this instance, however, the investor has a very direct interest in the matter,

* The author is indebted to the Prudential Assurance Company and Coral Index Ltd. for providing the necessary data for this study, and to Prof. H. B. Rose, Dr. D. J. Chambers and Mr. S. D. Hodges of the London Business School for comments on an early draft of the paper.

for, if the market does progress in a random fashion, systems of technical analysis and chartism that depend on the existence of patterns in these changes would be doomed to failure. In these circumstances, the investor who seeks superior performance must concentrate his effort on the quest for superior information about the events that directly determine the market level. The topic is also relevant to those who are concerned about the efficiency of the market place, for any dependence between successive price changes would constitute prima facie evidence that prices were not at any single point in time reflecting all the information available to the market.

Finally, there are some incidental advantages to investigating both questions, for in the process we shall be forced to explore some matters that are of interest in their own right. In particular we shall consider the effect on price movements of the British account system and the behaviour of shares on ex-dividend dates.

The two sections that follow will be concerned principally with an analysis of the empirical findings. The implications of these findings will be examined briefly in a final section.

DISTRIBUTION OF MARKET RATES OF RETURN

In recent years a number of studies have appeared in the U.S.A. on the distribution of rates of return from common stocks. Of particular interest for present purposes is the work of Fama and Mandelbrot.[1]–[3] Both have produced evidence suggesting that the distributions have been marked by higher peaks and fatter tails than is the case with the familiar Gaussian or normal distribution. They have gone on to argue that the returns from an individual stock are instead drawn from a single non-Gaussian Pareto Levy distribution. Since the normal distribution is the only member of the Pareto Levy family to possess a finite variance, such a suggestion raises questions about the appropriateness of statistical methods that depend on the existence of a second moment.

Our primary concern is whether successive rates of return from the British market are likewise characterised by a larger proportion of extreme values than would be likely if they were drawn from the same normal distribution. As a measure of the market factor we shall use the Financial Times–Actuaries All Share Index (F.T.–A. Index). This is formed from 600 shares, though the number has varied slightly since its inception. It is a base-weighted index of the price relatives, adjusted for scrip issues and the scrip element in rights issues and employing market capitalisation as the weights. The index therefore measures the changes in the capital value of a portfolio that consisted of all the shares outstanding at the base date in each of the 600 companies. No allowance is made for dividends received. Hence, whenever a share goes ex-dividend, other things being equal, the index will reflect the resultant fall in that share's price. To the extent that conclusions in this study are based on data that include these ex-dividend days, they refer only to price changes as opposed to rates of return. However, by omitting these days from the analysis, it should be possible to assess whether the findings are equally true of rates of return.

Because the F.T.–A. Index is based on a limited sample of shares, it provides only an imperfect measure of the market factor. Nevertheless, the firms represented are among the largest quoted British companies, so that any such imperfections should be minor. It is worth noting in this context that King obtained a correlation of 0·97 between the American Standard and Poor Index and the market factor.[4] Since the F.T.–A. Index is similar in construction and scope to the Standard and Poor Index, and since the market factor appears to be no less important in this country,[5] we suspect that comparable results would hold in the present case. Not only should the F.T.–A. Index serve well as a measure of the market level, but there is also good reason to suppose that changes in the index are highly correlated with changes in the value of

managed portfolios.[1] Thus our conclusions are likely to be true both of the market in general and of actual diversified portfolios.

The basic data for this study consist of the daily values for the index between 10th April, 1962, and 28th October, 1968, a total of 1,665 days. The daily change in the Index was measured by dividing each day's level by that of the preceding day and taking the natural logarithm of the result. This logarithmic transformation provides a measure of the rate of return with continuous compounding.[2]

The first thing to notice about the distribution is that it is highly symmetrical. Of the observations, 50·7% lay above the mean and 49·3% below. The median change differed from the mean change by only 0·00035 standard deviations.

An important characteristic of the normal distribution is that a known proportion of observations fall within a given number of standard deviations from the mean. The frequencies for certain selected ranges are shown in the first column of Table 1. For the purposes of comparison the changes in the F.T.–A. Index were also expressed in terms of the number of standard deviations by which they differed from the mean. The proportion of observations lying within the selected ranges is shown in the second column of Table 1. Compared with the normal distribution there is an excess of very small and very large changes and a deficiency of medium-sized changes. These results are similar to those observed by Fama for individual American stocks.

The divergences from a normal distribution may be further demonstrated by ranking the data in ascending order and plotting the cumulative frequencies on normal probability graph paper. This

---

[1] See, for example, A. Russell and B. F. Taylor 'Investment Uncertainty and British Equities', *The Investment Analyst*, 22 (December 1968), 13–22.

[2] Implicit in the use of the logarithmic form is the assumption that investors behave as if they had an instantaneous horizon interval. The arguments for such an assumption are presented in M. C. Jensen, 'Risk, the Pricing of Capital Assets and the Evaluation of Investment Portfolios', *Journal of Business*, 42 (April 1969), 167–247. In the present context, the difference between continuous compounding and daily compounding is likely to be negligible.

TABLE 1: Comparison of frequency distribution with unit normal

Intervals in standard deviations	Unit normal	All F.T.A. changes	F.T.A. Tuesday Friday	F.T.A. Monday	F.T.A. first Monday of acct.	F.T.A. second Monday of acct.	F.T.A. first Friday of acct.	F.T.A. second Friday of acct.
0·5	38·30%	50·30%	49·85%	52·02%	53·57%	50·97%	45·41%	54·29%
1·0	68·26	78·13	78·45	76·88	75·00	78·16	71·35	83·57
1·5	86·64	90·32	90·74	88·73	87·86	89·32	89·19	91·43
2·0	95·45	95·13	92·56	92·77	92·86	92·72	96·22	92·14
2·5	98·76	97·30	97·80	95·38	95·71	95·15	97·84	95·00
3·0	99·73	98·44	98·41	98·55	98·57	98·54	98·38	97·14
4·0	99·99	99·70	99·62	100·00	100·00	100·00	99·51	99·29
5·0	99·99994	99·82	99·77	100·00	100·00	100·00	100·00	100·00
>5·0	0·00006	0·18	0·23	—	—	—	—	—
No. of observations		1664	1318	346	140	206	185	140

paper is so scaled that for a normal distribution the points lie along a straight line. A plot of the daily changes of the index is shown in Figure 1. The S-shaped line is again evidence of the fat tails to the distribution.

We should recognise the possibility that the high incidence of extreme changes may simply be a con-

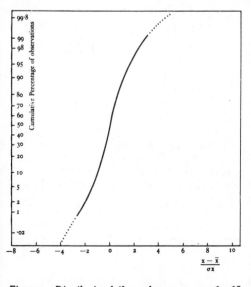

Figure 1   Distribution daily market returns—1962–68

sequence of measurement error. If the index moves in a random fashion, any random errors in the recorded level of the index are liable to produce an excess of large changes. The same effect could arise if jobbers have a tendency to repeat their quotation of the previous day unless the 'real' price has changed by a minimum amount. Fortunately both types of error are less likely to be a serious problem than in the case of individual securities.

An alternative explanation is that the changes in the index are not drawn from a single homogeneous universe. If changes on certain days characteristically display higher dispersion than on other days, it would be quite possible for the combined distribution to be characterised by fat tails, even if the distribution of the separate classes were normal.

Such a mixed distribution would be found if the variation in the price of the share increased in proportion to the total number of hours elapsed between the times at which the prices are recorded, This may be especially true of the type of news that is liable to induce market-wide moves. If this is the case, the changes in the index between Friday and Monday should show a greater degree of dispersion than between the close on successive weekdays.

A further reason for believing that the distribution of Monday changes may differ from that of other days is that normally shares go ex-dividend on the first Monday of the Account before the company closes its books. Since the prices of shares on all

51

other days will incorporate the accrued value of the dividend, omission of the Friday to Monday change may help towards an unbiased estimate of the distribution of daily rates of return.

Assume for a moment that successive market changes are independent. Then the standard deviation of the sums of N daily changes should be $\sqrt{N}$ times as great as the standard deviation of the daily changes themselves. Since three days elapse between Friday close and Monday close, the standard deviation of Monday changes should be $\sqrt{3}$, or 1·7 times that of weekday changes. In fact it was just over 1% lower.[3] Furthermore, when the Monday and Tuesday to Friday changes are considered separately in Table 1, the distributions continue to be characterised by fat tails.

A related possibility is that the amount of dispersion in price changes, or even the average change, may differ from one part of the Account to another. In particular, a large proportion of speculative activity may cause the market to fluctuate more widely at the beginning and end of the period. The first column of Table 2 shows the amount of dis-

TABLE 2: Dispersion and central tendency of changes on given days of Account

	Interquartile range $\times 10^3$	Median $\times 10^3$
First Monday (156)*	6·87	0·66
First Thursday (202)	7·24	1·73
First Friday (205)	6·12	1·28
Second Monday (227)	6·29	−0·99
Second Thursday (154)	5·85	−0·29
Second Friday (156)	5·66	−0·65

* Denotes numbers of observations.

persion of changes for six different points of the Account.[4] This provides some evidence that the

market is subject to greater variations at the beginning of the Account.

A further characteristic of interest is that the distributions of changes at different parts of the Account appear to differ in their measures of central tendency. This is illustrated in the second column of Table 2. It should be remembered that the absence of adjustment for dividend payments has already exerted a downward bias on the changes for the first Monday of the Account. Despite this, the difference between the medians for the first and second Mondays is significant at the 95% level on a one tailed test. No other tests of significance were undertaken. An attempt was made, however, to discover whether these differences were solely a result of the upward trend in prices during the period. This did not seem to be the case. Not only did the market fall proportionately less often on the first Monday and first Friday of the Account, but the average fall was no greater for the first Monday than for the second and was less for the first Friday than for the second.

These differences in dispersion and central tendency are insufficient to explain the high peaks and fat tails to the distribution. Table 1 demonstrates that, when sets of daily changes were analysed separately, the same characteristics were observed.

An alternative form of the mixed distribution hypothesis is that the series comprise a number of distributions successive in time. According to this view, the variations in the market during any sufficiently short period constitute a stable, and possibly Gaussian, distribution, but the process is not stationary and the parameters change between time periods. The suggestion of non-stationarity has intuitive appeal. Since the 1930's more skilled economic management and a better regulated stockmarket seem to have produced a downward shift in the risk and required return from equity investment. Within this framework, political and financial crises are liable to generate bouts of increased uncertainty.

Our record of market changes is not sufficiently

[3] Throughout this paper a set of simple rules was employed to handle complications posed by Stock Exchange holidays and three week accounts.

[4] For this analysis of account effects, the sample was extended to a total of 1,841 changes. The findings are consistent with the existence of a two-week cycle observed by

J. D. Hey in 'Spectral Analysis of Stock Market Prices', unpublished M.Sc. dissertation, Edinburgh University, 1968.

long to be able to cast any light on the question of long term shifts in the riskiness of equity investment. However, by studying the unusually large market moves, we should be able to learn something of the incidence of less prolonged changes in the amount of dispersion. During this 79-month period there were forty-five occasions on which the market change departed by more than 2·5 standard deviations from the mean. Of these instances, nineteen were clustered within four different calendar months. These unusually violent fluctuations were coincident with the Wall Street decline of June 1962, the Cuban missile alarm of October 1962, and the currency crises of November 1964 and November 1967. It seems reasonable to suppose that such events as the Cuban confrontation increase the conditional probability of further sharp price movements.

One necessary, but not sufficient, condition of shifts in the amount of dispersion would be some dependence between the absolute values of successive rates of return. For this reason the normalised changes in the index were converted to absolute amounts and the first order serial correlation co-efficient was computed. The co-efficient of 0·376 [$\sigma = 0.025$] indicates some highly significant dependence in the size of the changes. In addition contingency tables were constructed for the absolute changes on successive days and lagged days. This revealed that a below median change was succeeded by another below median change on 59% of the occasions and that it was followed on the next day but one by a below median change on 57% of the occasions. A chi square test indicated that both percentages differed from the expected figure at the one per cent level of significance.

Implicit in the preceding argument is the supposition that important items of news tend to cluster together in time. An alternative reason for expecting some serial dependence between the absolute values of changes was put forward by Mandelbrot. New information, it was suggested, is unlikely to be evaluated precisely by the market, so that the price may overshoot or fall short of the level dictated by more mature reflection. Since important items of news are not only likely to generate larger price

shifts but also greater initial errors in evaluation, the process of subsequent adjustment on these occasions is likely to involve larger price changes. The process, according to this view, appears to be akin to a servomechanism with major price movements being followed by dampened price oscillations. It is difficult to choose between these explanations on a priori grounds, nor indeed is there any reason that they could not both be valid.

If the fat tails are in part caused by periodic shifts in the dispersion parameter, we might expect to find that the distribution of changes over the appropriate sub-interval approaches the Gaussian. There are obvious objections to distinguishing these intervals so as to conform with our hypothesis. Nevertheless it was decided to separate out for further analysis the years 1963 and 1965, which were relatively free of wide fluctuations. The proportion of observations lying within selected ranges

TABLE 3: Comparison of frequency distributions with unit normal—selected years

Intervals in standard deviations	Unit normal	1963 Changes	1965 Changes	1962–68 Changes
0·5	38·30%	40·55%	43·53%	50·30%
1·0	68·26	74·80	75·69	78·13
1·5	86·64	86·22	89·80	90·32
2·0	95·45	93·70	94·12	95·13
2·5	98·76	98·43	96·47	97·30
3·0	99·73	99·61	98·43	98·44
4·0	99·99	99·61	100·00	99·70
5·0	99·99994	100·00	100·00	99·82
>5·0	0·00006	—	—	0·18
No. of observations		254	255	1664

is shown in Table 3. In both instances there is a smaller concentration of observations within the range of 0·5 standard deviations from the mean and the 1963 distribution approximates quite closely the normal. Thus it may not be necessary to postulate very short-lived periods of stationarity to retrieve the Gaussian case.

One other characteristic of the series is worth noting. If the members are drawn from a single

53

TABLE 4: Effect on frequency distribution of longer differencing intervals

Intervals in standard deviations	Unit normal	One-day changes	Four-day changes	Eight-day changes
0·5	38·30%	50·30%	47·60%	45·67%
1·0	68·26	78·13	72·84	74·04
1·5	86·64	90·32	87·98	87·50
2·0	95·45	95·13	94·71	94·71
2·5	98·76	97·30	97·36	97·60
3·0	99·73	98·44	98·80	99·52
4·0	99·99	99·70	99·76	99·52
5·0	99·99994	99·82	100·00	100·00
>5·0	0·00006	0·18	—	—
No. of observations		1664	416	208

Pareto Levy distribution, the distribution should be invariant under addition. Table 4 shows that, whilst the distribution is not seriously unstable, there is a tendency for it to approach normality as the interval is increased. Again the most satisfactory explanation of the long tails seems to be some degree of non-stationarity in the system.

INDEPENDENCE OF RETURNS

Dependence between the absolute values of changes in the market level cannot be used to achieve superior investment performance. The knowledge that tomorrow's change will be large, given that today's change was large, is in itself of relatively little value to investors. In contrast, any dependence between successive signed changes might indicate profitable trading opportunities.

There is a considerable body of evidence that successive returns from individual U.S. stock approximate a random progression.[5] However, not only might any non-randomness in the market component be obscured by noise, but, if there was cross-

serial correlation between the returns of individual stocks, there would be serial correlation in the average returns of a group of stocks. At first blush, some modest amount of dependence does appear to be present. For example, between 1951 and 1958 the serial correlation between the weekly changes of an index of American stocks was 0·15.[6] Similarly, the co-efficient of correlation between adjacent daily changes in the Dow Jones Average from 1952 to 1963 was 0·11.[6] When we turn to British data, there is a dearth of evidence either for individual shares or for the market. One study that is relevant for present purposes is that of Kendall, who observed a first order serial correlation of 0·23 and second-order correlation of 0·11 between the weekly changes in the Actuaries Index 1920–38.[7] More recently, Dryden has applied a number of tests that appear to confirm Kendall's results.[7] The behaviour of the F.T.–A. Index between 1962 and 1968 also seems to suggest some tendency for market changes to persist. The first order serial correlation co-efficient between the daily rates of return was 0·219 and the second order 0·018.

The difficulty with all these tests of market behaviour is that the first order co-efficient will be biased upward if the prices used to calculate the index do not occur simultaneously. In such circumstances the index in effect measures the average level of the market during the afternoon. It is known that the correlation of first differences of averages in a random chain can induce correlations not present in the original data and that the co-efficient will tend

---

[5] The most important empirical work conducted before 1964 is reproduced in P. H. Cootner (ed.), *The Random Character of Stock Market Prices*, Cambridge: The M.I.T. Press, 1964. Notable among more recent evidence is that provided by E. F. Fama in 'The Behavior of Stock Market Prices', *Journal of Business*, 38 (January 1965), 34–105. The statistical tests employed in this section closely parallel those of Fama.

[6] A. B. Moore, 'Some Characteristics of Changes in Common Stock Prices', in P. H. Cootner (ed.), *The Random Character of Stock Market Prices*. It is worth noting that Wise in an unpublished paper has shown that, where the observations conform to a stable Paretian distribution with $\alpha < 1$, the serial correlation co-efficient provides a consistent unbiased estimate of the true serial correlation in the population. If the series is non-stationary, corresponding inferences are of course not strictly possible.

[7] See, for example, M. M. Dryden, 'Short Term Forecasting of Share Prices: An Information Theory Approach', *Scottish Journal of Political Economy* (November 1968), 227–249, and by the same author 'Filter Tests of U.K. Share Prices', *Applied Economics*, I (January 1970), 261–76. In an appendix to the latter article, Dryden also notes the existence of fat tails to the distribution of his data.

rapidly towards 0·25 as the number of periods averaged is increased.[8] This problem is likely to beset the use of all popular market indexes. In the case of American indexes the prices employed are typically the last transaction of the day. In the British case they are usually the prices provided by a jobber when he closes his book in each share.

In an attempt to measure and eliminate this bias a new market index was constructed (the New Index). This spanned 202 days from February 1968 to November 1968. The 29 shares composing this index were identical to those used in the Financial Times Index except for the omission of Marks and Spencer, which was not incorporated in that index until October 1968. The New Index was constructed from blue-button quotations obtained at approximately 2 p.m. each day. Although there was some slight variation in the time at which prices were recorded, the quotations for any one day were, as near as possible, simultaneous.

These prices were adjusted for scrip issues, the scrip element in rights issues and dividend payments. This last task required an estimate of the expected effect on prices of dividend payments. It is frequently assumed that when a share goes ex the dividend the price will tend to fall by the full amount of the dividend. In the U.S.A. this assumption is for most purposes adequate, for several studies of the behaviour of American stocks on ex-dividend dates have indicated that the price on such occasions declines by about 90% of the value of the dividend.[9] It was felt that the very high marginal rates of tax on income in the U.K. could well cause a somewhat smaller fall off. During the period under consideration the 29 shares went ex-dividend 52 times. The change in price that occurred on each of these

occasions was obtained by subtracting the first quotation available for the ex-dividend day from the closing price on the previous day. The decline in price was then expressed as a percentage of the gross amount of the dividend. The results are shown in the first column of Table 5. As a check on these findings, a test was made of the behaviour of all shares that both went ex-dividend on 13th January, 1969, and that are quoted on the back page of the Financial Times. The closing price on the ex-dividend date was first adjusted for any change in the overall market level from the preceding day and then subtracted from the closing price on the preceding day. The result was again expressed as a percentage of the gross amount of the dividend. The results are shown in the second column of Table 5. Not only did relatively few

TABLE 5: Fall in price as % of gross dividend

| % of Dividend | No. of observations | |
	Sample A	Sample B
Below 16	8	15
16–25	3	2
26–35	4	5
36–45	6	3
46–55	10	7
56–65	9	3
66–75	4	2
76–85	0	2
Above 85	8	21
Total	52	60
Mean	52·5%	—
Median	51·3%	49·6%

shares qualify but those that did were for the most part thinly traded. Because of the resultant dispersion in the figures, only the median decline was calculated. This, however, closely approximated that of the first sample. In the light of these findings, the dividend correction was made by adding back to the price on the ex-dividend date half the amount of the dividend.

The market index, that was constructed from these prices, was a base weighted arithmetic

---

[8] See H. Working, 'Note on the Correlation of First Differences of Average in a Random Chain', *Econometrica*, 28 (October 1960), 916–18.

[9] See P. B. Readett, 'The Price Behavior of Stocks on their Ex-Dividend Dates', unpublished S. M. Thesis, M.I.T., 1956; J. A. Campbell and W. Beranek, 'Stock Price Behavior on Ex-Dividend Dates', *Journal of Finance*, 10 (December 1955), 425–29; D. Durand and A. M. May, 'The Ex-Dividend Behavior of American Telephone and Telegraph Stock', *Journal of Finance*, 15 (March 1960), 19–31.

average of the price relatives, with each security receiving equal weight. In other words, the index measured the subsequent performance of a portfolio, which consisted of an equal investment at the beginning of the period in each of the 29 shares. The daily return from this portfolio was measured by dividing each day's level of the index by that of the preceding day and taking the natural logarithm of the result.[10]

The relatively small body of data employed in the construction of this index limits its usefulness. No careful assessment was made of the adequacy of a 29-share index as a proxy for the market factor. More seriously, the very short period covered by the data provides a severe restriction on the significance of any tests that may be conducted on the data in isolation. However, by comparing the results with those of similar tests on the F.T.–A. Index for the same period, it may be possible to obtain some measure of the bias inherent in more comprehensive studies of the F.T.–A. Index.

It is now possible to return to the problem of serial dependence between market returns. Consider initially the second two columns of Table 6.

TABLE 6: Serial correlation co-efficient for signed changes in index

	F.T.–A. Index 1962–68	F.T.–A. Index 1968	New Index 1968
First-order co-efficient	0·22	0·32	0·19
Second-order co-efficient	0·02	−0·04	−0·10
σ	0·02	0·07	0·07

The second order correlation co-efficient is rather lower for the New Index than for the F.T.–A. Index. Since second-order relationships are unlikely to be biased by the use of non-simultaneous prices, it looks as if other differences in the construction of the two indices are affecting the corre-

---

[10] It is worth noting that the frequency distribution of the the 201 changes in both the F.T.–A. Index and the New Index was not substantially different from the Gaussian.

lations. This makes it difficult to be sure that the sharp drop in the first order co-efficient is due to the use of simultaneous prices, but it is at least a plausible explanation. The magnitude of this first-order co-efficient for the New Index is also not easy to interpret. On the one hand the co-efficient is significantly different from zero at the 95% level. Yet a comparison of the first two columns of the table shows that the first order correlation for the F.T.–A. sub-sample overestimates the correlation for the whole sample. It is likely, therefore, that the co-efficient for the New Index also provides a high estimate of the true first-order correlation for the whole 1962–68 period. Even if an adjustment is made for this fact, one is still left with positive first-order correlation. The evidence is by no means clear-cut but there does appear to be some slight dependence between market returns on successive days.

The serial correlation model offers a test for the presence of linear relationships only. Consequently, a co-efficient of zero would constitute a necessary but not sufficient condition of independence. It is taking an implausibly simple view of the world to suppose that economic variables can only be related in a linear fashion. Therefore, although it is not possible to test the infinite number of alternative hypotheses with only a finite body of data, it is at least prudent to extend the analysis to cover simple non-linear dependence.

Unfortunately, the apparent bias induced by non-simultaneous prices is not confined to serial correlation, but also applies to any test of first order dependence. The same approach can be used to judge the effects.

The first section of Table 7 shows two-by-two contingency tables for the changes in the F.T.–A. Index between 1962 and 1968. The table for adjacent changes appears to indicate that there is a 62% probability that an annual rise in equity prices today will be succeeded by an unusual rise tomorrow. The second section shows that during 1968 the probability of successive changes in the same direction had decreased to 59%. The third section demonstrates that the use of the New Index reduced the conditional probability by a further 4%. The

TABLE 7: Contingency tables of signed changes in index

	Successive changes		Lagged changes	
	Below median	Above median	Below median	Above median
F.T.–A. Index 1962–68				
Below median	518	314	429	403
Above median	314	518	403	429
	$x^2 = 24\cdot4$		$x^2 = 0\cdot4$	
F.T.–A. Index 1968				
Below median	59	41	49	51
Above median	41	59	51	49
	$x^2 = 6\cdot5$		$x^2 = 0\cdot0$	
New Index 1968				
Below median	55	45	48	52
Above median	45	55	52	48
	$x^2 = 1\cdot6$		$x^2 = 0\cdot2$	

results are again disappointingly inconclusive. Taken in isolation the differences between cells for the New Index are not significant at the 5% level. However, the evidence of the F.T.–A. Index suggests that, if the data were available for the New Index for the whole 1962–69 period, the differences between cells might be larger. The most satisfactory interpretation is that there is a weak tendency for the direction of change to persist.

This contingency test may be broadened to provide a runs test, where the direction of change is again defined in relation to the median. Table 8

TABLE 8: Runs of daily changes in index above or below median

	F.T.–A. Index 1962–68	F.T.–A. Index 1968	New Index 1968
Expected no. of runs	832·9	101·4	101·4
Actual no. of runs	629	80	91
Se	20·4	7·1	7·1

compares the actual number of runs with the expected number. As in the contingency tables, the shift to the New Index results in an increase in the total number of runs, which is no longer significantly different from the expected figure at the 5% level. Yet a comparison of the two sets of results for the F.T.–A. Index does suggest that repeated sampling for the New Index would produce a slightly higher divergence between the actual and expected number of runs. A further division of runs by length is given in Table 9. The use of the New Index again produces a sharp narrowing, but not the complete disappearance, of the gap between expected and actual runs.

TABLE 9: Expected and actual distribution of runs by length, given actual total number of positive and negative runs

Length of run	F.T.–A. Index 1962–68				F.T.–A. Index 1968				New Index			
	Negative Runs		Positive Runs		Negative Runs		Positive Runs		Negative Runs		Positive Runs	
	Exp.	Actual	Exp.	Actual	Exp.	Actual	Exp.	Actual	Exp.	Actual	Exp.	Actual
1	159·1	118	155·4	108	19·1	14	20·9	13	22·9	21	22·6	17
2	78·5	75	78·7	81	10·0	12	10·0	13	11·5	11	11·2	12
3	38·7	48	39·9	51	5·2	6	4·8	7	5·8	8	5·6	9
4	19·1	28	20·2	26	2·7	1	2·3	4	2·9	1	2·8	4
5	9·4	17	10·2	22	1·4	1	1·1	1	1·5	1	1·4	2
6	4·7	9	5·2	13	0·7	3	0·5	1	0·7	3	0·7	1
7	2·3	7	2·6	2	0·4	2	0·2	0	0·4	1	0·3	0
8	1·1	5	1·3	6	0·2	1	0·1	0	0·2	0	0·2	0
9	0·6	3	0·7	3	0·1	0	0·06	1	0·09	0	0·08	0
10	0·3	3	0.3	0	0·06	0	0·03	0	0·05	0	0·04	0
11	0·1	0	0·2	0	0·03	0	0·01	0	0·02	0	0·02	0
12	0·07	1	0·09	1	0.02	0	0·01	0	0·01	0	0·01	0
13	0·03	0	0·04	1	0·01	0	0·00	0	0·01	0	0·01	0
14	0·02	0	0·02	1	0·00	0	0·00	0	0·00	0	0·00	0

Whilst these findings do not violate seriously the random walk hypothesis, they do support the view that there exists a slight positive dependence between successive daily rates of return. Several explanations are possible. For example, jobbers may be slow to adjust their quotation in shares displaying little activity, so that the price movement of these issues would tend to lag that of the rest of the market. A cursory attempt was made to test this hypothesis by examining the profitability before dealing costs of the following decision rule:

'If by the end of the day the market has risen, purchase any share whose price has remained unchanged. Conversely, if the market has fallen, sell short the share whose price has not changed. In either case close the position at the end of the subsequent day.'

The effectiveness of this procedure was tested with the aid of the 29 share sample. In only 14 of the 29 cases did the shares provide a higher rate of return after they were purchased than after they were sold, and, although the average return was fractionally higher in the case of the purchases, the median was slightly lower. An alternative naive strategy produced substantially similar results. These findings do not, therefore, support the hypothesis that dependence in market rates of return is caused by some shares reacting more rapidly to information than others.

A more plausible suggestion is that share prices in general do not discount instantaneously the implication of new information. There are several pieces of evidence to suggest that in the U.S.A. news that is relevant to the price of an individual share is not fully reflected in the price until several days afterwards.[11] This delayed response is not though sufficient to offer the opportunity for any significant profit after allowance for dealing costs. Again there is no similar body of evidence as to the

[11] See, for example, J. V. Davis, 'The Adjustment of Stock Prices to New Information', unpublished Ph.D. dissertation, Cornell University, 1967; M. Scholes, 'A Test of the Competitive Market Hypothesis: The Market for New Issues and Secondary Offerings', unpublished Ph.D. dissertation, University of Chicago, 1969; R. Ferber, 'Short Run Effects of Stock Market Services on Stock Prices', *Journal of Finance*, 13 (March 1958), 80–95.

speed of reaction of the British equity market. For this reason we examined the reaction of the F.T.–A. Index to the publication of the monthly trade figures between 1962 and 1969. Each month's announcement was classified as a pleasant surprise or a disappointment according to whether the net balance was above or below the long term average balance. Table 10 shows the average progress of the

TABLE 10: Average performance of market during periods of good and bad trade figures

Day relative to announcement	Good trade figures	Bad trade figures
D−4	−0·053%	+0·144%
D−3	+0·117	+0·021
D−2	+0·048	+0·100
D−1	+0·159	−0·178
D	+0·106	−0·049
D+1	+0·035	−0·188
D+2	−0·102	−0·018
D+3	−0·162	−0·073
D+4	−0·167	+0·161
D+5	−0·119	+0·080
D+6	+0·006	+0·055
D+7	+0·195	−0·014
D+8	−0·022	−0·040
D+9	+0·354	+0·071

market in the days surrounding both kinds of event. Probably because a number of observations were incorrectly classified, the market movements are disappointingly small. Nevertheless it is interesting that on the day before the announcement and the next two days the market rose if the trade balance was relatively favourable and fell if it was unfavourable. Since the government press office frequently leaks the information one day before the official announcement, it is reasonable to interpret this three-day price adjustment as a reaction to the trade figures. This is consistent with the view that the market customarily takes more than one day to react to news.

CONCLUSION

At first glance the distribution of daily rates of return from the British equity market resembles the

58

familiar bell-shaped pattern of the normal distribution. The first thing to notice about it is that observations are evenly distributed about the mean, so that on any one occasion there is an equal chance that the return will be above or below the long-term rate. Such symmetry is important, for it suggests that the investor in ordinary shares is principally concerned with just two aspects of the distribution—the expected return and the dispersion of returns.

Closer examination of the frequency distributions reveals an important difference from the normal pattern. There is an excess of very small changes, a deficiency of medium-sized changes and an excess of very large changes. This inevitably provides sampling problems, for the mean change and the variance over any past period will be heavily affected by the presence of one of these extreme observations. By the same token an investor's performance will depend to a considerable extent on his ability to foresee the very unusual market move rather than on his success at predicting a whole succession of relatively small movements.

Much of the first section was devoted to seeking an explanation for the fat tails to the distribution. One possibility is that the rates of return belong to the Pareto Levy family of distributions, of which the normal is but an extreme case. An alternative explanation is that the distribution is non-stationary, so that the dispersion and even the central tendency are periodically shifting. It is difficult to be dogmatic on this subject but several features seemed to favour the latter suggestion. In particular it was found that the extreme changes tended to cluster together in time and to occur on specific days of the Account. Moreover, when specific sub-periods were selected for analysis, the distribution came closer to the normal pattern, and this also happened when the differencing interval was increased. It was unrealistic to expect any economic time series to present a perfect image of a theoretical distribution or its parameters to be perfectly stationary. However, unless some degree of stationarity is assumed, statistical inference is impossible. The Pareto Levy explanation, therefore, has the practical merit of not being nihilistic. Nevertheless it is not clear that regarded simply as a working hypothesis, it has sufficient advantages over the normal hypothesis to compensate for the additional complexity.

The occurrence of a major change in the market level appears to offer some warning to investors that another major shift may be imminent. This knowledge is insufficient to provide superior profits, unless the investor has some means of knowing the direction of the additional movement. After making an allowance for the bias that can result from the use of non-simultaneous prices, there still appeared to be some slight tendency for a change in the market one day to be repeated on the next day. A plausible explanation of the phenomenon is that investors do not at once react fully to new information.

It is most important to keep a sense of proportion about this result. The observed persistence in market movement was very weak and could well have been coincidental. Other, more pronounced, patterns in market behaviour may subsequently be discovered, but the regularity observed in this paper is almost certainly insufficient to be profitably exploited and does not seriously infringe the random walk hypothesis.

One minor, but nevertheless interesting, pattern concerns the market behaviour at different parts of the Account. Since there is a unique settlement date one might have expected rates of return within the Account to reflect the reward for risk bearing but not the time value of money. Instead prices seem customarily to have risen during the first part of the Account and to have declined in the second part. Fluctuations also were more marked towards the beginning of the Account.

Contrary to American experience share prices on ex-dividend days seem to have fallen by approximately 50% of the gross dividend. The most obvious explanation lies in the high marginal rates of income tax. If it is true that British investors are significantly influenced by the differential rates of tax on income and capital gain, then we must be willing to admit the possibility that the price of British securities is responsive to the firm's dividend policy.

REFERENCES

[1] E. F. Fama, 'The Behavior of Stock Market Prices', *Journal of Business*, 38 (January 1965,) 34-105.

[2] B. Mandelbrot, 'The Variation of Certain Speculative Prices', *Journal of Business*, 36 (October 1963), 394-419.

[3] B. Mandelbrot, 'The Variation of Some Other Speculative Prices', *Journal of Business*, 40 (October 1967), 393-413.

[4] B. F. King, 'Market and Industry Factors in Stock Price Behavior', *Journal of Business*, 38 (January 1966), 139-190.

[5] See, for example, D. O. Ewart-James, 'A Factor Analysis of Stock Market Prices', unpublished M.B.A. dissertation, Manchester Business School, 1969.

[6] E. F. Fama, 'Tomorrow on the New York Stock Exchange', *Journal of Business*, 38 (July 1965), 285-99.

[7] M. G. Kendall, 'The Analysis of Economic Time Series, Part I', *Journal of the Royal Statistical Society*, 96 (1953), 11-25.

Filter Tests of U.K. Share Prices

Myles M. Dryden
Edinburgh University

1

THE RESEARCH reported in this article is aimed at answering the question of whether or not statistical dependence is displayed in the behaviour of U.K. share price changes. The answer to this question clearly has implications in a number of directions: the management of portfolios, the construction and use of index numbers of share prices, the evaluation of the efficiency of capital markets as allocators of the nation's capital and so on. The statistical examination of share prices—and indeed of speculative prices in general—has been carried furthest in relation to American data and mainly by American economists[1]. A justification of this study lies in the danger of extrapolating the results of American investigations to U.K. situations[2]. Smaller studies carried out by the author [DRYDEN (1968) and (1969)] suggest that the American results are in fact not reliable guides to U.K. share price behaviour.

The question of whether or not there is dependence in time series of U.K. share prices is examined in relation to three sets of data[3]. All three series are index numbers of share prices and each covers a period of approximately 4 years. Since the data are collected on a daily basis this means that well over 1000 prices were collected for each series. Section 2 provides a description of the technique used to test each series for dependence. The results of the tests are then discussed and compared with similar U.S. studies. Section 3 simply offers a few concluding comments.

2

Does the future course of the price of a particular share depend on its prior behaviour? If so, how long is the memory of a share's pricing mechanism? What form does the dependence, if it exists, take? Are increases in prices more likely to be followed by increases than by decreases? Is the size of the change in price, as opposed to its sign, relevant? Quite naturally researchers have tried to examine these questions by applying orthodox statistical techniques. For example, the correlation between the change in price during one period and the change in the preceding period can be computed. If this first order serial correlation coefficient is statistically significant then the hypothesis of independence is rejected. Similar tests can be carried

---

1. The best single source is COOTNER (1964) which reprints many of the important articles on this subject. Cootner's introductions to the various topics are invaluable as summary statements of the key issues.
2. The need for research on British share prices is discussed by TAYLOR (1969). See especially pp.15–16 of his article for reasons why we should expect British share price behaviour to differ from American experience.
3. For a description of the data, sources, etc., see the Appendix.

out for two, three, and longer lags. While these and other statistical tests have often suggested the acceptance of the independence hypothesis there are several difficulties. Standard correlation tests detect the presence of linear dependence. Strong dependence of other forms may be present yet yield small and statistically non-significant correlation coefficients. In addition a very small serial correlation coefficient could be highly significant statistically but imply dependence which had virtually no 'significance' in terms of economic considerations. Finally although much of the statistical testing which has been carried out suggests the absence of dependence in series of share price changes yet some of the empirical work suggests the presence of statistical regularities not conveniently explained by the hypothesis of independence but which are not sufficiently influential to lead standard statistical tests to reject that hypothesis.

On balance, however, the data when confronted by the usual statistical tests of time series analysis suggest that changes in share prices can be represented by a simple random walk model. This model implies that the probability of a change in price of any given magnitude is independent of the past history of such changes, that is:

$$P\left(\Delta P_t = X \mid \Delta P_{t-1}, \Delta P_{t-2}, \ldots\right) = P\left(\Delta P_t = X\right),$$

where $\Delta P_t = P_{t+1} - P_t$. Alternatively the price at time t can be represented as equal to the price at time $(t-1)$ plus a random variable, that is:

$$P_t = P_{t-1} + e_t$$

where e_t is distributed independently of e_{t-1}, e_{t-2}, etc. There are variations of the random walk model; for example that the changes in the logarithms of prices follow a random walk. In this case $\Delta \log P_t = \log P_{t+1} - \log P_t$ replaces ΔP_t in the above expression. The random walk model has gained considerable support as being an adequate representation of share price movements[4].

An alternative way of testing the random walk hypothesis—and one which meets some of the objections to the use of standard statistical tests noted above—is to examine the profitability of applying a mechanical trading rule to the price series[5]. If a series of price changes followed a random walk with zero mean then it is impossible to formulate a trading rule which would on average do better than earn zero profit. Any such rule, based on the history of the prices known to the trader, would—by definition—give no insight into future prices and hence to an expectation of positive profits. To the extent that a rule can achieve this then there is evidence for rejecting the notion of simple random walks. It is possible, however, for a mechanical trading rule to produce positive profits on average simply because the expected price changes do not have a zero mean, although still following a random walk; that is the model is a random walk with drift. In this case the test of the random walk hypothesis must be based on a comparison of the profits of the trading rule not with zero profits but with the profitability expected on account of the drift.

This approach to the testing of the random walk hypothesis has been explored by ALEXANDER (1961 and 1964) and later refined by FAMA and BLUME (1966). The mechanical trading rule considered by these authors works as follows. Buy and sell decisions are triggered

---

4. For a theoretical discussion see SAMUELSON (1965).
5. I am indebted to Professor Seymour Smidt (Cornell University) for an opportunity to work along this line of investigation in 1961. See SMIDT (1965).

off by changes in the share's price which are at least equal to x per cent (filter size). The percentage change, however, is not necessarily computed from the price at which the transaction was initiated. Thus, for example, if a share is bought at 100 and moves on the next day to 110 then a 5 per cent filter would trigger a sell decision if the next day's price is less than (or equal to) 104·5 (that is, 110 minus 5 per cent of 110). Thus the trading rule attempts to guard against the erosion of the profit achieved by a series of favourable price changes. But it does not *ensure* this. In the above example if the decision to sell was indeed triggered by a price of 104·5 then the profit (undiscounted) is 4·5 units. But the sell decision of a 5 per cent filter rule may be triggered instead by a price of 95 thus leading to a loss of -5 units. Thus in order to compute the profits of the filter rules it is not assumed that the trader can terminate (or initiate) transactions exactly at the filter points themselves[6].

In addition the rule attempts to protect the trader by not revising the reference point in the event of adverse price changes. If, in the above example, the price fell on the second day to 96, that is by 4 per cent, then a 5 per cent filter rule would not initiate a sell decision. The reference point would still be 100 thus preventing the gradual erosion of the trader's capital by a long series of adverse price changes each one of which is less than 5 per cent. The rule is symmetrical in the sense that a decision to sell a share is equivalent to a decision to buy one and *vice versa*. The trader is always in the market alternately holding long and short positions. The behaviour of the price series determines whether the first position is long or short, successive positions being dictated by the filter rule in the manner described. In the following discussion only completed transactions are considered. This may mean that a small part (at the end) of the price series being analysed is omitted since there is no guarantee that the last observation of any given price series corresponds to a trigger point.

Applying this filter rule to a series of share prices results in the identification of a second series of prices, namely those at which buy and sell decisions are taken. This second series in turn allows profits to be calculated. These take the form of rates-of-return, initially computed for each transaction separately and then aggregated to produce an over-all rate-of-return. Finally this return is expressed in terms of its equivalent annual rate-of-return. These steps can be illustrated by a simple numerical example. Say a 5 per cent filter rule resulted in buying at 100 and selling at 121 two days hence. The daily rate-of-return for the transaction is r where r is the solution of the equation:

$$100 = 121/(1 + r)^2$$

Hence r equals 0·1 or 10 per cent. If, on the other hand, the filter rule had signalled selling at 100 and buying at 121 then the short rate-of-return for the transaction is $-11·1$ per cent[7]. If, for the price series under consideration, the 5 per cent filter rule indicated T transactions, the ith transaction having a rate-of-return (as computed above) equal to r_i then the over-all rate-of-return is R as defined by the following equation:

$$(1 + R)^N = \prod_{i=1}^{i=T} (1 + r_i)^{n_i}$$

---

6. ALEXANDER's (1961) original filter study was criticised by MANDELBROT (1963) for making this assumption. The more recent studies, including this one, do not suffer from this defect.
7. This lack of symmetry between the short and long rates-of-return is a source of bias in the results of FAMA and BLUME (1966). In their analysis they assume that the short rate-of-return for a transaction is simply the negative of the corresponding long rate-of-return. The source of the bias, its magnitude, and its effect on their conclusions is the subject of a note to be published in the *Journal of Business*.

where n_i is the length (in trading days) of the ith transaction and N equals the total number of days represented by all transactions, that is, $N = \sum\limits_{i=1}^{i=T} n_i$. The final step is to convert this daily rate-of-return into its equivalent annual rate-of-return. Assuming approximately 260 trading days per annum the equivalent annual rate-of-return is then $260R$. By including only long (short) transactions in the above equation the corresponding long (short) rate-of-return can be calculated. The over-all rate is clearly an average (but not simple) of these long and short rates. These are the calculations which underlie the results reported in rows (4), (5), and (6) of Tables 1, 2, and 3.

The initiating price (and date) of the first transaction and the terminating price (and date) of the last transaction will generally vary with the size of the filter. For each filter size these prices and the number of days separating them (N) allow the calculation of the buy-and-hold rate associated with the corresponding filter. These rates are computed in the same way as the rates for individual transactions. This rate is positive, negative, or zero depending on whether the terminating price of the last complete transaction signalled by the filter rule is greater than, less than, or equal to the first price identified by the filter in question. To allow comparisons to be made this rate is also multiplied by 260.

If a series of share prices follows a random walk then the application of the filter rule described above would produce over-all rates-of-return which on average would be less than the corresponding buy-and-hold rate. Secondly these filter rates would tend to produce short rates approximately[8] equal to the negative of the long rate and the long rate of the filter would approximately equal the buy-and-hold rate.

FAMA and BLUME's (1966) filter analysis of each of the thirty shares which comprise the Dow–Jones Industrial Average produced results[9] which are roughly in agreement with what would be expected on the assumption that prices follow a random walk. For our purposes the key results are the following: averaging over the thirty shares and the twenty-four filters which they employ the average rate-of-return is 1·85 per cent but the corresponding buy-and-hold rate-of-return is considerably higher, namely 9·86 per cent. This latter rate corresponds quite well with the long rate-of-return produced by the filters, 8·22 per cent, while the short rate was —12·79 per cent.

The results of applying the filter rule to the three sets of data are summarized in Tables 1, 2, and 3. Row (1) of the Tables indicates the total number of transactions resulting from applying different filter sizes. For each filter these transactions are divided between long and short transactions almost equally—the difference between the number of long transactions and the number of short transactions cannot be greater than one. Row (2) shows the average length (in trading days) of the transactions for each filter and row (3) shows the ratio of the number of days during which the filter rule had the trader holding long positions to the number of days during which the trader was holding short ones. Rows (4), (5) and (6) show the over-all rate-of-return earned by the filter and the rates earned on long and short transactions shown separately. Finally, row (7) shows the buy-and-hold rate earned by the trader over the period corresponding to the period during which the filter rule rates were calculated. The length of this period, in trading days, is equal to row (1) times row (2).

---

8. See footnote 7. Short rates would in fact be less than the negative of the long rates.
9. FAMA and BLUME (1966) used series of daily prices with approximately 1500 observations per share.

TABLE 1. *Results of applying filter rule to F.T. actuaries index (capital goods group)*

Filter size	0·001	0·003	0·005	0·010	0·015	0·020	0·025	0·030	0·035	0·040	0·045	0·050
Transactions	302	202	132	66	50	31	25	23	18	12	12	8
Average length of transactions	3·63	5·43	8·31	16·62	21·94	31·48	39·28	42·65	53·22	78·92	79·25	119·38
Long/short	1·24	1·34	1·32	1·38	1·34	1·76	1·52	1·27	1·85	2·87	1·61	2·60
Long rate of return	0·38004	0·29880	0·26305	0·21413	0·14130	0·10342	0·06733	−0·00929	0·01428	0·04450	−0·01320	−0·01402
Short rate of return	0·38597	0·30058	0·27232	0·22342	0·16560	0·09772	0·07748	0·01752	0·01665	−0·03462	−0·00541	−0·01447
Rate of return	0·37268	0·29643	0·25078	0·20130	0·10865	0·11344	0·05193	−0·04321	0·00990	0·07284	−0·02576	−0·01285
Buy-and-hold rate of return	0·03770	0·03770	0·03770	0·03682	0·03682	0·01039	0·01648	0·01812	−0·00380	−0·00209	0·00160	0·00501

TABLE 2. *Results of applying filter rule to F.T. actuaries 500 share index*

Filter size	0·001	0·003	0·005	0·010	0·015	0·020	0·025	0·030	0·035	0·040	0·045	0·050
Transactions	338	218	138	66	48	37	28	20	12	14	4	6
Average length of transactions	3·25	5·03	7·95	16·61	22·85	28·35	36·68	48·75	79·92	69·43	234·25	156·33
Long/short	1·17	1·29	1·40	2·07	1·74	2·10	1·98	2·01	1·76	2·04	1·72	1·73
Long rate of return	0·32299	0·25300	0·20237	0·14153	0·09465	0·03937	0·02392	−0·02564	−0·0700	−0·03060	0·07844	0·02199
Short rate of return	0·32893	0·25277	0·20153	0·12569	0·09780	0·04515	0·02577	−0·01795	−0·05184	−0·02495	0·05466	0·00995
Rate of return	0·31603	0·25328	0·20355	0·17432	0·08919	0·02721	0·02025	−0·04110	−0·10203	−0·04211	0·11926	0·04280
Buy-and-hold rate of return	0·02567	0·02567	0·02567	0·02287	0·02387	0·01745	0·00342	−0·00498	−0·01107	−0·00969	−0·01363	−0·01350

TABLE 3. Results of applying filter rule to Daily Mail ordinary industrial share price index

Filter size	0·001	0·003	0·005	0·010	0·015	0·020	0·025	0·030	0·035	0·040	0·045	0·050
Transactions	422	245	175	85	61	44	28	23	19	13	10	8
Average length of transactions	2·96	5·07	7·10	14·55	20·07	27·45	43·04	46·74	60·32	88·69	105·20	131·50
Long/short	1·03	1·09	1·25	1·40	1·99	2·03	1·76	2·77	2·11	2·44	2·51	3·52
Rate of return	0·25798	0·24409	0·17448	0·10341	0·01399	− 0·00724	0·02751	− 0·02106	− 0·02228	− 0·01331	− 0·00222	− 0·01375
Long rate of return	0·25343	0·23510	0·15731	0·08798	0·01049	− 0·00439	0·02204	− 0·00022	− 0·02688	− 0·00423	0·03143	0·02088
Short rate of return	0·26265	0·25384	0·19592	0·12504	0·02097	− 0·01302	0·03717	− 0·07882	− 0·01259	− 0·05615	− 0·08654	− 0·13543
Buy-and-hold rate of return	− 0·00753	− 0·00595	− 0·00595	− 0·00654	− 0·00522	− 0·00447	− 0·00346	− 0·01865	− 0·01870	− 0·02294	0·04451	0·04451

While the primary focus of this study are rows (4), (5), (6) and (7) perhaps a few comments on the other results are appropriate. There seemed little point in considering filters which are larger than 0·050 since beyond this point relatively few trigger points were found and, therefore, very few transactions take place. Calculation of rates-of-return would, therefore, be rather unreliable guides. Preliminary analysis also indicated that filters less than 0·001 although initiating more transactions did not produce rates-of-return which seemed to differ from those obtainable with larger filters. For example a filter of size 0·0001 when applied to the *F.T. 500-Share Index* produced a filter rate-of-return of 0·34907, representing 412 transactions with an average length of 2·66 trading days. Obviously smaller filters tend to generate more transactions than larger ones and this is reflected in the results[10]. The decline in the number of transactions with increasing filter size appears to be most rapid at the lower end of the filter scale.

The ratio of the number of days during which long positions were held to the number of days during which short positions were held is always greater than unity and also tends to increase with the size of the filter but somewhat erratically. This implies, since the number of transactions is almost evenly split between long and short transactions, that the average length of short transactions is less than the average length of long transactions and also less than the average length of all transactions, both long and short. For example if the ratio of long to short days [row (3)] is two then this implies that the average length of short transactions is approximately two-thirds of the average length of all transactions. There seems to be no adequate explanation for this other than the presence of some sort of dependence in price changes. The presence of an upward trend in prices might explain the fact that row (3) is invariably greater than unity. However, the presence of trend, at least as measured by the average size of price changes ($\overline{\Delta P}$), seems an inadequate explanation, certainly so far as the *Daily Mail* data is concerned.

All three sets of data generate filter rates-of-return which tend to decrease with increasing filter size. The general level of these rates is somewhat different—the *Daily Mail* being generally lowest and the *F.T. Capital Goods Index* highest. This difference tends to be maintained irrespective of filter size—at least for filters less than 2·5 per cent approximately. Around this point filter rates-of-return are approximately zero and beyond this the rate-of-return tends to fluctuate in an erratic fashion. For each of the three price series the most profitable filter is the smallest one.

For each series the variation in short and long rates as filter size varies tends to follow a pattern similar to that followed by the over-all rate-of-return. For the *F.T.* data there is relatively little difference between the long and short rates and both of these rates are similar to the over-all rate-of-return obtained by employing the filter rule. The *Daily Mail* data, however, almost invariably produced filter rates-of-return on short transactions which, in absolute value, are in excess of the corresponding long rates. The most significant feature of the results, however, is the complete absence of the pattern of rates which would be expected if prices followed random walks. Clearly the data generate filter returns, both long and short, well in excess of the buy-and-hold rate-of-return. The reader is reminded, however, that none

---

10. Clearly the net profitability of different filters depends on the number of transactions since account must be taken of commissions, taxes, etc. All profit rates reported here are gross—but see Part 3—and should be compared with the corresponding rates of other studies. The fact that dividends are not explicitly accounted for is also relevant in interpreting the rates-of-return presented above.

of these rates has been corrected for transaction costs.

There are a number of reasons why these results cannot be directly compared with those of other filter studies. These will be discussed later. The high rates-of-return, however, obtainable from the application of filters together with the absence of the pattern of relationships which would be expected in the presence of series following random walks suggest that considerably more dependence might exist in U.K. shares than in those of U.S.[11] One of the earliest studies of U.K. share price behaviour, that of M. G. KENDALL (1953), implied that random walk models may be an appropriate description of U.K. share price behaviour. Although not explicitly oriented towards testing this hypothesis his calculations of the auto-correlation coefficients for lags of 1, 2, . . . , and 29 weeks provided results broadly consistent with much of the subsequent U.S. research. Kendall concluded (*inter alia*) that "an analysis of stock-exchange movements revealed little serial correlation within series and little lag correlation between series. Unless individual stocks behave differently from the average of similar stocks, there is no hope of being able to predict movements on the exchange for a week ahead without extraneous information". Almost all of the correlation coefficients computed by Kendall were small, fluctuating around zero. He singles out only three of his nineteen series as possibly presenting opportunities for prediction. ALEXANDER (1961) regards Kendall's work as "the most impressive recent findings confirming the random walk hypothesis".

It is of interest, therefore, to consider whether the apparently strong dependence (relative to U.S. studies and subject to the qualifications noted later) implied by the filter results reported in Tables 1, 2, and 3 are reflected in serial correlation analysis. Table 4 shows the

TABLE 4. *Daily serial correlation coefficients*

| | F.T. | | |
Lag	Capital goods	500 Share	Daily Mail
1	0·3103*	0·2870*	0·1648*
2	0·0679*	− 0·0008	0·0077
3	0·0309	− 0·0059	− 0·0320
4	0·0471	0·0004	0·0159
5	0·0506	0·0064	− 0·0325
6	− 0·0022	− 0.0555	− 0·0351
7	0·0337	− 0·0265	− 0·0071
8	0·0968*	0·0638	0·0537*
9	0·1537*	0·1514*	0·0752*

* Indicates statistically significant coefficients (see footnote 12)

results of that analysis for each of the three sets of data. Although many of the coefficients are small and not statistically significant[12] each series has a statistically significant first order serial correlation coefficient which is larger than most of those computed by Kendall. The three largest of the nineteen first order serial correlation coefficients computed by Kendall had the following values: 0·301, 0·237 and 0·234—although it should be emphasized that these

11. The results of my filter tests support the evidence of two other analyses I have carried out: See DRYDEN (1968) and (1969).
12. The standard error of a serial correlation coefficient based on a lag of k days is $(N - k)^{-\frac{1}{2}}$ where N is the length of the series. To reduce the volume of computation $(N - 5)$ was used for each series and two standard errors was regarded as the level required for results to be deemed statistically significant.

were computed for series of weekly price changes. Similar calculations by MOORE (1964, p. 147) using *Standard and Poor's 500 Stock Index* (but using weekly changes in the logarithms of the index) supports Kendall's results. While there appears to be no published results on the behaviour of serial correlation coefficients using daily index data FAMA (1965, p. 72) reports the results of serial correlation analysis in daily changes in the logarithms of prices. Of the thirty individual shares he considers only eleven have significant first order serial correlation coefficients and of these nine are positive and two are negative. The largest, in absolute value, is 0·123. In a subsequent study of this data FAMA and BLUME (1966) found that the results of filter tests confirmed the serial correlation analysis and corroborated their view of independence or near independence in time series of share price changes.

3

The conclusions drawn from comparisons made between the serial correlation analysis and the filter tests of this study and those of other studies must be regarded as extremely tentative. Some of the reasons for this caution have already been suggested. The bases of the various studies differ in several respects. Some researchers have analyzed the behaviour of index numbers while others have studied individual shares[13]. Sometimes the series studied are daily but sometimes a monthly or other period is used. In addition some authors have chosen to examine the behaviour of simple arithmetic first differences of their price series while others prefer to analyse the first difference of the logarithm of the price.

One reason for exercising caution in accepting the foregoing results is that they are based on the behaviour of index numbers of share prices and not on the behaviour of individual shares. Several readers of an earlier version of this report felt quite certain that the results would not extend to the individual shares—and an almost equal number felt that they would! The following paragraphs do not purport to provide a definitive answer to this question. Further research is clearly indicated.

Table 5 provides the results of applying the filter rule to a series of 500 daily observations of the price of an individual share. The share (*Tesco Stores*) is one of a group of shares which had been selected (randomly) for analysis in connection with another study[14]. This share is also a member of both the *Financial Times Actuaries' 500-Share Index* and of the *Daily Mail Index*.

Since the number of observations on the individual share was considerably smaller the number of transactions reported in Table 5 is not directly comparable with the corresponding figures in Tables 1, 2 and 3. For the smaller filters the average length of transaction is similar but for filters greater than 15 per cent the averages for the indexes and the individual share start to diverge. As noted earlier the number of transactions for larger filters is often quite small and consequently these results could be fairly unstable as between shares. The ratio of the number of days a filter was associated with long transactions to the number of days it was short was almost always less than unity for the individual share analysis. This is quite different

---

13. For an excellent discussion of the relationship between individual share prices and indices of share prices, see KING (1966).
14. I am indebted to Mr. John D. Hey for the opportunity to use this data. The series was adjusted to take account of stock splits, etc. The details of these adjustments are contained in his M.Sc. thesis, HEY (1968).

TABLE 5. *Results of applying filter rule to an individual share* *

Filter size	0·001	0·003	0·005	0·010	0·015	0·020	0·025	0·030	0·035	0·040	0·045	0·050
Transactions	101	99	99	69	38	30	27	23	21	19	11	9
Average length of transactions	4·90	5·00	5·00	7·17	12·84	16·27	17·37	20·35	22·29	25·00	32·64	39·89
Long/short	0·77	0·76	0·76	0·79	0·64	0·83	0·75	0·84	0·79	1·07	0·52	0·46
Rate of return	0·3080	0·3210	0·3210	0·3025	0·3142	0·1194	− 0·0686	− 0·1909	− 0·2010	− 0·2625	− 0·2093	− 0·2323
Long rate of return	0·5352	0·5526	0·5526	0·5161	0·5970	0·2924	0·0671	− 0·0612	− 0·0731	− 0·1094	− 0·1519	− 0·2015
Short rate of return	0·1337	0·1447	0·1447	0·1331	0·1325	− 0·0249	− 0·1703	− 0·2991	− 0·3016	− 0·4256	− 0·2392	− 0·2464
Buy-and-hold rate of return	0·1382	0·1382	0·1382	0·1382	0·1418	0·1418	0·1218	0·1294	0·1294	0·1406	0·0961	0·0961

* *Tesco Stores*—500 daily observations (December 1962–December 1964).

to the value of this ratio for the index number analyses. There seems to be no immediaet explanation for this difference.

The main objective of the individual share analysis, however, is to find out how the rates-of-return compare with those found by applying the filter rule to indexes of share prices. In comparing rows (4), (5), (6) and (7) with the corresponding rows of Tables 1, 2 and 3 several patterns emerge. The greater profitability of small filters as compared to large filters found in the analysis of index numbers is reinforced in Table 5. The break from profitable to un-profitable rates-of-return occurs at approximately the same filter size but in the individual share analysis the break is clear-cut and not erratic as with the indexes. The most important result of all, from the point-of-view of this research, is that the individual share analysis fails to suggest—even remotely—the pattern of rates which would be expected in the event that the share's price followed a random walk. The long rates associated with the filter are well in excess of the buy-and-hold rates and the short rates although less than the long rates do not approximate the negative of the long rate. Thus the evidence—albeit limited—provided by analysing an individual share is quite clear in its support of the earlier conclusions, based on the analyses of index numbers, concerning the absence of random walks in U.K. share prices.

It is perhaps important to stress again the focus of the research carried out in this paper. The objective was *not* to find profitable trading rules but rather to test the random walk hypothesis in relation to share price behaviour. The possibility that after transaction costs are paid the profitability of even the most profitable filters may seriously be reduced is not a consideration central to the argument of this paper. This point has been most effectively stated by ALEXANDER (1964). If a share price followed a random walk with zero drift then trading rules would produce, on average, zero profit before transaction costs and net profits equal (approximately) to $-Nc$, where c is the cost of trading per transaction and N is the number of transactions. The argument that profits, after paying transaction costs, are negative cannot be used to infer that the *price series* is not a driftless random walk. It was for this reason that the rates computed above ignored transaction costs, etc.

Although the profitability of filter rates-of-return after adjusting for transaction costs may not be crucial to the main argument it is of interest to consider whether or not filter rules could produce profits for traders. A precise answer to this question would require a considerable volume of book-keeping to have been carried out. It would, for example, have been necessary to record whether or not transactions were completed within the same Stock Exchange Account period or not. In addition transaction costs depend on the volume of trading, the timing of trading in relation to other transactions, and the type of security traded. Since the book-keeping necessary to make precise computations of this type was not carried out the following remarks must be regarded as very rough approximations.

Table 5 indicates an average of about fifty transactions per trading year for each of the three smaller filters (0·001, 0·003 and 0·005). Transaction costs, on the assumption that costs average 0·625 per cent per transaction, account for about 30 per cent and this would reduce filter rates-of-return to approximately 0 per cent. A buy-and-hold policy would, on these assumptions, clearly be preferable. But if it is profits the reader wishes to seek he may wish to consider operating the filter rule and following its signals on the long transactions only!

The results of the foregoing analysis—both the filter results and the first order serial correlation coefficients—together with the comparison of the results with those of other researchers would appear to suggest sufficient divergence from the random walk hypothesis to justify a more extensive analysis of the behaviour of individual shares quoted on the London Stock Exchange.

REFERENCES

*ALEXANDER, S. S. (1961) Price movements in speculative markets: Trends or random walks, *Ind. Mangmt. Rev.* **2**, 7–26 (May).
*ALEXANDER, S. S. (1964) Price movements in speculative markets: Trends or random walks, No.2. *Ind. Mangmt. Rev.*, **5**, 25–46 (Spring).
COOTNER, P. H. (Editor) (1964) *The Random Character of Stock Market Prices.* M.I.T. Press.
DRYDEN, M. M. (1969) A source of bias in filter tests of share prices, *J. Bus.* (July).
DRYDEN, M. M. (1968) Short-term forecasting of share prices: An information theory approach, *Scot. J. Polit. Econ.* (November).
DRYDEN, M. M. (1969) Share price movements: A Markovian approach, *J. Finance* (March).
FAMA, E. F. (1965) The behaviour of stock-market prices, *J. Bus.* **38**, 34–105 (January).
FAMA, E. F. and BLUME, M. E. (1966) Filter rules and stock-market trading, *J. Bus.* **39**, 226–241 (January).
HEY, J. D. (1968) Spectral analysis of stock market prices, M.Sc. thesis, University of Edinburgh.
*KENDALL, M. G. (1953) The analysis of economic time series—Part 1: prices, *J. R. Statist. Soc.* **96**, 11–25.
KING, B. F. (1966) Market and industry factors in stock price behaviour, *J. Bus.* (January).
*MANDELBROT, B. (1963) The variation of certain speculative prices, *J. Bus.* **36**, 394–491 (October).
MOORE, A. B. (1964) Some characteristics of changes in common stock prices, in *The Random Character of Stock Market Prices*, edited by P. H. COOTNER. M.I.T. Press.
SAMUELSON, P. A. (1965) Proof that properly anticipated prices fluctuate randomly, *Ind. Mangmt Rev.* **6**, 41–49 (Spring).
SMIDT, S. (1965) A test of the serial independence of price changes in soybeans futures, *Fd. Res. Inst. Stud.* **5** (2), 117–136.
TAYLOR, BASIL (1969) Investment: art, science or what? *Lloyds Bank Rev.* (January).

APPENDIX

The following notes describe the main characteristics of the data[15]. All three series are index numbers of share prices; two are *Financial Times-Actuaries Share Indices;* the third is the· *Daily Mail Industrial Share Price Index.* Each series is reported on a daily basis. The two *F.T.* indices are not independent since the *Capital Goods Index* is a component of the 500-*Share Index.* Although the number of shares included in the indices fluctuated over the period of the study the *Capital Goods Index* represents approximately 37 per cent of the number of shares in the 500-*Share Index* and the *Daily Mail Index* is based on approximately 650 shares.

Although the details of calculation of the *Daily Mail Index* varied over the period of the study the object has been to provide an index which reflects price changes which occur because of changes in market conditions. Thus corrections to the index are made in order to eliminate share price changes due to rights issues, etc.

The *F.T.* indices are based on the share prices of companies which generally must have a market capitalization of over £4,000,000. Companies with extensive trading activities outside of the U.K. are excluded as are holding companies. The *F.T.* indices considered here are weighted arithmetic averages of price relatives with the weights being the corresponding

15. The following paragraphs are largely based on pamphlets available from the *Financial Times* and the *Daily Mail* which describe how their indices are constructed. I am grateful to the staff of the *Daily Mail* for providing me with a listing of their index thus sparing me the tedious task of collecting the data from the individual issues of the *Daily Mail.*
*Also Reprinted in COOTNER (1964).

capitalization market values. The occurrence of rights issues, etc., require adjustment in these weights.

TABLE 1A.

Series	Period		T	Max/min	$\bar{P}$	$\overline{\Delta P}$	$\overline{\Delta \text{Log } P}$
F.T. Actuaries							
Capital goods index	January	1963/	1101	123·94/	110·14	0·017	0·0002
	April	1967		92·99	(7·42)	(0·608)	(0·005)
500 Share index	January	1963/	1101	119·75/	108·17	0·012	0·0001
	April	1967		93·28	(6·37)	(0·595)	(0·006)
Daily Mail index	January	1962/	1253	182·1/	162·82	− 0·005	0·0000
	November	1966		133·4	(10·58)	(0·951)	(0·006)

Table 1A summarizes the characteristics of each series. The length of the series (T) is expressed in trading days. The column headed Max/min shows the highest and lowest values of the index during the period investigated. $\bar{P}$, $\overline{\Delta P}$, and $\overline{\Delta \log P}$ represent, respectively, the means of the price series, the series of its first differences, and the series of the first differences in the logarithm of the price. The entry in brackets below each of the means is the corresponding standard deviation. The information on $\Delta \log P$ is included since many share price studies use this variable rather than ΔP. Not unexpectedly the results for the two *Financial Times* series are quite similar.

Some readers may be interested in the extent to which the series indicate the presence of dependence as measured by serial correlation coefficients computed from the series of logarithmic differences. The results of that analysis for each series are presented in Table 2A. Clearly Tables 4 and 2A are very similar and there would seem to be no reason for modifying the earlier conclusions based on analysing the serial correlation coefficients of the simple arithmetic price differences.

TABLE 2A. Daily serial correlation coefficients

	F.T.		
Lag	Capital goods	500 Share	Daily Mail
1	0·3096	0·2848	0·1415
2	0·0752	0·0008	0·0098
3	0·0299	− 0·0036	− 0·0399
4	0·0387	− 0·0034	0·0105
5	0·0411	0·0000	− 0·0402
6	− 0·0044	− 0·0538	− 0·0245
7	0·0327	− 0·0278	0·0000
8	0·0973	0·0648	0·0566
9	0·1571	0·1511	0·0612

In this connection it is important to note the dangers of errors in the data. These can arise through errors in the original computations of the index, in its publication, and finally in preparing the data for computer input. Unfortunately plus and minus errors do not cancel themselves out so far as serial correlation analysis is concerned. Errors in the original price series will tend to bias the serial correlation coefficient downwards. Also since any extreme value in a given series would play a prominent part in triggering decisions to buy and sell in the application of the filter rule it is important, as far as is possible, to eliminate errors in the data. To this end extreme care was exercised in preparing the data for computer input. Prior to analyzing the data—either by correlation analysis or filter tests—all deviations of the index

73

from its mean in excess of twice the standard deviation were scrutinised. This resulted in the detection of several errors many of which were misprints in the newspapers. A variety of other checks were also carried out.

Although not directly relevant to this study the author was interested in discovering whether the apparent difference in U.K. share prices—as compared with U.S.—with respect to the question of dependence was also reflected in differences in the manner in which share price changes are distributed. Lack of space prevents full reporting on this topic for all series

TABLE 3A. *Distribution of price changes* in standardized form compared with normal distribution*

Intervals	Left-hand tail	Right-hand tail	Total	Normal	Actual minus Normal
0·50	0·2200000	0·2609091	0·4809091	0·3829249	+
1·00	0·1300000	0·1663636	0·2963636	0·2997645	−
1·50	0·0545455	0·0709091	0·1254545	0·1836961	−
2·00	0·0236364	0·0227273	0·0463636	0·0881141	−
2·50	0·0200000	0·0054545	0·0254545	0·0330809	−
3·00	0·0045455	0·0036364	0·0081818	0·0097195	−
3·50	0·0036364	0·0009091	0·0045455	0·0022345	+
4·00	0·0036364	0·0018182	0·0054545	0·0004019	+
4·50	0·0018182	0·0009091	0·0027273	0·0000565	+
5·00	0·0009091	0·0009091	0·0018182	0·0000062	+
> 5	0·0018182	0·0009091	0·0027273	0·0000006	+
Total	0·4645455	0·5354545	1·0000000	——	−

* F.T. (Capital Goods) Index

but Table 3A shows the results for one of the series. The first three columns show the relative frequency of price changes—negative, positive, and total respectively—computed from their mean and falling in different intervals defined in terms of standard deviations. Thus the table represents the distribution of price changes in standardized form. The first row shows the proportion of observations less than or equal to 0·5 standard deviations (S), the second row shows the proportion greater than 0·5S and less than or equal to 1S, and so on. The last interval shows the relative frequency in excess of 5S. In addition to the distribution of actual price differences the distribution of observations following the normal law of probability is also shown for purposes of comparison. The last column shows whether the actual distribution has an excess ($+$) of frequency or a deficiency ($−$) of frequency as compared with the normal distribution. This column confirms results found by FAMA (1965, p. 46 ff.) and others, namely, that the distribution of price differences although roughly of normal form has an excess of extreme values as compared with what would be expected on the assumption that the distribution of price differences is normal. That is the distribution has 'long tails'. Secondly, there is an excess of frequency of price changes which are within about one standard deviation from their mean. The corresponding deficiency of frequency, relative to the normal distribution, is in the region of observations which are two or three standard deviations from the mean. While this analysis is obviously not definitive it does at least suggest that U.K. share prices may exhibit more dependence than U.S. share prices but that the distribution of price changes is roughly similar.

CHARTS AND THE RANDOM WALK

D. H. Girmes and D. C. Damant

Introduction

In recent years statisticians who have studied the Stock Exchange have made certain claims about the characteristics shown by the share price series and have constructed certain models to explain these characteristics. The most comprehensive model is the Efficient Market Theory which holds that all price sensitive information is immediately discounted in the relevant share prices, thus making traditional investment analysis difficult and perhaps impossible. One of the main consequences of this theory is that the series of share prices is such that past prices are of no value in predicting future prices. Quite apart from the conclusions of this theory, it is also held that randomness in Stock Exchange prices is established by statistical tests. If this is the case, technical analysis is undermined: if share prices follow a random walk, patterns appearing on the charts cannot forecast the future with any useful degree of probability.

A good deal of argument has been centred on the logic of the Efficient Market Theory and its statistical infrastructure. Less attention has been given to the other approach to the problem: that is, to test by suitably objective means the claims of the chartists themselves.

Apart from the interest of a study which contributes to a possible resolution of the controversy about technical analysis, which existed for many years before the Efficient Market Theory was developed, it should be noted that the testing of technical analysis is of essential importance to the Efficient Market Theory. If objective tests of chartist techniques should establish for them a certain degree of significant validity then, since the random nature of Stock Exchange prices is one of the fundamental consequences of the Efficient Market Theory, that theory itself would have to be reformulated.

This paper describes the techniques which have been developed for testing the forecasting ability of the various patterns which chartists have detected in share price movements, and the application of this method to one particular pattern, the head and shoulders top. A significant degree of success for this pattern is noted. The future programme of work is indicated in the hope that comments and suggestions may be received from others interested in the questions under discussion.

Data Bank

Although the relative simplicity of the approach as described by the chartists would in principle allow the success or failure of the various patterns to be decided by inspection, the nature of the problem renders it essential to exclude the human element in decision making. Suitable computer programmes were therefore developed for use as analytical tools. The basis of this empirical study is formed by a data bank consisting of daily closing price relatives (Note 1) for a period of 1,304 days, roughly a five year period on the London Stock Exchange, from 1969 to 1973; the data bank covered in all 484 individual stocks (Note 2).

Smoothing

The computer assisted analysis of patterns in a series of share prices is likely to be complicated by the effects of short term fluctuations (which are held by some commentators to be random "noise") whatever the characteristics of the larger movements. A smoothing technique was therefore designed, aiming at the elimination of the short term movements without affecting the development of any pattern in the longer term picture. Previously published smoothing techniques such as moving averages or exponential smoothing were found unacceptable because of the time lag which occurs between observed and smoothed series when using these techniques; and also because of their "inertia" in situations where share price changes are both sharp and essential to a consideration of the pattern. It is vital to avoid any "cutting off" effect at important turning points. The so-called "gradient smoothing" was therefore developed as described in Note 3; essentially this approach ensures that long and relatively undisturbed trends in the price action are smoothed heavily while relatively sharp and essential turns are smoothed with greater care. The smoothing technique is vital to both the statistician and to the chartist in approaching this problem. It may be added that when chartists put forward certain standard patterns in the elaboration of their techniques they are, by imposing these standards on the variations which occur in practice, in fact carrying out a *de facto* smoothing.

Head and Shoulders Top

The first pattern tested by this method was the head and shoulders top, on the grounds that this was perhaps the most famous of the chart patterns. For the smoothed series, all local maxima and minima were determined. These are the points in time which make up reversal patterns and only such points were subjected to any further analysis. The illustration to this paper which shows the "average" head and shoulders top pattern (as discussed below) may be taken as a general picture of this pattern. In practice varied types of head and shoulders patterns may be observed: the constraints adopted for this programme are set out in Note 4. In spite of possible variations in these constraints it may be said that if the pattern as here defined produces a useful number of head and shoulders tops from the data bank then a valid exercise will have been carried out. It will be part of the further work on this subject to modify the constraints used, not only in the case of head and shoulders tops but also in the cases of head and shoulders bottoms, of the other major reversal patterns mentioned by chartists, and, perhaps, in the development of tests for the more irregular patterns which do not appear in the chartist textbooks but which are nevertheless used by chartists in practice.

It will be seen from Note 4 that a valid head and shoulders is taken as completed when the suitable penetration of the neckline gives the signal. Only patterns producing this signal were accepted in the analysis. The success of the patterns was judged by observing the lowest price reached by each share after the completion of a valid pattern, within a period of days extending to one and a half times the width of the pattern. It is recognised that as investment is a very practical matter future work on this problem will be improved if a more detailed description of the share price performance is developed for application in the period after a valid head and shoulders is signalled. Nevertheless the present straightforward test gives a positive result.

Results

The results were analysed in simple tables, histograms, scatter diagrams and correlation coefficient matrices. No attempt was made to design a mathematical model for describing the numerical results. The empirical results were contrasted with those obtained by a simulation study (Note 5). The figure shows the "average" head and shoulders top found to appear in the data bank; the numbers along the horizontal indicate the average number of days taken up by each element in the pattern. (Note 6.)

All together 462 head and shoulders top patterns as defined were selected by the computer. The number of occurrences of these heads and shoulders tops in the various charts is given as follows:

Number of Tops	0	1	2	3	4	5	6
Number of Price Series ..	196	158	82	22	2	1	1

In the simulation study (Note 5) only 71 head and shoulders tops were found and none of the generated time series in the simulation study had more than one such pattern occurring in it.

The declines experienced by the various time series after a head and shoulders top was seen are given in the table below:

Percentage Drop (Class Boundaries)	0–5	6–10	11–15	16–20	21–25	26–30	31–35	36–40	41–60	61–75
Frequency (i.e., Number of Drops of each %) ..	72	121	93	64	40	29	10	9	9	13

The mean percentage drop out of the top areas in question is given at 13·7%, (Standard Deviation 9·9) which is adequate to cover dealing expenses. On the basis of this first approach to the problem therefore a confirmation of the use of head and shoulders tops seems to have been achieved.

Further analysis by correlation matrices and scatter diagrams was carried out in order to see whether any characteristic of the head and shoulders top was correlated with the percentage drop at the end of the pattern, that is with the degree of success observed. In particular, and in accordance with chartist textbooks, an enquiry was made to see whether there was any correlation between the percentage rise observed before the pattern and the percentage drop; and between the percentage height of the head above the neckline and the percentage drop. No significant correlation was found. Of the various possibilities so far tested, the only significant correlation discovered was between the width of the right hand shoulder (that is, the shoulder before the drop) and the percentage drop. Before proceeding to look for other possible correlations, however, the changes already mentioned in this paper will be implemented; that is, separation of the smaller head and shoulders and the refinement of the definition of success, that is of the percentage drop.

Conclusion

The data bank has produced a significant number of head and shoulders tops which show a significant degree of success. The simulated series showed markedly fewer patterns. On this basis further and more elaborate investigations seem worthwhile and will be carried out (Note 7).

Notes

1. All daily closing prices have been re-scaled so that the starting prices of the data bank equal 100. This re-scaling does not affect the statistical nature of the price series. The authors acknowledge the use of the data bank administered by the City University.

2. It may be remarked that the data bank records a time when the London Stock Exchange was moving in a particular manner, with clear bull and bear markets, in which the majority of stocks generally followed the market trend. Indeed this is true for the period from mid-1966 to the current date. Less volatile markets and possibly more mixed markets were seen perhaps in the earlier 60s. Against this it may be said that a period of observation of five or so years, for the second largest and second most sophisticated Stock Exchange in the world, cannot be dismissed as not statistically representative. Also, the chartist himself might argue that in a sophisticated market he is prepared to change his techniques from time to time as market characteristics alter. It is interesting to compare the clear markets seen in London in the period covered by the data bank with the very much more confused markets on Wall Street, which have provided the background for the considerable amount of work on the Efficient Market Theory in the States.

3. The "gradient smoothing" moves backwards. The first smoothing step begins by taking the last observed value and calculating the slopes of lines connecting this point (called the origin of the first smoothing loop) with the N preceding values of the time series, where N is a parameter to be determined by experience. These N slope values are then averaged and the first smoothed point is obtained by adding the average slope to the last origin. The new smoothed value thus obtained is taken as the new origin and the averaging procedure is repeated until the N-th value of the observed price series is reached. A special facility (dynamic element) is added to the smoothing routine to assure greater sensitivity of smoothing at times of changes in trend.

4. The following constraints were imposed for head and shoulders top patterns:

(i) The gradient of the neckline must lie between $-45°$ and $+45°$.

(ii) The height of the head above the neckline must exceed the heights of the two shoulders.

(iii) The width of the pattern must be at least 15 days, where "width" is defined as the length of the pattern supported above the neckline (that is, between the beginning of the left shoulder and the end of the right shoulder).

(iv) The initial rise had to be greater than the height of the head above the neckline. The "initial rise" was defined as the difference between the beginning of the first shoulder and the lowest value of the price series in a period preceding the beginning of the first shoulder and extending to one and a half times the width of the pattern.

(v) The point of contact between the price and the neckline in the movement between the head and the right shoulder must be below the highest point in the formation of the left shoulder.

(vi) The head and shoulders top pattern is said to have established itself if (i) to (v) above are found to be correct and if a breakthrough of 3 per cent. through the neckline is seen after the completion of the second shoulder. This signal is therefore given at point X on the chart of the "average" head and shoulders.

5. The simulation study used the random walk model to generate 484 share prices with lengths of 1,304 values each. The means and variances of the observed data bank were used when generating normal deviates. A detailed account of the generation process and its implications will be given elsewhere. In the present context the simulation study results may serve merely as an encouragement for undertaking such research.

6. The "average" head and shoulders is not a large one and many of the heads and shoulders in the study are therefore rather small, as compared with the time scale of medium and long term investment management. It is hoped to analyse the patterns further by size measured in days.

7. In view of the fact that in the period covered by the data bank the London market moved in such clear trends one might have expected, on the basis of simple inspection, that the tops as defined by the chartists would produce significant success. Thus the market averages showed a very clear top pattern in 1972 (with volume confirmation). Although this study has concentrated entirely on factual tests of actual share price movements rather than any logical argument, there is one part of the Efficient Market Theory which is directly relevant: that is, it is argued that any "mechanical" method of forecasting the future will be seized on by an influential number of investors and therefore very shortly become useless. This argument is applied to all types of analysis and it would no doubt be applied to the 1972 top. How far money in London is determined by investors who watch the technical evidence must be a matter of subjective opinion, but in view of one author (D.C.D.) the determining weight of money in London is moved by investors who do not use charts and who in many cases have no real knowledge of them.

Illustration

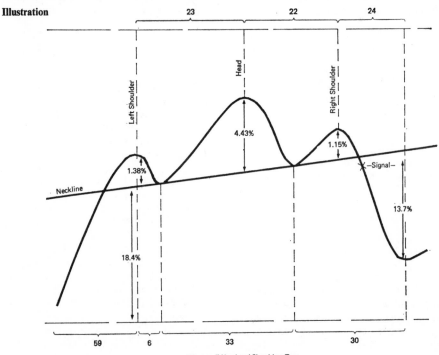

"Average" Head and Shoulders Top

CHAPTER 2

Risk and Return

Chapter 1 raised one very important question which goes right to the heart of investment management. What is good performance? The operation of a system or trading rule can often generate profits. What is not clear is whether such profits are high or low, or, good or bad. In other words is there a better alternative investment available? Indeed the whole question of determining what is or is not good performance can really only follow from a statement of the objective of the investment strategy adopted. Obviously until the investment aims are specified no definition of 'good performance' can be attempted.

This chapter develops the one key parameter which is central to the formulation of strategy, namely risk. As will be demonstrated, a choice of investment strategy is simply a choice of risk strategy. Once the level of risk the investor is prepared to suffer has been chosen, an appropriate investment strategy can be formulated and its success monitored thereafter.

Indices

Performance can be measured by comparison with an index. The idea of using an index is to provide a comparison or opportunity cost. The most popular index, and there are of course many, is the FT 30 share index. This is popular in the sense that it attracts much press comment and is generally regarded as 'the' market indicator.

Day	Share Price		Index	Portfolio
	X	Y	$\sqrt{X \times Y}$	$=\frac{1}{2}(X + Y)$
	£	£	£	£
1 (Base)	1	1	1	1
2	1	4	2	$2\frac{1}{2}$
3	4	$6\frac{1}{4}$	5	$5\frac{1}{8}$
4	4	4	4	4
5	16	4	8	10
6	9	25	15	17
7	8	$12\frac{1}{2}$	10	$10\frac{1}{4}$
8	16	$12\frac{1}{4}$	14	$14\frac{1}{8}$
9	4	9	6	$6\frac{1}{2}$
10	1	16	4	$8\frac{1}{2}$

This index is constructed of 30 shares which are chosen to be representative of British industry. Changes are made from time to time (eg after takeovers) to ensure that this representative feature continues. However, the index cannot be considered to be representative of a portfolio comprising the same 30 shares. This is because the index is a geometric average of the 30 share prices and as such has a number of important mathematical properties. To illustrate this let us calculate our own geometric index comprising two shares X and Y and compare its performance against a portfolio of the same two stocks. For simplicity let us suppose that on the base date both share prices are £1. The index and portfolio can be constructed of equal amounts of X and Y. At any point in time the index will be the square root of the product of the two share prices: this is where the unusual mathematical properties arise. The portfolio will take the value of half the sum of the two share prices. A possible series of prices is shown above.

It can be seen that the index does not equate with the portfolio except when the two share prices are identical (days 1 and 4). On all other days when the share prices are different so too are the index and portfolio. Most significant is the fact that the portfolio value is always equal to or greater than the index. Thus a portfolio based on the 30 FT index shares will, when compared over the period from the base date (1st July 1935), always (except when the 30 share prices are equal) perform better than the index. This feature is due entirely to the method of calculating the index.

There are further consequences. Looking at performance during the period, several anomalies are thrown up:

Period	Index	Portfolio
Day 1 to Day 2	+ 100%	+ 150%
Day 2 to Day 4	+ 100%	+ 60%
Day 5 to Day 9	– 25%	– 35%

It is clear that this type of index should be treated with caution. Obviously on a larger scale (ie 30 shares) the above effects become less noticeable. Nevertheless the fact remains that the FT 30 share index does not represent an alternative investment since no portfolio exists which will provide the same performance.

The logical alternative is to turn to an index which is calculated in the same way as a portfolio is valued: for example the FT all-share index. This is a simple arithmetical average of the share prices of the constituent shares weighted by their market capitalisations. Such an index would behave in the same way as a portfolio of the same constituents. However, if our particular portfolio includes foreign shares how appropriate is it to make a comparison to a solely UK index? Indeed this problem of matching index to investment objective can occur wholly within the UK. For example an oil industry based portfolio may not perform in the same way as the FT all-share index and it should not be expected to do so.

Even if a valid comparison could be made, the problem of consistency arises. The difficulties in performance measurement, including consistency, have been set out in most amusing fashion by Brew [20]. By consistency we refer to the situation where a portfolio outperforms an index over year 1 but underperforms on year 2 and of course during each year both outperforms and underperforms. The question that arises is whether on not this is good performance. Is year 1 the right year to examine? Is 12 months long enough or short enough? And so on. These questions are asked by Brew but not answered. This problem is merely a restatement of the question asked at the beginning of the chapter. What are investment objectives and how can we measure success in achieving these objectives? Risk is the key parameter in formulating investment strategy.

Risk

One risk concept has already been developed namely that of expectation. This concept was developed in Chapter 1 in the context of tendering for a contract. Consider instead two investment opportunities each of 12 months' duration and each costing £100 with the following outcomes:

Investment A	Return	Outcome	Probability	Calculation of Expectation
	8%	£108	0.25	£ 27
	20%	£120	0.25	£ 30
Invest £100	32%	£132	0.25	£ 33
	44%	£144	0.25	£ 36
			1.00	£126
Investment B				
	−80%	£ 20	0.1	£ 2
	20%	£120	0.4	£ 48
Invest £100	40%	£140	0.4	£ 56
	100%	£200	0.1	£ 20
			1.0	£126

Each outcome represents a different rate of return. Investment A has four equally likely outcomes. The expectation is calculated in the usual way by multiplying the value of each outcome by its probability and then adding these together for all possible outcomes. Note that Investment B does not have the same distribution: the outcome is different in its range of values and in the probability of each outcome. Nevertheless each investment has the same expectation, namely £126, which represents a rate of return of 26 per cent. The real question to be answered is whether or not the investor should be indifferent as to these alternatives.

The principal difference between the two is that Investment B provides the opportunity to lose £80 and at the same time gain £100 while the returns on Investment A are clustered more closely together. The widow's choice would be likely to be Investment A. Although she would thereby pass up the chance of doubling her money, she will avoid the possibility of losing 80 per cent of it.

This problem occupied the attention of leading mathematicians in the 18th century when it was posed in the form of the Petersburg Paradox:

Peter agrees to toss a coin and pay to Paul £2 if the coin shows heads on the first toss, or £4 if the coin first shows heads on the second toss, or £8 if the coin first shows heads on the third toss, and so on. The game ends as soon as heads appears. The problem is to determine what Paul should pay to Peter to play such a game.

The first step is to calculate Paul's expectation:

Event: first appearance of heads on the:	Outcome	Probability	Calculation of Expectation
1st toss	win: £2	$\frac{1}{2}$	£ 1
2nd toss	£4	$\frac{1}{4}$	£ 1
3rd toss	£8	$\frac{1}{8}$	£ 1
nth toss	£2^n	$\frac{1}{2}^n$	£ 1
			£∞

Each possible outcome contributes £1 to the expectation: so as there are infinitely many outcomes, the total expectation is infinite. The implication therefore is that Paul should pay £∞, but this is something few people would accept let alone pay.

Would-be solvers have pointed out that the game cannot be played indefinitely. The participants could die, after a lifetime tossing coins, before the result is known. More important than this, Peter's liability would after only a modest number of throws take on enormous dimensions. Heads on the 20th throw would cost him £1 million while heads on throw 30 would involve a payment in excess of £1 billion. Obviously there cannot be too many Peters around with a spare £1 billion. From Paul's point of view, even if he was confident he would get paid no matter what result, he would probably not risk all his wealth on the game. There is after all a 50 per cent chance that he would win only £1 and 99 per cent chance that he would win only £128 or less - hardly worth risking say £10,000 for. This is essentially the beginning of a solution. Bernoulli solved the paradox by introducing the concept of utility. He argued that each £1 won had a different value (ie different usefulness) to Paul depending on his own individual resources. Accordingly, the richer Paul was, the more he could risk. Likewise he would be indifferent between winning £1 million and £2 million but, given limited resources, be very concerned about losing say £10,000. It is this reason which explains why Paul will not be prepared to pay the expectation price to play.

Reverting to our two investments, the widow's choice, Investment A, can be explained in terms of her utility preference. As we observed before, she cannot afford to lose much, she is risk-averse, so will always choose the safer investment. This process of choice occurs for all investors no matter what their utility or risk preference. But not all investors have infinite wealth. So, for high-risk investments (like the Petersburg game) investors will not pay the full expectation price. In other words they want a higher rate of return to compensate for the risk. In the example, if investors are prepared to pay £100 for Investment A then, given that Investment B has identical expectation but higher risk, the investors would pay less than £100 for such an opportunity, say £90. These investment opportunities can be classified as follows:

Risk	Cost	Expectation	Expected Return
Investment A: Low	£100	£126	26% pa
Investment B: High	£90	£126	40% pa

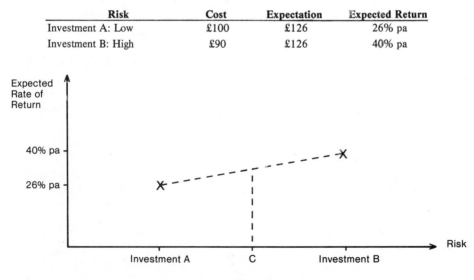

Note that any position on the dotted line can be achieved by splitting one's funds between both A and B. For example, spreading funds equally between Investments A and B would produce an expected rate of return of 33 per cent pa for a medium risk investment — point C in the diagram.

Risk Measurement

In the comparison of the two investment opportunities we have decided simply by looking at the distributions of outcomes that Investment B is riskier than A — not a very precise method. What is needed is an exact measure of the risk of an investment given that we know its distribution of outcomes. Such a measure must take account of the dispersion of possible outcomes from which the risk derives. It was an analysis of the dispersion of the outcomes which enabled our widow to make her choice. There are a number of statistical formulae which provide a measure for comparison. One such is the standard deviation (σ). This is calculated as follows:

- determine the expectation
- sum the squares of the differences between the expected outcome and each outcome multiplying each square by the frequency (ie probability) of the outcome. Then take the square root.

The various calculations for the two investments are:

Investment A:

Expectation £126

$$\begin{aligned} \text{Sum} - (126 - 108)^2 \times 0.25 &= 81 \\ (126 - 120)^2 \times 0.25 &= 9 \\ (132 - 126)^2 \times 0.25 &= 36 \\ (144 - 126)^2 \times 0.25 &= \underline{144} \\ & 270 \end{aligned}$$

Taking the square root gives a standard deviation of £16.4

Investment B:

Expectation £126

$$\begin{aligned} \text{Sum} - (126 - 20)^2 \times 0.1 &= 1123.6 \\ (126 - 120)^2 \times 0.4 &= 14.4 \\ (140 - 126)^2 \times 0.4 &= 78.4 \\ (200 - 126)^2 \times 0.1 &= \underline{547.6} \\ & 1764.0 \end{aligned}$$

Taking the square root gives a standard deviation of £42, considerably more than for investment A.

This comparison provides us with a quantitive measure of the difference in risk. (It is interesting to note that the standard deviation of the Petersburg game is infinity, a very high risk game.)

Application

It is easy to see how this process of risk measurement or assessment occurs in the stock market. The chief difference is that the range of outcomes of an investment in the ordinary shares of, say, company X, will not comprise four distinct possibilities as in the example above. Instead, the range of outcomes will be very wide. The worst outcome could be −100 per cent (it cannot be worse, providing that company X has limited liability) whilst at the other end of the spectrum, the sky is the limit (eg Poseidon). However the same calculations of expectation and dispersion are performed in order to arrive at a buy/sell decision. It is unlikely that specific computations are performed. Instead the investor will compare forecast outcomes for X with other similar companies and at the end of the day make a subjective judgement.

When a company is contemplating investing in new plant a similar decision has to be taken. Management will usually produce estimates of three outcomes,
— most optimistic outcome
— most likely outcome
— most pessimistic outcome

Probabilities will be attached to each outcome and the expectation calculated in the usual way. Management will then use this information to help make the correct investment decision.

Diversification

As any fund manager will tell you, diversification is at the heart of successful fund management. Markowitz [21] provided the theoretical foundation for this in 1952. The essential point is that if a portfolio of investments is considered then the chances of all the investments comprising the portfolio achieving their worst results simultaneously is much less than any single investment achieving its worst outcome. The reason for this is that the outcomes of the investment are not perfectly correlated. Thus when Investment A achieves its best result it does not necessarily follow that Investment B will also achieve its best result, and vice versa. In a corporate context, the profits of two different industries do not move exactly in line although they both show upturns when the world economy in general enjoys an upturn. Thus it can be seen that investment results are not perfectly correlated although some degree of correlation is always present since such investments are inevitably made in the same economic environment.

The benefits of diversifying into two different investments are best illustrated by a simple example. Suppose Investments A and B each have two outcomes:

	Cost	Outcome	(1 year later)	Rate of Return
Investment A	£100	A1	£115	15%pa
		A2	£125	25%pa
Investment B	£100	B1	£110	10%pa
		B2	£130	30%pa

As mentioned above, some degree of similarity in the outcome of these two investments is inevitable. Let us therefore suppose (i) that the outcomes depend on the state of the economy which may be,

either 'boom' (probability = 0.6)

or, 'bust' (probability = 0.4)

and (ii) that the outcomes and their respective probabilities can be categorised as:

State of economy (and probability)		Probabilities of each outcome Investment A		Investment B	
		A1	A2	B1	B2
'boom'	0.6	0.25	0.75	0.20	0.80
'bust'	0.4	0.75	0.25	0.80	0.20

From this table it is easy to calculate the probabilities of each outcome (eg the probability of A1 = probability of 'boom' $\times$ 0.25 plus the probability of 'bust' $\times$ 0.75, ie 0.45). The expectations and riskiness (standard deviation) may be calculated in the usual way.

	Outcome	Probability	Expectation	Rate of Return	Standard Deviation
Investment A	A1 £115	0.45	£ 51.75		
	A2 £120	0.55	£ 66.00		
			£117.75	17.75%	£2.50
Investment B	A1 £113	0.44	£ 49.72		
	A2 £126	0.56	£ 70.56		
			£120.28	20.28%	£6.50

Note that Investment B offers a higher expected rate of return as compensation for the greater risk (as measured by the standard deviation).

Adopting a policy of diversification we may now consider an investment of equal amounts (say £50) in A and in B. There are now 4 possible outcomes to this investment:

Outcome	Probability	Expectation	Rate of Return	Standard Deviation
'A1, B1' £114	0.27	£ 30.78		
'A1, B2' £120.5	0.18	£ 21.69		
'A2, B1' £116.5	0.17	£ 19.81		
'A2, B2' £123	0.38	£ 46.74		
		£119.02	19.02%	£3.80

Standard Deviation = £3.80

(The probability of outcome 'A1,B1' is probability of 'boom' x probability of A1 x probability of B1 plus probability of 'bust' x probability of A1 x probability of B1, and so on for the other outcomes.)

As would be expected, the expected rate of return generated by this investment is the exact average of the rates of return for Investments A and B. However, the risk of this diversified investment is less than a simple average of the standard deviations of Investments A and B, which amounts to £4.50. This is best illustrated graphically:

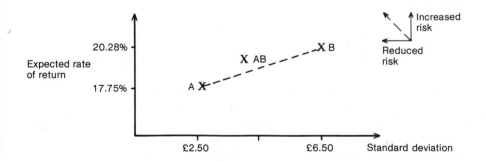

This in essence is the benefit of diversification. The point AB is to the north west of the dotted line. This is the region which offers better investment prospects since the return is

85

higher and the risk is lower. Other combinations of A and B also provide improved investment terms.

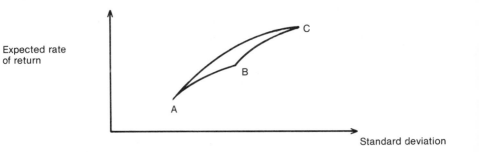

The curve AB plots out the alternatives available by varying the proportions of A and B comprising Investment AB: similarly the curve BC where C is another investment. The curve AC plots out the alternatives obtainable by combinations of A, B and C. Thus it can be seen that the addition of another investment pushes the curve further towards the north west of the diagram improving the rate of return and reducing the level of risk.

This process of diversification can be continued indefinitely to the extent that investments are available which are not perfectly correlated to existing investments in the portfolio, (and of course no two investments ever are perfectly correlated). Maximum benefit will be reached when all quoted equities are included in the portfolio, ie any point on the curve below, each point representing a different combination of investments.

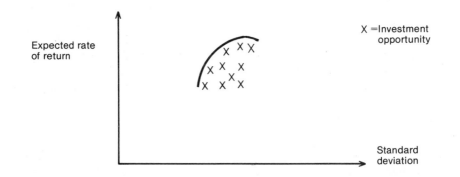

The curve represents the risk/return of a portfolio consisting of varying combinations of the investment opportunities also plotted. To this diagram can be added a 'risk-less' investment, for example a 3 month treasury bill. This is risk-less in the sense that over the life of the bill, the rate of return is fixed and therefore the standard deviation is zero. (This reasoning only works if the bill is actually redeemed, ie we are assuming that the credit worthiness of HM government is beyond question. This may or may not be reasonable.) There will be no correlation between the return on the treasury bill and the return on other investments. We can now consider including treasury bills in our portfolio.

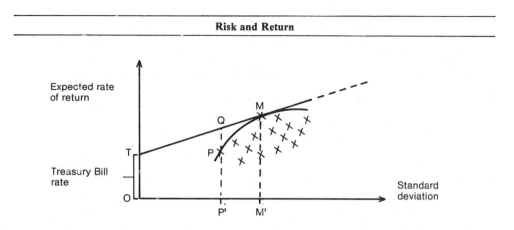

The introduction of the treasury bill (point T above) immediately clarifies our choice of portfolio on the curve. In order to be nearest the north-west corner (ie maximum return, minimum risk) the point M is chosen so that the line TM just touches the curve at M: TM is a tangent. Furthermore any point on the line TM can be achieved by splitting the portfolio between portfolio M and treasury bills. The advantage we have now is that if an investor desires less risk than the riskiness of the optimum portfolio (point M^1), say a risk level of P^1, then the curve alone would give him point P. Now however, by the inclusion of treasury bills in the portfolio, his expected return at that risk level is increased to point Q. Thus all portfolios having a risk level between zero and M^1 should consist of treasury bills and portfolio M in appropriate proportions. This argument applies to any single investment since these are not even on the curve. Points on the dotted line correspond to risk levels greater than M^1 and are obtained by borrowing and investing in M. Thus returns on portfolios to the right of point M on the curve can be increased, for the same level of risk, by borrowing and investing. (It is assumed that one can lend and borrow at the risk-free rate.)

Since point M is the optimum portfolio it follows that it will be the same as the portfolio of all securities in the proportions in which they are capitalised. Hereafter, references to 'the market' and 'the market portfolio' shall mean a portfolio of all shares in the proportions of their capitalisations.

Mathematically, this model expresses the return on a security or portfolio as follows:

$$E(R) = I + \frac{Cov(R,Rm)}{Var(Rm)} (E(Rm) - I)$$

where $E(R)$ = expected rate of return of the security or portfolio.
I = risk-free rate of interest.
$Cov(R,Rm)$ = covariance of the returns on the security or portfolio, (R) and the return on the market (Rm).
$Var(Rm)$ = the square of the standard deviation of return on the market (Rm).
$E(Rm)$ = expected rate of return on the market.

The main problem with using this model is complexity, as is amply demonstrated by the above formula. For a large portfolio the amount of data and computation required would be enormous. Some attempts have been made to use it in practice (Richards [22]) but for most purposes a simplification is used — the Sharpe or Diagonal model. The importance of this is that it is frequently used in studies of share price behaviour and in particular in some of those quoted in Chapter 3 and 4.

The Sharpe Model

The Sharpe model is based on the proposition that the rate of return on any individual share can be related to the rate of return on the market. Here 'market' has the same meaning as in the Markowitz model implying the inclusion of all shares. Any other share price movement not deriving from movements of the market as a whole can be explained by a factor 'u'. Algebraically, the return on a share, R, is given by:

$$R = \alpha + (\beta \times Rm) + u$$

where α (alpha) and β (beta) are constants and Rm is the return on the market. This model can be represented diagrammatically:

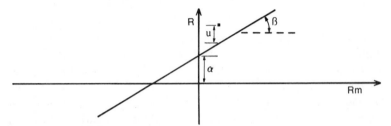

Note that alpha represents the rate of return on the share when the market rate of return is zero. The 'u' factor explains the difference between the actual price change and that which would be expected from consideration of the line. The expectation of 'u' is zero. Essentially, this model explains share price behaviour in terms of overall market movement plus a random factor 'u' which averages out to zero.

Shares are often categorised as those to hold in a rising market and those to hold when the market is falling. The first category is expected to out-perform a rising market and the second category should under-perform a falling market. Brealey [23] has referred to these two categories as 'aggressive' and 'defensive' respectively. This type of argument is often put forward by investment trust managers. They argue that because of the gearing in an investment trust, the investment trust shares are 'aggressive' and can be expected to out-perform a rising market. Since gearing is a major source of risk this could well be true provided that the portfolio of the trust is not too defensive which would otherwise tend to negate the effects of gearing.

The model is capable of further refinement. If the riskless rate of interest is I then all lines should pass through the point P on the diagram where R = I.

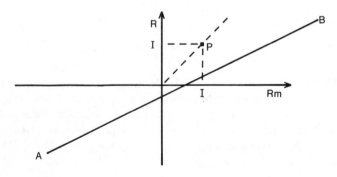

This can be seen quite easily if a line AB (below the point P) for share X is considered. If this line has slope s, then a portfolio can be constructed as follows:

> invest £s in the market
> invest £(1–s) in the riskless asset
> then the rate of return (Rp) on this will be
> Rp = (1–s) I + s.Rm

and the slope of the line of this portfolio will be s or line CD on the diagram below. Furthermore when Rm = I, the return on the portfolio will be Rp = (1–s)I + sI or Rp =I. Thus the line CD must pass through the point R = I.

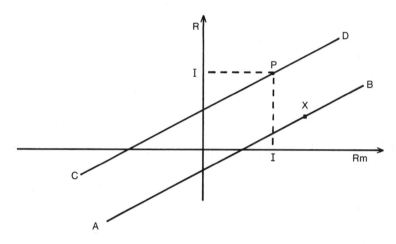

It will be obvious that share X would not be bought since a higher return could be obtained from the portfolio constructed above. The price of share X will therefore fall until it offers a return commensurate with line CD. Thus the line AB will move until it is parallel to CD and passes through the point P. Individual shares therefore would not lie below the point P. Also since the market line R = Rm is an average of all shares, no shares can lie above point P. Hence all lines must pass through P. It then follows that the intercept α is equal to (1–β)I. Thus beta is the only factor which characterises the behaviour of an individual share in relation to the market.

The term aggressive therefore describes shares with beta of more than 1 and defensive denotes beta factors of less than 1. For example, a share with beta of, say, 1.2 would mean that it would show a greater return than the market when the market is rising but fall further when the market is falling.

Diversification

The Sharpe model also explains how diversification works. On any individual share the return is expressed as (α +βRm+u); u is the factor in share price behaviour not explained by market movements.

The expected value of u is zero but takes positive or negative values. Clearly it is a source of risk. Consider how the equal combination of two securities changes the risk:

89

Share 1 $R_1 = \alpha_1 + \beta_1 Rm + u_1$

Share 2 $R_2 = \alpha_2 + \beta_2 Rm + u_2$

A portfolio would have a rate of return R_{12} given by:

$R_{12} = \frac{1}{2}(\alpha_1 + \alpha_2) + \frac{1}{2}(\beta_1 = \beta_2) Rm + \frac{1}{2}(u_1 + u_2)$

Apart from the averaging of the α and β factors, the main change lies in the reduced risk. The standard deviation of the u factor will be reduced. On the assumption that each u factor is independent of the rest, the combined standard deviation will be given by:

$$\sigma_{12} = \frac{1}{2} \sqrt{\sigma_1{}^2 + \sigma_2{}^2}$$

where σ_1 and σ_2 are the standard deviations of u_1 and u_2 respectively. Thus σ_{12} is less than $\frac{1}{2}(\sigma_1 + \sigma_2)$ and risk is reduced. For equal investments in n shares, the standard deviation of the u factor becomes:

$$\frac{1}{n}\left[\sqrt{\sigma_1{}^2 + \sigma_2{}^2 + \cdots\cdots + \sigma^2}\right]$$

For example, if all the σ's were equal then a portfolio of 100 shares would have a standard deviation of one tenth of that of each individual share. Thus the risk arising from the u factor can be diversified away while the beta market factor cannot be avoided.

Brealey [23]

So far the model appears workable in theory but how does it compare with the real world? Professor Brealey has examined the workings of this model by estimating the beta factors for 29 of the shares comprising the FT 30 share index.

One source of beta estimates would be the analyst. However, such estimates are likely to be subjective and not very accurate. One of the problems inherent in such an exercise is that of distinguishing between diversifiable and non-diversifiable risk. Highly geared companies, whose mainstream activities are related to the general level of economic activity, would be expected to have a high beta and be high risk. On the other hand an exploration company, an equally high risk investment, would be expected to have a low beta since success would only be remotely linked to the market as a whole. In this particular case the risk lies in large part in the u factor which can be diversified away.

Beta can be determined by examining the way the share has behaved in comparison to the market's behaviour. This is not inconsistent with the efficient market hypothesis since we are merely using an historic relationship to forecast a prospective one. The only possible validity for this method is if beta factors are stable over time. This Brealey examined.

Brealey collected share prices over a 200-day period for each of the 29 shares and made the necessary adjustments for dividends and scrip/rights issues. Proportionate changes in these prices were then compared with the corresponding changes in a market index using regression analysis. A similar exercise was undertaken for 138 shares using weekly prices over the period 1967-68. The extreme beta values obtained were:

	29 shares (1968)	138 shares (1967/68)
High	1.36 (Courtaulds)	1.88 (Plessey)
Low	0.46 (Watney Mann)	0.10 (Rowntree)

Brealey noted that 'the shares that were revealed as the most aggressive or defensive accorded fairly well with popular conceptions'. He also noted that the aggressive shares included consumer durable and building material companies where profitability is related to economic activity in a quite highly geared way. Low beta companies included food manufacturers, brewers and publishers where changes in economic activity have little if any effect.

Further tests were made to determine the stability of the beta factors over time. Brealey looked at estimates of beta in successive 5-week periods and observed significant correlation. Overall he was able to conclude that 'shares differ significantly in the way in which they are affected by the market and that these differences largely persist over time'.

Of course there may be good reason for the beta factor to change over time. For example a change in gearing brought about by a rights issue or an acquisition could lead to a revised beta factor. Such a change would not be allowed for in historic price data but could be covered by the analyst making an adjustment.

In a later article, Hodges and Brealey [24] described the workings of a computerised Sharpe model based on the FT Actuaries sector indices as opposed to individual shares. Regression was used to estimate sector beta factors over the period and the FTA 600 index was employed as a proxy for the market. Factors quite close to unity were observed:

Sector	Beta
Aircraft	0.999
Building materials	1.062
Contracting	1.164
Electricals	1.001
Engineering	0.961
Machine tools	0.886
Shipbuilding	1.114
Electronics	1.161
Household goods	1.042
Motors	1.127
Breweries	0.826
Entertainment	1.133
Food manufacturing	1.059
Newspapers	0.834
Paper and packaging	0.694
Stores	0.914
Textiles	0.907
Tobacco	1.135
Chemicals	1.021
Oil	0.928
Shipping	0.834
Financial group	1.075

The lowest sector beta measured was for Paper and packaging at 0.694 and the highest was Electronics at 1.161.

Cunningham [8] studied the beta factors for 950 shares using Wednesday closing prices over a 6-year period (1965-70). In particular he found that the alpha factors were so close in value to each that they were virtually equal. In this respect this is a divergence from the Sharpe model which suggests that each alpha is equal to $(1 - \beta)I$, where I is the riskless interest rate. The beta factors showed marked differences from share to share and varied only slowly over time.

Forecasting with Beta

The evidence reviewed above suggests that beta is a reliable guide to risk and, because of its stability, can be expected to persist over time. This quality can be used to forecast prices. This is especially useful when studying the effects of particular events (eg acquisitions, scrip issues, earnings announcements etc) since a forecast price can be compared with the actual price and so the effect on the share price can thereby be quantified. This technique, which will hereafter be referred to as residuals analysis, is used in the work reviewed in Chapter 3. The alpha and beta factors are estimated using share price data which excludes the period surrounding the event under study. Once these factors are known and the rate of return on the market calculated over the period immediately preceding the event then the expected rate of return can be computed and compared with what actually happened.

Example: Company announces a scrip issue at the end of the month.

Suppose α =   0.003 β =   0.90

and the FT index at the beginning of the month is 500 and at the end 525. The return on the index is given not just by the increase in capital value as dividends must be taken into account. This can be done by taking 1 month's dividend yield of the yield on the market (also published by the FT). This is only an approximation (albeit quite accurate) since the market yield is an annualised figure and does not represent actual dividends which would be received by a holder of the market portfolio in that particular month. Suppose that dividends account for another point on the index then the market rate of return is given by:

$$RM = \frac{525 + 1 - 500}{500} \times 100 \quad = 5.2\%$$

Hence the return on the share over the same month should be:

$$R = \alpha + \beta \; Rm \quad = 0.003 + (0.9 \times 0.052) \quad = 5.0\%$$

This can then be compared with the actual return in that particular month. Let us suppose that at the beginning of the month, the share price is 100p and at the end of the month immediately after the announcement of the scrip the price of 107p (no dividends being paid during the period). The return is therfore 7% over the month which is in excess of that forecast. The residual is 2% (ie 7% less 5%) or 2p. This residual can be attributed to the event under study. However, there is a possibility that the residual could be due to some other influence which would be explained by the 'u' term. To avoid this problem, large samples are taken so that the entraneous influences not connected with the scrip announcement will tend to cancel out.

Risk Classification

The other use for beta is in the analysis of risk. In Chapter 4, techniques are used which involve beta whereby portfolio performance can be compared. The theory is that higher risk should be rewarded by higher return. Thus over a long period of time a high risk fund should out-perform a low risk fund. This will not therefore necessarily imply anything about the ability of the two fund managers. Hence any comparison should make allowance for risk and this is where beta comes in.

THE TRUSTEES' MEETING—A CITY DAYDREAM

J. M. BREW

"Well", said the Chairman, "you have all had a few days to consider the figures of our pension fund's investment performance. Before handing over to the Secretary who will explain them in detail I must thank him for his foresight in instituting a scheme which makes performance so easy to assess. I hear at the club that some other funds have been having a good deal of trouble in this area. What it comes down to is that they don't really know whether their pension funds have been invested well or badly. I am confident that in our case the question has been made unusually straightforward and we shall be able to reach a decision fairly quickly".

Before seeing the Secretary's comments on the situation the reader should be told the story so far. Some time ago this pension fund decided to divide its equity portfolio into six equal parts and to entrust their management to six organisations which had offered investment management services. The Trustees presciently took the view that ordinary share prices would probably drift down during the period and accordingly made arrangements to put all their new money into property. In order that there should be no ambiguity about the investment performance the powers of management were restricted to investment in shares which were constituents of the F.T.A. All-Share Index with, of course, permission to hold cash and reinvest the dividend income. It was further stipulated that investment should be conducted within the normal bounds of prudence. The Trustees did not know quite what that meant, but it seemed the right sort of thing to say. So the reader will agree that the problem could hardly be simpler. Each management was subject to the same constraints and each portfolio could accurately be compared with the Index. The specific reason for this meeting was the fact that more money was now available for equity investment. Decisions were needed on the allocation of this new money and also, perhaps, on the re-allocation of the management of existing portfolios.

The first table produced by the Secretary showed the result of quarterly valuations between the starting date, 29 June 1968, and 2 October 1970, all expressed as a percentage of the starting value. The Secretary took the trouble to estimate what the periodic results would have been if the valuations had been exactly in line with the F.T.A. Index and income from the Index constituents had been reinvested as it was received. This is Table 1.

Table 1

Quarterly Valuation Totals allowing for reinvested income

Valuation date				F.T.A. Index	Fund A	Fund B	Fund C	Fund D	Fund E	Fund F
29. 6.68	..	..	..	100	100	100	100	100	100	100
4.10.68	..	..	..	107.17	135.13	112.10	104.50	115.20	107.30	93.10
3. 1.69	..	..	..	114.89	142.04	127.91	109.73	122.23	115.24	101.12
3. 4.69	..	..	..	108.83	130.86	117.68	105.89	116.61	110.17	97.90
4. 7.69	..	..	..	95.70	111.36	95.32	98.48	89.79	97.17	87.13
3.10.69	..	..	..	94.86	107.79	95.32	97.79	98.14	96.68	87.13
2. 1.70	..	..	..	101.65	113.50	104.85	103.66	107.95	103.84	94.20
3. 4.70	..	..	..	99.49	108.66	102.23	102.11	101.47	101.97	94.20
3. 7.70	..	..	..	88.75	95.62	85.87	95.98	86.25	91.26	88.29
2.10.70	..	..	..	98.83	105.56	103.04	103.66	103.33	102.21	101.65
Effective total quarterly rate of return as calculated by the Secretary..				−0.131%	+0.603%	+0.333%	+0.400%	+0.365%	+0.243+	+0.182%
Trend rate of quarterly return as calculated by the Economic Adviser ..				−1.420%	−2.237%	−1.839%	−0.425%	−1.685%	−1.044%	−0.420%

93

"Well, Sir, fortunately the figures are sufficiently clear-cut to speak for themselves", the Secretary began, "but perhaps I could be allowed to elaborate very briefly. The first thing to notice is that, even allowing for reinvested income the F.T.A. Index showed a negative rate of return over the period, a rate of minus ·131 per cent. per quarter to be exact. We should have been much better off to sell out completely and put the proceeds out on loan. So to some extent we can congratulate ourselves on the decision to channel our new money elsewhere during the period. I think most of us believe that the future for equities is now a little more rosy and, with new money to invest, it seems to me that we should take this opportunity of reviewing the performance of our managers. You will see that they all achieved a positive rate of return, and within the brief we gave them it was very satisfactory that they all beat the Index by a significant amount. I have designated the managements by letters, and my recommendation is that we should give all the new money to the one at the top of my league table, namely A".

The Chairman asked for comments and the first one to speak was the Economic Adviser. His economic advice had not been conspicuously successful in the immediate past and he was not in a mood to let anyone get away with praise too easily. "I should like to know why you have given us all these intermediate valuation results if the end figure is the only one that matters", he said. "I thought I ought to keep an eye on what was going on" replied the Secretary, "and having arranged for quarterly valuations I thought the Trustees would be interested to see the full result. But you are quite right that my recommendation is based on the last valuation".

"That is very interesting", said the Economic Adviser, "because I have been looking at the intermediate figures and I should like to ask you if there is any sort of intermediate fluctuation which might have made you change your mind". "I think I see your point" replied the Secretary, "but I am bound to say that it seems to me to be a trifle academic. After all there is no getting away from the fact that A has done a good deal better with our money than any of the others".

But the Economic Adviser was not quite finished. "If you want my specific recommendation it is that we should give the new money to those who are likely to do the best with it in the future rather than give it to those who have done best in the past. Your motive for the study of performance seems to be to reward those who have made the most money for us, on the basis that these will do the best for us in future. I think we should study your performance tables much more carefully."

Having made this suggestion the Economic Adviser produced Table 2 which shows the performance of each fund each quarter allowing for both capital and income.

"Is it so obvious now", he said "that A is such a good manager? He started off like a shot from a gun and was miles ahead of the field at the end of the first quarter. After that he has done noticeably worse than the Index every single time. Contrast this with F who started very badly and has done outstandingly well since. Would you stake any

Table 2

Quarterly Rates of Return allowing for both capital changes and income

Quarter				F.T.A. Index	Fund A	Fund B	Fund C	Fund D	Fund E	Fund F
1	..	..	..	+ 7.17%	+35.13%	+12.1%	+ 4.50%	+15.20%	+ 7.30%	− 6.90%
2	..	..	..	+ 7.20%	+ 5.11%	+14.1%	+ 5.00%	+ 6.10%	+ 7.40%	+ 8.61%
3	..	..	..	− 5.27%	− 7.87%	− 8.00%	− 3.50%	− 4.60%	− 4.40%	− 3.18%
4	..	..	..	−12.07%	−14.90%	−19.00%	− 7.00%	−23.00%	−11.80%	−11.00%
5	..	..	..	− 0.87%	− 3.21%	Nil	− 0.70%	+ 9.30%	− 0.50%	Nil
6	..	..	..	+ 7.15%	+ 5.30%	+10.00%	+ 6.00%	+10.00%	+ 7.40%	+ 8.12%
7	..	..	..	− 2.12%	− 4.26%	− 2.50%	− 1.50%	− 6.00%	− 1.80%	Nil
8	..	..	..	−11.80%	−12.00%	−16.00%	− 6.00%	−15.00%	−10.50%	− 6.27%
9	..	..	..	+11.36%	+10.40%	+20.00%	+ 8.00%	+19.80%	+12.00%	+15.13%
Arithmetic Mean			..	+ 0.194%	+ 1.52%	+ 1.19%	+ 0.53%	+ 1.31%	+ 0.57%	+ 0.50%

money on A beating F between now and next year, because I certainly wouldn't? My impression is that F is much the better horse but that the finish came a furlong too soon for him. In fact I think we should seriously consider dropping A altogether. He is easily bottom of my league table".

The proposition being put by the Economic Adviser was that F, the management which had put up easily the worst end-to-end performance of all the six, was the one likely to do best in the future. He had some figures to prove it too. He had applied regression methods to the valuation figures (or, to be more accurate, the logarithm of the valuation totals) and derived a trend line for each management which can be used to estimate the rate of total return each is likely to achieve in future. The result is shown in the last line of Table 1. This new method of assessment turns the ranking order just about completely upside down and shows that only three managements have a trend rate better than the Index. There are other ways of fitting a trend line but the results would not differ substantially. But if the Economic Adviser had been allowed to fit a second degree curve the trend would have been even more strongly in favour of F. His second favourite was C.

At this stage the Finance Director introduced the question of variability and risk which became the subject of a somewhat lengthy argument. It is evident from the tables that some managements produced results which were much more variable than others. But it is not obvious how we should assess variability. Should one consider the periodic valuation totals, or the totals relative to the Index? Perhaps we should consider the variability of the quarterly rates of return, or, probably best of all, the difference between the actual rates of return and those achieved on the Index. The Chairman very much liked E on these grounds, but nobody quite knew how much the better performance should be required or expected before one is justified in pursuing a more risky policy. Still it was evident that E, though he produced rather unexciting results, did so in a way which gave confidence that he would rarely produce a bad performance and would nearly always be above average.

"But there is another, and much better, way of looking at it" said the Finance Director. "Ever since the Chairman and I went to talk to them about

the company I have subscribed to the Journal of The Society of Investment Analysts. I read an article in the December 1968 issue by Taylor and Russell which explained what I think is the correct approach. This article applied an idea of an American called Jack Treynor to the analysis of U.K. Unit Trusts. The idea is that some managements consistently have portfolios which both go up more and down more than the Index. Others have portfolios which go up less and down less. By examination of Table 2 you can see roughly what I mean. Fund C moved the same way as the Index each quarter but its movement was always a good deal less pronounced. By contrast, Fund B was more volatile than the Index in both directions. The problem is easily analysed statistically by making a regression of each fund's quarterly rate of total return on the Index return". The results are shown in Table 3, which shows the equation of the regression line for each management. The variable x represents the performance of the Index expressed as a total return and the variable y represents the performance of the management under analysis. The gradient of the line for A is 1·39 which means that a 1 per cent. increase in the Index tended in the past to be accompanied by a 1·39 per cent. increase in the portfolio managed by A. Management C, on the other hand only showed a 0·645 per cent. increase in the same circumstances. This line is called the "characteristic line" and there is some evidence that its slope is relatively stable in time".

Table 3

Regression Equations for each management

x = Quarterly Return on F.T.A. Index
y = Quarterly Return on the Fund

		Correlation
Fund A	y = 1.25 + 1.39 x	r² = 0.782
Fund B	y = 0.88 + 1.61 x	r² = 0.996
Fund C	y = 0.41 + 0.65 x	r² = 0.994
Fund D	y = 1.00 + 1.58 x	r² = 0.939
Fund E	y = 0.38 + 0.99 x	r² = 0.999
Fund F	y = 0.35 + 0.79 x	r² = 0.789

The Finance Director contended that the choice lay squarely between B and D because these managements had the steepest slopes to their characteristic lines and would therefore perform better in the rising market which the Trustees had agreed was likely to occur. He had a marginal preference for D because though its line was not quite so steep it intersected the vertical axis at a slightly higher point—which is supposed to reflect the amount by which the fund would beat the Index given a nil rate of return on the Index. But the Economic Adviser pointed out that the lines intersected at a point given by an Index return of 4 per cent. which was surely less than one could expect in a normal year. The Finance Director then agreed that B was slightly preferable.

The Chairman was a bit dazed by now, but he felt obliged to put in another word for E. "I just don't believe it", he said. "You chaps are being much too clever about it all. Look at E's performance. He beat the Index by a perceptible amount every single time which is more than any of the others did. My second choice would be F who beat it eight times out of nine".

So there we have it. The Secretary chose A. The Economic Adviser chose C and F. The Finance Director chose B and D, and the Chairman chose E and F. About a hundred years ago Mr. Punch summed it up aptly when he said "You pays your money and you takes your choice".

Postscript

In real life the figures will never be as conveniently clearcut as those in the tables. But the reader will have noticed one respect in which this daydream is realistic. At the time of the meeting there was only one thing on which the trustees were in agreement—that the equity market was likely to rise. At the time of going to press the index is about 10% lower. But given the fact that they agreed to be bullish it would have been right to prefer B and D whatever Mr. Punch said. If you are going to make quarterly valuations you surely ought to use them.

We can all agree, though, that the matter is not quite so simple as the Secretary supposed.

THE IMPACT OF THE MARKET ON BRITISH SHARE PRICES

RICHARD BREALEY

Investors frequently classify shares as either aggressive or defensive holdings. The former consist of those issues that can be expected to advance most in a rising market and the latter comprise those that are likely to decline least in a falling market. According to this description what distinguishes the two groups is the way that they react to different market conditions. A share that is expected to give a stable rate of return is defensive, but so also is a volatile share as long as it is just as likely to advance in a falling market as it is to decline. In other words the aggressive or defensive characteristics of a share depend both on whether its price is volatile and on whether its performance is closely related to that of the market.

A possible way to measure whether in the past a stock has behaved in a defensive or aggressive manner would be to draw a diagram similar to Figure 1. The vertical axis represents the proportionate change in the price of a hypothetical share and the horizontal axis the corresponding change in the level of the market. Each point depicts the experience during a different week. Least squares regression was then used to pass through these points a line of best fit. The gradient of this line measures the average affect on the share of a difference of one per cent. in the performance of the market. Thus in Figure 1 the slope of 1.5 indicates that an additional 1 per cent. change in the market index would have induced on the average an additional 1½ per cent. change in the price of the stock. On these grounds the share could reasonably be classified as an aggressive holding. If the slope were less than one, it would constitute a defensive investment. This measure of the sensitivity of the share price to market changes accords well with the earlier stipulation that the degree of aggressiveness should depend both on the share's volatility and on the extent to

which its movement echoed that of the market. This becomes clear if one thinks of the slope of the fitted lines as the product of two quantities. The first is the ratio of the standard deviation of the share price changes to that of the market changes. The second is the co-efficient of correlation between the two series.

It should be stressed that the slope of the line measures the impact of the market at the margin. Thus in the case of the stock illustrated in Figure 1 the slope of 1.5 suggests that when the market rose by 2 per cent. the gain in the share price tended to be 1.5 per cent. greater than when the market rose by 1 per cent. However the actual magnitude of the share change in either case depends not only on the slope of the line but also on the point at which it crosses the vertical axis. For reasons that will not be elaborated here these lines may be expected to intersect each other in the region of the interest rate, so that in an unchanged or very gently rising market the defensive issues should provide superior performance.

These regression lines offer a very simple means

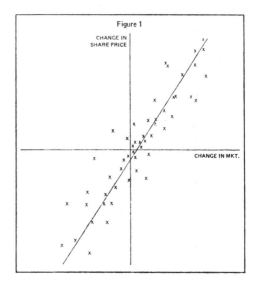

Figure 1

The bulk of the data for this article was contributed by Wood, Mackenzie & Co. and Coral Index Ltd., both for the purpose of research by members of the London Business School and for a privately sponsored project. This article would not have been possible without their kind assistance.

of depicting the way in which different shares have reacted to the market. However, one cannot be confident that they depict the true relationship unless certain conditions are met. To ensure that in practice they do accurately measure the market impact a study was made of the behaviour of twenty-nine of the shares used in the computation of the F.T. Index. For each company share prices were collected for a 200 day period and adjusted for capital issues and dividend payments. The proportionate changes in these share prices were then regressed on the corresponding changes in a market index. An assessment was first made of the assumption that the relationships between share and market could be accurately represented by a straight line. Inspection of the scatter diagrams and statistical tests confirmed that this view was justified. In other words a share's sensitivity to the market appears to remain constant over the whole range of market changes. It follows that the defensive and aggressive categories are mutually exclusive. An aggressive share will display the best performance in rising markets but will also perform least well when share prices are generally declining.

A second feature of this exercise was that the deviations from the fitted line appeared to be independent of one another. This not only provides encouragement that the estimated slope of the line will be unbiased but it is also an interesting observation in its own right. In these circumstances the fact that a share performed better in one period than it usually did in such a market is immaterial to whether it is likely in the next period to perform better or worse than the movement of the market would lead one to expect.

A further useful characteristic of the data was that the successive changes in the level of the market were also almost independent of each other. Consequently the expected slope of the line would not have been affected if, for example, daily or monthly price changes had been employed instead of weekly variations.

In other ways too the analysis suggests that this is an efficient approach to estimating the impact of the market. In particular the amount of variation in the price changes of each share does not increase with the magnitude of the change in the market. Only the relatively high frequency of extremely large changes suggests that there may be better methods for estimating the slope than least squares regression.

Our prime concern so far has been with whether this approach can be employed to provide reliable estimates of the way in which shares have responded to the market. We now turn to the much more interesting question of whether these lines have the necessary characteristics for them to prove useful. In order for the analysis to have any practical value two requirements must be met. Firstly one needs some assurance that shares really do differ significantly in the way that they react to the market and secondly one needs to be sure that a share that responds unusually sharply in one period will behave in a similar way in the next period. The first of these questions is easily answered. In the case of 29 shares examined the range of slopes proved to be quite wide, despite the fact that they were all leading industrial issues. The most aggressive share, Courtaulds, moved 1.36 per cent. for each additional 1 per cent. change in the market and the most defensive share, Watney Mann, varied by 0.46 per cent. for an extra 1 per cent. change in the market. In another study of 138 shares the slopes of the lines ranged between 1.88 (for Plessey) and 0.10 (for Rowntree). American studies have also revealed a wide range of gradients. For example, one analysis of 950 New York Stock Exchange issues revealed a spread of 1.95 to −0.10.[3] It should be recognised that these figures are estimates based on a limited number of observations and that they do not necessarily measure in each case the true relationship between share and market. Therefore, even if all the shares were in fact equally affected by the market, an examination of their performance during specific days or weeks would create an illusion of differences in their behaviour. For this reason it is to be expected that the above figures overstate in each case the spread between the most aggressive and defensive shares. However, the large number of observations suggests what later tests will confirm. Even when allowance is made for estimate errors, there is a substantial difference between the ways in which defensive and aggressive shares react to the market.

It is interesting, if not strictly relevant, to note that the shares that were revealed as the most aggressive or the most defensive accorded fairly well with popular conceptions. The aggressive

Table 1

Co-efficients of Correlation between Estimated Slopes in Successive Periods

Source of Data	No. of Shares	No. of Observations per Period	Length of Period	Years Spanned	Correlation Co-efficients	Average Co-efficient
U.K.	29	40	8 weeks	1968	0.42 0.54 0.71 0.30	0.49
U.K.	138	25	25 weeks	1967-1968	0.31 0.19 0.36	0.29
U.S.A.[b]	251	100	8 years	1927-1960	0.72 0.76 0.67	0.72
U.S.A.[c]	36	12	1 year	1957-1963	0.55 0.37 0.00-0.24 0.24 0.33	0.21
U.S.A.[d]	801	25	25 months	1964-1968	0.45	0.45

[a] NB. the expected value of these co-efficients varies with the number of observations per period.
[b] See Blume[3].
[c] See Ahlers and Steglitz[1].
[d] See Fisher[4].

issues have included a large number of the shares of consumer durable and building material companies, whose fortunes not only vary widely but are also closely dependent upon the degree of economic activity. At the other end of the spectrum are the shares of a number of food manufacturers, of brewers and of publishers. Many of these firms are characterised by steady earnings progression and all are relatively unaffected by boom and recession.

The second condition for the usefulness of these measures is that they should be relatively stable over time. After all there is little value in knowing that over the past year a share has responded 1.2 per cent. for each additional 1 per cent. change in the market, if the figure for the first six months was 0.7 per cent. and for the remainder of the year was 1.7 per cent. If the slopes do persist over time, one could not only make more useful comments about the behaviour of specific shares in some past period, one could also predict the way in which they should react to the market in the future. In these circumstances one might expect consumer durable shares to perform well in a rising market and brewery issues to be relatively good holdings when prices are generally declining.

To test the stability of these relationships, estimates were derived of the manner in which each of the 29 shares responded to changes in the market during five successive eight week periods. The estimated slopes in one period were then correlated with those in the next. The average correlation co-efficient was 0.49 (the separate co-efficients are shown in the first row of Table 1). The fact that all the co-efficients were significantly positive constitutes evidence that the relationships between share and market did persist to some degree from one period to another. Moreover the fact that the estimates of the slopes are subject to a certain amount of random error suggests that these co-efficients probably understate the true extent of the persistence of each share's response to market changes.

If, instead of looking at individual shares, consideration were given to the average sensitivity of a group of shares, these estimate errors could be expected partly to cancel out. In this way it should prove possible to get a better idea of the extent to which the market has the same affect on a share in two different periods. The 29 shares were, therefore, classified into five portfolios on the basis of their apparent sensitivity to market changes in the first eight week period. The first column of Table 3 shows that on the average the most aggressive issues tended during these weeks to move 1.48 per cent. for each one per cent. change in the market and that the least aggressive performers tended to move 0.47 per cent. The second column of this table records the manner in which the same portfolios tended to respond in the next eight week period. The correspondence between the two columns is very clear. This exercise was repeated for other pairs of adjacent eight week periods and the results set out in the remaining columns of Table 3. In each case there was a close relationship between the sensitivity of the portfolios in adjacent periods.

It is now possible to consider jointly the two conditions of usefulness by asking the question " Could this approach have been employed to select stocks which were likely in another period to respond very differently to fluctuations in the market?" The answer is an unequivocal " Yes ". On the average in the subsequent eight week period the most aggressive shares responded 1.8 times as

Table 2

Ratios of the Slopes of the Regression Lines of Shares that had formerly been most and least Sensitive to Market Changes.

Source of Data	No. of Shares	Ratios	Average Ratio
U.K.	29	1.6 2.0 2.0 1.5	1.8
U.K.	138	2.0 1.1 1.8	1.6
U.S.A.	251	2.9 2.6 2.6	2.7
U.S.A.	36	7.1 3.5 1.0 1.0 1.5 1.8	2.7
U.S.A.	801	1.9	1.9

Table 3

Average Sensitivity to Market Changes of 29 U.K. Shares Grouped According to Sensitivity in Earlier 40 Day Period

Group	1st & 2nd Periods		2nd & 3rd Periods		3rd & 4th Periods		4th & 5th Periods	
	1st	2nd	2nd	3rd	3rd	4th	4th	5th
1	1.48	1.14	1.43	1.21	1.32	1.18	1.31	1.15
2	1.10	1.12	1.12	0.93	1.08	0.99	1.06	0.84
3	0.88	1.09	0.96	0.88	0.94	0.91	0.82	0.87
4	0.73	0.67	0.74	0.90	0.70	0.65	0.62	0.92
5	0.47	0.71	0.43	0.61	0.46	0.59	0.50	0.76

sharply to market changes as did the defensive shares (the figures for the individual eight week periods are shown in the first row of Table 2).

For investment purposes eight weeks is a very short time, so that it would be useful to know whether this persistence extends over longer periods. The absence of any comprehensive data bank of British share prices limits the possible scope of such tests but it did prove possible to repeat the above exercise for several successive six month periods.

Weekly share prices of 138 companies were obtained for a period of nearly two years ending in December 1968. For each of four successive six month periods an estimate was made of the way in which each share responded to the market. The estimates of price sensitivity in one period were then correlated with those in the next. The average correlation co-efficient was 0.29 (see the second row of Table 1 for the separate co-efficients). When comparing this statistic with the earlier test one should bear in mind that the smaller number

of observations is liable to have resulted in greater estimate errors and thus biased downward the correlations.

Again an attempt was made to minimise the impact of these estimate errors by allotting the shares to five portfolios according to their apparent sensitivity to the market in one six month period. An analysis was then made of the behaviour of these shares in the next six month period. The results are shown in Table 4. A strong degree of persistence can be observed between the first and second periods and between the third and fourth periods. Between the middle periods there is a detectable but weaker relationship.

On the average the most aggressive shares proved to be 1.6 times as sensitive to market changes in subsequent months as the least aggressive issues. This average conceals a diversity of experience. In one case the most aggressive stocks were 2.0 times as sensitive, in another they were 1.8 times as sensitive and in the remaining case they proved only 14 per cent. more responsive to market changes.

Table 4

Average Sensitivity to Market Changes of 138 U.K. Shares Grouped According to Sensitivity in Earlier 25 Week Period

Group	1st & 2nd Periods		2nd & 3rd Periods		3rd & 4th Periods	
	1st	2nd	2nd	3rd	3rd	4th
1	1.52	0.98	1.46	1.00	1.52	1.31
2	1.09	0.71	0.95	1.01	1.14	1.01
3	0.83	0.72	0.66	0.89	0.90	0.81
4	0.58	0.61	0.39	0.79	0.65	0.77
5	0.24	0.50	0.01	0.88	0.32	0.71

This much larger sample of shares provided additional support for the view that shares differ significantly in the way in which they are affected by the market and that these differences largely persist over time. It also, however, emphasised that the relationships are much more constant in some periods than others. There is a good justification for believing that the relatively weak correlation between the slopes in the second and third of the six month periods is a rare phenomenon. Towards the end of the earlier period sterling was devalued, an event which caused a major reassessment of the qualities needed for profit growth. Even in the U.K., events with an economic impact of this magnitude are uncommon.

It is instructive to compare these results with similar studies of American stock behaviour. The first and most comprehensive of these analyses was undertaken by Marshall Blume[2]. Blume examined the performance of 251 stocks during four successive periods of approximately eight years each. Table 1 indicates that the degree of correlation between the slopes of the regression lines in successive periods was uniformly very high and Table 5 demonstrates that when these shares were collected into portfolios this stability was even more apparent. Finally Table 2 shows that the most aggressive portfolio in one period proved to be subsequently 2.7 times as responsive to market changes as the issues that had appeared the least aggressive.

Blume's results are impressive both because the degree of correspondence between the slopes of the regression lines in different periods is very high and because he was able to demonstrate that these relationships endured over quite long time spans. In contrast to Blume, Ahlers and Steglitz[1], have argued that the usefulness of these measures is considerably limited by the number of occasions in which there appears to be no consistency in the manner in which individual shares are affected by the market. Ahlers and Steglitz support their argument with measures of the sensitivity of 36 shares to market changes in each of the years 1957-63. Their findings, rearranged to be comparable to those already described, are shown in Tables 1, 6 and 2.

On the average the most sensitive shares in one period responded in the next year more than 2.7 times as sharply to market changes as the shares that appeared least sensitive. This result was not significantly different from the findings of other researchers. However the authors were disturbed by the fact that the correlation analysis suggested no relationship between the slopes that were observed in 1959 and those observed in 1960, and that there appeared to be an inverse relationship between the slopes in 1960 and 1961. However these estimates were derived with only twelve observations so that the slopes of the regression lines are subject to considerable error and the correlation between these slopes is in consequence

Table 5.

Average Sensitivity to Market Changes of 251 U.S. Shares Grouped According to Sensitivity in Earlier 8 Year Period

Group	1st & 2nd Periods		2nd & 3rd Periods		3rd & 4th Periods	
	1st	2nd	2nd	3rd	3rd	4th
1	1.47	1.46	1.65	1.42	1.51	1.42
2	1.14	1.14	1.19	1.15	1.15	1.13
3	0.90	0.97	0.92	1.02	0.97	1.05
4	0.69	0.77	0.68	0.76	0.75	0.87
5	0.43	0.50	0.39	0.55	0.48	0.55

Table 6.

Average Sensitivity to Market Changes of 36 U.S. Shares Grouped According to Sensitivity in Earlier 1 Year Period.

Group	1957 & 1958		1958 & 1959		1959 & 1960		1960 & 1961		1961 & 1962		1662 & 1963	
	1957	1958	1958	1959	1959	1960	1960	1961	1961	1962	1962	1963
1	1.59	1.64	2.11	2.03	2.39	1.08	1.66	0.98	1.78	1.20	1.61	1.54
2	1.10	1.32	1.37	1.28	1.14	1.00	1.16	1.06	1.28	1.12	1.22	0.95
3	0.84	0.72	0.94	0.88	0.98	0.84	0.99	0.98	1.08	1.22	1.05	0.78
4	0.62	0.63	0.63	0.62	0.67	0.94	0.73	0.79	0.75	0.96	0.87	0.84
5	0.21	0.23	−0.42	0.59	0.28	1.10	0.50	1.01	0.06	0.79	0.56	0.88

biased heavily downward. At the same time the sample of companies is very small, so that the magnitude of these correlation co-efficients can be expected to vary widely from year to year. It is indicative of the low significance of these results that, if one stock is omitted from the sample, the correlations in both the questionable years become respectably, though not of course significantly, positive. While, therefore, these findings do constitute evidence of a general persistence in shares' reactions to the market, they are not able to cast any useful light on the frequency of exceptions to this rule.

A third study of U.S. data was undertaken by Eric Fisher[4]. Fisher examined the persistence of the market impact on 801 stocks over two successive periods of 25 months each. His findings, stated in a comparable form, are shown in Tables 1, 2 and 7. While less encouraging than Blume's the study suggests a degree of stability similar to that of British issues.

Table 7.

Average Sensitivity to Market Changes of
801 U.S. Shares Grouped According to Sensitivity
in Earlier 25 Month Period

Group	1st Period	2nd Period
1	1.82	1.33
2	1.25	1.08
3	0.97	0.98
4	0.69	0.87
5	0.25	0.71

The results of these tests have differed in detail. These distinctions undoubtedly reflect in part a genuine tendency for the market effect to be more constant in some periods than others but they are probably also in large part a consequence of chance differences in the samples and of slight variations in the method of analysis. However, in one thing they are all agreed. Shares differ sharply in the manner in which they react to the market and these differences persist to some degree over time.

It is worth returning for a moment to Figure 1 to consider the significance of this conclusion. The consistency of the relationship makes it possible to distinguish between the expected price changes of any two shares given the state of the market. It is important to remember the limitations to this statement. The fact that only a quarter of a share's price movement can be explained by the market is testimony to a wide scatter about the line, so that,

even if its position were known with certainty, a share's performance on any single occasion may differ quite markedly from what was expected. These regression lines therefore provide the best estimate of a share's behaviour in the absence of any special foreknowledge of the events affecting that share alone.

These qualifications are less serious than may at first sight appear. In the first place the fact that successive deviations from the line are nearly independent means that the average performance of a share over a number of periods is likely to be much closer to the average of the predicted changes. Secondly the fact that the deviations from the line for any two companies are also in large measure independent means that the average performance of a group of shares in any one period is likely to be much closer to the average of the predicted changes. This implies that by measuring the historical effect of the market on individual holdings it should be possible to distinguish fairly accurately between the future changes of any two portfolios given the condition of the market (see Treynor et al.[6] for a practical demonstration of this).

The consistency of the market effect is a very useful phenomenon both in the analysis of past performance and the prediction of future performance (one application to the problem of performance measurement was described by Albert Russell and Basil Taylor in the December 1968 issue of this Journal[5]). However, perhaps the most important aspect of these findings is that they suggest a new way to look at the portfolio manager's job. If two investors are equally competent at selecting superior investments the difference between the expected performance of their portfolios will depend solely on whether one is invested in more aggressive issues. Even if the two managers are not of equal ability a very substantial part of the variation in performance will depend on the sensitivity of their portfolios to the market. It follows that a major part of the manager's job must be to select issues with a degree of aggressiveness that is in accordance with his assessment of market prospects and with the fund's objectives. Not only the portfolio manager but also his superiors are affected by this. Legislators and company boards have devoted considerable ingenuity to controlling the risks that the manager of an institutional portfolio may take. He is required to invest only in trustee stocks, to buy shares with certain yields or certain historical records, submit his proposals for board approval. In many cases these controls have dictated the company's organisational structure. The difficulty is that either these restrictions have undesirable side effects or they are evaded by the ingenious manager. It would therefore be more efficient if risk could be controlled directly. The only event likely to cause the performance of a diversified portfolio to be worse than expected is a poor market. Company managements may not be able to prevent this but they can control the impact of such markets on the value of their portfolios. The portfolio manager can be informed of the maximum degree of aggressiveness that the fund should be allowed to adopt and this can be periodically compared to its actual

position. The other merit to setting limits in this way is that it is easy to appreciate the opportunities for gain that are being given up through not holding more aggressive shares. Who knows what affect the Trustee Act is likely to have on the performance of trusts ? Finally it is worth noting that the development of an accurate and easily comprehended measure that simultaneously sums up the risks and opportunities from any portfolio might alter the relationship between institution and client. It could, for example, prove far more useful in describing a unit trust's objectives than a hundred pictures of Blue Streak.

These reflections are necessarily brief, but they suggest interesting fields for further research. This, we hope, will follow.

References

[1]D. Ahlers and M. Steglitz, " The Use and Misuse of Security Evaluation Models ". Unpublished paper prepared for the Seminar on the Analysis of Security Prices, University of Chicago, May 1968.

[2]M. Blume, " The Assessment of Portfolio Performance —An Application to Portfolio Theory ". Unpublished PhD dissertation, University of Chicago, 1968.

[3]E. F. Fama, L. Fisher, M. C. Jensen and R. Roll, " The Adjustment of Stock Prices to New Information ". *International Economic Review*, 10 (February 1969), 1-21.

[4]E. Fisher, " More about the Stability of Measures of Volatility of Individual Stocks ". Unpublished paper prepared for the Seminar on the Analysis of Security Prices, University of Chicago, November, 1968.

[5]A Russell and B. Taylor, " Investment Uncertainty and British Equities ". *The Investment Analyst*, 22 (December 1968), 13-22.

[6]J. L. Treynor, W. W. Priest, Jr., L. Fisher and C. A. Higgins, " Using Portfolio Composition to Estimate Risk ". *Financial Analysts Journal*, 24 (September-October 1968), 93-100.

USING THE SHARPE MODEL

S. D. HODGES and R. A. BREALEY

(London Graduate School of Business Studies)

Introduction

Participants in the recent Portfolio Investment Research Seminar at the London Business School were shown how to use our Sharpe portfolio selection programme at an on-line computer terminal. They worked in small groups on a number of projects to examine different aspects of the Sharpe model.

In this paper we bring together these and some other results which have been obtained using this computer programme, and describe some of the lessons we have learnt about the design and use of such systems.

The paper falls into three main sections. We first outline what the programme itself can do and how it is used. In the second section we discuss the data inputs required by the programme. Some of these were estimated statistically and provided by us and others were given subjectively by the participants. The final section of the paper presents results on the sensitivity of the Sharpe model to changes in its data inputs. We also look at the implications of these results for the use and usefulness of the Sharpe model.

The Sharpe Model

The computer programme is for a Sharpe diagonal model extended to include some additional useful features[1]. It was written at the London Business School by S. D. Hodges ; much of its design is due to suggestions by R. A. Brealey. It is a Fortran programme, written for use on an on-line time-sharing computer system which makes its operation very flexible and yet also very simple.

As in other portfolio selection models the aim is to decide how to balance the level of return expected from a portfolio up to some fixed horizon point, against the uncertainty of actually achieving it. The standard deviation of the return is taken as a measure of this uncertainty. The situation is illustrated in Figure 1.

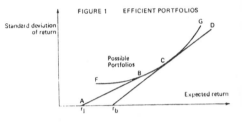

FIGURE 1   EFFICIENT PORTFOLIOS

We want to select a portfolio with high expected return but low standard deviation. One lying on the lower-right efficient frontier FG of the area of all possible portfolios should therefore be chosen. This can be narrowed down further to the portion lying between B and C if the possibilities of lending or borrowing at fixed rates are acknowledged. By lending part of our investment at the risk free rate r_l and investing the rest in portfolio B, we discover portfolios along AB preferable to those of FB. A similar argument for borrowing extra money at a rate of interest r_b disposes of portfolios along CG. The portion of our portfolio invested in shares should therefore ideally constitute one of the portfolios between B and C. The portfolio selection models enable us·to compute these portfolios, provided only that we can define our beliefs about the likely future performance and riskiness of the individual securities in a sufficiently accurate manner. Since we may often be unsure of our various estimates, a flexible system is essential so that a close check can be kept on the implications of changing them.

The Sharpe diagonal model achieves economy in both data estimation and computation by relating the return on each stock to the return on the market index. The return R_i on the ith stock is assumed to be given by

$$R_i = \alpha_i + \beta_i I + u_i$$

In the equation, α_i is the return expected from the

stock in an unchanged market, β_i is the volatility or gearing of the stock to the return I on the market index. Finally u_i is a term accounting for all other variations in the return. To implement a Sharpe model, values must be estimated for α_i, β_i and the standard deviation of u_i (which will be denoted by $sd(u_i)$) on each stock. The expected return $E(I)$ and standard deviation $sd(I)$ of the index must also be estimated.

Our model differs from the model described by Sharpe in two important features. Instead of being purely a model to compute an ideal portfolio to hold, ours is an adaptive one which will compute the best portfolio to change to. We take into account the transaction costs in making changes to an existing portfolio. In order to do this, the programme has to be supplied with details of what constitutes the current portfolio and what level of costs is appropriate. The second extension we have made is the fairly common one of allowing upper limits to be imposed on the amounts held of individual securities. This enables the model to avoid recommending the purchase of a security in quantities which would be regarded as unmarketable.

When the programme is used, the first thing it does is to read the contents of a data file which contains standard settings for the programme and values which have previously been estimated by statistical methods. The user must then supply some additional data on a subjective basis and he is also free to make changes to the standard values. Although the programme is quite flexible, it is also very easy to use and the seminar participants (who with few exceptions had little or no previous experience of computers) seemed to get the hang of things very quickly. The output corresponding to each set of assumptions was restricted to a single " optimal " portfolio by pre-setting the risk-free lending and borrowing rates at the same value. The user can observe the sensitivity of this portfolio to changes in the data from which it is calculated.

The Data Inputs for the Model

Instead of selecting portfolios of shares, our analyses were carried out in terms of 22 of the FT Actuaries share indices. This was done solely to avoid the problem of choosing a small set of shares that all our participants would be familiar with and

in no way affects the principle of the method. The main difference it produces in the data is that the indices are more closely correlated to the market index (which we take as the FTA 600 index) than would be the case with individual shares. Consequently, the $se(u_i)$ terms are relatively small and since it is these which effectively cause the model to diversify, our portfolios may consist of fewer holdings than would similar analyses of individual shares.

Most of the data required by the programme is pre-set from its permanent data file. The initial portfolio was taken as close to the weightings which make up the FTA 600 index as possible and the analysis is to produce the best portfolio to change to and hold for a one-year period. This horizon period assumption certainly does not mean that the portfolio should only be changed again after another year. The transaction cost of a switch was originally set at $2\frac{1}{4}$ per cent. (representing stamp duty on the purchase and half commission on both the purchase and sale) but this was later changed to 4 per cent. to allow for the jobber's turn. We decided not to impose any upper limits on holdings, so that the degree of diversification retained without them could be studied. The programme was set to print out the efficient portfolio corresponding to a lending rate of 6 per cent. (i.e., $r_l = r_b = 6$ per cent.).

Regression analyses of the 22 FTA indices against the FTA 600 index were used to estimate most of the remaining data. Forty-seven monthly changes were used and the results were adjusted so as to be on a yearly basis. This gave values for the β_i's the $sd(u_i)$'s and for $sd(I)$. The 22 indices and these data values are displayed in Table 1. The numbering of the indices differs from that given in the FT.

The rest of the data is supplied by the programme user. The return expected from the index $E(I)$ is straightforward enough, though very low or negative values may produce seemingly odd recommendations from the analysis : the computer has no qualms about taking everything out of equities to invest in fixed interest holdings. Most of our analyses were done using 10 per cent. as the level of return expected from the market index.

Finally, the α_i values had to be obtained from the user in some way. These are the returns expected from each industry index if the 600 index remains unchanged and we found these values the hardest part of the data to organise sensibly. The method we adopted was to ask the participants to rank the 22 indices in terms of their supposed α_i values and then estimate the range covering the middle 12 indices of this ranking. The programme then calculates their values from this ranking and interquartile range by assuming a normal distribution. We had some difficulties in explaining what the quantities involved really meant and we now think that this method is rather a clumsy one. Our chief problem was to persuade people not to give absurdly high values for the interquartile range. Roughly speaking the α_i values represent the difference between the market's and the individual's expectations for that sector. More strictly, it follows from the Capital Asset Pricing Model[2] that this difference is $\alpha_i + (\beta_i - 1)E_m(I)$, where $E_m(I)$ denotes the market's expectation from the index. By giving the α_i's a large interquartile range the participants were asserting that they could be fairly certain that the sectors at the top of their lists would perform substantially better than those at the bottom. Since people with widely differing rankings of the sectors still gave high values for the interquartile range, we know that some degree of exaggeration must be present. For this reason, after some initial computer runs, we persuaded the participants to adopt a standard value of 3 per cent. for the interquartile range.

Our participants were divided into six groups and supplied us with a total of nine independent rankings, groups one and six trying out more than one. These are set out in Table 2, the final column of which gives for comparison the " lowest β first " ranking we should expect from the Capital Asset Pricing Model of Sharpe[2]. In considering these rankings, it should be borne in mind that our participants were given little time for reflection and so they represent a very hurried expression of their views. On some sectors there is remarkable unanimity. All were agreed that in an unchanged market, store shares (no. 016) and breweries (no. 011) would perform well, and that aircraft (no. 001) and shipbuilding (no. 007) would do badly. However, for the most part there is only a relatively weak degree of correspondence between the rankings. Kendall's coefficient of concordance for the nine rankings (see for example Siegel[3]) was 0.187 which is statistically significant at the 5 per

cent. level, but not at 2 per cent. There also appears to be a weak correspondence between the participants rankings and the " lowest β " ranking. This was significant at 2 sd's for two out of the nine rankings.

Results

The Sharpe portfolio selection model assumes that the user can define his beliefs with complete accuracy. In this final section, we assess the importance of this assumption by inspecting the effect of making systematic changes to each of the following seven of the inputs to the programme :

1. The interquartile range of the distribution of α_i's.
2. The level of transaction costs.
3. The return expected from the index, $E(I)$.
4. The standard deviation of the index return, $sd(I)$.
5. The price of a sector.
6. The β value of a sector.
7. The residual variation $sd(u)$ of a sector.

At the L.B.S. Seminar, each group of participants used its own ranking to examine just one of these questions. For better comparibility in this paper we have standardised on the rankings designated 1(a) in Table 2. Our conclusions do not appear to be very sensitive to this choice. The empirical results are displayed in the seven tables at the end of the paper, and below we comment briefly on their more interesting features. The tables share a common format which is explained in our remarks on Project 1.

Project 1

The first project was concerned with the impact of varying the dispersion of the α_i's. The first two rows of the table, Project 1, set out the standard deviation SD, and the expected return R of the original portfolio for various values of the interquartile range. The next row, " changed portfolio ", gives a figure for the investor's return, if he acts optimally on the basis of our standard assumptions. This portfolio is selected using an interquartile range of 3 per cent., when the true value is that shown at the head of the column. Its rate of return has been adjusted to correspond to the same level of risk (SD) as the original portfolio, by assuming appropriate borrowing or lending at

106

6 per cent. The fourth row gives a similar equivalent return for the optimal portfolio, further details of which are given in the remainder of the table.

The " changed portfolio " row is in many ways the most interesting as it enables us to measure the cost of false assumptions. This portfolio is calculated under the assumption of an interquartile range of 3 per cent. Notice that if this range is actually 2 per cent. or less, then the supposedly optimal portfolio provides a lower rate of return than the original portfolio. Clearly, given the high costs of transactions, it is dangerous to trade on the basis of an overestimate of the extent of one's knowledge. Not surprisingly, the converse is also true. The gains from altering the original portfolio are greatest if wide differences between the sectors can be accurately distinguished. For an interquartile range of 2 per cent. or less the optimal portfolio is well diversified and close to the original portfolio. The ranking used has a correlation of 0.47 with the lowest β ranking, so for low values of the interquartile range, the α's are close to those suggested by the capital asset pricing model. For an interquartile range of 1 per cent., the differences are insufficient to cover the costs of trading and the optimal portfolio is the original one. For an interquartile range of 3 per cent. the portfolio is diversified across thirteen sectors with a maximum of 44 per cent. of the investment in a single sector. If the interquartile range is 8 per cent., then only four sectors should be held and 71 per cent. is concentrated in stores shares. Those participants who believed that they could distinguish such very different prospects between sectors, baulked at the suggestion that they should hold such a concentrated portfolio. Despite their bold assertions, most investors seem to act as if they have no reason to expect one group of securities to perform very differently from any other group.

Project 2

This project considered the effect of varying the level of transaction costs, with all the other data held at our standard values. Uncertainty in these costs arises in two ways. The magnitude of the jobber's turn is uncertain and in addition the appropriate cost to use depends on the length of time over which the investor aims to write it off. As one might expect, the larger the costs, the smaller the opportunities to profit from trading.

Again the structure of the optimal portfolio is extremely sensitive to the input data. If transaction costs are ignored completely, a very high degree of concentration is indicated. With costs at 5 per cent. the changes required to the initial portfolio become much more modest. Even under the 4 per cent. assumption of the changed portfolio, not many changes are made and so little harm is done if this understates the real costs. If these are less than 4 per cent., then the investor could increase his return by as much as 0.7 per cent. For most investors, the possibility of this kind of opportunity loss is likely to be of less concern than the effect of ignoring or estimating very low transaction costs when they are in fact significant. In these circumstances, the supposedly optimal portfolio could well prove to be considerably less desirable than the investor's original holdings. When one considers the rarity with which transaction costs are incorporated in portfolio selection models, it is no wonder that they have met with such little acceptance in the investment community.

Project 3

This project demonstrated that the improvement in equivalent return given by the optimal portfolio is relatively insensitive to changes in the outlook for the market. The cost of a poor market estimate can in this sense be very slight. The composition of the optimal portfolio too is relatively unaffected though increasing the market return does generally lead to an optimal equity portfolio which is slightly more diversified and involves less risk. The reason for this is that with a high $E(I)$ value, the α_i's become rather less important than before, and more justification is required for spending money on transactions.

In interpreting this, and some of our later findings, it is important to bear in mind that they apply only to the composition of the equity part of a total portfolio. Serious losses can be incurred if a poor market estimate leads to an incorrect balance between equities and fixed interest securities.

Project 4

The fourth project was concerned with variations in the investor's uncertainty as to the market prospects. Our standard value for this was the standard deviation of historical returns, which we suspect implies a higher degree of uncertainty than most participants would have admitted to. The gain offered by the optimal portfolio varies comparatively little for different values of $sd(I)$. Our results indicate that it only becomes dangerous to use the historical standard deviation when the investor has a much lower degree of uncertainty. This leads to the seemingly paradoxical conclusion that when using the Sharpe model, the conservative procedure is to adopt a relatively low figure for $sd(I)$. The variation in the content of the optimal portfolio is also interesting. Because a high level of $sd(I)$ effectively reduces the importance of the individual standard errors (the $sd(u_i)$ terms), an investor should adopt a less diversified position when the market outlook is unusually obscure. The familiar advice to be particularly selective at such times is more to the point than one might have supposed.

Project 5

In this project participants examined the effect of changing the price of one security, with everything else held constant. The table shows what happens when the level of industry index 016 is progressively increased. A less than 1 per cent. increase in the price of store shares is sufficient to make the investor reduce his buying programme sharply. The equivalent return from the changed portfolio shows the cost of acting as if the price of these shares had not changed. This is again substantial.

In practice investors do not drastically revise their buying programmes for every minor change in price. It is possible that they underestimate the danger of raising their buying price, but we suggest the principal explanation is that the individual investor continually revises his assessment of the outlook to neutralise the effect of such day-to-day changes. His buying and selling programme is characterised by gradual shifts, not because the prospective returns are large, but because the price changes reflect adjustments which he largely agrees with, in the market's assessment of the shares.

Project 6

Project 6 examined the effect on the optimal portfolio of altering the volatility of a single sector. The problem may be considered in the light of Sharpe's mutual fund model[1]. This requires the investor to purchase those securities with the highest values for the expression :

$$\frac{\alpha_1 - r + \beta_1 E(I)}{\beta_1}$$, where r is the interest rate.

By rearranging this expression as $\frac{\alpha_1 - r}{\beta_1} + E(I)$

we immediately see that so long as α_1 is less than r, the effect of increasing β_1 is to make the security more attractive. On the rare occasion that α_1 is greater than the interest rate, the security is so desirable that a higher value of β_1 would only introduce more risk than return. The value of α for sector 016 was 4.4 per cent., only a little below the assumed 6 per cent. interest rate. Despite this, reducing the value of β by just one standard error led to a significant reduction in the size of the optimal holding. The cost of poor estimates of β is surprisingly low, but these might cause the investor to adopt a portfolio with an inappropriate level of riskiness.

Project 7

The final project considered the effect of changing the residual dispersion $sd(u)$. In the absence of transaction costs, it is this residual dispersion which alone justifies diversification. Consequently, increasing $sd(u)$ for sector 016 produces a significant reduction in the size of the holding. A serious underestimate of $sd(u)$ can result in the supposedly optimal changed portfolio offering a lower prospective return than the initial holdings.

Conclusions

This article was prompted by the dearth of published empirical evidence on the behaviour of portfolio selection models. The usefulness of these models is often questioned on the grounds that they lead to unacceptable solutions. In particular, many people have suggested that the models indicate a degree of concentration and of portfolio turnover that is completely foreign to established practice. We believe that these criticisms are in large measure misplaced. Once we recognise that individual investors do not typically possess substantial superior insight and that there are significant transaction costs, the solutions we obtain become far more sensible.

A more serious concern centres on the sensitivity

of the results to errors in the inputs. The composition of the optimal portfolio is highly dependent on the ordering and dispersion of the α_i's and on the level of transaction costs. It is significantly affected by the measures of β_i and $sd(u)_i$, and modestly affected by $E(I)$ and $sd(I)$. When these data are incorrectly estimated, the user will obtain portfolios which are not truly optimal, and, if he is mistakenly led into making large changes to his initial portfolio, he may well succeed in worsening

his position. These difficulties apply equally strongly to the fund manager who relies entirely on his own judgment and intuition. It is clear that portfolio selection models must be designed so that the inevitability of errors in the estimates is recognised, and the user is enabled to experiment freely with the implications of a variety of assumptions. This is the approach which we try to emphasise in our work at the London Business School.

REFERENCES

[1]Sharpe, W. F. " A Simplified Model for Portfolio Analysis ". *Management Science* (Jan. 1963), pp. 277-293.

[2]Sharpe, W. F. " Capital Asset Prices : A Theory of Market Equilibrium under conditions of Risk ". *J. of Finance* (Sept. 1964), pp. 425-442.

[3]Siegel, S. " Nonparametric Statistics for the Behavioural Sciences ". McGraw Hill, 1956, p. 229.

[4]Sharpe, W. F. " A Linear Programming Algorithm for Mutual Fund Portfolio Selection ". *Management Science* (March 1967), pp. 499-510.

APPENDIX A

Table 1

FTA Indices used in the Sharpe Model

Code	Index	Original Holding	β	se of β	se(u)
001	Aircraft	0.82	0.999	.132	15.39
002	Building materials	2.95	1.062	.078	9.08
003	Contracting	1.38	1.164	.134	15.59
004	Electricals	3.65	1.001	.262	30.53
005	Engineering	6.01	0.961	.061	7.15
006	Machine Tools	0.37	0.886	.101	11.74
007	Shipbuilding	0.12	1.114	.188	21.91
008	Electronics	4.13	1.161	.099	11.52
009	Household goods	0.79	1.042	.113	13.18
010	Motors	0.75	1.127	.120	14.04
011	Breweries	4.78	0.826	.108	12.57
012	Entertainment	2.75	1.133	.083	9.68
013	Food manufacturing	3.09	1.059	.082	9.52
014	Newspapers	1.33	0.834	.090	10.54
015	Paper and packaging	2.16	0.694	.099	11.59
016	Stores	9.90	0.914	.089	10.36
017	Textiles	3.28	0.907	.086	9.98
018	Tobacco	2.68	1.135	.132	15.43
019	Chemicals	7.67	1.021	.090	10.48
020	Oil	16.55	0.928	.138	16.05
021	Shipping	1.65	0.834	.118	13.81
022	Financial group	23.19	1.075	.058	6.78

Estimated s.d. of the 600 index $= 17.22\%$.

Table 2

Rankings of the Indices

Codes of the F.T. Indices

Group		1(a)	1(b)	1(c)	2	3	4	5	6(a)	6(b)	Rank by lowest β
Order	1	016	022	022	009	008	008	010	003	016	015
	2	011	011	011	008	018	009	009	022	012	011
	3	009	012	016	016	002	022	012	012	008	014
	4	022	020	012	012	011	010	022	011	013	021
	5	010	016	021	014	016	011	008	013	011	006
	6	012	009	008	019	003	005	013	016	018	017
	7	015	002	004	020	022	003	016	008	017	016
	8	021	013	005	010	015	016	011	009	010	020
	9	018	014	013	011	019	017	017	002	009	005
	10	004	019	019	022	012	019	005	018	002	001
	11	008	017	020	013	004	012	006	021	003	004
	12	019	005	018	017	005	015	019	019	015	019
	13	020	006	009	004	009	013	003	014	004	009
	14	002	018	017	005	014	021	020	015	022	013
	15	003	021	015	021	017	002	018	007	014	002
	16	013	015	014	003	021	004	014	010	020	022
	17	014	010	010	001	010	020	015	017	021	007
	18	017	008	002	006	013	018	021	006	005	010
	19	005	007	003	018	020	006	004	005	006	012
	20	006	003	001	015	006	001	002	004	019	018
	21	001	004	006	007	007	014	001	001	007	008
	22	007	001	007	002	001	007	007	020	001	003

Project 1

Sensitivity to the Interquartile Range

Interquartile Range %	0	1	2	3	4	5	6	7	8
Initial Portfolio :									
SD	17.52	17.52	17.52	17.52	17.52	17.52	17.52	17.52	17.52
R	9.94	10.23	10.52	10.81	11.10	11.39	11.68	11.97	12.26
Equivalent R from :									
Changed portfolio ..	8.51	9.40	10.29	11.17	12.05	12.94	13.82	14.71	15.60
Optimal portfolio	9.94	10.23	10.52	11.17	12.16	13.33	14.54	15.77	17.02
Optimal Portfolio :									
SD	17.70	17.52	17.63	17.78	17.96	17.96	17.97	17.99	17.99
R	9.97	10.23	10.55	11.25	12.31	13.51	14.76	16.03	17.32
No. of sectors held ..	21	22	17	13	9	7	6	5	4
Per cent. held ·of :									
016	4.1	4.1	13.8	43.6	60.4	66.7	67.7	70.5	71.2
011	4.8	4.8	4.8	4.8	4.8	4.8	4.8	4.8	4.8
099	0.8	0.8	0.8	0.8	0.8	0.8	0.8	0.8	0.8
022	23.2	23.2	23.2	23.2	23.2	23.2	23.2	23.2	23.2

" Changed Portfolio " means the portfolio which is optimal under our standard assumptions of :

Interquartile range	= 3%
Return on Index	= 10%
Level of Costs	= 4%
Standard deviation of index	17.2%

Project 2

Sensitivity to Transaction Costs

Costs %						0	1	2	3	4	5
Initial Portfolio :											
SD	..	..	..	..	..	17.52	17.52	17.52	17.52	17.52	17.52
R	..	..	..	..	..	10.81	10.81	10.81	10.81	10.81	10.81
Equivalent R from :											
Changed Portfolio	..	..	.			12.49	12.17	11.83	11.50	11.17	10.84
Optimal Portfolio	..	..	..			13.18	12.57	12.03	11.53	11.17	10.96
Optimal Portfolio :											
SD	..	..	..	..	..	17.96	17.91	17.97	17.94	17.78	17.59
R	..	..	..			13.36	12.72	12.18	11.66	11.25	10.98
No. of sectors held	..	..	..			4	6	8	10	13	16
Percent. held of :											
016	..	..	..	..	..	71.9	63.9	61.3	58.1	43.6	21.8
011	..	..	..	..	..	4.8	4.8	4.8	4.8	4.8	4.8
009	..	..	..	..	..	11.7	4.7	0.8	0.8	0.8	0.8
022	..	..	..	..	..	11.6	23.2	23.2	23.2	23.2	23.2

Project 3

Sensitivity to Return Expected from FTA 600 Index

E(I) %						5	7½	10	12½	15	20
Initial Portfolio :											
SD	..	..	..	..	..	17.52	17.52	17.52	17.52	17.52	17.52
R	..	..	..	..	..	5.84	8.32	10.81	13.30	15.78	20.75
Equivalent R from :											
Changed portfolio	..	..	..			6.30	8.73	11.17	13.61	16.04	20.92
Optimal portfolio	..	..	..			6.30	8.73	11.17	13.62	16.10	21.05
Optimal Portfolio :											
SD	..	..	..	..	..	17.86	17.78	17.78	17.72	17.59	17.64
R	..	..	..	..	..	6.31	8.77	11.25	13.71	16.14	21.15
No. of sectors held	..	..	..			10	13	13	16	16	16
Percent. held of :											
016	..	..	.	..	..	55.6	43.6	43.6	38.8	33.4	27.0
011	..	..	..	..	..	4.8	4.8	4.8	4.8	4.8	4.8
009	..	..	..	..	..	0.8	0.8	0.8	0.8	2.4	5.7
022	..	..	..	..	..	23.2	23.2	23.2	23.2	23.2	23.2

Project 4

Sensitivity to Standard Deviation of FTA 600 Index

sd(1) %	5	10	15	20	25
Initial Portfolio :					
SD	6.22	10.62	15.37	20.23	25.13
R	10.81	10.81	10.81	10.81	10.81
Equivalent R from :					
Changed portfolio	10.61	11.01	11.14	11.20	11.22
Optimal portfolio	11.17	11.10	11.14	11.20	11.22
Optimal Portfolio :					
SD	6.12	10.77	15.68	20.44	25.26
R	11.09	11.17	11.24	11.25	11.25
No. of sectors held	16	16	14	13	13
Percent. held of :					
016	19.7	32.5	42.9	43.6	43.6
011	4.8	4.8	4.8	4.8	4.8
009	6.9	3.0	0.8	0.8	0.8
022	23.2	23.2	23.2	23.2	23.2

Project 5

Sensitivity to Price of Sector 016

% Price change to sector 016	0	0.2	0.4	0.6	0.8	2.0
Initial portfolio :						
SD	17.52	17.52	17.52	17.52	17.52	17.52
R	10.81	10.79	10.77	10.74	10.72	10.59
Equivalent R from :						
Changed portfolios	11.17	11.07	10.98	10.88	10.78	10.21
Optimal portfolios	11.17	11.07	11.01	10.94	10.88	10.74
Optimal Portfolio :						
SD	17.78	17.78	17.58	17.58	17.74	17.82
R	11.25	11.15	11.03	10.96	10.94	10.82
No. of sectors held	13	14	16	16	16	16
Percent. held of :						
016	43.6	40.5	34.4	25.2	13.6	9.9
011	4.8	4.8	4.8	4.8	4.8	4.8
009	0.8	0.8	0.8	5.3	12.4	14.7
022	23.2	23.2	23.2	23.2	23.2	23.2

Project 6

Sensitivity to β of Sector 016

Size of change (s.e.'s)								−2	−1	0	+1	+2
β value								0.736	0.825	0.914	1.003	1.092
Initial Portfolio :												
SD	..	..	..	..	..	..	..	17.22	17.37	17.52	17.67	17.82
R	..	..	..	..	..	..	..	10.63	10.72	10.81	10.90	10.99
Equivalent R from :												
Changed portfolio		..	..	..	.	..		10.66	10.93	11.17	11.40	11.63
Optimal portfolio		..	..	..	..	..		10.78	10.96	11.17	11.41	11.64
Optimal Portfolio :												
SD	..	..	..	..	..	..	..	17.53	17.16	17.78	18.47	19.64
R	..	..	..	..	..	..	..	10.87	10.90	11.25	11.65	12.22
No. of sectors held	..	..	..	..	..			16	16	13	12	9
Percent. held of :												
016	..	..	..	..	..	..	..	2.2	27.3	43.6	46.6	59.0
011	..	..	..	..	..	..	..	4.8	4.8	4.8	4.8	4.8
009	..	..	..	..	..	..	..	14.7	4.1	0.8	0.8	0.8
022	..	..	..	..	..	..	..	23.2	23.2	23.2	23.2	23.2

Project 7

Sensitivity to SD(U) for Sector 016

Change made							×½	none	×2	×3
Value of sd(u)							5.18	10.36	20.72	31.08
Initial Portfolio :										
SD ..	..	..	..	..	..	..	17.50	17.52	17.61	17.76
R	..	..	..	..	..	..	10.81	10.81	10.81	10.81
Equivalent R from :										
Changed portfolio		..	..	..	..		11.29	11.17	10.76	10.26
Optimal portfolio		..	..	..	..		11.29	11.17	10.91	10.95
Optimal Portfolio :										
SD ..	..	..	..	..	..	..	17.30	17.78	18.08	18.11
R	..	..	..	..	..	..	11.23	11.25	11.12	11.05
No. of sectors held		..	..	..	..		13	13	16	16
Percent. held of :										
016	..	..	..	..	..	..	46.4	43.6	23.1	11.8
011	..	..	..	..	..	..	4.8	4.8	4.8	4.8
009	..	..	..	..	..	..	0.8	0.8	6.6	13.5
022	..	..	..	..	..	..	23.2	23.2	23.2	23.2

CHAPTER 3

The Semi-strong Form of the Efficient Market Hypothesis

The evidence presented in Chapter 1 indicated that historical share prices could not be profitably used to forecast future price movements. The logical question to ask then is to what extent other publicly available information relevant to a particular company (eg balance sheets) can be used to forecast price movements? In other words, would the analysis of published information lead to estimates of the value of share prices more accurate than merely taking actual share prices, as suggested by the weak form hypothesis? The answer to this question is contained in the statement of the semi-strong hypothesis:

> The share price of a company, at any point in time, represents and fully discounts all the knowledge that is publicly available and relevant to that company and the valuation of its shares.

It will be immediately clear that the weak form hypothesis is merely a special case of the semi-strong form. Historic share price data is part of the available knowledge relating to a company and, according to this form of the hypothesis, any value this information might have is already discounted in the share price. If the semi-strong form of the hypothesis is true then *a fortiori* the weak form must be true.

This does not mean that publicly available information has no impact on share prices nor does it mean that such information is irrelevant. It is simply that the information is discounted into the share price at the moment it is released. There is no opportunity between the moment of publication of new information and the time when the share price has adjusted to reflect fully that information, during which to buy or sell shares advantageously.

This proposition is based on studies of the effects of particular events (eg scrip issues) on share prices which have shown how quickly the discounting process works and that opportunities for profit-making do not exist.

A distinction has to be drawn as to whether the recommendation of investment analysts should be included under the umbrella of 'publicly available information'. Clearly if an analyst's recommendation is made public then it can be treated like any announcement and unless the analyst can add to the information which is already known either by some inside information, new insights or by superior judgment, then the share price should remain unchanged. Whether an analyst can add to the general body of information surrounding a particular share is really the subject of Chapter 4. However, publication of analysts' recommendations will be treated like other information generating events.

Studies of this form of hypothesis seek to analyse share price movements to see exactly how long it takes for the share price to digest and respond to new information. Depending on how quickly and accurately prices react it may or may not be possible to use the duration of the digestion process to make abnormal profits. Alas the evidence is not encouraging. It appears that the digestion process is quick, indeed almost instantaneous and, further, that it is accurate. By the time one investor has absorbed and understood a piece of news, other investors will have done exactly the same and probably come to the same conclusions. An understanding of the dissemination process may help. Consider an announcement made by a company through the Stock Exchange. In a very short time via word of mouth, observing the actions of others, walkie-talkie, closed circuit TV, telephone, etc, the news reaches a very large group of people. If the news is readily understandable in terms of its effect on the share price then price adjustment will be virtually instantaneous. If however the news takes longer to value then there could conceivably be a situation almost like a race between investors to be the first to complete the valuation. Most probably a large number come to the same conclusion at the same time. Even if there were only a few winners there would still be the problem of persuading the jobber to deal since, if he has not finished the course, he is most likely to quote a defensive price (ie a wide spread between bid and offer) if indeed he is prepared to quote a price at all. Tests of the semi-strong hypothesis attempt to discover whether there is a race and if so if it is possible to enter and win and make abnormal profits.

The fact that investors do not all hold the same views nor come to the same conclusions does not affect the race. The winner of the race will decide whether or not to buy or sell, in the light of the then market price, in exactly the same way as he would if there were no race. Thus differences of opinion or interpretation are entirely consistent with the accurate interpretation of news.

Differences of opinion as to the value of any particular share may prevail at any point in time. The market price is the reflection of market opinion being a hybrid or average of all the views of market participants. There are several institutional constraints which can distort estimates of value as well as different interpretations of information. Tax is one of the most important of these. Unit trusts, pension funds, life assurance companies and private individuals are all treated differently for tax purposes. This means that if each class of investor held the same investment, the after-tax rate of return could well vary. The return an investor in ordinary shares expects is made up of capital gain and dividend both of which are subject to a rate of tax peculiar to the status of the investor. For example, consider two private investors with different marginal rates of tax. This could lead to what has been called the 'clientele effect' where investors with particular tax rates chase particular shares eg high or low dividend payout companies. Richards [25] calculated the marginal rate of tax at which a private investor (paying capital gains tax at 30 per cent) would be indifferent to the payout ratio to be 54 per cent: those with higher marginal rates would prefer capital gain to dividend and vice versa. This clientele effect is readily observable in the gilt edge market where low coupon gilt stocks, offering the prospect of a return by way of capital gain (taxed at 30 per cent at most), tend to sell at a premium to other comparable high coupon stocks. This tax effect is distorting since a variable rate of return is offered for the same level of risk. For a high rate taxpayer, this is clearly a disincentive to invest in both gilts and shares and may well explain the dwindling numbers of private investors in the market place.

Brealey [7]

Brealey's article on the distribution of returns (see Chapter 1), also contains one of the first tests of the semi-strong hypothesis. Brealey examined the average performance of the market (FT all-share index) around the time of publication of the monthly trade figures between 1962 and 1969. Each set of figures was classified as 'good' or 'bad' depending on whether the net balance was above or below the long term average. The results show that the market rises on the day of the announcement of 'good' results and also on preceding and following days.

Similarly the market falls on the three days surrounding the announcement of 'bad' figures. The market movement preceding the announcement is explained by frequent deliberate leaking of the results. Brealey concludes that '. . . it is reasonable to interpret this three-day price adjustment as a reaction to the trade figures. This is consistent with the view that the market customarily takes more than one day to react to news'.

This suggests that profits could be made in the three-day process of digesting trade figures. However, one glance at the percentage increases and decreases and we are reminded of the difference between an efficient and a perfect market. The market movements are so small as to rule out the possibility of any dealing profits. Thus for all practical purposes the adjustment process may be regarded as efficient.

Brealey's results are not necessarily inconsistent with a rapid process of price adjustment. If the contents of the announcement are sometimes leaked but sometimes not, then, even if price adjustment occurs instantaneously, the above test should still show increases on the announcement day and on the preceding day (the day the news is leaked). This does not of course explain the movement on the day after announcement. However, as we have already seen in Chapter 1, there is a tendency for price changes to persist. Thus it is quite likely that a rise (or fall) on announcement day would be followed by a rise (or fall) on the following day. Thus movement on the following day may not be due to any further adjustment to the trade figures and Brealey's results are not therefore necessarily inconsistent with a price-adjustment process which takes less than one day.

It is worth noting the design of the test employed in this study. The classification of the trading results as 'good' or 'bad' does not involve the exercise of judgment but merely comparison with an existing and known quantity (the long-term average). This is not a test of analytical ability. If there was any inefficiency, in the semi-strong sense, then it could be exploited by devising a simple trading rule based on this test. No special analytical expertise would be required.

Capitalisation Issues

Firth has made two studies of the effects of capitalisation issues on share prices. In theory a capitalisation issue will have no effect on the share price save the usual dilution effect relating to the terms. For example a one-for-one will reduce the share price by half (although stamp duty may have a temporary effect on price adjustment). Essentially there is no special merit in capitalisation issues but nevertheless they still seem to be quite popular with management.

Firth [26] examined 441 capitalisation issues announced in the period 1968-70. He found that companies tended to make capitalisation issues when their share prices had been doing relatively well. This could be seen in the steady price increase exhibited by the shares prior to announcement. There was a significant price increase on the day of the announcement. However, in practice, capitalisation announcements often accompany the announcement of above average trading results and dividend increases. This factor could explain the whole of the share price movement: the capitalisation issue, as theory would suggest, may have no effect whatsoever. The difficulty of linking cause and effect is a recurrent problem in statistics. The observation that two events tend to occur at the same time does not necessarily imply that one causes the other. Both events may be caused by something else. In this case it may be the above-average results which put the share price up and which encourage management to make a capitalisation issue and not the capitalisation issue which puts the share price up. To establish whether trading results and dividends were the sole cause of the share price movement, Firth used a regression model to explain share price movement in terms of the earnings increase, dividend increase and the capitalisation issue. This result he compared with price movements for companies announcing good results but without any capitalisation issue. The equation used was:

(% increase in share price) = a + b x (% earnings increase) + c x (% dividend increase) + d x S.

where a, b, c, d are constants to be calculated by regression and S=1 if a capitalisation issue is announced, otherwise S=0

The coefficients obtained were:

(% increase in share price) = 1.281 + 0.621 (% earnings increase) + 0.158 (% dividend increase) - 0.003 S

The very low value for 'd' clearly indicates that the capitalisation *per se* has virtually no effect on the share price. It is the other news accompanying such an announcement which is responsible for the subsequent price movement.

Although it is established that theory is borne out in practice, no light has been cast on market efficiency. However, we may regard the event under study as 'the announcement of earnings and/or dividend increases' and see how quickly such information is incorporated into the share price. Firth discovered no unusual share price movement on the day following the announcement, thereby implying a rapid discounting of information and he concluded that 'this lends support to the efficient markets theory'.

The second Firth study [27] covered 227 capitalisation issues announced in the period 1973-74. The methodology included the Sharpe model, described in Chapter 2 (residuals analysis). This model was used to estimate what each price should be in the absence of the capitalisation announcement. This estimate was then compared with the actual share price and the difference, the residuals, were then computed. These residuals are that part of share price behaviour which can be attributed to the particular event under examination (ie the capitalisation announcement). Positive and increasing residuals were observed in the 30 days preceding the announcement. On announcement day, there was a share price increase of 5.7 per cent not explained by market movements. Most of the price increase was completed on announcement day but there were distinct increases on the following 3-4 days. On the day following the announcement there was an average rise of 2.6 per cent. (Note that in the first study, no unusual movement was observed on the following day.) However, only 61 per cent of the shares studied showed increases and the spread of movement, as measured by the standard deviation, was wide. Given the small increase, the likely expenses, the jobbers turn and probably above-average risk, it is unlikely that consistent profits could be earned. Firth concluded that the results were further evidence of the efficiency of the pricing mechanism.

This study also repeated the exercise to determine whether the capitalisation *per se* could explain any of the share price movement. The result was the same with the share price movement being determined solely by earnings and dividends.

Morris [28]

The debate about an appropriate system of inflation accounting has become almost permanent. A number of different systems have come and gone without actually being fully implemented. Various alternatives have been advanced quite vigorously from different interested parties. Some have argued that a system which reduces profits, and most systems by separating stock profit will do this, will reduce earnings and therefore reduce share prices: that is, if earnings are halved, then to maintain the same rating share prices will also halve. Of course this is not the case. The act of separating and classifying profits does not destroy them. Presentation of accounts in a different format, providing no new information is revealed, should have no effect on the share price whatsoever. Indeed it is likely that most analysts, using non-inflation-adjusted accounts, have a reasonable knowledge of the size of companies' stock profits. The main requirement for an inflation accounting system is that it can describe the fortunes of a company by including any benefits or otherwise arising from the effects of inflation. From the investor's point of view, the new system should provide for the disclosure of at least as much information as at present and, to reduce uncertainty, preferably more.

During the course of the debate a number of brokers have published their own reviews of the effects of an inflation accounting system. Some of this work was published in accounting journals and also subsequently in the national press. Phillips and Drew were particularly prominent, producing estimates of how the share price would alter to reflect the inflation-adjusted accounts. Morris, using residuals analysis, examined the effect of publication of this information on three dates:

Inflation-adjusted accounts	Companies	Publication Date
(estimated by Phillips	59 companies :	December 1971
and Drew)	136 companies :	March 1973
	53 companies :	April 1974

Morris found no evidence of any abnormal share price movement which could be attributed to the new inflation-adjusted accounts. In the case of the April 1974 publication, a comparison was made between an investment strategy based on the information and recommendations published and an investment in a market portfolio. Over an 11-week period the market portfolio outperformed the recommendations by 8 per cent. (Note the use of the market portfolio as a yardstick.)

Morris concluded that '. . . as yet there is little sign that the market has responded to the information. This partly reflects the fact that the incidence of inflation at an industry level has already been discounted into prices'; this supports the semi-strong form hypothesis, and 'it may also indicate a certain distrust of the figures'. This latter remark hints at one explanation for the results, simply that the brokers' estimates were regarded as so far from reality as to be worthless. In fact, in the case of those companies which published accounts adjusted for inflation on the same basis, the estimates turned out to be very close proxies for the real thing. This is a reflection on the expertise of Phillips and Drew

119

and, because there was no observable price movement, on the expertise of the market in general.

Published Investment Recommendations

Firth [29] examined the recommendations made in three newspaper portfolios *(Observer, Guardian* and the *Investors Chronicle)* and one advisory service (Moodies Review). The object of the exercise was to see if the tipsters out-performed the market and to determine how quickly new information (if any) contained in the 'tip' was discounted into the share price. Two tipsters claimed large profits while the other two just about broke even: profits were based on a comparison with the FT all-share index. These claims were based on prices ruling before publication. But when Firth used prices for the day following the tip, the profits in all cases, except the *Guardian*, disappeared.

Factors common to the best performers included concentration on smaller companies, to which little research effort is devoted. This was evidenced by a hefty mark-up of the price following the tip and usually to the price level recommended by the tipster. Thus any potential profit-making opportunity was eliminated before any profit could be made.

The price rise itself was according to Firth due to the fact that each tip contained new information usually gleaned from the company itself. In the case of the smaller companies this information was relatively of much more value. Also, as each tipster developed a track record based on declared profits, so too did the price rise tend to reflect more exactly the content of each tip. The market was 'learning' and placing increasing weight on the information provided.

The major part of this analysis was based on data gathered over short time periods and the results must therefore be treated with caution. Nevertheless it does seem clear that once a tip has been published it is impossible to profit thereby if only for the simple fact that newspapers are available to all. The only one who could benefit from this (apart from an insider of course) is the tipster. He can claim recommendations at pre-tip prices and claim profits that never could have been achieved in practice. Whether it is possible for tipsters or indeed analysts to discover such tips is the subject of Chapter 4.

Large Investment Holdings

Firth has completed studies of two other information generating events: earnings announcements and declarations of large investment holdings. This latter event follows from a requirement of the Stock Exchange that listed companies announce the receipt of any notification of a large holding as required under the Companies Acts 1967, 1976. Prior to the 1976 Act, the disclosure level was 10 per cent, reducing, as a result of that Act, to 5 per cent. Firth [30] analysed all such announcements made in 1973 excluding those which contained additional information, for example, profits and dividends. In all, 85 such announcements were studied. Residuals analysis was used to examine share price behaviour subsequent to the announcement. An immediate price rise averaging 3.3 per cent was observed. The rise is of course due to a change in expectations about the likelihood of a bid materialising. In fact, 10 of the 85 companies announcing 10 per cent stakes were bid for within 3 months of the announcement. After the immediate rise, the price slowly fell back over the 20-day period following the announcement by approximately 2 per cent. Without inside knowledge, the only way profits could be made would be by selling the shares short after the announcement and buying them back at the end of the 20 days. However, in view of the expenses and jobbers turn and the very small price fall involved, profits look only a remote possibility. Thus despite a long adjustment period, the market discounts the bulk of the new information quickly and may be regarded as efficient. Interestingly, Firth observed abnormal share price behaviour in the 30 days preceding the announcement. This could be explained by the activities of the investor in the market place becoming known or information leaks.

Earnings Announcements

When a company announces unexpectedly good or bad trading results, there is always by definition a share price rise or fall since otherwise such results would not have been unexpected. Such an announcement conveys new information to the investor. This information is not limited solely to the announcing company. The investor can infer either that the company alone is responsible for the exceptional nature of the results, or, that the results are symptomatic of a trend within that particular industry, or, a combination of both factors. In any event it is most likely that exceptional results will have some influence on the share prices of companies in similar industries. Firth [31] looked at four sectors: breweries; food retailers (supermarkets); shipping; and banks. Share price behaviour was studied using residuals analysis around the time of the announcement of preliminary results during 1973 and 1974. Each set of results was classified as exceptionally good or bad depending on whether the price-residual was positive or negative following the announcement. Each category was taken separately and the residuals of the remaining companies in the sector were measured at the same point in time. Exceptionally good results were matched by price rises in the rest of the sector averaging 2.1 per cent while exceptionally bad results produced falls averaging 3.7 per cent. Virtually all of the abnormal price adjustment occurred on announcement day thus providing no opportunity for dealing and confirming the efficient and rapid incorporation of new information into share prices.

In value, the price changes of each sector represented between 50 per cent and 80 per cent of the share price rise/fall of the announcing company. The market attributes the major part of the exceptional nature of individual results to industry factors which affect similar companies. Of the sectors included, Banks showed the highest degree of correlation between the residuals of the announcing company and the residuals of the other members of the sector.

Saunders and Woodward [32]

American studies which are reviewed in the Saunders and Woodward article, have demonstrated that money supply variables tend to lead share prices. For instance, one study showed that the level of money supply and its rate of growth were able to explain 96 per cent of the variation in the Standard and Poors stock index. The method employed was a statistical comparison of the two money supply variables with changes in the Standard and Poors stock index occurring 3 months later.

Saunders and Woodward investigated the effects of UK money supply variables on the FT all-share index in the period 1971-75. The publication of money supply figures is clearly an event conveying information about the economy and hence may influence share prices. The information will have varying effects on individual companies but as it is a reflection of general economic activity, will tend to affect the market as a whole. Saunders and Woodward tested the semi-strong hypothesis by examining the effect of the money supply variables on the market to see how quickly the market incorporated such new information.

No opportunity to use residuals analysis arises here because the normal predictive process which uses the market index cannot be used to predict itself. Therefore we have no way of calculating a residual and cannot quantify the effect of money supply variables on the index. Instead various statistical comparisons of monthly changes in the index and money supply variables were used. No relationship however could be discovered. This could perhaps be due to three factors:

(i)   the money supply has no effect on share prices. This is unlikely. Even if there was no direct relationship, government increasingly responds to changes in the money supply with measures which undoubtedly do have an impact on the market — special deposits, the 'corset', HP controls, higher interest rates, etc;

(ii) the market always correctly anticipates the money supply figures. In such a case there would be no change in the market index. The UK money supply data are in any case considered suspect and so the market may tend to ignore single items but look at longer term trends; and

(iii) the choice of methodology was inappropriate. Monthly changes in the index were used. This could be too long a time period and probably includes movement due to other factors (eg exchange rates) which swamp that part due to money supply. While a relationship may exist, it may not be possible to detect it using only monthly price changes. A technique of looking at daily index changes in conjunction with a classification of money supply figures as good or bad (say by reference to the long-term average as Brealey [7] used for trade figures) might have been better.

The results, which may be due to a combination of the above factors, are therefore perhaps somewhat inconclusive.

Franks, Broyles and Hecht [33]

Takeovers or, more politely, mergers are often the subject of examination for a variety of reasons. This particular study covered 70 successful mergers in the Breweries sector between 1955 and 1972. Residuals analysis was employed to study abnormal share price behaviour around the time of the merger. The objective was to see how the gains, if any, were allocated between acquiror and acquiree.

Abnormal Rate of Return	Acquiree	Acquiror
a) during the month up to and including the day of the merger announcement	+14.8%	+0.1%
b) during the month following the merger announcement	+2.9%	-1.1%

It is clear that virtually all the price movement ensuing from the merger announcement is completed before the month is up. An investment in the acquiror immediately after the announcement would probably not yield sufficient over the month to cover transaction costs. These results only confirm that the market takes less than one month fully to discount merger information.

Nevertheless, a number of refinements were incorporated into the methodology which are worth noting. The non-trading effect which was discussed in Chapter 1, can introduce bias into the results especially for smaller companies. As an illustration, the first estimate of beta for the sample produced an average of 0.50. Then those items of data which were more than 14 days old were excluded: these items are defined as those monthly prices (as per the FT where there was a gap of at least 14 days between that date and the previous mark as recorded in the Stock Exchange Daily Official List (SEDOL). Certain transactions must be 'marked' by the broker concerned and such marks are recorded in SEDOL. The marks can be used to identify days when some trading definitely did occur. Removing data items where the previous mark occurred more than 14 days previously increased the estimate for beta to 0.53. But when the age barrier was reduced to 3 days, the estimate rose to 0.72 underlining the seriousness of non-trading.

The above method of screening introduces bias of its own. Screening out the infrequently traded shares generally means excluding the small companies leaving the sample dominated by the large companies. This problem was circumvented by changing the time period for those data items suffering from age to end on the day of the mark immediately preceding that particular month end. The index reading and time base were also adjusted to correspond. In this way, non-trading problems were avoided without seriously biasing the sample towards large companies.

To calculate beta the natural logarithms of the price relatives are used. Earlier studies used simple rates of return over various time periods (a week, two weeks, a month, etc). Logarithms merely provide for continuous compounding. After all, returns are expected to be earned continuously rather than in lumps.

The study covered quite a large time period during the course of which there may have been changes in the industry which may have given rise to spurious observations of residuals. To check this, the residuals for both acquirors and acquirees (weighted by market capitalisation) were examined in the 80-month period surrounding the merger announcement. A distinct positive trend was noticeable throughout indicating the sample to have performed better than predicted by 22.7 per cent. This trend is most likely due to changes in the industry. To compensate for this, the forecasting model was altered to include the appropriate sector index. As a result, the positive trend disappeared and the predictive model was therefore more accurate.

Firth [34] has studied UK mergers announced in 1973/74. As did Franks, Broyles and Hecht, Firth observed abnormal share price behaviour (a consistent price rise) in the acquiree's share price prior to the bid. Firth used this phenomenon to derive a simple trading rule to see if profits could be made. The rule was a simple filter applied to the size of the residual. A purchase or sale was triggered when the residual exceeded the filter. Of the filters tested, only one (the 8 per cent filter) yielded profits (1.6 per cent net of expenses of 1.5 per cent: this compares with an investment in debt of 0.5 per cent). This result may therefore be due to chance alone. The transaction costs are in any case on the optimistic side.

Firth tested other systems, only one of which generated profits: buying shares in the acquiree after it had announced a rejection of the offer. In his data there were 36 instances of bid rejections. In 14 cases, rejection was followed by a successful revised bid and in 5 cases a successful counterbid was made. In the remaining 17 cases, the bid was allowed to lapse. A policy of buying after the rejection announcement and holding until the revised/counterbid was declared unconditional or lapsed, produced an average return of 4.3 per cent or 2.8 per cent net of expenses of 1.5 per cent. Unfortunately no comparison was provided against which these profits could be measured. The market might well have shown profits of 10 per cent over the same period. Such an investment strategy also has greater than average risk. During the period the investment is held, the acquiree's share price is not only subject to the usual vagaries of investment sentiment, but also to the much larger uncertainty of whether a bid will succeed. An above average rate of return would be required for such risk.

Merrett, Howe and Newbould [35]
The above analysed 110 rights issues made in 1963 and looked in particular at price performance over the 12-month period following announcement. A somewhat clumsy adjustment was made for movements in the market by using the Daily Mail index. No account was taken of the differing levels of risk of each individual share. However, an above average return of 1.2 per cent over the issue date and 3.2 per cent over the following year was observed. This is evidence that the market is not perfect as once again transaction costs would swamp profits.

Marsh [36]
Marsh, in an extensive study of rights issues, examined market efficiency in the light of the rights announcement using residuals analysis. Over the 12-month period following the announcement, significant abnormal price behaviour took place suggesting market inefficiency. Over the 5 months following announcement, an average abnormal return of 10 per cent is achieved which increases to a peak at the end of 12 months of 11 per cent. Thereafter, there is a gradual tailing off and 12 months later the total abnormal return is down to 6 per cent, a level which is maintained 4 years later. If this effect could be relied upon to persist, it would be easy to devise a trading rule (merely buying on announcement and holding for 12 months) which took advantage of this phenomenon.

These results are somewhat surprising. It seems almost inconceivable that the bulk of information contained in a rights issue announcement is not incorporated into the share price until 5 months later. This is unlikely even accepting a very lengthy decision process. Marsh made a number of tests to see whether his results were due to chance or some special feature of his data. He noted that the abnormal returns were calculated from the beginning of the month of announcement and therefore included pre-announcement returns which could not be earned under the trading rule defined above.

To see if the effect persisted, the analysis was repeated on the data over two separate periods (July 1962-August 1967, and September 1967-December 1972). The patterns were slightly different but abnormal returns of 13 per cent and 9 per cent respectively were earned over the 6 months following announcement.

The tests were repeated after excluding several exceptional data items, (eg one investment trust which increased by 650 per cent over the 2-year period) but with little effect on the results. It is worth recalling that the averaging process to calculate abnormal returns ascribes no special weight to large companies. Small and large companies have equal weighting.

Finally, since only a part of his data bank had been used in these tests, Marsh examined the remaining data to see if the subsample was typical of the whole. It appeared that the subsample was overstating the behaviour of the whole and that the measured levels of return could not necessarily be earned from all rights issue announcements.

However, although a number of mitigating factors have been put forward, this work cannot be regarded as supportive of the semi-strong form hypothesis.

AN EMPIRICAL INVESTIGATION OF THE IMPACT OF THE ACCOUNCEMENT OF CAPITALISATION ISSUES ON SHARE PRICES

MICHAEL FIRTH*

The current prevailing description of share price behaviour in competitive capital markets is the 'efficient markets theory'. This says that there are so many competing expert analysts and investors that all publicly available information relating to the value of a security is immediately and correctly incorporated in the share price. The theory has been based upon the findings of a large number of empirical studies into American stock prices and these have largely supported market 'efficiency'.[1] Studies in other capital markets have been more sparse, however, and much more research is required before any firm conclusions can be drawn as to their share pricing processes. The purpose of this paper is to report the findings of an investigation into the adjustment of share prices quoted on the United Stock Exchange in the U.K., to the announcement of capitalisation issues.[2] This provides a direct test of the semistrong version of market efficiency,[3] and as will be shown adds to the growing body of support for the efficient markets model in the U.K.

THE NORMATIVE IMPACT OF CAPITALISATION ISSUES

As will be described later, the research methodology invólves comparing the actual price behaviour of securities against the price behaviour expected under efficient market conditions. It is therefore necessary to hypothesize the information content of a capitalisation issue. Other things being equal, the announcement of a capitalisation issue should have no impact on the share price at all, and at the exscrip date the share price should adjust precisely for the scrip terms. However it has been argued that share prices may be expected to rise at the time of the announcement of the issue and this was found to happen in an earlier study by Firth (13) into capitalisation issues (in the years 1968, 1969 and 1970) in the U.K.

The reasons suggested by Firth for this price impact were –

a) the capitalisation issue was nearly always announced at the same time as the fundamental news of the dividend and earnings for the year or half year,

b) in the majority of cases these dividend and earnings announcements showed an above average increase.

*The author is Lecturer in Accountancy at the University of Stirling. (Paper received October 1975, revised March 1976)

Firth ran a regression model on his data which measured the impact of capitalisation issues when the effects of dividends and earnings are controlled (this model is described later and applied on the current data). The results of the regression indicated that the scrip factor had no influence on the share price movements at the time of the announcement. It was therefore hypothesised that the price increase associated with the announcement of a scrip issue (which averaged 3.1% in 1968, 1.0% in 1969, and 3.1% in 1970) was occasioned solely by the dividend and earnings figures published at the same time.

A similar hypothesis was suggested by Fama, Fisher, Jensen, and Roll (9) who measured the impact of stock splits[4] on share prices in the U.S.A. They found that firms which split their securities tended to have superior price performance prior to the announcement, but they ascribed this all to the dividend and earnings expectations.

It is therefore hypothesised that scripping securities will have a superior price performance shortly before the announcement. It is further hypothesised that the share price performance will be a function of dividend and earnings records and expectations, and that the scrip factor itself has no impact.

DATA POPULATION

The data used in the study consisted of 227 capitalisation issues made by quoted companies in the years 1973 and 1974. This information was extracted from the *Financial Times*.[5] Financial characteristics of the population were extracted, but they showed no great difference from those reported in the 1968–1970 study by Firth (13). Specifically —

a) there was no significant industry concentration,
b) there was no significant grouping by market capitalisation,
c) earnings rates prior to the capitalisation issue tended to be high,
d) share price levels prior to the capitalisation issue tended to be high,
e) in the vast majority of cases dividend and earnings performance reported at the date of the scrip announcement showed an above average performance when compared against the market average. The statistics relating to dividend and earnings performance are used later in the regression modelling.

METHODOLOGY

The research methodology used in the study was to measure the behaviour of share prices around the date of the scrip announcement. This was done by comparing the actual price performance against the 'expected price'. The 'expected price' performance was given by the market model of the form suggested by Sharpe (17); that is

$$R_{jt} = a_j + B_j I_t + e_{jt}$$

where R_{jt} = return for period t on the jth security, i.e. –

$$\frac{P_t - P_{t-1}}{P_{t-1}}$$

where P_t = Price at period t, and P_{t-1} = Price at period t-1.[6] I_t = average return for period t on all shares in the stock exchange or some representative index, i.e.

$$\frac{MI_t - MI_{t-1}}{MI_{t-1}}$$

where MI = Market index at day t, and MI_{t-1} = Market index at day t-1. a_j and B_j are parameters that vary from security to security. e_{jt} = the random disturbance term for period t. The e_{jt} term is assumed to satisfy the usual requirements of a linear regression model, i.e. –

1. the e_{jt} are serially independent
2. the distribution of e_j is independent of I
3. e_{jt} has a mean of zero and variance independent of t.

The R_{jt} term is therefore used as the expected return against which the actual returns are compared. The rationale behind the model is that the major factor affecting a security's price is the movement in the general market index.[7] By controlling the impact of movements in the market index, the market model allows the impact of items specific to the particular security to be isolated. Any difference between the actual return and the predicted return on a security is ascribed to specific factors relating to the individual security. In the current study the difference is ascribed to the dividend, earnings, and scrip announcement.

The data used for deriving the regression coefficients for each company in the population, comprised the latest 57 four weekly recordings of proportional security price changes and proportionate index changes; the recordings being taken on Wednesdays. The index used was the Hoare & Co., Govett index – this is calculated daily from 1130 stock prices and is weighted by the number of shares in issue. The index·is adjusted for share splits and capitalisation issues but no adjustment is made for dividends. The 'a' term was found to be not statistically different from zero for all stocks[8] and so was ignored from the model.

The actual daily returns on securities, that is

$$\frac{P_t - P_{t-1}}{P_{t-1}} \,,$$

were compared against the returns predicted by the market model, i.e.

$$B_j \left(\frac{MI_t - MI_{t-1}}{MI_{t-1}} \right)$$

The differences between actual and predicted returns were computed thus –

$$U_{jt} = \frac{P_t - P_{t-1}}{P_{t-1}} = B_j \left(\frac{MI_t - MI_{t-1}}{MI_{t-1}} \right)$$

The differences, designated U_{jt}, are known as the prediction errors or residuals. These residuals were computed on a daily basis for the period thirty days prior to the scrip, to thirty days after.[9] The residuals as computed above form the data used in the analyses and results presented in the rest of the paper. Away from the impact of the dividend, earnings and scrip announcement, the U_{jt} term has a mean of zero. The deviations from zero around the time of the announcement represent the impact of the dividend, earnings and scrip news.

RESULTS – PRICE RETURNS AT THE DATE OF THE ANNOUNCEMENT

The cross-sectional average of the residuals for each security was computed for each day relative to the day of announcement (day 0). The cross-sectional average was computed from the expression

$$U_D = \frac{1}{N} \sum_{j=1}^{N} U_{j,D}$$

where U_{jD} is the residual for security j on day D relative to the announcement day. The results of the cross-sectional average of the residuals are shown in the second column of Table 1 along with their associated standard deviations. Figure 1 plots the residuals in pictorial form.

Table 1 also gives the cumulative average residuals, which is defined as

$$CU_D = \frac{1}{N} \sum_{j=1}^{N} \left[\prod_{d-30}^{M} (1 + U_{j,D}) \right] - 1$$

129

ANALYSIS OF DAILY AVERAGE RESIDUALS

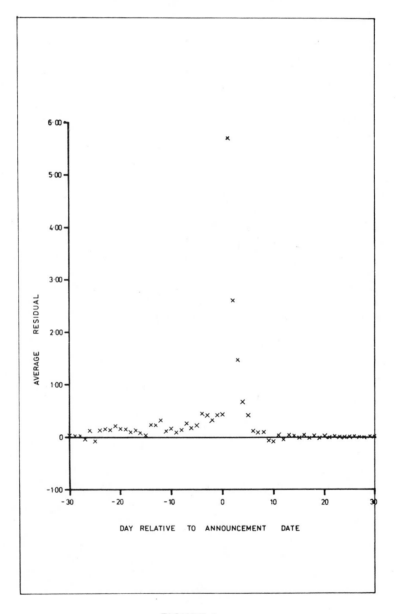

FIGURE 1

TABLE 1

ANALYSIS OF RESIDUALS IN THE 60 DAY PERIOD SURROUNDING THE ANNOUNCEMENT

DAY	Average Residual U_D	Standard Deviation	Percentage Positive	Cumulative Average Residual from Day − 30; CU_D
− 30	0.014	0.001	50	0.0
− 29	0.009	0.003	49	0.0
− 28	0.009	0.002	49	0.0
− 27	−0.013	0.004	50	0.0
− 26	0.125	0.012	51	0.1
− 25	−0.096	0.017	48	0.1
− 24	0.127	0.025	49	0.2
− 23	0.159	0.013	50	0.4
− 22	0.134	0.035	50	0.5
− 21	0.213	0.062	51	0.7
− 20	0.174	0.102	50	0.9
− 19	0.162	0.089	52	1.1
− 18	0.094	0.074	53	1.2
− 17	0.135	0.126	52	1.3
− 16	0.094	0.131	53	1.4
− 15	0.031	0.201	51	1.4
− 14	0.240	0.184	53	1.7
− 13	0.216	0.131	53	1.9
− 12	0.321	0.264	54	2.2
− 11	0.104	0.171	51	2.3
− 10	0.162	0.312	55	2.5
− 9	0.095	0.269	55	2.6
− 8	0.143	0.284	57	2.7
− 7	0.272	0.365	57	3.0
− 6	0.184	0.612	56	3.2
− 5	0.213	0.704	57	3.4
− 4	0.462	0.629	58	3.9
− 3	0.412	0.713	58	4.3
− 2	0.317	0.737	57	4.6
− 1	0.417	0.794	57	5.1
− 0	0.432	0.821	59	5.5

DAY	Average Residual U_D	Standard Deviation	Percentage Positive	Cumulative Average Residual from Day − 30; CU_D
1	5.719	4.161	85	11.5
2	2.614	2.107	61	14.5
3	1.472	1.364	54	16.1
4	0.672	0.474	52	16.9
5	0.412	0.302	49	17.4
6	0.103	0.113	50	17.5
7	0.099	0.046	51	17.6
8	0.097	0.047	48	17.7
9	−0.071	0.061	49	17.6
10	−0.098	0.042	50	17.6
11	0.043	0.032	49	17.6
12	−0.041	0.027	49	17.6
13	0.021	0.015	52	17.6
14	0.017	0.007	50	17.6
15	−0.016	0.010	51	17.6
16	0.031	0.013	50	17.6
17	−0.012	0.006	50	17.6
18	0.010	0.001	49	17.6
19	−0.013	0.008	48	17.6
20	0.007	0.004	50	17.6
21	−0.001	0.004	50	17.6
22	−0.004	0.003	51	17.6
23	−0.003	0.006	49	17.6
24	−0.005	0.007	50	17.6
25	0.007	0.008	50	17.6
26	0.006	0.013	50	17.6
27	−0.003	0.009	50	17.6
28	0.002	0.003	50	17.6
29	−0.001	0.006	51	17.6
30	−0.005	0.003	50	17.6

ANALYSIS OF CUMULATIVE AVERAGE RESIDUALS

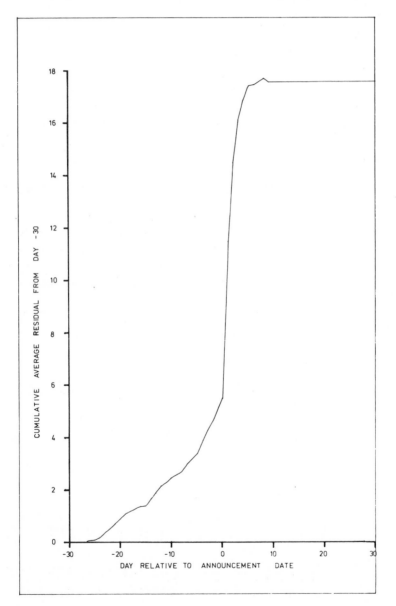

FIGURE 2

The cumulative average residual from day −30 (i.e. 30 days prior to the announcement) gives the cumulative deviation of actual returns from those computed by the market model. The cumulative average residual for each day from day −30 is given in the final column of Table 1. The movement of the cumulative average residuals are shown in Figure 2.

Table 1 and Figure 1 show a very slight increase in relative price[10] up to the announcement day, this suggesting that investors were anticipating better-than-expected results to be reported.[11] At day 1 (the day when trading was first possible after the announcement − this was the day of announcement if the news was released before the close of the market) there was a large increase in the share price, averaging 5.7% greater than the market index. The positive residuals on day 1 were quite widespread with 85% of the population showing increases. For the next few days the residuals were again quite large as investors and analysts appraised the dividend, earnings and scrip news. The standard deviation of the residuals, shown in Table 1, were quite high around the date of the announcement showing that the impact of the news varied significantly between securities. Subsequent to the first week after the announcement, the share prices of the population settled down to their normal relationship with the market index and thus the residuals approached a mean of zero: the number of days on which the average residuals were negative equalled the number of days on which they were positive. The results were also computed for periods prior to day −30 and for periods beyond day +30, but the average residuals had a mean of zero, showing that the market index accounted for all the price changes.

The results from Table 1 have shown that there was a significant relative price rise around the period of the announcement, which averaged over 17% from thirty days prior to the news release. Most of this increase came within the week of the announcement, showing that the incorporation of the information contained in the announcement was completed fairly speedily.

The information contained in the announcement consisted of three main items, namely dividends, earnings and the capitalisation issue. The hypothesis is that the residuals were the result of the dividend and earnings information, and that the capitalisation issue itself had no impact (in 187 out of 227 cases dividend and earnings news was released at the same time as the scrip announcement). In order to test this hypothesis a regression model was constructed showing the relationship of the percentage change in earnings and the percentage change in dividends to the residuals. To test the hypothesis that the announcement of a capitalisation issue has no significant impact on prices when the effect of earnings and dividends are controlled, a scrip factor is included as a qualitative (dummy) variable which is designated S. The model is expressed notationally[12] as

$$U_{jt} = a + bE + cD + dS$$

where U_{jt} is the residual recorded on day 1
  E = percentage change in earnings
  D = percentage change in dividends
  a, b, c, d = regression coefficients

The data for the model consisted of the 227 companies which had made capital-isation issues, and a control group consisting of a random sample of 227 non-scripping companies which reported their results during the same period (i.e., a non-scripping company reporting its financial result in the same month as the scripping stock was chosen for the control group). The scrip securities were assigned a value of 1 for the dummy variable S, and each non-scripping security was assigned the value 0 for S. If the news of the capitalisation issue does have an impact on share price behaviour, then this will be shown up by there being a significant 't' value for the regression coefficient d of the scrip factor S. The results of the regression are shown in Table 2.

TABLE 2
REGRESSION OF RESIDUALS ON MEASURES OF EARNINGS AND
DIVIDEND PERFORMANCE AND SCRIP–NONSCRIP ACTION
$$U_{jt} = a + bE + cD + dS$$

Degrees of freedom	a	b	c	d	R^2	F Value	Durbin Watson
449	1.483	0.823	0.361	0.017	.53	15.46*	1.8712
	3.617*	6.421*	6.001*	0.412			
450	1.296	0.794	0.305		.53	14.76*	1.8010
	3.472*	6.217*	5.872*				

Top line gives the regression coefficients.
Bottom line gives the 't' values for the regression coefficients.
  * Significant at the 0.05 level.

Although the equation only explained 53% of the total variance in the residuals, the F values were significant. The 't' values for the regression coefficients of earnings and dividends are both significant, showing the importance of these variables in explaining the residuals. The 't' value for the scrip-nonscrip factor is however not significant at the 0.05 level. This indicates that the capitalisation issue itself does not have any impact on the residuals. When the model was rerun after omitting the scrip-nonscrip factor (the results of this are shown in the lower half of Table 2), the R^2 statistic was unaltered showing that the inclusion of the capitalisation-issue variable, did not lead to a better explanatory model of share price behaviour: the F statistic was again significant with a value of 14.76. Further regressions were run using different figures for the dependent variable:

for example the cumulative average residual from day −30 to day +1 was used. These additional models revealed the same results as above. Whilst the population securities showed substantial relative price increases at the time of the announcement, this it is argued, is attributable solely to the dividend and earnings news, whilst the scrip itself has no impact.

Several other studies have adopted a regression approach to isolating the impact of capitalisation issues. Both Finn on Canadian data (11) and West, Hausman and Largay on American data (18) derived similar conclusions to those in the current study. In contrast Johnson in an investigation of American data in 1959, found that "there is a significant relative price change associated with a stock split" (16). Johnson's research did however agree with the other studies when he found it difficult to establish a profitable investment strategy: "The knowledge that, on the average, a positive relationship exists between price change and splitting would appear to be useful to investors only insofar as they can predict several months in advance that a stock split will occur".

INVESTMENT STRATEGIES

No significantly consistent profitable investment strategy could be substantiated by the study. Although the population showed a superior price performance over the period, most of this was earned prior to the announcement. There was no mechanical method for correctly predicting the occurrence of a capitalisation issue in advance. Table 1 shows that there was a positive price performance in the three days after the announcement, and this suggests there may be some scope for a smallish profitable trading rule. The returns were very volatile however, with many shares showing large relative price declines in this period (presumably reflecting an over-enthusiastic initial reaction to the financial results). In summary, the results have shown that for the data involved and before transaction costs, a smallish profitable investment strategy may exist. It is doubtful however if this strategy in practice would turn out to be worthwhile.[13]

SHARE PRICE BEHAVIOUR AT THE DATE OF GOING EXSCRIP

In addition to ascertaining the impact of the scrip announcement, an analysis was also carried out on the effect of going exscrip on share prices (the exscrip date was on average 7 weeks after the announcement). If the market is efficient, the share price of a scripping security should adjust precisely.[14] If it does not, then this has serious implications for market efficiency, as the adjustment process should be straightforward. Previous studies by Chottiner and Young in the U.S.A. (6) and Firth in the U.K. (12) indicated that share prices do adjust correctly.

The methodology involved adjusting the prescrip price by the scrip factor and by the movement in the market index and then comparing this with the actual exscrip price.

This is described notationally as

$$U_{jt} = P_t - \left(\frac{P_{t-1}}{SF} \right) \left[1 + \left(B_j \frac{I_t - I_{t-1}}{I_{t-1}} \right) \right]$$

where P_t = Price immediately exscrip (day t)
P_{t-1} = Price immediately prescrip (day t - 1)
SF = Scrip factor
B_j = beta coefficient (as constructed previously)
I_t = Market index at day t
I_{t-1} = Market index at day t - 1
U_{jt} = residual. This is expected to be zero for each stock.

The adjustment for the market index had to be made, as it proved impossible to obtain quotations immediately the market opened *post* the scrip.[15]

TABLE 3
ANALYSIS OF RESIDUALS IN THE TEN-DAY PERIOD SURROUNDING THE SCRIP DATE

DAY	Average Residual U_D %	Standard Deviation	Percentage Positive	Cumulative Average Residuals from 5 days before the scrip, CU_D %
-5	0.001	0.011	50	0.0
-4	0.003	0.014	49	0.0
-3	-0.003	0.010	48	0.0
-2	0.006	0.001	48	0.0
-1	-0.012	0.001	51	0.0
0	0.003	0.016	50	0.0
1	-0.003	0.021	49	0.0
2	0.006	0.017	52	0.0
3	0.004	0.006	48	0.0
4	-0.005	0.032	50	0.0

Table 3 shows the recordings of the residuals analysis from 5 days prior to the scrip date, to five days after. The average residual was calculated thus

$$U_D = \frac{1}{N} \sum_{j=1}^{N} U_{j,D}$$

and the cumulative average residual as

$$CU_D = \frac{1}{N} \sum_{j=1}^{N} \left[\prod_{d-30}^{M} (1 + U_{j,D}) \right] - 1$$

These results show that the prices did adjust as expected, and thus the study confirms the prior findings in the U.K. and the studies from America. The results were classified by the scrip terms to see if there were any significant subgroups. None were found.

SUMMARY

The conclusions drawn from the study are —

a) that capitalisation issues themselves have no impact on share prices. The superior share price performance usually associated with scripping securities is attributed solely to the concomitant dividends and earnings information.

b) there is no mechanical way of forecasting the occurrence of a capitalisation issue. Without having inside knowledge of when an issue is to be made, no consistently profitable investment strategy appears to exist.

c) the stock market adjusts the exscrip prices in the manner expected. Any other result would suggest a fairly serious imperfection in the market's pricing mechanism.

d) the results have added evidence that the pricing mechanism of the United Stock Exchange is 'efficient'. It also suggests that capitalisation issues have no relevance for investors, and it confirms prior conclusions (13) that in general they are a wasteful exercise.

NOTES

[1] See the review works of Brealey (4), (5), Fama (10) and Granger and Morgenstern (15).

[2] Also commonly referred to as scrip issues. Both terms are used in the paper.

[3] See the review article of Fama (10) for a description of the various forms of efficiency.

[4] Stock splits and stock dividends in the U.S.A. are the equivalents of capitalisation issues in the U.K. For a description of the terminologies see Firth (13).

[5] A total of 286 capitalisation issues were recorded in the two years. Of these 59 had to be omitted from the analyses because of lack of share price data; these were companies with small market capitalisations. Scrip issues made in lieu of cash dividends, which became popular in 1974, were excluded from the study.

[6] Data limitations prevented the inclusion of dividends in the R_{jt} term.

[7] This is partly due to earnings prospects for different companies being positively correlated, partly that the economic policies of Governments often have common cross industry influences and because changes in the returns of alternative types of investments alter the expected returns of equities as a whole.

[8] This being in line with most of the American results. For a description of the testing of the market model in the U.K. see Cunningham (7) and (8).

[9] These periods were extended, but the recordings therefrom had no impact on the results of the study.

[10] And column four in Table 1 shows that on average just over 50% of the securities in the sample had positive residuals.

[11] This anticipation proved well founded.

[12] This is a similar model specification to that used by Firth in the earlier study (13).

[13] A number of researchers have looked at the profitability of investment strategies based on stock splits and stock dividends occurring in the U.S.A. Most of these were unable to establish a profitable strategy (see Barker (1), (2), Bellemore and Blucher (3), Graham (14), Johnson (16) and West, Hausman and Largay (18)).

[14] No other information is usually released at the exscrip date, and so apart from the movement in the market index there should be no other influences on the share price.

[15] In addition the opening prices quoted in the stock market also include any other information released or opinions formed since the previous day's close.

REFERENCES

(1)   Barker, C.A., "Effective Stock Splits", HARVARD BUSINESS REVIEW, Jan–Feb, 1956.

(2)   Barker, C.A., "Stock Splits in a Bull Market", HARVARD BUSINESS REVIEW, May–June, 1957.

(3)   Bellemore, D.H. and Blucher, L., "A Study of Stock Splits in Postwar Years", FINANCIAL ANALYSTS JOURNAL, November, 1956.

(4)   Brealey, R.A., AN INTRODUCTION TO RISK AND RETURN FROM COMMON STOCKS, M.I.T. 1969.

(5)   Brealey, R.A., SECURITY PRICES IN A COMPETITIVE MARKET: MORE ABOUT RISK AND RETURN FROM COMMON STOCKS, M.I.T., 1971.

(6)   Chottiner, S. and Young, A., "A Test of the A.I.C.P.A. Differentiation Between Stock Dividends and Stock Splits", JOURNAL OF ACCOUNTING RESEARCH, Autumn, 1971.

(7)   Cunningham, S.W., "The Sensitivities of Individual Share Prices to Changes in an Index" in MATHEMATICS IN THE STOCK EXCHANGE, The Institute of Mathematics and its Applications, 1972.

(8) Cunningham, S.W., "The Predictability of British Stock Market Prices", APPLIED STATISTICS, No. 3, Vol. 22, 1973.

(9) Fama, E.F., Fisher, L., Jensen, M., and Roll, R., "The Adjustment of Stock Prices to New Information", INTERNATIONAL ECONOMIC REVIEW, X, February, 1969.

(10) Fama, E.F., "Efficient Capital Markets: A Review of Theory and Empirical Work", JOURNAL OF FINANCE, 25, May, 1970.

(11) Finn, F.J., "Stock Splits: Prior and Subsequent Price Relationships", JOURNAL OF BUSINESS FINANCE AND ACCOUNTING, Spring, 1974.

(12) Firth, M.A., "An Empirical Examination of the Applicability of Adopting the A.I.C.P.A. and N.Y.S.E. Regulations on Free Share Distributions in the U.K.", JOURNAL OF ACCOUNTING RESEARCH, Spring, 1973.

(13) Firth, M.A., "The Incidence and Impact of Capitalisation Issues", Occasional Paper No. 3, The Institute of Chartered Accountants in England and Wales, October, 1974.

(14) Graham, B., THE EFFECT OF STOCK SPLITS ON THE NUMBER OF STOCK-HOLDERS AND MARKET PRICES, Hardy & Co., New York.

(15) Granger, C.W.J. and Morgenstern, O., PREDICTABILITY OF STOCK MARKET PRICES, Heath Lexington, 1970.

(16) Johnson, K.B., "Stock Splits and Price Change", JOURNAL OF FINANCE 21, December, 1966.

(17) Sharpe, W.F., "A Simplified Model for Portfolio Analysis", MANAGEMENT SCIENCE, January, 1963.

(18) West, R.R., Hausman, W.H. and Largay, J.A., "Stock Splits, Price Changes and Trading Profits: A Synthesis", JOURNAL OF BUSINESS, Vol. 44, No. 1, 1971.

Evidence of the Impact of Inflation Accounting on Share Prices

R. C. Morris

I The impact of general indexed earnings on share prices

Inflation accounting and the investing public

In recent discussions on inflation accounting it seems to have been widely assumed that one of the main bodies to benefit from the publication of supplementary information will be the investing public. However, it is far from clear how such information can directly help *individual* investors since published data will immediately be impounded in share prices – assuming, of course, that it is regarded as having valuable informational content by the market at large. Individual investors can only benefit by having prior knowledge or by chance at the expense of other investors.[1]

The market itself, of course, still has to determine share prices. To establish such intrinsic values, essentially it has to decide what pieces of current information are good predictors of prices that will be set in the future.

It should thus be apparent that inflation accounting along the lines proposed in SSAP7 [2] will have little impact on the stock market unless brokers, jobbers and the institutions feel that inflation adjusted figures are those they should use in determining current share prices.

Investment analysts, of course, have always been aware that figures shown relating to the *past* are but one piece of information available to them, and an examination of a small sample of the multitude of brokers' company forecasts at a particular point in time makes it quite clear that non-accounting information is of the utmost importance in enabling analysts to produce crude budget predictions.[3] Equally it is well known that qualitative and to some extent quantitative adjustments to published accounting figures are made to present information on a more comparable basis. Thus, for instance, attempts by management to manipulate reported profit figures by what is variously known as cosmetic reporting or reserve- or creative-accounting have probably been largely self-defeating, so long as the nature of the manipulation has had to be disclosed in the accounts.[4] Similarly, some broking firms are known to have calculated adjusted figures to allow for changes in price levels – an apparently common procedure being to attribute an approximate current value to long-lived assets such as land and buildings; others have made allowance for the impact of general price level movements.

It should be clear, then, that there is little value from the investment point of view in making these adjustments to published accounts *unless* the market

---

[1]For a brief description of this view of the market, see R. C. Morris, 'Corporate Reporting Standards and the 4th Directive', Occasional Paper No. 2 of the Research Committee of the Institute of Chartered Accountants in England and Wales, 1974, p. 57–60. For a fuller discussion, see E. F. Fama, 'Efficient Capital Markets: A Review of Theory and Empirical Work', *Journal of Finance*, 1970; and for an examination of its far reaching implications for accountants, see W. H. Beaver, 'The Behaviour of Security Prices and its Implications for Accounting Research (Methods)', *Accounting Review*, 1972: Supplement of the Committee Reports of the AAA; and N. J. Gonedes, 'Efficient Markets and External Accounting', *Accounting Review*, 1972.

[2]'Accounting for Changes in the Purchasing Power of Money', Provisional Statement of Standard Accounting Practice (SSAP 7), *Accountancy*, June 1974.

[3]This is hardly surprising in view of the fact that according to studies by A. C. Rayner and I. M. F. Little, 'Higgledy Piggledy Growth Again', Basil Blackwell, Oxford: 1966; R. Ball and R. Watts, 'Some Time Series Properties of Accounting Income', *Journal of Finance*, 1972; and others, earnings figures appear to have little predictive significance. See also R. C. Morris, op. cit., p. 63

[4]See, for instance, R. Ball, 'Changes in Accounting Techniques and Stock Prices', *Journal of Accounting Research*, 1972: Supplement on Empirical Research in Accounting: Selected Studies; R. S. Kaplan and R. Roll, 'Investor Evaluation of Accounting Information: Some Empirical Evidence', *Journal of Business*, 1972; and other studies referred to by R. C. Morris, op. cit., p. 59, footnote 18.

impounds the information into share prices; or the data themselves are better predictors of future share prices than are existing (unadjusted) accounting indicators.

There are thus two important questions which need to be asked.

(1) To what extent does the market impound inflation adjusted data into share prices? and

(2) are price level adjusted data better predictors of future share prices than unadjusted data?

Some research has been undertaken on the latter point in the United States to see whether or not there is stronger serial correlation through time for adjusted profit figures than for conventional income statistics.[5] On the whole the results have been somewhat inconclusive – which is hardly surprising since the researchers have either unrealistically had to adjust real-world data with the advantage of hindsight; or instead have had to resort to sophisticated but artificial laboratory experiments. As far as one is aware, however, little or nothing has been done to provide an answer to the first question, though a number of surveys suggest analysts regard price level adjusted data (especially where replacement cost values are used) as being helpful additional information.[6]

The impact of inflation on market prices

Empirically there is evidence that the market has allowed in part at least for the effects of inflation in recent years. Thus by industry categories those sectors most vulnerable to inflation have in general performed worse than the FT-Actuaries all share index in the period 1968–1973, while those with high external gearing and owning property have shown the greatest gains over the six year period.[7]

However, at the present time the market appears to have reacted little to the SSAP 7 inflation adjusted results so far published by some 20–25 companies, and indeed the financial press seems to have greeted the statements with little more than mild curiosity. (For the most part, anyway, the companies concerned have not reported supplementary figures which the market regards as severely damaging: GKN, for instance, with an adjusted 20 per cent fall in profits, was described by the *Investors Chronicle* as 'coming out well in its accounting for inflation statement'!)[8]

Nevertheless, even if most companies have yet to apply SSAP 7 it is perfectly possible for outsiders to make approximate adjustments to allow for the effects of changing price levels. This can even be done using special price indices appropriate to different types of non-monetary assets owned by companies if asset categories are sufficiently well-defined and the nature of the fixed assets involved is apparent. It is rather easier, however, to make general price-level adjustments of the nature envisaged in SSAP 7. (Indeed, the fact that such adjustments can be fairly easily made by outsiders has been advanced as one very good reason why current cost accounting should be preferred to mere general index adjustments.)[9]

Pioneer work on producing price-level adjusted figures for quoted companies on a regular basis has been undertaken over the past few years by R. S. Cutler of the brokers Phillips and Drew. The companies whose results have been adjusted are amongst the largest in the country, accounting for about 75 per cent of the capitalized market value of equities quoted in London (excluding investment trusts). Certainly the information thus made available covers a wide enough spectrum to make it feasible for the investing public in the form of institutional investors and brokers to use this price level adjusted data in setting the relative market values of equities.

Cutler's first analysis covered 132 quoted companies, and the results were published in the *Phillips and Drew Market Review*, December 1971.[10] The

[5] See, for instance, W. Frank, 'A Study of the Predictive Significance of Two Income Measures', *Journal of Accounting Research*, 1969; R. A. Samuelson, 'Prediction and Price-Level Adjustment', *Journal of Accounting Research*, 1972; M. N. Greenball, 'Evaluation of the Usefulness to Investors of Different Accounting Estimators of Earnings: A Simulation Approach', *Journal of Accounting Research*, 1968: Supplement on Empirical Research in Accounting: Selected Studies; J. K. Simmons and J. Gray, 'An Investigation of the Effect of Differing Accounting Frameworks on the Prediction of Net Income', *Accounting Review*, 1969; and E. V. McIntyre, 'Current Cost Financial Statements and Common Stock Investment Decisions', *Accounting Review*, 1973.

[6] e.g. T. R. Dyckman, 'Investment Analysis and General Price-Level Adjustments', Studies in Accounting Research 1, American Accounting Association, Evanston, Ill.: 1969; R. W. Estes, 'An Assessment of the Usefulness of Current Cost and Price Level Information by Financial Statement Users', *Journal of Accounting Research*, 1968; and V. C. Brenner, 'Financial Statement Users' Views of the Desirability of Reporting Current Cost Information', *Journal of Accounting Research*, 1970. A similar inference can be drawn from the submission to the Sandilands Committee by the Society of Investment Analysts: 'Inflation Accounting', the *Investment Analyst*, May 1974.

[7] P. W. Parker and P. M. D. Gibbs, 'Accounting for Inflation – Recent Proposals and their Effects', *Journal of the Institute of Actuaries*, 1974, paras. 36–37.

[8] *Investors Chronicle*, 17th May 1974, p. 822.

[9] D. A. Egginton and R. C. Morris, 'Borrowing Costs, Price Level Changes, and ED8' *The Accountant*, 11th October 1973, who are merely developing the theme of E. O. Edwards and P. W. Bell, 'The Theory and Measurement of Business Income', University of California Press, Berkeley: 1965, p. 264–6.

[10] R. S. Cutler, 'Inflation and Accounting', *Phillips and Drew Market Review*, December 1971.

information, though circulating widely in the City, apparently 'appeared to have very little effect on stock exchange prices'.[11] Nevertheless, the possibilities and implications had been aired, if only to a relatively narrow audience.

In the autumn of 1971, just before Cutler's calculations were published, the Institute of Chartered Accountants in England and Wales released a discussion document on inflation accounting.[12] Over the next few months interest in inflation accounting quickened and was heightened by the publication in January 1973 of an exposure draft of proposed standard accounting practice (ED8).[13] This was followed soon afterwards by the publication of a second and more detailed analysis of the adjusted results for almost the same population of companies in the March 1973 issue of *Accountancy*.[14] The article, authored by Cutler and C. A. Westwick of the Institute, aroused widespread interest and comment in the financial press.[15] Certainly it is safe to say the results reached a far wider audience, and by showing the extent to which share prices might have to be adjusted to reflect the effects of inflation the implications were obvious.

Since then several other broking firms have been experimenting with inflation adjustments applied to conventionally published accounting figures. However, it appears Phillips and Drew still lead the field in this area, promoting seminars on the topic, updating the adjusted figures, and producing a detailed study of the incidence of inflation in the engineering sector. Most importantly, though, two of the firm's partners presented an influential and widely reported paper to the Institute of Actuaries in April 1974.[16] In this the authors, P. W. Parker and P. M. D. Gibbs, did not merely examine the relative merits of current cost and general index accounting, but also reproduced the updated figures for inflation adjusted

earnings for 120 companies.

Clearly, the market has had access to inflation adjusted earnings for most sizeable companies since December 1971, and it is possible to identify three separate occasions when a full and comparable list of inflation adjusted earnings figures has been published. Of course, while it is true that the adjustments made by Cutler and his associates have had to be approximate in nature, there is little reason to believe their estimates are very wide of the mark. Indeed, where companies have published SSAP 7 statements the results can be compared with Phillips and Drew estimates – and in most cases the brokers' calculations seem to have been remarkably close.[17] Moreover, it should be pointed out that all that is really wanted is an approximate indication of the size of the inflationary error – accuracy is an elusive quality in terms of earnings figures, which anyway may be very poor indicators of future likely performance.

In the circumstances, as Kirkman has observed, it would be extremely interesting to see whether or not the stock market has taken any notice of the Phillips and Drew data.[18] Rather surprisingly no-one yet seems to have tried to test this, so it was to remedy the situation that the current study was undertaken.

The methodology

A widely accepted model of share price movements is the Markowitz 'market model',[19] which defines the stochastic process generating share price changes (or returns on investment in a share) as

$$R_{it} = \alpha_i + \beta_i R'_{mt} + u_{it}$$

where R_{it} = the return of share i in period t

R'_{mt} = the market factor in period t

α_i, β_i = intercept and slope of the linear relationship between R_{it} and R'_{mt}

u_{it} = stochastic portion of the individualistic component of R_{it}

Simply put the model proposes that there is a linear relationship between the price movements of a share (i) and the market-wide factors. Any residual movement after market-wide effects have been removed is reflected as the u_{it} term, which is expected to be stochastic.

[11]P. R. A. Kirkman, 'Accounting Under Inflationary Conditions', Geo. Allen and Unwin, London: 1974, p. 115.

[12]Institute of Chartered Accountants in England and Wales, 'Inflation and Accounts', Discussion Paper of the Accounting Standards Steering Committee: *Accountancy*, September 1971.

[13]Institute of Chartered Accountants in England and Wales, 'Accounting for Changes in the Purchasing Power of Money', Proposed Statement of Standard Accounting Practice, ED8: *Accountancy*, March 1973.

[14]R. S. Cutler and C. A. Westwick, 'The Impact of Inflation Accounting on the Stock Market', *Accountancy*, March 1973.

[15]e.g. *Sunday Times* 4th March 1973; *Guardian* 5th March 1973; *Daily Telegraph* 5th March 1973.

[16]P. W. Parker and P. M. D. Gibbs, op. cit. Since this study was completed in July 1974, more recent Phillips and Drew figures have been published: P. W. Parker and P. M. D. Gibbs, 'Inflation Accounting and its Effects', *Accountancy*, September 1974.

[17]See R. S. Cutler, text of a talk given at the Phillips and Drew seminar on 'Accounting for Inflation' at the Plaisterers' Hall, London Wall, 24th July 1973: Table 1. But see also J. M. Boersma, 'Can General Price-level Adjusted Statements be Approximated by the Outsider?', *Accountancy*, May 1974.

[18]P. R. A. Kirkman, op. cit., p. 116.

[19]For a clear exposition of the model in this context, see W. H. Beaver, op. cit.

In practice share price movements reflect not merely market-wide effects but also an industry factor. Operationally it is possible to approximate these factors by calculating the return on the market- and an industry-portfolio and thus isolate the residual reflecting that part of return on a share which reflects information peculiar to it. For this purpose, however, the security under scrutiny should technically be excluded from the portfolio. Empirical studies in the United States in fact show that about half the movement in the price of an individual share can be explained by its co-movement with the market factor and a further ten per cent relates to industry-wide events.[20]

In the present study a simple approach has been used. It has been assumed that the FT-Actuaries all share and industry indices provide adequate indicators of market- and industry-wide price movements, thus enabling residual price changes to be isolated. However, it should be remembered that these indices are weighted according to the capitalized market values of securities.[21] Since the indices include almost all the shares under scrutiny, and the companies are among the largest in the country, there is a bias in the procedure. For the market-wide factor it is probably unimportant, but in abstracting industry effects it could cast serious doubt on the validity of the results. Consequently more attention should probably be paid to the findings where only a market-wide factor was taken out of the price movements, especially as the impact of industry effects is relatively insignificant. Nevertheless, some results derived when industry-wide events were taken out of the data have also been presented, though the reader should treat these findings with caution.

There are various ways of testing residual price movements to see whether they relate to any particular piece of information available to the market. One method is to see whether the residual price changes (u_{it}) are larger in a period when information is available to the market than at other times, the inference being that the news has led to changed expectations. This method is appropriate for testing over short time spans and where the news announcement can clearly be identified in time; it can also be backed up by an examination of the level of trading activity, which is another indicator of changed expectations on the part of investors.[22]

An alternative approach, which has been widely used in the United States in recent years, is to see whether the price residuals (u_{it}) move in the expected direction following the publication of a piece of news. The data can be examined in various ways, but the methods most widely adopted nowadays were pioneered in an accounting context by Ball and Brown.[23] In fact a simplified version of their approach has been employed in this study since it seems most appropriate.

Two tests have been applied to the data. The first is a simple comparison between the signs of the actual residual price movements and those 'forecast' by the inflation adjusted earnings figures. Thus if the 'real' earnings are lower than the conventional profit figures reported, it seems not unreasonable to expect the relative price of a share to fall; if higher, the market might be expected to mark it upwards. (Indeed, in the Cutler and Westwick article this was specifically suggested and notional 'new' prices given). It should therefore be possible to see whether the direction of the price movements was as predicted. This can be achieved quite simply by using a chi-square test to see whether one can reject a null hypothesis that the combination of the signs of price movements (either in the same direction as 'predicted', or in the opposite) occurred by chance.

The second test requires the use of a simplified version of the Ball and Brown 'Abnormal Performance Index' (API). This can be defined as

$$API = \frac{1}{I} \sum_{i=1}^{i=I} u_i$$

where the u factors represent residual percentage gains and losses on shares after the appropriate 'bull' or 'bear' strategies suggested by the differences between actual and inflation adjusted earnings have been adopted. The API can be calculated for each time span examined to give the relative profit for £1 'invested' in equal amounts in all shares $(i = 1, 2, \dots I)$

---

[20]B. F. King, 'Market and Industry Factors in Stock Prices Behaviour', *Journal of Business*, 1966; S. L. Meyers, 'A Re-examination of Market and Industry Factors in Stock Price Behaviour', *Journal of Finance*, 1973.

[21]'Guide to Financial Times Statistics, the *Financial Times*, London: 1973.

[22]The method has been used in the US by W. H. Beaver, 'The Information Content of Annual Earnings Announcements', *Journal of Accounting Research*, 1968: Supplement on Empirical Research in Accounting: Selected Studies; and by R. G. May, 'The Influence of Quarterly Earnings Announcements on Investor Decisions as Reflected in Common Stock Price Changes', *Journal of Accounting Research*, 1971: Supplement on Empirical Research in Accounting: Selected Studies. In the UK the lack of facilities similar to Standard and Poor's Compustat tapes and the fact that until recently not all deals were recorded has meant that such procedures have hardly been practical.

[23]R. Ball and P. Brown, 'An Empirical Evaluation of Accounting Income Numbers', *Journal of Accounting Research*, 1968.

over that period.

To amplify briefly, the relative profit is found in the following manner. Firstly, the percentage change in each share price is calculated and the proportion of expected change due to market- or industry-wide effects eliminated. The resultant residuals are then summed in two subsets, according to whether the difference between actual and inflation adjusted earnings suggests that a rise or fall in share price can be expected. Then, after appropriate adjustments to the signs, the results are added together and divided by the number of shares under scrutiny to produce the overall API coefficient. (Normally one would have to allow for dividends received as well, but for reasons which will be given presently this refinement was not adopted in this study.)

The API can intuitively be interpreted as showing the net gain an individual would have made over a period by constructing a portfolio specifically using the information before it was published in the hope of subsequently beating the market. This would be achieved by taking 'bull' positions on shares which inflation adjusted earnings indicated were 'under-valued', and 'bear' positions on those which appeared to be 'overvalued'.

The empirical evidence

In testing the data most attention was concentrated on the Cutler-Westwick article, since the figures contained in it received a good deal of publicity. For the first test market reaction was examined for 136 of the 137 companies they dealt with over an arbitrary period, approximately two weeks after publication of *Accountancy*. (The 137th company was ignored, in fact, as there was no material difference between its reported and inflation-adjusted earnings). The bench marks used for calculating movements in share prices were the quotations given in the article showing closing prices on February 1st, 1973[24] – i.e. there was a six week span over which price movements were calculated.

It can be seen from Tables 1 and 2 that the null hypothesis based on the simple sign test is not rejected, and the API values are negative in the case where market residuals were examined and are too low even to cover dealing costs when industry effects are removed. The inference is clear that the market found little information content in the publication of the inflation adjusted figures – either because it

had already made its adjustments; or because it chose in general not to regard such data as being relevant to its deliberations.

It might be suggested that for many companies the differences between actual prices and those suggested by Cutler and Westwick were negligible and would either have been ignored anyway by the market or would have been saturated by general noise. As a result it was decided to re-run the tests for a subset of companies showing sizeable price (or earnings) 'errors'. The criterion used was a difference of 30 per cent or over.

Again it can be seen that at two weeks the indicators suggest the market did not find the information particularly valuable. The APIs are negative and the sign movements were actually in the opposite direction to what might have been expected. Moreover, when these data were further partitioned to isolate those shares most over- and under-valued, the API values were even less suggestive of there being informational content in the figures as far as the market was concerned.

Further tests of the subset of companies where the error was 30 per cent and over were tried for three other intervals on the Cutler-Westwick data: at four weeks from the publication of *Accountancy*, at five months, and at eleven months. It can be seen that the results are not materially different, even at eleven months, when the market was spiralling downwards in face of the three day week. This is particularly interesting since at a distance of one year from the bench mark date the new prices must have been influenced by new (conventional) earnings figures.

As for the less widely exposed Cutler data, published in December 1971, similar tests on companies showing earnings errors of 20 per cent or above confirm Kirkman's unsupported assertion that the data appeared to have had little effect on share prices. Here intervals of approximately one month, two months and six months were used to examine the behaviour of 'market residuals'. As can be seen from Table 1 both tests indicate there was negligible informational content in the data.

The most recently published figures are those of Parker and Gibbs, released in April 1974. Only one period was examined with this data, the 'market residuals' being calculated one month after publication. However, the bench mark date for calculating price movements was taken seven weeks prior to publication to allow for 'leakage' of information in the City.

On this occasion both tests indicate the market if anything has acted in the opposite direction to that one might expect. The API coefficient suggests that

---

[24] 'This date was chosen as the base to cover the possibility of leakages of information prior to publication. The two week lapse following official publication should have been sufficient time for the market to react – as is noted in footnote 15, three newspapers reported the results on March 4th and 5th.

TABLE 1

Test statistics on 'market residual' data

Approx. time since publication (months)	Data source	No. of companies	Sign test null hypothesis χ^2 statistic	API (£)
0.5	Cutler-Westwick	136	1.441 •	−0.008
0.5	Cutler-Westwick : earnings errors over 30%	65	4.446 •	−0.020
1.0	earnings errors over 30%	65	1.246 •	−0.010
5.0	earnings errors over 30%	65	1.862	−0.002
11.0	earnings errors over 30%	65	3.462	+0.024
1.0	Cutler : earnings errors over 20%	59	0.017	+0.008
2.0	earnings errors over 20%	59	0.831	+0.022
6.0	earnings errors over 20%	59	0.424	+0.020
1.0	Parker and Gibbs : earnings errors over 30%	53	11.792 •	−0.077

•Majority of sign movements in opposite direction to that expected.

TABLE 2

Test statistics on 'industry residual' data

Approx. time since publication (months)	Data source	No. of companies	Sign test null hypothesis χ^2 statistic	API (£)
0.5	Cutler-Westwick	136	0.029	+0.003
0.5	Cutler-Westwick : earning errors over 30%	65	0.385 •	0.000
1.0	earning errors over 30%	65	0.015 •	+0.004
5.0	earning errors over 30%	65	4.446	+0.007
11.0	earning errors over 30%	65	0.754	−0.002

•Majority of sign movements in opposite direction to that expected.

Percentage points of the chi-square distribution at one degree of freedom are as follows :

Probability factor	χ^2 statistic
0.25	1.323
0.10	2.706
0.05	3.841
0.025	5.024
0.001	10.827

i.e. values in the tables for χ^2 below 3.841 indicate the null hypothesis cannot be denied.

a strategy based on the information would over the period have produced a loss almost 8p in the £ greater than if a market average portfolio had been selected. Similarly, for the sign test the chi-square statistic (which in all other instances is significant or nearly so at the 95 per cent probability level) does not sustain the null hypothesis that the direction of the residual price movements could have arisen by chance. However, this hardly suggests that the market has used the data since some two thirds of the price changes were in the *opposite* direction to that which might have been expected.

A possible explanation could in fact be that companies which do well under inflation accounting tend to be heavy borrowers benefiting from the recognition of monetary holding gains. In the uncertain economic conditions prevalent in the period in question these very same concerns tended to suffer most from doubts about corporate solvency.

As a final point it should be noted that the returns for individual securities in this study have been calculated simply as the change in share prices, adjusted where appropriate for rights and bonus issues, but ignoring dividend income. The omission of the latter is justified on the grounds that in taking the market factor out of the data one should also have abstracted from the effect of dividend policies on share prices, since the FT all-share index will itself contain an element representing the market's discounted value of expected distributions for its component firms. Thus if it is assumed that the groups of companies whose share prices have been the subject of study have similar dividend policies and on average declare dividends at the same times as the market index population, it is only necessary to examine residual price movements.

It should also be recognised, of course, that the inclusion of dividends would almost certainly further weaken the case for arguing that the Phillips and Drew figures have had some impact on the market. In each set of data tested over three-quarters of the historic earnings figures were greater than their inflation-adjusted counterparts, so there is a strong likelihood that the positive API coefficients would be reduced and the negative ones increased.

II The case for current cost income statements[25]

Readers may be surprised that the market appears to respond so little to the information disclosed in inflation adjusted statements, and may even believe it refutes the efficient markets hypothesis. This, however, does not do for reasons already given. Firstly, there is some evidence that the market has

already adjusted for the effects of inflation at the industry level; and, secondly, the market may not at present regard the more detailed company information as being relevant when setting share prices.

In taking this latter view, in fact, who is to say the market is wrong? Certainly not the accountancy profession, which has done little enough to determine whether general indexed data are of any value to investors; and which, together with the CBI, seems more intent on trying to get the income tax burden shifted away from the corporate sector. Moreover, as some writers have observed, it may well be that no accounting figures reporting on *past* events can be very helpful as predictors of the future, except where bankruptcy is impending.[26]

This, however, seems to be too pessimistic a view. It should in fact be possible to identify the *type* of information which is most likely to prove helpful to investors. On this basis it seems fairly clear that two factors above all interest analysts: firstly, they would like to isolate any recurrent element in a firm's profits; and, secondly, they would like to be able to compare the performances of companies against each other.

Fortunately there is a type of income measure which provides economically meaningful information of this kind, and this is produced by current cost accounting.[27] Under this method of income calculation all firms in a particular period charge against their operating revenues depreciation based on the current purchase cost of an asset. So long as the method of depreciation adopted measures fairly accurately the incidence of capital consumption,[28]

[25] The term 'current cost income' has been used here to refer to the fully adjusted 'real business profit' concept developed by E. O. Edwards and P. W. Bell, op. cit. Succinct summaries of the Edwards and Bell type arguments are given by P. W. Bell, 'Price Changes and Income Measurement', in 'Readings in the Concept and Measurement of Income', ed. R. H. Parker and G. C. Harcourt, Cambridge University Press, London: 1969; by R. H. Parker and G. C. Harcourt in their 'Introduction' to the 'Readings' just referred to; and by L. R. Amey and D. A. Egginton, 'Management Accounting: A Conceptual Approach', Longman, London: 1973, chapter 3.

[26] e.g. M. N. Greenball, 'The Predictive-Ability Criterion: Its Relevance in Evaluating Accounting Data', *Abacus*, 1971: K. V. Peasnell, 'The Usefulness of Accounting Information to Investors', International Centre for Research in Accounting: Occasional Paper No. 1, Lancaster: 1973.

[27] The importance of current cost accounting as a means of producing an income figure which measures performance is clearly and strongly emphasised in L. R. Amey and D. A. Egginton, op. cit., chapter 3.6. See also D. A. Egginton and R. C. Morris, op. cit.

[28] Conceptually this is probably best achieved in this context using so-called 'equivalent replacement cost' depreciation. Once again the clearest and best exposition seems to be given in L. R. Amey and D. A. Egginton, op. cit., p. 114–118.

firms are put on a common footing, and it should thus be possible to make reasonable comparisons of their operating performances in a particular period.

Unless current costs are used, of course, the figures become distorted, since long-lived assets are purchased by companies at different times. By using current costs a firm which has just purchased a particular asset should charge depreciation against operating revenues on exactly the same underlying basis as one which purchased a similar asset some years earlier when its *relative* price was different. The value thus placed on each unit of service potential consumed should in fact be the same in a given period for all business with similar types of assets. Any advantage or disadvantage a company receives by buying the asset earlier in time is quite reasonably treated separately as a capital gain or loss incurred at the time when the current cost of that asset changed.

It should therefore be clear that for a particular period the current operating profits of similar businesses should be comparable under a full current cost accounting system. Moreover, where firms separate out their capital (or more specifically 'holding') gains in this way, the *recurrent* trading element of their activities is isolated. Presumably over time one might expect this element would be the best base on which to build predictions of future (operating) profits, and this task would be made easier where a breakdown of fixed and variable costs was given. Another advantage of current cost accounting is that some economic meaning can be attached to the values placed on assets shown in the corresponding balance sheets, since they can be interpreted as one set of external opportunity costs. Thus this method of income calculation provides the best hope of producing data which might be helpful to investment analysts.

Unfortunately the point about performance measurement and comparability is too often overlooked, even by experienced investment analysts who do not rebut the extravagant claims of proponents of mere general index adjustments that their historic cost based figures are somehow made comparable over time and as between companies.[29] The simple truth is that they are not – and cannot be – so long as 'realizable cost savings' (i.e. holding gains) are not distinguished, but are recognized in an arbitrary manner.

Unhappily the accountancy profession seems unwilling to examine critically the conventional historic cost system of income calculation. The fact that it

appears to be acceptable (and even desirable) at law as a basis for calculating taxable income and for determining the maximum fund out of which dividends can be paid without impairing the position of unsecured creditors does *not* mean the figures meet the needs of investors and others trying to assess the economic performance of firms.

A great deal has been written about current cost accounting over the last 30 years – indeed, one is sorely tempted to say far too much has been written and too little read, understood and digested! Various versions have masqueraded under titles such as 'current value' or (more usually) 'replacement cost' accounting. The former term is hardly appropriate since 'value' is an undefined concept, while the latter is positively misleading and produces some hoary old chestnuts. Current cost accounting in fact really implies *nothing* about the amount that can be distributed as dividends; nor does it imply that assets can be sold at their current purchase costs. Moreover, the question of whether or not a particular asset is going to be replaced is irrelevant in assessing performance; what one really needs for this purpose is a measure of the change in the current (opportunity) cost of an asset in a period.[30] For the same reason the rather dubious argument that real capital should be maintained intact by 'capitalizing' holding gains so that a company can replace its existing assets by similar ones without recourse to the capital market is also irrelevant.[31]

The above brief discussion should make it clear that if any supplementary information needs to be published by companies it ought to be an income figure based on current cost calculations. Moreover, in practice it is unrealistic to deal with general and relative price level changes separately. To apply mere general index adjustments means that some holding gains are recognized while others are not.[32] (The distinction depends on whether an asset is 'monetary' or 'non-monetary' in nature, of course). This seems illogical. What is surely required is a system whereby both specific and general price level changes are taken into account. There may, of course, be a good deal of argument about how such a system should be implemented, but this should not affect the basic issue. Regrettably in the past academics have all too frequently squabbled over details when what is

---

[29]e.g. P. W. Parker and P. M. D. Gibbs, 'Accounting for Inflation – Recent Proposals and their Effects', *Journal of the Institute of Actuaries*, 1974, para. 14.

[30]P. W. Parker and P. M. D. Gibbs, 'Accounting for Inflation – Recent Proposals and their Effects', op. cit., paras. 17 and 18, again fail to rebut the fallacy in the argument.

[31]Despite the fact that the point is irrelevant if one is trying to measure *performance* it has greatly exercised a number of academics, notably Gynther in various writings.

[32]D. A. Egginton and R. C. Morris, op. cit.

really needed is a concerted effort to make the profession see the need for the supplementary publication of an income figure, which, by recognizing the impact of unrealized changes in relative prices, differs sharply from that produced by the conventional historic cost system.

III Conclusions

Reasonably accurate inflation adjusted earnings figures for most major quoted companies have now been available to the City for almost three years, but as yet there is very little sign that the market has responded to the information. This partly reflects the fact that the incidence of inflation at an industry level has already been discounted into prices; and it may also indicate a certain distrust of the figures. Since there is little evidence that these disguised historic cost figures are good predictors of future outcomes, such a scepticism has much to commend it. However, it may well yet be that irresistible pressures will be mounted forcing analysts to rush lemming-like into an acceptance of the new figures. Such a development would be regrettable since there

are few grounds for believing that such figures are more relevant to either the deliberations of individual investors or to the efficient allocation of resources through the capital market. The latter goal – inasmuch as it can ever be achieved anyway[33] – requires that analysts have a better means of making comparisons of performance between firms and of predicting more accurately future outcomes. In practice, as has been argued elsewhere,[34] it seems the crystal-ball gazing required to make any capital market system work effectively is only reasonably accurate in predicting marginal profit levels for periods of up to about a year. However, on a priori grounds there seems to be a strong case for publishing a fully indexed set of supplementary accounts incorporating current cost principles since such a method of calculating income offers investors the best chance of making meaningful comparisons between companies and of improving their predictive abilities.

[33]See R. C. Morris, op. cit., ch. IV.

[34]Ibid., p. 60–64.

The performance of share recommendations made by investment analysts and the effects on market efficiency

by Michael Firth

There has been considerable dialectic over the past decade or so on the validity of the random walk theory as a description of share price behaviour. The protagonists of the random walk theory contend that, on average, investment analysts cannot out-perform the market index and that it is not worthwhile for investors to engage in any additional research. This paper briefly summarizes the arguments put forward and the evidence to date, and publishes findings of an investigation into recommendations made by investment analysts working for financial papers, journals and stockbrokers.

EFFICIENT MARKET AND SHARE EVALUATION MODELS

THE main proponents of the random walk model theory, the academics, argue along the lines of an expected return theory. Fama [1] describes such a model notationally as:

$$E(V_{j, t+1}/X_t) = (1 + E(r_{j, t+1}/X_t)) V_{jt}$$

where E = expected value,

V_{jt} = price of security j at time t,

$V_{j, t+1}$ = price of security j at time $t+1$ with the reinvestment of dividends,

$r_{j, t+1}$ = percentage return for the period

$$\left(= \frac{V_{j, t+1} - V_{jt}}{V_{jt}} \right)$$

X_t = set of information assumed to be fully reflected in the price at t,

$\left. \begin{array}{c} V_{j, t+1} \\ r_{j, t+1} \end{array} \right\}$ = random variables at time t.

The formula implies that the information set, X_t, is fully incorporated in the dynamic equilibrium model which produces the price at time t.

The assumption of market equilibrium rules out the possibility of trading systems, based only on the information set X_t, having profits in excess of equilibrium expected profits. Let

$$Y_{j, t+1} = V_{j, t+1} - E(V_{j, t+1}/X_t)$$

If Xt fully reflects the information on which the share price is based

then $\qquad E(Y_{j, t+1}/X_t) = 0$

Thus the process is a fair game with respect to the information sequence X_t.

The random walk model is an extension of the expected return or fair game model. It implies that successive one period price changes are independent. Statistical tests to date have shown that there are some dependencies in successive price changes[1] but they are too small on which to base profitable trading rules—such a model can be described as a submartingale process. The model says that if all publicly available information, X_t, is incorporated in a share price, then trading rules based on such information cannot make profits in excess of following a buy and hold policy. Both the random walk and the martingale models require that the market value of a security be a good estimate of its intrinsic worth and that no further detailed analysis will, on average, provide profitable results. A stockmarket based on such processes has become known as "efficient".

Potential sources of inefficiencies to the model exist in the forms of transaction costs, information that is not freely available to all, and to differences among investors about the implications of the given information. Much of the empirical work has been in measuring the effect that inefficiencies have on share prices.

Investment analysts employed by financial institutions set out to find an intrinsic value of a share. The intrinsic value can be thought of as the discounted value of all future dividends, ie,

---

[1] It has been pointed out that stock price changes do not follow a gaussian distribution and that therefore the statistical tests used in measuring dependencies are not valid. However the distribution of price changes does not affect the findings that no profitable trading rules have been based upon such dependencies.

$$P_0 = \frac{D_1}{(1+K_1)^1} + \frac{D_2}{(1+K_2)^2} + \frac{D_3}{(1+K_3)^3} + \ldots + \frac{D_n}{(1+K_n)^n}$$

D = Dividends
P_0 = Intrinsic value
K_i = Discount rates

Because of the difficulty of estimating dividends each year a constant growth rate is often used in evaluation models such that

$$P_0 = D_0 \int_0^\infty \exp(gt)\exp(-kt)\,dt$$

Thus the current share price is equal to current dividends growing at rate g and discounted by the rate k over infinitely small time periods dt. The discount rate k is held constant in the above formula. When this formula is integrated or infinitely summed it reduces to the form

$$P_0 = \frac{D_0}{k-g}$$

This formula will yield meaningful results only if the value of the discount rate k is greater than the growth rate g.

Investment analysts are traditionally divided into two camps, fundamentalist and technical. The fundamental analysts attempt to find the intrinsic value of a share and use economic and industrial factors, interfirm comparisons, company statements and any other relevant information in their assessment. In practice the discounting of all future estimated dividends is impractical: analysts tend to project the earnings and dividends per share for the near future and then estimate a future growth rate so that

$$P_0 = \frac{D_1}{(1+K_1)^1} + \frac{D_2}{(1+K_2)^2} + \cdots + \frac{D_n}{(1+K_n)^n} + \frac{D_n/(K-g)}{(1+K_n)^n}$$

The formula says the intrinsic price is the discounted estimated dividends for the next n periods plus the

discounted value of the share price at time n. This price is found by using a constant growth rate g and a constant discount rate K. From these projections, and from an assessment of what the stock market and the economy are likely to do as a whole, the fundamentalists arrive at a value for a company's shares.

Technical analysts predict share prices and stock market levels by using various mechanical trading rules such as chart projections, filter tests, moving averages, relative strength tests, fixed investment proportion maintenance strategies, the advance decline line and the breadth of market theory. The chartists and technical analysts assume that facts existing at one time will determine the prices at some future time—they study price movements of the immediate past for telltale indications of movements in the immediate future.

IMPLICATIONS AND THE EVIDENCE

The implication of the efficient markets model for fundamental analysts is that they cannot outperform the market average. This is due, the model says, to there being so many competing analysts that they should cause the market price to wander randomly around the intrinsic value. Indeed the intrinsic value may be said to be represented by a dynamic equilibrium model, ie, the weighted mean of all investors' evaluations at that point in time.

The intrinsic value of a security does of course change across time as a result of new information, actual, anticipated or putative. Prices incorporating the new information will usually over or under adjust initially. The time taken for the security's price to settle down to the intrinsic value is a stochastic variable: the process of adjustment is the reflection of the changing uncertainty remaining in the minds of investors. If there are many astute traders in the market then, on average, the full effects of new information on the intrinsic value of a share will be reflected instantaneously: any under and any over adjustment and the time taken to adjust are randomly distributed and therefore no profitable trading rules can be based upon them.

If differences arise between intrinsic and actual prices owing to dependencies in the process generating new information or if disagreements over the intrinsic price are systematic, then knowledge of such would help analysts to outperform the market index. However the efficient market theorists say that there are so many rational market operators with sufficient resources who are able to take advantage of such profit opportunities, that they compete with each other until all non-random fluctuations about the intrinsic value become so small that they cannot be exploited for profit.

According to the efficient market theory it does not pay investors to engage in any additional analysis. Wallich [2], in taking this view, said "Incorrect pricing can produce serious disturbance. Here is the main social contribution of securities analysis. But approximately correct pricing could probably be obtained with a fraction of the manpower now employed in securities analysis. Once the best available judgment has put prices where they belong, there is no social benefit in duplicating the work . . . correct pricing of securities . . . is a public good available free to all, even though it costs money to produce. Anybody can get the benefit of the combined best judgment by simply accepting the prices set by the market".

Analysts, especially those employed by advisory and management companies, obviously disagree with Wallich. Rinfret [3] said, "In the market economy we live in, the ultimate test of anything is what the market will pay. The market pays for investment advice because investment advice is worth paying for." The vast number of services, especially in America, gives testimony to Rinfret's comments. However, the success of investment services may be the result of investors' eternal hopes of earning spectacular returns, irrational though such hopes may be in the light of all the evidence to date.

The fundamentalists argue that there are not sufficient intelligent analysts to make the market efficient and that information is not incorporated in share prices immediately. It has been pointed out that the London Stock Market is less subjected to

investment research than, say, the U.S.A. where much of the statistical evidence on the "efficiency" of the stock market has come from.

The random walk model says that successive one period price differences are independent, that a series of price changes has no memory and that past history cannot predict the future in any profitable way. Both the random walk and submartingale models preclude earning returns in excess of a buy and hold policy by using charts and the various trading rules.

Technical analysts defend themselves from criticism coming from academic quarters by saying that the statistical tests employed in supporting the random walk hypothesis are not sophisticated enough and that they, the analysts, use longer time periods for their selection methods.

The research into the efficient markets theory has been conducted along four main lines:

1) *Statistical testing of the dependence of price changes.* Most research, both in the U.S. and the U.K., has revealed some dependence, although there has been no consistency of positive and negative correlations. Such dependencies have been found to be insufficient on which to base profitable trading rules. Spectral analysis techniques, pioneered by Granger and Morgenstern [4], have been used to investigate longer term dependencies but none has been found sufficient to earn profits in excess of a policy of buy and hold. Granger and Morgenstern concluded, "The evidence of 'cycles' obtained in our studies is so weak that 'cyclical investment' is at best only marginally worthwhile. Even this small margin will rapidly disappear as it is being made use of. The extreme weakness of the seasonal components is an example of a cycle which has been practically removed by utilizing the opportunities it seemed to offer."

2) *Testing the various trading rules used by chartists and technical analysts.* None of the research has shown that any of the technical rules investigated could consistently beat a buy and hold policy. Jensen and Benington [5], in testing and refuting a claim by Levy [6] that the "relative strength" rule could outperform the market, said ". . . given enough com-

puter time, we are sure that we can find a mechanical trading rule which 'works' on a table of random numbers—provided of course that we are allowed to test the rule on the same table of numbers which we used to discover the rule. We realize of course that the rule would prove useless on any other table of random numbers, and this is exactly the issue with Levy's results."

3) *Testing the ability of published portfolios to outperform the market average.* The majority of such research has been undertaken in the U.S.A. It was found that most funds fared worse than the market index and there was no consistency of success from one year to the next, showing that no one set of analysts could consistently evaluate information better and quicker. Jensen [7] found that even when loading and expense charges were added back the majority of mutual funds failed to match the market index. Louis [8] showed that most mutual funds would have done better most of the time had they not traded but simply held the portfolio that they started with, thus showing that active management detracted from the initial selections. Sharpe [9] in a study of mutual funds found that good performance was associated with low expense ratios (of which research costs formed a large part). The monthly magazine *Money Management* publishes statistical information on unit trusts in the U.K. In the February 1971 edition it gave a long-term performance table for unit trusts which showed that in the seven years to the end of 1970, 27 of the 51 trusts operating throughout that period failed to do as well as the F.T. All Share Index. The magazine also gives current year performances of unit trusts and again the majority do not match the F.T.A. Index, although such shortfall may well disappear if costs were added back.

4) *Testing whether share prices instantaneously and accurately adjust to new information.* Such tests have included research on the information content of scrip and rights issues, annual and quarterly earnings and dividend announcements, bank rate changes, ex-dividend price behaviour, sales and production figures and secondary stock issues (large underwritten sale of stock by institutions). Practically all the research has shown that share prices adequately and correctly adjust to new information in a very short period of time. Under and over adjustment was found to exist but was not systematic enough to earn profits from.

SHARE RECOMMENDATIONS

A study was made of portfolios run by John Davis in *The Observer*, John Coyne in *The Guardian*, *Moodies Review* and Mr. Bearbull of the *Investors Chronicle*, over varying periods to 30 June 1970. The aim was threefold:

1) to assess whether investors following recommendations from papers and journals could increase their starting capital and outperform the market index.

2) to see whether the information content of recommendations was immediately reflected in the share price.

3) to see if there are any reasons for the varying performances of the analysts.

The graphs of the individual portfolios show the published value per the analyst and the performance using the day after recommendation prices (the average mark was taken). Both the *Sunday Observer* and *The Guardian* claim to have beaten the F.T.A. Index by a handsome margin and the latter has also substantially increased its starting capital. However, when the day after recommendation prices are used the margins are reduced considerably with only *The Guardian* portfolio having kept investors' starting capital intact.[2] It must be noted, however, that the research ended in a major bear market; the analysts may well argue that an increase on starting capital is not the relevant yardstick (investors would no doubt disagree!).

The results indicated that *The Observer* and *The Guardian* had a great influence on their readers with the initial mark up by the jobbers reaching over 50% in some cases. The shares recommended by these two newspapers were usually quite small in equity

---

[2] Increase on starting capital is not a fair inter-portfolio comparison as the various funds were started at differing dates.

capitalization terms and were probably not analysed to any great extent by professional analysts. Thus it was possible for such shares to be undervalued and, because of the small and often tightly held equity capital, the small but consistent demand from private investors would be sufficient to move the share price substantially.

Investors following recommendations, especially those of *The Observer* and *The Guardian*, usually found that by the next trading day the price of the share had risen, often to the intrinsic value estimated by the analyst. The jobbers, who make the initial markups, are influenced partly by the analysts' reasons for the recommended share and partly by

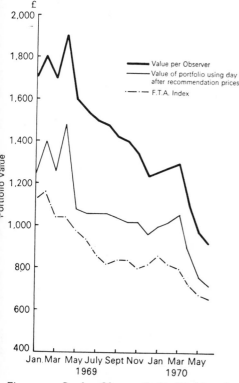

Figure 1: Sunday Observer Go-Go Fund (starting capital 25 February 1967 = £1,000)

the demand they expect from investors. The price rise by the first trading day often takes all the upside potential of the share so the investor has bought a correctly priced security with no expectation of a future price rise. Because of this the value of an investor's portfolio following *The Observer* and *The Guardian* recommendations may well be more correlated with the F.T.A. Index than with the values published by the two newspapers.

John Davis's "go-go" fund was started in February 1967 and did very well in the bull market that existed until the beginning of 1969. Investors following his recommendations would have made useful profits in excess of the F.T.A. Index: most of these profits would have been earned in the earlier part of the period before John Davis's ability was fully recognized. Since February 1969 the portfolio has fallen sharply in line with the market and investors following the share selections have fared similarly. Using the day after recommendation prices investors would have lost around 28% of their starting capital by June 1970. Figure 1 shows the performance of the fund since January 1969.

John Coyne's portfolio was started in October 1969 and by the end of June 1970 the fund showed a significant increase of over 35% on starting capital which is very impressive in such a poor market. However, when the prices ruling on the day after recommendation were used, investors would have just about maintained their starting capital.[3] During the early part of the portfolio's existence the initial markups, while being considerable, by no means took all the upside potential from the recommendations. Jobbers were not at that time fully discounting Coyne's ability and influence. Figure 2 shows the performance of the portfolio over the period investigated.

Mr. Bearbull began his portfolio in July 1967 and it was terminated in June 1970. The object was "to beat the Ordinary Share indices by as wide a margin as possible, taking advantage of any special situation

[3] In November 1970 Coyne estimated that the average markup placed by jobbers on his recommendations was around 11%. He arrived at this figure by taking the Wednesday after recommendation price and was the average of the markups over the 14 months to the end of November 1970.

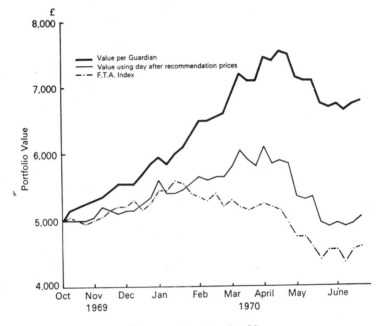

Figure 2: *Guardian Portfolio*

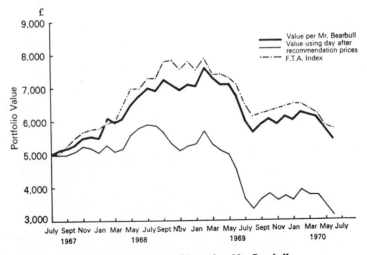

Figure 3: *Investors Chronicle—Mr. Bearbull*

which comes to my knowledge". His performance has certainly not had the success of *The Observer* and *The Guardian* portfolios: the value of his portfolio has, in fact, been highly correlated with the F.T.A. Index (correlation coefficient ·80). Figure 3 shows the performance over the portfolio's existence. Using the day after recommendation prices an investor would have lost around 30% of his starting capital (Mr. Bearbull started with £5,000 in July 1967.) The initial markups of his selections varied considerably: many of the more recent recommendations have barely moved after publication. This was possibly due to the fact that readers were not buying the shares as they had made little or no profit from the previous recommendations and because of the bear market.

Moodies Services Ltd. issues a weekly review which analyses a certain sector of shares and also runs recommended portfolios. Two such portfolios, one composed of financial stocks, the other "recovery" stocks, were investigated from their birth in January 1969 to June 1970. The two portfolios started with capitals of £10,000 each and were fully invested from the start. Very few alterations were made to the initial selection of the "recovery" portfolio and none at all to the financial. The portfolios managed to beat the market index over the period investigated but both lost 30% of their starting capital (see Figure 4). If the *Review* claims success in beating the F.T.A. Index it can certainly claim no laurels on market timing, starting when the market was just about to reach its highest ever peak then to decline into a major bear market. The recommendations of both portfolios had no effect on share prices. The reasons for this could be largely attributable to the following:

1) the shares selected tended to be well known and to have been well analysed by the city institutions.
2) the funds were fully invested from the start in ten stocks. Few investors would have sufficient resources to invest in all selections and therefore the weight of investors' money was spread between the ten stocks.
3) Few alterations were made to the portfolio and it was reviewed irregularly with little comment. This

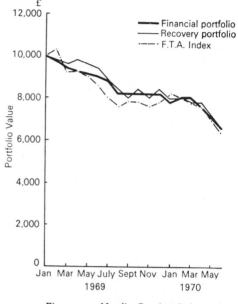

Figure 4: Moodies Services Ltd.

sort of presentation fails to create or to keep the interest of investors. John Davis of *The Observer* ran a number of funds other than the "go-go" portfolio: these other portfolios were similar to the *Moodies Review* portfolios in that they were reviewed irregularly and without alteration. Like the portfolios run by *Moodies Review* the recommendations had little effect on share prices.

The policies of the successful portfolios could be characterized by:

a) selecting shares which have small equity capitalizations, where the demand from private investors can force a price up considerably. The analysts rely on readers to push the price of a share up and so give the published portfolio a good performance. It is doubtful if the selected shares, even if achieving the forecasted results, would have risen so much without the recommendation.

b) publishing the portfolios regularly and reviewing the constituent shares consistently.

c) giving forecasts of earnings and asset values, and giving a price or range of prices which the analyst believes the share to be worth. The more information given on a company the more it seemed to attract investors.

Once an analyst has gained a reputation it becomes very difficult for investors following the recommendations to profit—the initial mark-ups usually leave the share price at the intrinsic price suggested.

The share recommendations made by Coyne and Davis usually contained a fair amount of information, much of which was new. Information was often given of current and near future trading prospects which were in many cases gained from interviews with company officials. Some recommendations gave current asset values when the company had large property interests and often gave price limits up to which shares should be bought.

A criticism often levelled at analysts who publish their recommendations is that when they have gained reputations they can recommend almost any share and be sure of the price moving up very quickly owing to readers following their advice; the analysts could be fairly certain of making a lot of money if they invested in the shares they recommend. In a report on Investment Services to the U.S. Congress House Committee on Interstate and Foreign Commerce it was stated, "One of the publisher's two regular subscription services, which regularly recommended purchases of securities, had a paid circulation of 5,000 and in addition was distributed free on some occasions to as many as 100,000 non-subscribers. During a nine-month period in 1960 the publisher traded in securities which it recommended, purchasing shortly before the recommendation and selling shortly after the publication of the recommendation, without disclosing the facts to its subscribers. . . . In one instance the publication compared two companies in the same industry. As to one where the publisher had a short position, it suggested the stock had reached its peak, while in the other, where it held call options, it recommended purchase." In an investigation of the price behaviour of shares

recommended by Davis, Coyne and Mr. Bearbull no evidence was found of any violent price fluctuations or any heavy buying prior to publication.

The *Money Which* magazine of September 1968 reported a survey of New Year share recommendations by six papers—*Financial Times, Investors Chronicle, Sunday Express, Sunday Telegraph, Investors Chronicle Newsletter* and the *Sunday Times.* The object of the investigation, which was titled "Share Tipsters", was to determine how good the publications' advice was. £100 was allotted to each recommendation at 1 January 1967 and the results are shown below. No account was taken of dividends brokerage fees or capital gains tax.

Average performance based on 1,500 randomly selected shares 1967	127
Average performance of recommendations 1967	155
Average performance of recommendations using day after recommendation price	151

The performance of the 1966 recommendations.

Average performance based on 1,500 shares	92
Average performance of recommendations	99

The 1967 recommendations were very successful but the returns for 1966, although beating the contrived index, showed a loss on the opening capital. The investigation showed no one paper gave consistently above-average performance for all recommendations. A surprising feature of the survey was that the *I.C. Newsletter*'s "riskier portfolio" had the best performance in the bear market and the worst in the bull market. The report said that the order of merit can be expected to change from year to year "for luck will clearly play a part in the success of their predictions. The tipsters' average performance will depend very much on just how good are the good shares he happens to pick".

Money Which concluded that the risks the investor takes in choosing from the various selections (it is doubtful if they have the resources to buy all the recommendations) are not much less than if the investor had picked the shares entirely on his own.

In the U.S.A., Ferber and Cowles have both in-

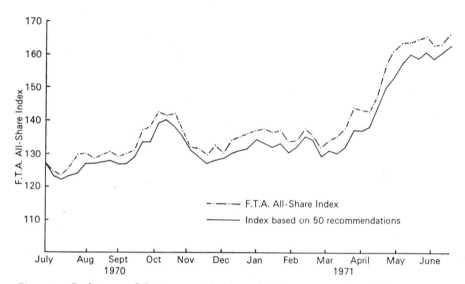

Figure 5: Performance of share recommendations made by investment analysts during June 1970

vestigated the effect investment services have on share prices. Ferber's [10] research centred on the effect four widely distributed market services (Investors' Service, Standard and Poor's, United Business Service and Value Line) had on share prices in 1953. He found there was a small but statistically significant shift in the price of the stocks in the direction that would be expected, but at the same time the magnitude of the effect was not substantial. Ferber found that the general pattern of the recommended stocks during the first week after issuance of the recommendations appears to be a relatively sharp price increase in the selected stocks in the first day, a decline for a day or two thereafter, and then another, though secondary, upsurge. The change apparently persisted, there being no evidence of a movement in the opposite direction for at least four weeks.

Cowles [11] investigated the ability of 11 leading financial periodicals and services to forecast the course of the stock market during the period June 1928 to July 1943. He concluded that there was no evidence of superior performance from the services.

It should be noted that the period under investigation was one of the longest in which stock prices failed to move into new ground.

These American studies show a distinct lack of success for stock market forecasting services. A strict comparison with the investigation into the recommendations of analysts in the U.K. is not tenable owing to differences in time periods and the type of forecasting. However, it would appear that British journals and papers have more influence on share prices than their American counterparts, probably because smallish British companies are less frequently analysed. No analyst appears to be able significantly to affect the share price of large companies.

A further study of share recommendations in the U.K. was made by investigating the performances of shares recommended by weekly newspapers, journals and stockbrokers' reports between June 1969 and June 1970. A total of 1,100 different recommendations were taken and analysed. A chi-square test was conducted on the data, the hypothesis being that there was little difference between the various

157

analysts. This was was confirmed with a chi-square value of 23·0 for 21 degrees of freedom.

Figure 5 shows the performance of 50 shares recommended during June 1970 measured against the F.T.A. Index for the period July 1970 to June 1971. The recommendations were taken from newspapers and stockbrokers' research material. As can be seen the recommended stocks were highly correlated with the index (correlation coefficient was 0·89) and in fact had a slightly poorer performance throughout the year. The recommended shares would probably have not done as well as a random selection. A Kolmogorov-Smirnov one-sample test was used on the above data and the hypothesis that the recommended securities had not done as well as the market index was confirmed. No account was taken of dividends or brokerage expenses and the prices taken were those used in the recommendations.

Drawbacks encountered to the above research were:

1) the recommended shares were assumed to be kept right through the period. Analysts may argue that a particular selection of theirs should have been sold during the period—however no sale advice was given on the shares recommended.
2) no difference was attached to recommendations that had large write-ups and those that consisted only of a couple of sentences. From an examination of recommendations there was no reason to believe that the voluminous reports on companies produced by stockbrokers were any better at selecting shares than the two- or three-line recommendations of some newspapers.

The above recommendations did not appear to have any initial effect on share prices. This may be accounted for by the number of very large, well analysed shares that were selected and the lack of prior success of the particular analysts.

CONCLUSION

This investigation of share recommendations in the U.K. has produced no evidence against the efficient market hypothesis. Specifically, the information content of newspaper recommendations appeared to be fully incorporated in share prices almost immediately. Although there are fewer analysts in Britain there still seem to be sufficient numbers to make the market efficient for all but the smallest shares.

Because analysts cannot on average beat the market index does not mean they are otiose, for, as Wallich [2] pointed out, the proper allocation of scarce capital resources requires securities to be correctly priced. The newspaper analysts in selecting a share can be said to be performing a socially useful function by correctly pricing the shares of smallish companies. Incorrect pricing will lead to a non-optimal economy and will increase risk with the consequent lack of confidence in equity investment by the public. With new information coming out daily, investment analysts are needed to interpret the knowledge in share prices and this they have done well enough to call the market efficient.

REFERENCES

[1] Fama, E., "Efficient Capital Markets: A Review of Theory and Empirical Work", *Journal of Finance*, May 1970.
[2] Wallich, H.C., "What Does the Random Walk Hypothesis Mean to Security Analysts?" *Financial Analysts Journal*, March/April 1968.
[3] Rinfret, P.A., "Investment Managers Are Worth Their Keep", *Financial Analysts Journal*, March/April 1968.
[4] Granger, C.W.J. and Morgenstern, O., "Spectral Analysis of New York Stock Market Prices", *Kyklos* 16, 1963.
[5] Jensen, M.C. and Benington, G.A., "Random Walks and Technical Theories: Some Additional Evidence", *Journal of Finance*, May 1970.
[6] Levy, R.A., "Random Walks: Reality or Myth—Reply", *Financial Analysts Journal*, January/February 1968.
[7] Jensen, M.C., "The Performance of Mutual Funds in the Period 1945–64", *Journal of Finance*, May 1968.
[8] Louis, A.M.M., "Those Go-Go Funds May be Going Nowhere", *Fortune*, November 1967.
[9] Sharpe, W.F., "Mutual Fund Performance", *Journal of Business*, January 1966.
[10] Ferber, R., "Short-Run Effects of Stock Market Services on Stock Prices", *Journal of Finance*, March 1958.
[11] Cowles, A., "Stock Market Forecasting", *Econometrica*, July/October 1944.

THE INFORMATION CONTENT OF LARGE INVESTMENT HOLDINGS

MICHAEL FIRTH*

SECTION 33 of the Companies Act of 1967 contains provisions relating to the disclosure of the acquisition and disposal of shares by an investor carrying unrestricted voting rights in a company. When an investor makes a purchase such that he becomes the owner of 10 per cent or more of the equity shares of a company, he must notify the company of the fact within fourteen days beginning with the day following the occurrence. The investor must disclose the percentage of shares held and any addition or reduction in this stake must also be disclosed within fourteen days after the transaction. The Stock Exchange requires companies who have a quotation to inform the Exchange of any notification received regarding an investor's 10 per cent or more holding.

The object of such disclosure requirements is to give more information to the Directors of the company being invested in, their shareholders and the investing community as a whole. Knowledge of an investment holding being built up may indicate a possible takeover approach,[1] or the exercise of some managerial or shareholder influence by the investor. Additionally, the acquisition of a 10 per cent stake implies confidence in the share price potential and thus the existing and potential investors may use this as one indicator in their own decision making. No empirical study of the information content of such announcements has been made and thus the usefulness of the Companies Act provisions has not been tested. The selection of the 10 per cent level for disclosure was fairly arbitrary and if investors attach substantial importance to such news it implies that some lesser disclosure level would also provide useful information. This has been supported by the press and by companies themselves and some changes in the legislation are therefore likely in any new Companies Act.[2]

The research reported in this paper investigates the impact of the announcement of 10 per cent holdings having been made in quoted companies. It examines the impact of the building up of stakes on share prices, the initial reaction of investors to the news of large investment holdings, the longer term investor behaviour and whether the information content of the announcements has been correctly appraised by the market.

* University of Stirling, Scotland. The author wishes to acknowledge the data provided by Hoare & Co., Govett. Additionally, the paper has benefited from the advice of the referee, George Benston.

1. Prior to the Companies Act provisions the investing company could acquire a 49 per cent holding in a company and then mount a 'surprise bid.'

2. Changes advocated include the lowering of the disclosure level, reducing the notification time and the disclosure of the beneficial owners of shares held in nominee names.

I. PRIOR RESEARCH FINDINGS

The only research to date on the impact of large investment stakes on share prices has come from the U.S.A. Whilst the institutional and disclosure requirements in America are different from those in the U.K., the studies do provide useful reference points for the current research. The Securities and Exchange Commission (S.E.C.) and the New York Stock Exchange require disclosure and publish statistics relating to purchases and sales of large blocks of stocks and of secondary distributions. This information has provided the data for a number of studies concerned with the information content and the price behaviour attendant upon large share deals. Guthman and Bakay conducted an early study into the share price performance of the sales of large blocks of stocks in the period 1949 to 1964. They found there was, on average, a slight price decline associated with a block sale which pointed to "a very mild amount of pressure upon market price by the offering" [5]. In the case of public utilities the prices tended to recover whilst those of industrial companies drifted lower. After allowing for transaction costs, the authors were unable to construct any profitable investment strategies based upon the block sales. Guthman and Bakay did not explicitly recognise the 'information content' of the news and attributed all the price changes to inducements that were needed to attract buyers. Kraus and Stoll conducted a later study into block transactions made on the New York Stock Exchange during the period July 1968 to September 1969 [7]. They differentiated between 'purchase' and 'sales' influences by looking at whether the transaction was made at an above market price (purchase pressure) or below market price (sales pressure). The authors found that 'purchase' blocks had an information impact and that investors used this in their valuation of shares. For 'sales' blocks, however, they suggested that the price declines associated with them were a result of the sellers accepting lower prices so as to obtain immediate liquidity—the prices were found to recover quickly after the transaction therefore implying no fundamental change in the value of the company. Kraus and Stoll did not find any profitable mechanical investment strategy based on the news of a block trade—except if investors had advance knowledge of such. They suggested, however, that the large scale transactions of some institutions may have an unsettling influence on the stock market. Grier and Albin undertook a study of block transactions during a similar time period to that used by Kraus and Stoll [4]. They constructed an investment strategy based on buying securities on the announcement of a block transaction and classified these by prior price performance. Although the strategy produced small profits these were insufficient to cover the transaction costs associated with the strategy.

Scholes' study of secondary issues made in the period 1947 to 1965 found that the New York Stock Exchange was 'efficient' in its pricing of securities and that no consistent profit opportunities were available unless the investor has advance knowledge [8]. He suggests that the small negative price reaction associated with a secondary is more due to the 'information' that an investor is wanting to sell (that this investor may have inside knowledge) rather than any 'selling pressure.' This is based partly on the finding that the percentage size of the deal was not related to the share price performance. Scholes found that companies did not suffer significantly from having large scale investors as shareholders and concluded ''It is apparent from the analysis that the distribution of a large block of a corporation's stock by a holding company will not have a long-run depressing effect on share prices.''

These studies have not derived any consistent conclusions as to whether the price adjustment on a large block sale is due to the information content of the news or to selling pressures. Thus there is no unanimity in the findings for subsequent price performance although no profitable investment strategies have been found. Much less research has been carried out on purchases of large blocks, which is the main interest of this paper, but the evidence from Kraus and Stoll suggests that this does tend to have an 'information' influence for the intrinsic value of shares.

II. POPULATION AND METHODOLOGY

The population used in this study was of all announcements made during 1973 of an investment holding of 10 per cent or over having been built up in a quoted company. This excluded cases when merger and acquisition announcements were made at the same time as the declaration of a 10 per cent holding. Also excluded were cases when the company being invested in announced earnings and dividends figures, paid dividends or had an Annual General Meeting during the period within 6 weeks on both sides of the 10 per cent investment holding announcement. The population total came to 85 and Table 1 summarises the financial characteristics of the companies involved. Data relating to subsequent additions or reductions to the 10 per cent or over holding was also collected.

The acquirer of a stake was classified into either a 'trade investment' category or an 'investment bank' category: this necessarily involved subjective judgment. The reasoning behind this analysis was that an 'investment bank' stake is often short term and may indicate takeover possibilities. Thus greater price variability is hypothesised for 'investment bank' stakes. In deciding the categorisation the main criterion was whether the investor was in the same industry as the company being invested in: this was a trade investment, others being investment bank stakes. The number of trade investment stakes came to 38; the remainder, 47, being 'investment bank' stakes.

The criterion used to assess the impact of a 10 per cent stake announcement was to measure the difference between the actual share price and what the share price would have been if there had been no such announcement. This latter expected price is given by a market model of the form suggested by Sharpe [9]; that is

$$R_{jt} = a_j + B_j I_t + u_{jt}$$

where R_{jt} = return for period t on the jth security

TABLE 1
SUMMARY STATISTICS OF POPULATION

	Market Capitalisation (£millions)
.00- .50	4
.51- 1.00	11
1.01- 2.00	18
2.01- 5.00	20
5.01-10.00	15
10.01-25.00	13
>25.00	4
Mean	£7.74 million
Standard Deviation	£5.62 million

	Percentage Size of Deal*
10	16
10.1-15.0	29
15.1-20.0	14
20.1-25.0	12
25.1-30.0	14
Mean	18.05%
Standard Deviation	9.69%

* Number of shares acquired expressed as a percentage of the equity capital of the company being invested in.

RELATIVE PRICE EARNINGS RATIO AND ASSET VALUE

	P.E.R.[1]	Asset Value[2]
No Entry	8*	
.00- .50	1	35
.51- .70	10	14
.71- .80	10	10
.81- .90	5	4
.91- .95	3	3
.96-1.00	5	5
1.01-1.05	2	
1.06-1.10	3	1
1.11-1.20	8	4
1.21-1.30	6	3
1.31-1.50	4	3
>1.50	20	3
Mean	1.23	0.71
Standard Deviation	0.62	0.41

* Companies who were making losses.
[1] Price earnings ratio of company ÷ price earnings ratio of the appropriate Financial Times – Actuaries Industrial Index.
[2] Net asset value of company ÷ share price immediately prior to announcement.
The latest price earnings ratios and asset values for the companies were used.

I_t = average return for period t on all shares in the stock exchange or some representative index.

a_j and B_j are parameters that vary from security to security

u_{jt} = the random disturbance term for period t. The u_{jt} term is assumed to satisfy the usual requirements of a linear regression model.

Thus share prices are expressed in a linear relationship to the market index. The error term, u_{jt}, therefore includes all the other factors which influence prices, one of which will be any 'information' content contained in the news of large share stakes.

The market model has been used extensively in performance appraisal and formed the research methodology of the previously mentioned works of Kraus and Stoll and Scholes. Away from major fundamental news such as dividend and earnings announcements, the market index, reflecting investors' changing values for companies as a whole, is the major determinant of price changes.[3]

Thus away from the influence of financial performance statistics and prospects it is hypothesised that the market factor will account for virtually all of the change in share prices. The error term will therefore have a mean of zero. If the announcement of a large holding having been built up is used by investors to re-evaluate the price of shares, then the error term should move significantly away from zero. This study uses the measurements of the u_{jt}'s to derive hypotheses on the 'information' content of large share stake announcements.

The data used for deriving the regression coefficients for each company comprised the latest 57 4-week recordings (taken on Wednesdays) for proportionate price changes and index changes. The index used was the Hoare & Co. Govett Index. This is calculated daily from 1,130 stock prices and is weighted by the number of shares in issue. The index is adjusted for stock splits and scrip issues but no adjustment is made for dividends. A better explanatory model was achieved by ignoring the a's[4] and by adjusting the least squares estimates of the B's (the corrected version designated $\hat{\beta}^*$). The adjustment of the beta coefficients and the testing of the explanatory and predictive ability of the model is described by Cunningham [2] and [3]. The adjustment involved regressing the least squares estimates toward the mean,[5] thus

$$\hat{\beta}^* = b + (\hat{\beta} - b)\left(\frac{\text{Var b}}{\text{Var b} + \text{Var } \hat{\beta}}\right)$$

where

b = mean of true betas

Var b = variance of true betas

---

3. See King [6].

4. These were found to be virtually zero for all stocks. Other studies have similarly found the alpha term to be nil.

5. A method used by Blume [1].

$\hat{\beta}$ = least squares estimate of beta for a stock

Var $\hat{\beta}$ = variance of $\hat{\beta}$

For the current study the mean (b) and variance (Var b) of the true betas were taken as 1.00 and 0.07 respectively; a study of 807 stocks for three separate three year periods showed the mean and variance of the true betas to be (.987, .077), (.891, .063) and (1.066, .069). The ordinary least squares estimates of the $\hat{\beta}$'s and the associated variance were then substituted into the above formula to obtain the better forecasts of the true betas, $\hat{\beta}^*$. The price predicted by the market model is thus $\beta_j^* I_t$.

The predicted share prices as given by the model were compared against the actual daily closing prices and the prediction error, or residual, u_{jt}, computed for a period 30 days prior to the announcement to 30 days after the announcement. The prediction error is notationally described as follows

$$u_{jt} = AR_{jt} - \beta_j^* I_t.$$

where AR_{jt} is the actual proportionate change in share price in time period t and the $\beta_j^* I_t$ term is the price predicted by the market model. I_t is the actual proportionate change in the index.

III. RESULTS

Table 2 shows the cross-sectional average of the prediction errors of each share for each day relative to the day of the announcement. This is computed thus

$$u_D = \frac{1}{N} \sum_{j=1}^{N} u_{j,D}$$

TABLE 2
DAILY ANALYSIS OF PREDICTION ERRORS

Day	Average Prediction Error %	Standard Deviation	Percentage Positive	Cumulative Movement in Average Prediction Error from Day −30%
−30	0.327	0.060	55	.327
−29	0.251	0.041	53	.579
−28	0.212	0.021	54	.792
−27	0.254	0.009	59	1.048
−26	0.118	0.007	50	1.167
−25	−0.012	0.008	50	1.155
−24	−0.191	0.006	47	.964
−23	0.362	0.006	58	1.329
−22	0.212	0.007	54	1.544
−21	−0.090	0.012	53	1.452
−20	0.410	0.017	56	1.868
−19	0.262	0.001	55	2.135

TABLE 2 (*Continued*)

Day	Average Prediction Error %	Standard Deviation	Percentage Positive	Cumulative Movement in Average Prediction Error from Day −30%
−18	0.310	0.027	53	2.452
−17	0.090	0.016	53	2.544
−16	0.084	0.007	52	2.630
−15	−0.197	0.010	51	2.431
−14	0.253	0.021	52	2.690
−13	0.413	0.034	54	3.114
−12	0.017	0.007	53	3.132
−11	−0.216	0.006	51	2.910
−10	−0.098	0.012	50	2.803
− 9	0.163	0.014	51	2.971
− 8	−0.274	0.005	48	2.692
− 7	0.417	0.017	54	3.120
− 6	0.563	0.051	54	3.701
− 5	0.612	0.072	58	4.336
− 4	0.204	0.061	56	4.549
− 3	0.210	0.072	57	4.769
− 2	0.117	0.045	56	4.892
− 1	−0.072	0.049	54	4.819
0	0.061	0.072	53	4.880
1	3.301	1.185	94	8.342
2	0.012	0.172	51	8.354
3	−0.612	0.179	43	7.731
4	−0.254	0.091	42	7.473
5	0.217	0.161	47	7.706
6	0.019	0.254	50	7.729
7	−0.107	0.094	51	7.614
8	−0.245	0.087	51	7.351
9	0.261	0.016	51	7.631
10	−0.274	0.017	48	7.336
11	−0.272	0.016	47	7.044
12	−0.317	0.007	42	6.705
13	−0.101	0.021	48	6.597
14	0.097	0.016	49	6.700
15	0.002	0.017	48	6.703
16	−0.202	0.034	47	6.588
17	0.090	0.041	51	6.684
18	−0.219	0.032	47	6.450
19	0.066	0.002	51	6.520
20	−0.193	0.006	50	6.315
21	−0.141	0.007	47	6.165
22	−0.115	0.008	48	6.043
23	0.095	0.010	49	6.144
24	0.034	0.021	51	6.180
25	−0.006	0.026	50	6.172
26	0.087	0.024	50	6.264
27	−0.002	0.009	51	6.262
28	−0.016	0.003	48	6.245
29	0.016	0.008	49	6.262
30	−0.017	0.001	51	6.243

where the average residual u_D for day D, relative to the 'news' day (D = 1) is computed.[6] $j = 1 \ldots N$, is the number of shares in the sample. The table also gives the cumulative effects of the residuals in the days surrounding the announcement. The cumulative prediction error is given as

$$U_D = \frac{1}{N} \sum_{j=1}^{N} \left[\prod_{d-30}^{M} (100 + u_{jd}) - 100 \right]$$

This shows the movement in the prediction errors of the actual prices from those computed from the normal relationship to market movements from 30 days prior to the announcement day up to 30 days after (M taking the value $D-30, -29, -28 \ldots +29, +30$).

The table and Diagram 1 show clearly that there is a preponderance of quite significant positive residuals from thirty days prior to the announcement, to that date. The number of days on which the average residuals are positive outweighs those that show negative prediction errors by nearly three to one. The percentage of the population showing positive returns is generally over 50 per cent during this period. Diagram 2 shows the cumulative residuals calculated from the change in price from day -30. This shows a steady build up in price prior to the announcement which suggests either information leakage or the perhaps more likely explanation that the investing institution, once realizing its holding is to be disclosed, decides to build up its stake as quickly as possible prior to releasing the information.[7] Table 1 showed that the mean size of the investment stake to be 18 per cent and this lends some support to the contention that the price behaviour in the period prior to the announcement is influenced by investing companies rapidly increasing their stakes. The table and diagram 1 clearly show the impact of the announcement on share prices: there is an average rise in share prices over those expected of 3.3 per cent and 94 per cent of the population showed gains. The gains experienced during the day of announcement (d_1) were far in excess of any of the other residuals and this is due to the market incorporating the 'intrinsic value' information of the announcement. An examination of the number of bargains marked in the day of the announcement showed a marked increase over previous levels. Although the recording of bargains is an imperfect method of measuring investor activity the increases were so consistent that it would appear that the announcement does lead to greater investment interest and business. The degree of variability of share price returns also heightens during the initial adjustment of values thus representing some large increases, some very small.

The average residuals show a fair level of activity in days 2 to 7 and the standard deviations remain high. Thereafter the residuals settle down and towards the end of the period they approach a mean of zero. The residuals

6. The actual announcement takes place during day 1; the closing price on day 1 therefore reflects the information in this announcement.

7. Once a company has obtained a stake of 10 per cent it has fourteen days within which to notify that company. In this fourteen days they may purchase more shares at a price which does not reflect the 'information content' of the announcement. This is a likely description of the investment policies of investment bankers.

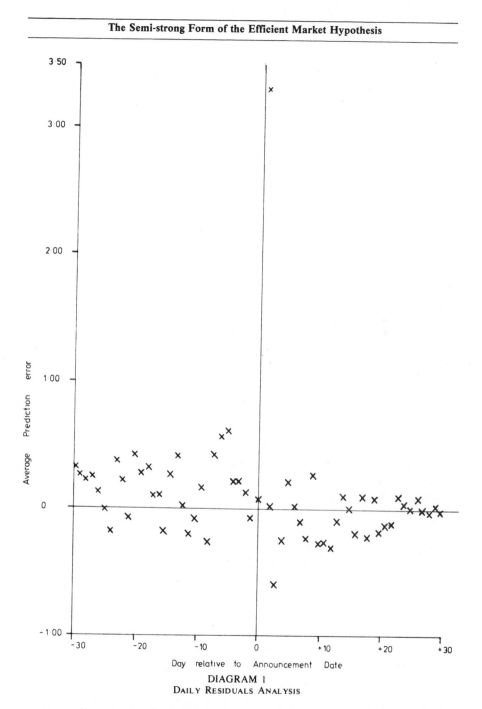

DIAGRAM 1
DAILY RESIDUALS ANALYSIS

are generally negative during the twenty or so days after the announcement and this reduction in prices is shown in Diagram 2. Beyond day 20 the prices settle down to the normal market relationship. The price adjustments indicate that the initial reaction to the news is too optimistic. This over

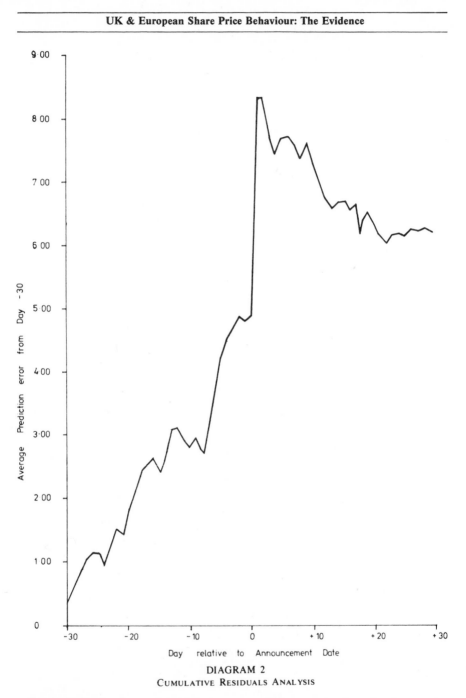

DIAGRAM 2
CUMULATIVE RESIDUALS ANALYSIS

adjustment is in the order of 2 per cent. This may be largely due to the withdrawal of the 10 per cent holder from the market and thus the withdrawal of considerable purchasing pressure.

Diagram 2 may be interpreted as showing that the '10 per cent holder' makes substantial purchases before the announcement day, as he realizes knowledge of his stake will increase prices, such that on average share prices stand nearly 5 per cent higher than the normal relationship with the market would suggest. Upon the announcement, investors' changing views of the company and their buying power produces an immediate price rise in the order of 3 to 4 per cent. Thereafter the '10 per cent holder' leaves the market and this reduction in buying volume and any over valuation of the 'news' causes a 1 to 2 per cent fall in prices. After about twenty days the share prices settle down to their predicted values. Over the whole period the prices have on average increased by 6 per cent and this may be interpreted as the 'information impact' i.e. the mean of investors' changed views as regards takeovers, bid premiums and the earnings and dividend prospects of the company. This mean increase had a wide dispersion, however, with over 10 per cent of the population showing positive prediction errors from day -30 to day $+30$ of 20 per cent or over.

The residual's analysis was carried back earlier than day -30 but the recordings clustered around zero and the cumulative average prediction errors were virtually zero. Thus there were no abnormal returns before day -30 indicating little 'buying pressure' or little leakage of news as regards substantial investment stakes. The share prices for each company at a date six months prior to the announcement were extracted. The prediction errors between this date and day -30 averaged $+5$ per cent showing that there was an above average rate of return being earned in this period: this is likely to be the result of a long but steady acquisition of a stake.[8]

Table 2 showed the average prediction errors computed from the market model and the positive impact of the announcement is very significant. Within this average, however, there may be subgroups which have a substantially different performance. The particular groupings which may have an impact include the relative price-earnings ratio, the relative asset values, the percentage size of the deal, the market capitalization and whether the purchaser had been classified as an investment bank or not.[9] Poor price-earnings ratios and asset value relatives (i.e. under 1.00) may, for instance, indicate poor financial performance by the company and that the acquirer of the stake has takeover ambitions where they hope to increase the return on assets employed. If this is the case, the bid may come at a substantially higher price (especially if the percentage holding of the acquirer is none too high. If the percentage acquired is say 40 per cent this may imply that the bidder will not have to pay much of a premium over the existing price). The percentage size of the acquirer's holding may, by itself, have implications for prices. A large holding probably implies a future bid as few investors would be prepared to own, say, 40 per cent of a company without having a voice in the management of that firm. Although as hypothesized before, the bid pre-

8. During this five month period most companies also published interim or final results which will have influenced prices.
9. The statistics are as computed in Table 1.

mium may be less, it may be more certain. An investment stake acquired by an 'investment bank' may indicate a more active share price as these investors are typically bidders or short-term holders. Thus the market may attach a premium to an announcement where the acquirer is an 'investment bank.'

To measure the importance of these factors a linear model was developed with the least squares multiple regression of the prediction residuals and measures of market capitalisation (MCAP), categorisation of acquirer (CAT), percentage size of deal (SIZ), asset value divided by share price (AVSP) and relative price-earnings ratio (RPER). The model specification is thus

$$U_{jt} = a + bMCAP + cCAT + dSIZ + eAVSP + fRPER$$

The results for the movement in the cumulative residuals between day 0 and day 7 are shown in Table 3. These dates were used as it was during this period that the greatest price adjustment occurs i.e. the 'information' impact of the announcement. The table shows quite clearly that the factors have little explanatory or predictive value in describing the differences in the abnormal returns between day 0 and day 7. Different equations were tried but all showed low R^2 values and except for equation 2 all revealed nonsignificant F statistics. Significant t-values were obtained for the 'percentage size of stake' factor: thus the higher the percentage of a company owned, which is given in the announcement, the greater the share price increase. The market therefore attached importance to the size of the investment holding. The partial regression coefficients and t-values for the other factors are not significant and investors do not therefore attach any importance to these financial measures.

The equations were also run for the cumulative residuals of other time periods namely day −10 to day 0 and day −30 to day +30. These analyses were undertaken in order to see if there were any significant explanatory factors for either the sharp preannouncement price increases or for the price performance over the whole period surrounding the announcement. The results from these regressions were similar to those of Table 3 with low R^2 values and nonsignificant t-values and F-values.

IV. INVESTMENT STRATEGIES

In order to see whether a successful investment strategy could be based upon buying shares in a company once an announcement has been made a portfolio was constructed which assumed a constant investment (say £1) in each of the population using the price immediately after announcement.[10] These prices were obtained from Extel tapes which give a minute by minute record of the latest quotations.

10. This is equivalent to the product of the residuals averaged over all the population; i.e. Portfolio Performance =

Information Content of Large Investment Holdings

TABLE 3

REGRESSIONS OF SHARE PRICE RESIDUALS* ON MEASURES OF MARKET CAPITALISATION, ACQUIRER, SIZE OF DEAL, ASSET VALUE AND PRICE EARNINGS RELATIVES ($U_{jt} = a + bMCAP + cCAT + dSIZ + eAVSP + fRPER$)

Equation No.	Degrees of Freedom	a	b	c	d	e	f	R^2	d.f.	F Value
1	69	0.8629 (10.88)+	−0.0017 (−1.3017)	0.0212 (0.6418)	0.0054 (2.1845)+	0.0603 (1.4640)	0.0162 (0.5879)	.1299	5,69	2.0595
2	70	0.8764 (11.60)+	−0.0016 (−1.2358)	0.0213 (0.6475)	0.0054 (2.2062)+	0.0675 (1.7222)		.1255	4,70	2.5114
3	71	0.8743 (14.12)+			0.0058 (2.4075)+	0.0677 (1.6600)		.1010	3,71	2.6598
4	72	0.9727 (20.66)+	−0.0017 (−1.3390)		0.0046 (1.8725)		0.0186 (0.3972)	.0783	2,72	3.0584

* The difference between the expected and actual movements in share prices between days 0 and +7.
Top line: Regression coefficient.
Bottom line: t-value.
+ Significant at 0.05 level.
Von Neumann statistic was not significant.

TABLE 4
RETURNS FROM AN INVESTMENT STRATEGY
BASED UPON BUYING IMMEDIATELY
AFTER ANNOUNCEMENT

Period	Mean %	S.D.
Day 1 to 7	−0.67	.58
1 to 14	−1.52	.73
1 to 21	−2.01	.69
1 to 30	−1.94	.70

DISTRIBUTION OF RETURNS

	Day 1 to 7	Day 1 to 30
<.850	3	7
.850- .900	8	8
.901- .920	4	4
.921- .940	6	6
.941- .960	9	12
.961- .980	8	10
.981-1.000	15	5
1.001-1.020	12	11
1.021-1.040	6	3
1.041-1.060	4	2
1.061-1.080	2	3
1.081-1.100	2	3
1.101-1.150	3	7
1.151-1.200		3
>1.200	3	1

Table 4 shows the mean results for holding the shares for various periods and the distribution of percentage profits or losses for holding until day 7 and day 30. These figures do not include any transaction expenses which would be quite significant if an active buying and selling policy around the date of the announcement were adopted.[11] The table shows that without advance knowledge of an announcement the mean returns were negative.

Table 4 also shows the dispersions of the returns from such a strategy over the time periods day $1*(d*_1)$[12] to day 7 (d_7) and day $1*(d*_1)$ to day 30 (d_{30}). There are a fair number of positive returns being made. In order to see if there were any similarities in the companies which earned

$$\frac{1}{N} \sum_{j=1}^{N} \left(\prod_{l=d}^{D} (1 + u_{jd}) \right)$$

This is the index value of £1 invested in equal amounts in each of N shares in the population at date d (the time of announcement) to the end of some future period, D, after allowing for market movement (D = 1, 2, 3 . . . . 29, 30).

11. Buying expenses range from around 2.25 per cent of consideration for small bargains to 1.625 per cent for larger deals. Selling expenses do not involve stamp duty and the total costs are around 1.25 per cent of consideration for small bargains to .625 per cent for larger transactions.

12. The price at day $1*(d*_1)$ is that taken immediately after the announcement; it is not taken at the end of the day as with other price recordings.

specific rates of return, the regression model described earlier was re-run with the prediction errors (d1*/d7) and (d1*/d30) used as the dependent variables. No significant factors explaining the differences in returns were found however. Thus no profitable strategy has been found based on purchasing shares immediately after an announcement has been made.

Besides looking at the impact of an announcement on share prices, analyses were also made of the 'information content' of announcements of additional purchases and of sales in holdings including those which reduced the investment to below 10 per cent. Forty-six cases of extra purchases in 18 companies were studied. The mean increase in share price from the announcement to the prices prevailing immediately after was 2.0 per cent with a range of −1.2 per cent to +5 per cent. The share price performance thereafter was in line with the normal market model relationship. There was a slight positive correlation between the level of price increase and the percentage of additional shares bought. No other financial characteristic seemed to have any impact on the size of the residual and specifically the number of investment holding announcements per particular share had no influence. No profitable investment strategies based on subsequent additions to investment stakes appear to exist.

Only fourteen cases of investment stakes being reduced were recorded and of these eight were reduced to below 10 per cent. In five cases the reductions in stakes were matched by a 'purchase announcement,' thus a large investor was still present and as expected the share prices showed little movement. For the other cases the immediate prediction errors by day 1 were as follows: 0, 0, −0.5, −2.0, −2.25, −2.5, −5.0, −7.0, −8.5 per cent. From day 1 the share price performance of these shares settled down to the predicted levels. Investors therefore interpret sale announcements by decreasing the value of the shares: the takeover probabilities are reduced and the selling institution may have inside information on the prospects of the company.

In the period up to three months after the announcement, there were 10 cases of the invested-in companies being bid for, thus justifying any takeover conclusions drawn from the announcement. The average bid premium over the price prior to announcement was 15 per cent and 12 per cent in the case of the price reigning at day 1: the dispersion of the results from day 1 was from a high of +38 per cent to a low of −10 per cent. Although the recognition of the above cases would have resulted in a very profitable investment rule there appears to be no way of foretelling which of the announcements would be followed by a bid. Thus all shares subject to an 'announcement' would have to be bought and, as shown previously, this proved unprofitable. In examining the share price performance between day 1 and the subsequent bid it was apparent that investors did not have the ability to select the takeover possibilities; whilst the premium from day 1 to the bid terms was 12 per cent, this was also the figure for the percentage increase between the price immediately prior to the bid and the takeover terms.

In five cases the price or average price paid for an investment stake was given. The share prices paid relative to that at day 0 were .85 (.80), .87 (.90), 1.05 (1.05), 1.07 (1.00), 1.10 (1.20). The figures in brackets give the price relatives to day 1. No particular pattern is given by these figures and there is nothing here to suggest any great profits for the buying institution.

V. CONCLUSIONS

The results have shown that the stock market attaches a significantly positive value to announcements of large stakes having been built up in companies. The immediate mean increase is of the order of 3.3 per cent. Price performance subsequent to the day after announcement shows a price reduction of around 2 per cent over the period to 20 days after the announcement; thereafter price behaviour returns to the normal linear relationship to the market index. This small price reduction suggests, of course, that investors' initial reaction to the news is too optimistic. These negative returns are quite small however and last for only 20 days at the most; this seems too small a discrepancy to reject the efficient market hypothesis. No profitable trading rules based on the announcements or on any of the announcements of additional purchases or sales could be derived. There was a consistent price rise just prior to the announcement and it is hypothesised that this was due to heavy purchases being made by the acquirer. This explanation suggests that the prediction residuals between day −30 and day +30 represents the fully incorporated information content of the announcement. This averaged just over 6 per cent and although there was a fairly wide dispersion there were no common attributes to these various levels. The research has not refuted the efficient market hypothesis and has shown that investors incorporate the information contained in the announcement in the share price immediately. This adjustment to share prices is done fairly accurately, and without inside information no excess profits can be earned from using the announcement as some trigger for mechanical share selection.

In view of the value placed by investors on the knowledge of a 10 per cent holding, there is perhaps a case for lowering the disclosure level. Lowering the threshold to, say, 5 per cent would give information to investors that much more quickly and would perhaps give more 'accurate' share prices. This would also mean smaller profits for insider dealings. However, the greatest area for tightening any regulations appears to be in the time allowed to announce a stake. The fourteen days grace gives the investing institution time to substantially increase their stake with the reasonably certain knowledge that the share price will rise after the announcement. This probably only produces initial paper profits as to attempt to liquidate their holding would almost certainly cause a sharp fall in price. There appears to be no reason why the investor should be given fourteen days within which to declare his interest; he will receive any broker's contract notes the day after the transaction and the bookkeeping recordings are straightforward. The reduction in the time available in which to disclose a holding will give less opportunity for the investor to substantially boost his holdings prior to the announcement which is in fact a form of 'insider dealing.' Investors who have sold just prior to the announcement may have legitimate complaints of inadequate knowledge if the purchaser turns out to be a large holder.

There appear to be few arguments against greater disclosure. First, the cost of disclosing a, say, 5 per cent investment holding would be minimal. Second, there is little reason for thinking that any decreased disclosure threshold would deter takeovers or management participation as the investor's holding would have to be far greater than even 10 per cent to effect these. Third, although the lower disclosure level may deter investors building up stakes and thus reducing selling opportunities for existing shareholders there was no reason for believing that there was any especially strong selling pressure existing as regards the population in the study.

In summary, the announcements do have an information content and this is efficiently incorporated into share prices. Greater efficiency might however be gained by lowering the disclosure threshold and reducing the notification time.

REFERENCES

1. M. Blume. "On the Assessment of Risk," *Journal of Finance*, 26, 1971.
2. S. W. Cunningham. "The Sensitivities of Individual Share Prices to Changes in an Index" in 'Mathematics in the Stock Exchange,' *The Institute of Mathematics and its Applications*, 1972.
3. S. W. Cunningham. "The Predictability of British Stock Market Prices," *Applied Statistics*. No. 3, Vol. 22, 1973.
4. P. C. Grier and P. S. Albin. "Non-random Price Changes in Association with Trading in Large Blocks," *Journal of Business*, Vol. 46, No. 3, July 1973.
5. H. G. Guthman and A. J. Bakay. "The Market Impact of the Sale of Large Blocks of Stock," *Journal of Finance*, 20, December 1966.
6. B. F. King. "Market and Industry Factors in Stock Price Behaviour," *Journal of Business*, 39, Special Supplement, January 1966.
7. A. Kraus and H. Stoll. "Price Impacts of Block Trading on the New York Stock Exchange," *Journal of Finance*, 27, June 1972.
8. M. S. Scholes. "The Market for Securities: Substitution Versus Price Pressure and the Effects of Information on Share Prices," *Journal of Business*, 45, April 1972.
9. W. F. Sharpe. "A Simplified Model for Portfolio Analysis," *Management Science*, January 1963.

MONEY SUPPLY AND SHARE PRICES: THE EVIDENCE FOR THE U.K. IN THE POST-CCC PERIOD

Anthony Saunders and Richard S. Woodward

In recent years, U.K. economists and analysts alike, have shown increasing interest in the timing relationship between the money supply and share prices. Yet compared with the United States, where a considerable body of literature already exists, the volume of empirical research has been disproportionately small.

There was until 1971, however, an important limitation on quantifying this relationship for the U.K., namely the Bank of England's stated objective of interest-rate stabilization in the gilt market. This effectively put the cash base beyond the authorities' control and made any prior assumption as to the "exogeneity" of the money supply untenable. In addition, the low weight given to the money supply as a policy objective had an indirect informational effect in that regular monthly M_1 and M_3 series did not appear until after the announcement of the Competition and Credit Control (CCC) reforms in June 1971.

This availability of monthly data, combined with the adoption of "monetary objectives"[1] under CCC has allowed us to formulate a number of money supply-share price tests similar to those conducted in the United States.

The first part of this article discusses the theoretical rationale for the existence (or non-existence) of a systematic timing relationship between these variables, the second briefly outlines some of the evidence from the United States and, in the third, our results for the post-CCC period (October 1971 to December 1975) are presented.

The Theory

There are two opposing views of the timing relationship between changes in the money supply and share prices. The first, which might be called the simple Quantity Theory, argues that one should normally find changes in the money supply preceding changes in stock prices. Put simply, the theory suggests that any increase in the money supply, induced by the authorities, will push wealth-holders asset portfolios into disequilibrium

such that their actual (real) money holdings would no longer equal their desired level. In attempting to adjust their portfolios wealth-holders will substitute out of money into other real and/or financial assets (including shares), pushing up the prices of these assets, until real balances are reduced to their former level. Consequently changes in share prices are predicted to follow (with an unspecified lag) changes in the money supply.

The second view is Efficient Market Theory, with proponents such as Fama,[2] arguing that if the (U.K.) stock market is efficient then competition among market participants will lead (on average) to a situation where at any point in time, the actual prices of individual shares will reflect information based both on events that have already occurred and on events which the market expects to take place in the future. That is, the full effects of new information, in this case on the money supply, should be reflected "instantaneously" in changes in share prices. This instantaneous adjustment of prices in an efficient market also implies that they will tend to be independent over time (technically, follow a random walk) and that past information cannot be consistently used to predict future share prices. If Efficient Market Theory is a good description of reality then one would not expect, for example, to discover any systematic relationship between current changes in share prices and current and past changes in the money supply. Indeed, if any relationship were to exist at all it would be between current changes in prices and "expected" future changes in the money supply, that is changes in stock prices should precede actual changes in the money supply, although empirically, this relationship will tend to be obscured by "noise" in the market.

United States Evidence

Most U.S. studies have found evidence, to support the view that money supply variables

---

[1]Backed by more flexible tactics in the gilt-edged market.

[2]Eugene Fama, "Efficient Capital Markets: A Review of Theory and Empirical Work", *Journal of Finance*, May 1970.

tend to lead share prices. Sprinkel,[3] comparing turning points in stock indices with turning points in the growth rate of the money supply found that over the period 1918–1960 "a bear market in stock prices was predicted fifteen months after each peak in monetary growth, and that a bull market was predicted two months after each monetary growth trough was reached".[4]

Whilst Sprinkel's turning point analysis provides some interesting results, it has several disadvantages compared to regression analysis (used in this, and most other U.S. studies). In particular, regression analysis allows much greater flexibility in the specification of lags, peaks and troughs in time-series do not have to be explicitly identified and, perhaps more importantly, the regression equation allows quantification of the relationship between variables.

Homa and Jaffee[5] using a regression model on quarterly data between 1954 IV—1969 IV found that the current level of the money supply, it's current rate of growth and the rate of growth lagged one quarter explained over ninety-six per cent of the variation in the Standard and Poors (S.P.) stock index. The fact that the level of the money supply was found to be a significant independent explanatory variable of stock price changes is *a priori* difficult to rationalize, since Quantity Theorists would maintain that it is changes in, rather than levels of, the money supply that matter.[6] However as a forecasting model it has proved to be highly accurate in predicting future changes in U.S. stock prices.

Palmer[7] using a simple regression equation explicitly based on a Quantity theory model found a high correlation (0·61) between monthly changes in the money stock (M_1) and changes in the S.P. Index over the period January 1966 to August 1969. The coefficient on the money stock variable was extremely large, suggesting that a 1 per cent. change in the money supply

would lead to a 10 per cent. change in stock prices within one month.

A more sophisticated study has been carried out by Hamburger and Kochin [8] using an Almon (polynomial) lag structure. Arguing that the variability in the growth rate of the money supply is an important determinant of variability in the economy, they regressed current and past changes in monetary growth rates on current changes in the S.P. index over the period 1956-I to 1970-II. Their results show an important independent effect of the past nine-quarters' money growth rate changes on current changes in the S.P. index, with 26 per cent. of its variation being explained by these monetary variables alone.

To sum up, then, the results from U.S. regression studies appear to show that there has been a direct and relatively stable relationship between current and past changes in (variously defined) money supply variables and current changes in stock prices over the most of post-war period. This evidence has provided strong support for the Quantity Theorists' view as to the transmission mechanism between money and prices.

U.K. Evidence

The results from a battery of U.K. tests are presented in the Statistical Appendix. Our approach was basically investigative in that we sought systematic relationships between current changes in the *Financial Times* "650" Share Index and current and past money supply variables. The money supply variables chosen paralleled those used in U.S. studies, namely the level of the money stock (M) the change in the level of the money stock (ΔM) and the change in the growth rate of the money stock ($\Delta \dot{M}$).

Our first set of tests (equations I-III) attempt to find what relationship, if any, exists between current monthly changes in share prices and current monthly values of the three money supply variables over the post-CCC period. As can be seen no significant statistical relationship was found for either M_1 or M_3.[9]

[3]Beryl Sprinkel, Money and Stock Prices, (Homewood, Illinois: Richard D. Irwin, Inc. 1964).
[4]*Ibid.*
[5]K. E. Homa and D. M. Jaffee, "The Supply of Money and Common Stock Prices", *Journal of Finance*, December 1971.
[6]An intuitive argument of this kind can be found in M. H. Miller, "Criticisms of Hamburger, Kochin and Keran", *Journal of Finance*, May 1972.
[7]M. Palmer, "Money Supply, Portfolio Adjustments and Stock Prices", *Financial Analysts Journal*, July/August 1970.

[8]M. J. Hamburger and L. A. Kochin, "Money and Stock Prices: the Channels of Influence", *Journal of Finance*, May 1972, use a fifth degree polynomial with no end constraints, lagged nine quarters.
[9]As measured by the high standard errors on the money supply coefficients and the poor "fit" (low R^2) of the equation.

The poor explanatory power of these equations clearly indicates that either some independent determinants of U.K. share prices have been ignored, or that the U.K. stock market is highly efficient. Economic theory suggests that other important determinants of the demand for shares include such variables as the expected yield on shares, expected yields on alternative assets and changes in the price-level. By including only money supply variables in the regression equation, indirect effects on stock prices working through interest rates and relative yields are ignored. It has been suggested by Jones, Poindexter and Williamson [10] that the inclusion of the change in share price index lagged one period as an independent variable will capture these (slower) indirect effects of money supply changes.

If these indirect effects are important then this variable will be statistically significant in the regression equation; if, however, it is found to be insignificant this will provide additional support for the contention of Efficient Market theorists that past changes in stock prices have no consistent relationship with current changes in stock prices.

The results presented in equation IV in the Appendix [11] provide additional support for the Efficient Market view, as the inclusion of the lagged stock price variable is statistically insignificant at any meaningful level and the explanatory power of the equation is hardly improved.

On the whole, though, this approach is unsatisfactory in that it explicitly excludes the past money supply variables themselves. Consequently our next approach was to follow Homa and Jaffee and include both current and lagged values of the level and rate of growth of the money supply as independent explanatory variables. A large number of combinations and lag structures were tried without success; in all cases the predictive power of equations were poor. For compari-son equation V presents the U.K. results for Homa and Jaffee's forecasting equation.

Finally, we decided to adopt the Almon lag technique so successfully utilised by Hamburger and Kochin in the United States. This test allows the employment of a number of past money supply variables in the same regression equation without incurring problems of correlation between the money supply variables themselves [12] and permits lagged effects to be more accurately captured.

Using monthly data, a number of (polynomial) lag structures were tested . [13] Our results suggest an initial negative relationship between current and preceding changes in money supply growth rates and share price changes extending over the first six months, with the positive effects being felt after seven months and continuing until the twelfth month. However, the standard errors on the coefficients were large enough to lower the degree of confidence we should have in these results. In addition the equation of best fit explained less than twenty per cent. of the variation in stock prices.

Conclusion

Our results appear to contradict the evidence from the United States by providing strong support for an Efficient Market view. At the very least they seem to discount any significant direct effect of U.K. money supply variables on stock prices inside one year. Whilst it may be argued that money supply variables effect economic activity and hence "prices" with a much longer lag (as found by Friedman and Schwartz [14] for the United States) analysis of these long-run effects must be deferred until sufficient quarterly data is available for the post-CCC period.

[10]C. P. Jones, J. C. Poindexter and R. H. Williamson, "The Money Supply, Portfolio Adjustments and Stock Prices", *Financial Analysts Journal*, March 1972.

[11]A regression of ΔP_{t-1} on ΔP_t over the same period yielded the following results.
$\Delta P_t = 1\cdot2 + 0\cdot047\Delta P_{t-1}$, $R^2 = 0\cdot002$, $D - W = 1\cdot7$
$\quad\quad(3\cdot4)\ (0\cdot14)$

[12]This is the statistical problem of multicollinearity.

[13]Briefly this approach involves fitting a past series of money supply variables to a polynomial curve with weights chosen to maximize the R^2 of the equation. The form used

was $\Delta P_t = B_t \sum_{i=o}^{N} \Delta \dot{M}_{t-i}$, $i = 1 \ldots 12$. The lag was terminated

at 12 months because of data limitations and the associated loss of degrees of freedom. Results from these regressions are available from the authors on request.

[14]M. Friedman and A. Schwartz, Monetary History of the United States (Princeton University Press, 1963).

STATISTICAL APPENDIX

TABLE A

Money—Share-Price Regression Tests

(Standard error of estimates in the parenthesis; superscript "N" indicates that the estimated coefficient is not significant at the 10 per cent. level)

Tests	Explanatory variables	α	M_t	ΔM_t	ΔM_t	ΔM_{t-1}	ΔP_{t-1}	R^2	$D-W$
I	[a]	0.784^N (1·8)	$(-)0.001^N$ (0·01)	—	—	—	—	0·0002	2·0
	[b]	4.01^N (10·75)	$(-)0.0002^N$ (0·00035)	—	—	—	—	0·005	2·01
II	[a]	$(-)3.17^N$ (2·9)	—	$+0.018^N$ (0·014)	—	—	—	0·035	2·08
	[b]	$(-)0.789^N$ (3·53)	—	$(-)0.001^N$ (0·0007)	—	—	—	0·0003	2·01
III	[a]	$(-)1.14^N$ (2·13)	—	—	$+145.5^N$ (101·84)	—	—	0·04	1·9
	[b]	1.33^N (3·55)	—	—	$(-)172.36^N$ (199·15)	—	—	0·015	1·96
IV	[a]	0.8^N (2·14)	—	—	151.8^N (102·03)	—	0.056^N (0·144)	0·053	1·92
V	[a]	2.64^N (18·76)	$(-)0.0003^N$ (0·001)	—	$+114.52^N$ (118·24)	$(-)79.18^N$ (118·01)	—	0·055	1·96

Notes: [a] refers to regression tests where M_1 is the independent variable, [b] refers to tests where M_3 is the independent variable, α = the intercept term of the regression equation, M_t refers to the level of the money stock, ΔM_t refers to the change in the money stock over time, ΔM_t refers to the change in the current growth rate of the money stock and ΔM_{t-1} is the same variable lagged one period, ΔP_{t-1} is the lagged change in the stock price series (share index), R^2 is the sample coefficient of determination and $D-W$ refers to the Durbin-Watson statistic. In all equations ΔP_t is the dependent variable.

Sources: Bank of England Statistical Abstract No. 2, 1975, Bank of England Quarterly Bulletin Vol. 16, No. 3, September 1976, *Financial Times.*

CHAPTER 4

The Strong Form of the Efficient Market Hypothesis

The evidence reviewed in Chapters 1 and 3 suggested that publicly available information (including historic share price data) cannot *per se* generate returns over and above those of a simple buy and hold policy. Many investors would take this as read. They would argue that a newspaper tip or the announcement of rights or dividend etc are news available to everyone and as such cannot be used to outperform anyone else. The area where individual differences can arise is in the interpretation of publicly available information by investment analysts. Investment analysts do not always come to the same conclusion. The question is, do some produce consistently better forecasts than others and if so can these forecasts be used to generate abnormal profits? The answer to this question can be found in the formulation of the strong form hypothesis:

> The share price of a company, at any point in time, represents and fully discounts all that can be known which is relevant to that company and the valuation of its shares.

Obviously the semi-strong form and weak form hypotheses are special cases of the strong form hypothesis. Historic share price data and publicly available information about a company can be 'known' extremely easily. If the strong form hypothesis is true then *a fortiori* the semi-strong and weak form hypotheses are also true.

A word of caution must be expressed about inside information. Such information is capable of being 'known' but by definition, as it is inside knowledge, is not reflected in the share price. The availability of such inside information to an investor would enable him to make superior returns. Investors do not generally have access to such information (although those who do, sometimes become investors). In any case such practice is expected to become a criminal offence once legislation is introduced. In view of this it is appropriate to exclude inside information and to assume that such information is not available and therefore not capable of being 'known'.

In addition to publicly available information, the recommendations of investment analysts are conclusions or pieces of information and are capable of being 'known'. Thus the strong form hypothesis is asserting that even with the advice of investment analysts, the investor still cannot hope to beat the market. Whilst accepting that analysts can differ in opinion, the evidence suggests that their recommendations are already discounted by share prices.

One feature of the evidence presented throughout is that it has either been published or has been publicly available. Now if work has been undertaken which has isolated market inefficiencies then it is possible that the researcher may first construct a system to exploit the efficiencies before publishing the results. In other words there may be a bias in the evidence presented in that only the research which confirms efficiency is published.

Either, no-one has discovered any inefficiencies, or, if someone has then they are still being exploited. Of course once details of an inefficiency are published, it should disappear. The published results will form part of the body of information about shares and will therefore be incorporated into share prices.

However these problems can be avoided to some extent by tests of the strong form hypothesis. Two types of test are reviewed here. Firstly a study of analysts' recommendations to see whether any analyst can consistently produce recommendations which would generate superior returns. Secondly an analysis of the performance of institutional portfolios. This latter test is without doubt the most powerful test of market efficiency. Compared with other investors, the institutions have their own full-time research and investment teams plus the benefit of the pick of the brokers' research work. Indeed they sometimes employ someone to analyse all the brokers' research which has been received. If such investors could not beat the market then this would be compelling evidence for market efficiency.

Analysts' Recommendations

Fitzgerald [37] has examined the recommendations of 25 stockbroking firms over the period January 1971 to March 1973. The firms were first classified into 6 different groups based on their answers to a questionnaire. The analysis was then performed on a group basis and also on the basis of taking all the firms included as a single group. Residuals analysis was used to study the behaviour of the share price around the time the recommendation was published. The results can be summarised as follows:

Group Type	No. of Recommendations	Average Abnormal Returns Days 1-30	Day 31	Day 32	Days 31-61
1. Large firms concentrating on highly sophisticated research	220	2.90%	0.08%	1.49%	6.53%
2. Highly specialised, institutionally orientated, moderate size, sophisticated research operation	38	2.71%	-0.65%	0.50%	-3.31%
3. Size and research level varies but major emphasis on marketing	60	22.61%	1.60%	1.74%	6.32%
4. Medium size and fast growing with emphasis on status and new business but not on research	126	0.74%	0.79%	0.59%	-3.38%
5. Well-established, medium size with separate research department and some emphasis on marketing	91	4.69%	0.01%	-1.00%	7.23%
6. Very small and localised with no research capability	100	0.17%	-0.33%	1.02%	2.29%
Total sample	635	5.64%	0.25%	0.72%	0.50%

NB Day 31 is the day the recommendation is released to clients. Days 31 to 61 therefore represent the period following the recommendation and during which time share price adjustment (if any) should occur.

Looking first at the results for the whole sample, it is readily apparent that no advantage can be taken of the recommendations. Abnormal returns over the 30 days following release average out at 0.5 per cent. On release day and the day immediately following, abnormal returns total approximately 1.0 per cent, still insufficient to cover transaction costs. Quite clearly any information contained in the recommendation is incorporated very quickly into share prices. Fitzgerald infers that this is confirmatory of the semi-strong form hypothesis. However this is only true if the recommendations become public knowledge. In practice this is generally true with brokers' circulars often being distributed to the press. Indeed even if a broker's recommendation did contain some new information, market operations of those investors involved would begin to affect the share price. Such an inference is in any case subject to the caveats below.

The magnitude of the abnormal return on the day of release (0.25 per cent) suggests that brokers' recommendations contain virtually no new information and thus supports the strong form hypothesis. The real weakness here is that the recommendations may not actually be released to all clients at the same point in time. It is not inconceivable that a broker could telephone the recommendation to his clients in descending order of size and possibly over the course of several days. Depending on how extensive this practice is, any information contained in the recommendation may be already discounted in the share price by the time the circular is received by clients. For the period prior to announcement there was an abnormal rate of return of 5.64 per cent. One possible explanation is that brokers' recommendations do contain new information and that through the process of leaking the recommendation to selected clients, this information becomes incorporated into the price before the circular containing the recommendation is physically received by the clients.

Another source of bias may arise as a result of the timing of recommendations. It is implicit in the Fitzgerald study that the recommendations are to buy shares. 'Sell' recommendations are much less common and would necessitate segregation in the analysis. (Otherwise rising share prices caused by 'buy' recommendations would tend to be cancelled out by falling share prices caused by 'sell' recommendations.) It is common practice for brokers to circularise clients with their views after the announcement of interim and preliminary trading results and sometimes when the annual accounts are published. This is an obvious opportunity for the broker to give his comments on current profitability and to update his recommendation. It is possible that where companies announce better-than-expected results the broker responds with a buy recommendation. Thus it could be above-average profits that are responsible for the abnormal share price behaviour preceding release of the recommendation.

This bias could be reduced by considering only the period between the day following the announcement of trading results and the day of the recommendation. In this way a clearer picture of the effects of brokers' recommendations would emerge.

The breakdown by category of broker is revealing although the results may perhaps be due partly to chance. Results for groups 1 and 3 were statistically significant throughout and for group 5 significant only in the pre-recommendation period. Thus it would appear that by careful choice of broker, superior returns can be earned after receipt of the recommendation. Fitzgerald characterised group 3 with the tag 'unethical' on the basis of their answers to the questionnaire. He suggests that this may not be inconsistent with the fact that pre-recommendation returns for this group are the highest. The best place to be is therefore at the top of such a broker's client list and to sit by a telephone until he rings.

Finally a note of caution must be recorded regarding the broker's listed clients. These are companies which have a listing on the Stock Exchange and for whom the broker acts in all matters relating to the Stock Exchange. As a result of this relationship it is not unusual for a broker to visit a client from time to time and to distribute circulars containing information gleaned from the client. Such information might well not be generally available and is therefore inside knowledge and could explain the results. The whole climate of opinion was different then (1971-73) and if the exercise were repeated today, different results could well be obtained. The one clear fact which does emerge from this study is that unless the investor is selective in the brokers he uses, the recommendations he receives via circulars will on average have little or no value whatsoever.

Portfolio Performance Tests

The difficulty of defining good performance was discussed briefly in Chapter 2. *Money Which?* [38] provided some interesting insights into performance when they surveyed the conventional wisdom surrounding the choice of unit trust. Annual data were used for the 5-year period ending February 1974. The sample appeared to include all trusts in existence at the end of the period (a source of bias which will be discussed later). The conclusions of the survey were:

1. Comparative past performance (of general trusts) not a useful guide to the future.
2. Comparative past record of management company not a useful guide to the future.
3. The type of investment adviser (stockbroker/merchant bank etc) is not a useful guide when picking a unit trust.
4. Capital trusts are not necessarily better than income trusts.
5. Capital trusts are not better than income trusts when shares are rising and vice versa.
6. The size of a unit trust fund does not affect performance.

On the actual levels of performance achieved, *Money Which?* concluded:

'Over periods covered by previous reports ... the performance of the average general unit trust has not been very different from that of shares as a whole — sometimes better sometimes worse...Over the long term, a general trust seems unlikely to do much better — or much worse — than shares as a whole.'
(The performance of shares as a whole was taken to be the FT all-share index.)

Clearly *Money Which?* found it impossible to distinguish good performance (and bad) among the trusts. The problem is to relate specific portfolio performance to the actions of the manager and to determine whether it is the manager's decisions which are responsible for the performance good or bad, or, simply chance.

Samuels [39]

Samuels attempted to identify portfolio performance which could be attributed to the actions of management. The portfolios of 10 unit trusts were classified into appropriate industry sectors and control portfolios were then constructed. These control portfolios were set up with the same proportionate investment in each sector but using the FT actuaries sector indices. The performance of 10 unit trusts was then compared with the appropriate control portfolios over 1964 - 66. The 3-year period is short but the unit trust portfolios changed while the control portfolios remained fixed. The unit trust managers therefore had the flexibility to be selective within each industry and of course to change the industry weighting.

His analysis discovered only insignificant differences in performance. This suggests that even if fund managers could choose the right industry, and this could not be ascertained from this study, their individual selections within each industry sector are no better than the sector average.

Samuels also undertook a number of other tests over a longer period of time which confirmed that unit trust portfolio performance was little different to the market average, marginally under-performing and out-performing in rising and falling markets respectively (an effect which is explained later).

Rutherford [40]

The article by Rutherford explains very clearly the statistical methodology (ranking correlation) which can be used to assess the consistency of relative performance. Here relative performance (of up to 142 unit trusts observed over 1963 - 68) is taken to be the position (rank) of the individual trust in the annual performance table. This type of analysis then determines a measure, the Spearman correlation coefficient, for the consistency or inconsistency of the rankings from year to year.

Rutherford considered his most important result was that '...nothing simple and definite emerges'. Tests for significance were also used to determine the extent to which the results could be due to chance. Most of the results proved to be statistically insignificant. Thus no degree of consistency in ranking could be recognised. Had there been some level of correlation then this might have been due to the relative skills of the managers. In fact, of the results which were measurably significant, many were negative indicating that high ranking was more likely to be followed by low ranking and vice versa.

Cranshaw [41]

During the late 1960s, there was much discussion in the financial press on the subject of the apparently unusually good performance of new unit trusts. For instance, it was noticed that new unit trusts tended to dominate the top twenty rankings to a greater extent than would be expected if the new unit trusts were evenly spread through the whole performance range. If we accept the findings of the Samuels study that unit trust portfolio performance is no different to the market average, then superior performance demonstrated by new unit trusts would be evidence against the strong form hypothesis.

Cranshaw investigated this effect for new unit trusts in the period 1962 - 69. The belief that new trusts outperformed old ones stemmed from the unusually high proportion of new trusts in the top twenty. The first test Cranshaw performed was to compare average investment performance of new unit trusts against all unit trusts: the rates of return were 9.2 per cent pa and 8.8 per cent pa respectively. Thus there is only a relatively small difference in performance which is not sufficient to explain the preponderance of new trusts in the top twenty.

One possible explanation is that new trusts may have more widely dispersed returns caused by poor diversification. Accordingly Cranshaw measured the dispersion and observed that in 7 out of the 8 years, dispersion of returns on the new trusts was higher. A higher level of dispersion can explain the preponderance of new trusts in the top twenty but would also indicate that there should be a similar preponderance of new trusts in the bottom twenty. This prediction Cranshaw confirmed. Thus a new trust has a greater than average chance of being in the top twenty but also a greater than average chance of being in the bottom twenty.

The higher level of dispersion of returns in new trusts is most likely due to the fact that they are invested in few shares to begin with. As Chapter 2 demonstrated, reduced dispersion (equivalent to risk) is achieved by diversification. Unit trusts perhaps are not sufficiently well diversified over the first months of their life.

The subject of new trusts raises a point about the data used in studies of performance. The usual procedure is to look at the trusts in existence at the date of the study and then to collect data relating to the preceding period. There is a source of bias in this process in that poorly performing trusts are often merged into successful trusts. Only the fittest survive. Thus the trusts in existence at any point in time are self-selecting in that they are generally the more successful trusts which the managers see fit to retain. To allow for this it would be better to collect data on all trusts in existence for any part of the period of study.

Risk

The studies summarised above only hinted at risk and did not explicitly make any appropriate allowance. However the Sharpe model, described in Chapter 2 and used extensively in Chapter 3, readily adapts for portfolios of shares. Instead of using data on an individual share to calculate the beta value, data on the portfolio are used to calculate a beta value for the portfolio. This is a measure of the riskiness of the portfolio.

Russell and Taylor [42]

Russell and Taylor were among the first to test this model on UK portfolios using the City University data bank. The portfolios were 20 British unit trusts although there were only 9 items of data for each trust representing 6-monthly values over the period December 1962 - June 1967. Nevertheless good results were obtained in that the Sharpe model appeared to be a reasonable description of reality. Russell and Taylor pointed to the high correlation between portfolio and market returns as evidence of the stability and validity of the beta values calculated.

One interesting feature of the results, which confirms an earlier observation, is that the majority of unit trusts in the sample had beta values less than unity. Such portfolios move up and down much less than the market. A portfolio with beta = 1 would simply comprise the market, the FT all-share index portfolio say. To construct a portfolio with beta = ½, the portfolio would be divided equally between the risk-free investment (treasury bills) and the market. The portfolio would then have a return Rp, given by

$$Rp = \tfrac{1}{2}I + \tfrac{1}{2}Rm, \text{ where } I = \text{risk-free return}$$
$$Rm = \text{return on the market (FT all-share index)}$$

This equation is similar to that of the Sharpe model (see Chapter 2), where $R = \alpha + \beta Rm$. Here beta = ½ . Hence it can be seen that portfolios with any beta value between 0 and 1 can be constructed by allocating the appropriate proportions of the portfolio to treasury bills and to the market. To arrange portfolios with beta greater than 1, a loan has to be raised which is then invested in the market (this is simply gearing up the portfolio). Suppose an amount equal to 50 per cent of the value of the portfolio was borrowed (at a rate of interest, I) and, together with existing funds, invested in the market. The return on the portfolio would be given by:

$Rp = -½ I + 1½ Rm$, and

by analogy with the above, the beta of this portfolio would be 1½.

Since a unit trust cannot borrow, gearing cannot be used to raise beta over 1 and hence the above results. It is possible however by concentrating on individual stocks to arrive at a portfolio with beta in excess of 1. The price for this is poor diversification. Unit trusts might not therefore be the best vehicle for a higher risk (higher beta) investment policy.

Summary of results:

Fund No.	Mean half-yearly Return	Standard Deviation	'Slope'** (beta)	Correlation with FTA *
1	0.0047	0.062	0.44	0.68
2	0.0319	0.062	0.43	0.65
3	0.0477	0.071	0.68	0.90
4	0.0277	0.096	1.00	0.97
5	0.0360	0.098	1.03	0.98
6	0.0250	0.088	0.89	0.95
7	0.0382	0.094	0.98	0.98
8	-0.0053	0.084	0.53	0.59
9	0.0332	0.125	1.27	0.95
10	0.0495	0.101	0.95	0.89
11	0.0373	0.097	0.99	0.95
12	0.0368	0.100	1.01	0.95
13	0.0334	0.082	0.86	0.98
14	0.0342	0.074	0.74	0.94
15	0.0196	0.098	0.99	0.95
16	0.0415	0.101	1.03	0.96
17	0.0298	0.069	0.69	0.95
18	0.0461	0.077	0.80	0.97
19	0.0480	0.078	0.74	0.89
20	0.0269	0.095	0.99	0.98
21*	0.0276	0.094	1.00	1.00

* FT Actuaries all-share index.
** Tangent of angle where the all-share index is the horizontal axis.

Briscoe, Samuels and Smythe [43]

A study of 14 unit trusts was undertaken by Briscoe, Samuels and Smythe for the period 1953 - 63. Their objective was to determine whether risk was rewarded by higher rates of return. Using regression analysis, they observed a negative relationship between the mean return and the standard deviation of returns (σ), given by:

mean return = $17.9 - 0.22\sigma$

Although the relationship is not significantly negative, theory suggests that it should be significantly positive. There could be a number of reasons for this. Poor diversification, chance, high transaction and tax costs associated with too vigorous an investment policy could each be the cause. Alternatively it may be that the following assumption is untenable.

Assumption

When considering whether the Sharpe model was a reasonable description of reality, it was noted that beta values for individual shares over time remained fairly constant. The use of betas for portfolios also requires stability. For example, a fixed portfolio (comprising shares which are never changed) would be stable because the beta values of the underlying shares are stable. However, suppose changes are made to the portfolio such that the beta values of the underlying shares change significantly. The beta value of the portfolio would therefore also change. However, the method of estimating betas is to fit the best single value to the data. This single value will not take account of any changes. It is not unusual for fund managers to go liquid. This might entail holding up to 50 per cent of the portfolio in treasury bills. Thus the beta value would be reduced from 1.0 to 0.5. Attempting to fit a single beta value would clearly be invalid.

Jensen [44] partially overcame this problem in his now famous article on US mutual funds. He made the assumption that each fund manager adopted a target beta level. This level would remain constant with exceptional changes occurring temporarily when the fund manager identified an opportunity to outperform the market. For example, if he thought that the market would rise (fall) he would increase (decrease) his investment in high risk stocks. Jensen proved that if this were true, then only if the fund manager possessed superior forecasting ability would the estimate of beta be affected. In fact, he showed that this effect would tend to exaggerate any superior investment performance.

Tests for Superior Performance

Jensen's article set out the first test for superior investment performance. The method employed was a simple modification to residuals analysis. The expected return on any portfolio is given by Rp,

$$Rp = Rf + \beta \ (Rm - Rf) \qquad Rf = \text{riskfree rate of interest.}$$

Jensen suggested that if the manager did have some superior skill then he might be able to earn a return of say Rp^1, superior to that level given by the above formula for the same level of risk (as measured by beta). Suppose this excess return is Rs (subscript 's' for superior).

Hence $Rp^1 = Rs + Rp$, but Rp is given by the above
and so $Rp^1 = Rs + [Rf + \beta(Rm - Rf)]$

The term 'Rs' is analogous to the excess returns measured by residuals analysis.

Jensen then used regression analysis to calculate the value if any of Rs. (In fact Jensen found no values for Rs significantly different from zero.)

This methodology constitutes a test of superior performance which explicitly takes account of risk. Other measures have been put forward:

Treynor [45]: $\dfrac{\overline{Rp} - Rf}{\beta p}$ Sharpe [46]: $\dfrac{\overline{Rp} - Rf}{\sigma (Rp)}$

where Rp = expected return on the portfolio (ie historical average);
  βp = the beta value for the portfolio;
  $\sigma(Rp)$ = standard deviation of Rp.

The main improvement these other suggestions contain is that any excess returns are divided by a measure of risk (βp and $\sigma(Rp)$ respectively). Thus they quantify excess returns per unit level of risk.

However, before examining the evidence, the work of Roll [47] must be considered. He has proved that the choice of proxy for the market (usually the FT all-share index has been used) can alter the performance rankings of a set of portfolios as measured by the above methods. In other words, the above methods may or may not identify good or bad performance but this may be due entirely to the choice of proxy for the market. Indeed Roll went further to prove that such good or bad performance was due entirely to the choice of market proxy. Only if the portfolios all appeared to do no better and no worse than expected could it be concluded that the right market proxy was being used. But then no comment on management's expertise could be made. This problem applies only to the Jensen and Treynor measures and not to Sharpe's.

The Sharpe Test

This test has a certain intuitive appeal. The riskiness of a portfolio is measured by the standard deviation of its historic rates of return. This is then compared with the average (mean) rate of return. This gives an indication of the trade-off between expected rate of return (as measured by the average historic rate) and risk (as measured by the standard deviation of returns). The FT all-share index, as a market proxy, is similarly treated and finally, the risk-free rate is recorded. The test can be illustrated graphically:

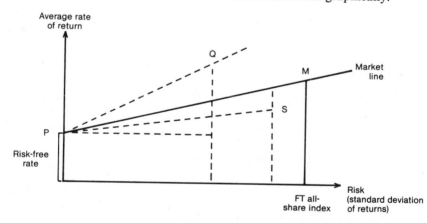

It is readily apparent that this is identical to the beta model described in Chapter 2 except that risk is measured by standard deviation instead of beta. Any point on the market line can be achieved by a combination of investment in the market and in treasury bills. It will also be apparent that the computation of the Sharpe performance measure is equivalent to measuring the slope of the line PQ. Thus this test can identify those portfolios beating the market and can rank all portfolios according to their performance relative to the market.

As with the beta model, there are problems in extrapolating from historic data: historic performance is not necessarily a guide to future performance; and if a portfolio changes composition and its risk over time then the measurement process may be affected. Thus, the risk measure may not relate to the actual risk suffered. Another problem is the choice of risk-free rate. A Sharpe test covering a number of years would have to use an average treasury bill rate. The model imputes zero risk to this investment although in practice, the actual rate varies from week to week. This average cannot therefore be projected forward. This will also affect any conclusion about, say, portfolio S. If we conclude from the Sharpe test that an investor would have been better off by investing on the market line (immediately above 'S') we are doing so with the benefit of hindsight to the extent that an average treasury bill rate is used.

In the evidence that follows, the Jensen, Treynor and Sharpe measures are used and, in some cases, a variety of different indices are used as a market proxy. Care must be exercised when evaluating the results of the Jensen and Treynor tests and the main emphasis is placed on the results of the Sharpe test.

Performance tests for unit trusts

Dixon [48]

In a comprehensive study of 50 unit trusts, over the period January 1966 to December 1971, in which weekly data were used, Dixon examined performance using all three of the above measures. Furthermore, three different market proxies were used:

FT industrial ordinary (30 shares)
FT 500 index (500 shares)
FT all-share index (651 shares)

To calculate rates of return for the unit trusts, offer prices (ie the purchase price as opposed to the sale price) were used. Unit trust managers are required by law to make prices within a band of about 12-13 per cent where the limits are fixed by reference to the value of the underlying portfolio. In practice, a much narrower spread of prices is quoted. The position of this narrower band within the band fixed by law can vary, usually depending on whether the trust is expanding or contracting. Thus the offer price could change without there being any change in value to the underlying portfolio. Whilst this is a source of error, it is not unreasonable to assume, as Dixon did, that there is no consistent bias in using offer prices throughout.

The choice of index made very little difference to the rankings of the trusts by each performance measure. Only in absolute terms was there a difference. In performance terms, Dixon's general conclusion was that 'the trusts on average do not do any better than a naive investment policy of buying a random portfolio and holding, and that they therefore do not justify their research expenditures'.

The results of applying the Sharpe measure are summarised graphically. Only 11 of the trusts were above the market line while many of the remainder were substantially below. Clearly poor diversification could be one explanation. For a given rate of return, concentration on relatively few stocks would push up the volatility of the portfolio and thus increase the risk as measured by the standard deviation of return. In addition management charges and transaction expenses further eat into the return.

Dixon noted that in the diagram, the points indicate a positive relationship between risk and return.

Ward and Saunders [49]

A similar study was carried out by Ward and Saunders on 49 unit trusts over the nine year period 1964-72. The three performance measures were computed as before. In particular, the Sharpe performance measure was calculated for each trust. Of the 49 trusts, only 7 managed to beat the market. As with the Dixon study, this is a small proportion of the total.

Firth [50]

Firth concentrated on 72 unit trusts (other than those which invested overseas) in existence from the beginning of 1965 through to the end of 1975 — a total period of eleven years. Once again the Sharpe measure of performance was calculated but this time only 3 trusts managed to beat the market.

These three studies thus provide cogent evidence of the difficulty of beating the market and thereby support the strong form hypothesis.

Moles and Taylor [51]

At this point it is worth reviewing a number of points arising from this type of analysis concerning the strategy adopted by fund managers. The study by Moles and Taylor highlights a number of these. Their study covered 86 unit trusts over 1965-75. Included in this sample were trusts invested overseas. However, the beta values were calculated with respect to the FT all-share index. It was found that the beta values so calculated were not stable over time and further that there was little or no correlation between betas measured in consecutive time intervals. Moles and Taylor concluded that 'Beta gave a poor showing'. Of course there is no reason why beta should be constant. Indeed it would be unusual if funds did not from time to time change beta, for example by taking a liquid position. In any event the beta factors so calculated must be viewed with suspicion. A fund containing overseas shares cannot be compared with an index relating solely to the UK. From the work of Roll [47] it is known that all funds should lie on the market line providing the correct proxy for the market is used. Moles and Taylor found a very wide divergence from the market line and this confirms that the choice of index was inappropriate.

The beta for a portfolio should be constant providing there are no changes within the portfolio. Thus the conclusion that beta was unstable and therefore unreliable should be taken instead as evidence of changes in the underlying portfolios. Moles and Taylor had expected to observe the following relationship:

Unit Trust Type	Beta Value
Income funds	low beta
Balanced funds	average beta
Growth funds	high beta

Such a relationship was not discovered (a 'staggering finding'). This may be due entirely to the mis-specification of the market proxy. However, there is no reason why the above classification should hold. Whether the objective is income or growth or whatever does not necessarily ensure that the fund manager will pick high or low beta shares. His perception of the appropriate strategy to achieve income or growth need not take risk into account but, if it does, may not coincide with the classification of Moles and Taylor.

Pension Funds

The above research concerns unit trusts only. As the problems with pension fund analysis will illustrate, unit trusts are particularly suitable for testing performance. The chief advantage is that they are valued regularly, usually on a daily basis. Thus new investment into the unit trust does not affect the unit price and performance measurement is straightforward. Pension funds differ in that there is no requirement for frequent valuations which is in any case a costly procedure. However, when measuring performance, distortion can arise. When cash is added into the fund (and most if not all pension funds have a positive cash flow) at any time between valuation dates, there is no way of knowing the proportionate increase in size of fund. Consider a simple example of two funds earning 10 per cent pa and 12 per cent pa respectively. Suppose each invests additional cash during the year as follows:

Fund A: Opening valuation: £100   Closing valuation: £165
        Invests further £50 immediately   Rate of return $= \dfrac{£165 - £150}{£150} = 10\%$
        after initial valuation

Fund B: Opening valuation: £100   Closing valuation: £162
        Invests further £50 immediately   Rate of return $= \dfrac{£162 - £150}{£150} = 8\%$
        before closing valuation

Thus although Fund B was in reality earning the higher rate of return, the above crude measure, distorted by the timing of cash flows, gives the wrong result. No improvement is achieved if allowance is made for the timing of cash flows since in an equity fund, the rate of return is not earned evenly over time. The only certain way to avoid distortion is to value the fund every time there is cash in or out. This is generally regarded as an unnecessary expense, and no such valuations are available.

This is therefore one major problem with the data. However, more crucial is the difficulty of obtaining the data. Fortunately a number of firms of actuaries are consulted regularly by trustees of pension funds to seek amongst other things information on the performance of the chosen fund managers. The actuaries are thus able, subject to the limitations of the data, to comment on the performance of the pension funds under scrutiny.

Holbrook [52]

Holbrook covered extensively the problems of pension fund investment and in particular considered the rate of return problem. He also tested performance on a sample of up to 93 pension funds over the period 1970-75. Annual valuations only were available but monthly cash flows were detailed. The rate of return was calculated to be the internal rate of return. This is an approximation to the actual rate of return as although it provides for the timing of cash flows, it assumes that the return is earned evenly throughout the year.

Holbrook looked at separate areas of pension fund investment — fixed interest and UK equities. To provide a yardstick for comparison, two control funds were monitored throughout the period: a fund comprising the FT all-share index, and a portfolio split equally between that index and long-dated gilts. These portfolios are analogous to portfolios having beta factors of 1 and 0.5 respectively. (The analogy is not quite exact since the risk-free asset is usually taken to be treasury bills.) The use of these portfolios can be regarded as an approximate risk adjustment. Holbrook argued that a suitable combination of the two control portfolios could have the same risk characteristics as the pension fund under examination. He compared the performance of each pension fund with both control portfolios.

The results were distorted by the inclusion of convertibles in the data (on UK equities) for 1974 and 1975. Nevertheless, his results did not indicate any significant over-or under-performance and he was able to conclude:

'... the median performance of equity portfolios was close to that of the FT actuaries all share index.

There were wide fluctuations in the performance of funds in the single years, but the dispersion of the results was appreciably less over periods of 3 years or more. Very few funds consistently achieved above- or below-average performance, either in the Main Fund as a whole or in the sectors. Because of the small numbers of funds which participated in the early years, judgments on the persistence of performance can only be provisional at this stage.'

The 'Main Fund' comprised UK equities and fixed interest including cash deposits.

The limited data is a drawback to this study but the results nevertheless provide support for the strong form hypothesis.

Bacon & Woodrow [53]

Since 1970 Messrs Bacon & Woodrow, consulting actuaries, have provided a service to pension fund clients which reports on the performance of each particular fund and compares it with others participating in the service. The data on which this analysis is based comprises quarterly rates of return. The effects of new cash in/out-flows during a quarter are allowed for by the method used by Holbrook [52]. Each flow is timed during the quarter and the internal rate of return for that quarter then calculated. This is an improvement on Holbrook's analysis which employed annual rates of return as opposed to the quarterly rates used here.

Each fund is split up into a number of categories including 'UK equities', 'British Funds', etc. To calculate rates of return on individual sectors is a little more complicated. Switching between sectors, which is regarded as equivalent to new investment (or disinvestment) in each sector, must be incorporated. A further assumption is therefore made that cash being switched between sectors is invested evenly throughout the quarter.

A total of 103 funds participate in this service (although not all participated for the whole period) varying in size from £0.3m to £300m. The majority of the funds are managed externally:

Type of Adviser	Number of Funds
Merchant banks	61
Stockbrokers	14
Others	11
Clearing banks	7
Managed internally	10
Total	103

In the report for 1970-76, Messrs Bacon & Woodrow comment that:

'So far, our findings show that generally there is no significant correlation between the factors investigated. For example, we have not found any significant differences in performance between small, medium and large funds. Neither have we found any significant difference between the performance of various types of manager, (eg Merchant banks, Stockbrokers, etc) and it is clear that no manager in our Measurement of Investment Performance service has managed to stay consistently ahead of his rivals.'

The report for 1970-75 contained the results of a 'comprehensive series of tests to determine whether there are any conclusions to be drawn from the 6 years of performance data'. In addition to the above comments, Messrs Bacon & Woodrow note that there is some evidence of similarity between the results and that over time the funds tend to converge.

This is not of course evidence that the funds studied did not beat the market since no index or control fund was included. However what is clear is that not a single fund could be identified as showing superior performance to that shown by the other funds. Indeed they all behaved in a similar fashion. It is possible (although perhaps unlikely) that all the funds did beat the market. Some of the funds are very large and would not easily be able to differentiate their portfolios from that of the market. Thus it is not unreasonable to conclude that professional managers are not able to distinguish themselves from their colleagues and probably are unable to beat the market.

Richards [54]

Richards has applied the Sharpe test to the data on pension funds collected by Bacon & Woodrow [53]. A number of improvements were made in the application of this test. Firstly, an allowance was made for new money. Because pension funds generally have a positive cash inflow, a distortion can arise in the measurement of the rate of return. New money would be invested in equities and the pension fund would have to pay offer prices for such investment. However, the valuation of such investments would be at bid prices. Hence this method of valuation will produce a bias against the calculated rates of return for pension funds which will vary depending on the rate of investment of new money. To compensate, rates of return were calculated for the market (the FT all-share index was used as a proxy) after allowing for a notional rate of investment of new money of 4 per cent per quarter and transaction costs plus a loss of value resulting from the difference between bid and offer prices totalling 4½ per cent. This adjustment can counteract the bias inherent in this particular method of valuation although to the extent that some funds have a rate of investment of new money in excess of 4 per cent per quarter, then the bias will still be present.

Secondly, a number of modifications were considered to the use of average treasury bill rate as the risk-free asset. The chief problem is that over a long time period, treasury bill rate will clearly vary and an average will have to be used. Because of this, the standard deviation of the returns of a repeated investment in treasury bills is clearly non-zero. Several alternatives are considered: making allowance for the non-zero standard deviation; and choosing cash (with interest rate zero) as the risk-free asset. However, these modifications made very little difference if any to the results.

The Sharpe test was applied to the UK equity portfolio of pension funds over the period 1970-77 and over a number of shorter time periods where data for more funds were available. The conclusion was that on average no superior performance was observed. However, superior performance was demonstrated by several individual funds, a result which is unlikely to be due to chance. Thus this can be regarded as evidence of a high degree of efficiency while admitting of the possibility, albeit remote, of producing superior performance.

The Performance of Unit Trusts[1]

J. M. SAMUELS

Investors and bankers are constantly being bombarded with unit trust advertisements and performance claims. In this report of his research Mr. Samuels, Senior Lecturer in Finance and Accounting at the Graduate Centre for Management Studies, Birmingham, concludes that unit trusts on average perform no better than portfolios made up of shares in the same industries as the unit trusts, but chosen with a pin. But this does not imply that one should pick a unit trust with a pin. It implies, rather, that one would do better with a pin rather than a poor (less than average performance) unit trust. Apparently most unit trusts get the right growth industries, but only one-sixth of the sample in this research did consistently better in those industries.

In recent years unit trusts have proved highly successful in attracting the savings of investors both small and large. They have offered the investor protection for the real value of his savings in inflationary times, as well as the services of highly skilled management for the selection of investment portfolios. Most, if not all, unit trusts can claim to have maintained, and perhaps increased, the real value of their investors' savings as compared with what would have happened if those savings had been invested in deposits at banks and other financial institutions. But it is by no means certain that the advantages of skilled and experienced management can be so easily demonstrated. Would not investors have done just as well if they themselves had managed their own portfolios?

This article attempts to answer this question by comparing the performance of unit trusts with randomly chosen investments in the industries in which the trusts themselves invest. The reason for adopting this approach

is that it is misleading to judge unit trust performance against average market behaviour. The market average, or an overall market index, is affected by the performance of certain declining industries, or declining or lagging firms, in which no reasonable unit trust would consider investing. In judging the gains from investing in unit trust it is considered more relevant to see how well they have done in the industries in which they themselves have invested compared with the average performance in these industries. The question that this raises is: have the managers of the trusts chosen the leading performers in the key industries in which they invest? This is the main point examined in this article.

Advertisements for unit-trust shares often show the dramatic performance of money invested in the trust compared with some average performance of all shares traded in the Stock Market. One crucial factor in the trusts performance is of course the date from which growth is calculated. If the lowest point of a year's prices is taken as the base, it is easy to show a high growth rate on the investment: if, however, an average price for a year is taken, the performance to the next average is obviously not so great. The significance of this fact is also brought out in the article.

Details of the study and of the data used are first described. The results of a three-year comparison, and of a ten-year comparison are then given. Finally, certain conclusions are drawn.

METHOD EMPLOYED

The performance of a sample of unit trusts is first examined over the three-year period 1964 to 1966 inclusive. Thirty six unit trusts were selected randomly from those in existence over the period. Investors in a unit trust in most cases receive their returns in two forms, dividends and capital growth. Certain unit trusts provide for investors who just want capital growth by accumulating unpaid dividends within the trust fund. None of this category was included in the sample. The measurement of capital growth depends on the dates chosen for the opening and closing prices. In the study this was done in two ways. One was to compare the opening price at

[1] The Author wishes to acknowledge the valuable research assistance of Mr. R. Fox.

1 January 1964 with the final price at 31 December 1966. The problem with this method is that the price at 1 January 1964 may not have been a representative price for unit trusts. In fact, as can be seen from the graph, 1 January 1964 was a reasonable starting point, prices having recovered from the low levels of 1963. However, 31 December 1966 was unfortunately not a representative date on which to finish as prices had only just begun to recover from the slump of Autumn, 1966. Whatever dates had been chosen however, the difficulty of a fair representation would have arisen.

This difficulty is not too important since the comparisons are made with random portfolios judged over similar time intervals. Ten random portfolios were produced from the investments portfolios of ten unit trusts as at 1 January 1964 or at as near that date as it was possible to obtain information. These actual company investments were then classified into industry groups, to find the percentage of each of the ten unit trusts in each industry. The performance of these industry groups over each of the three years was obtained from the

Financial Times Actuaries, 500-Share Index (FTA), the change in the index number of share prices between 1 January and 31 December being used together with the average dividends received, which was calculated from the dividend-yields index after adjusting for the standard rate of tax. This gave an average performance of an investment in these industries, year by year, allowing for unit price changes and dividends. The performance of the generated portfolios is then the average performance of a selection of industry groups, weighted by industry, in the same proportions as actual unit trusts invested their funds between different industries.

This means that a comparison was being made between, say, a unit trust that has invested in 120 companies with a portfolio divided between industry groups, in a similar manner to the distribution of the 120 companies. If, say, 25 per cent of the generated portfolio was in the chemical engineering industry, the change in the average share price index for this group over the period of the comparison was weighted by the 25 per cent and added to the weighted-average perform-

Unit Trust & Stock Market Prices (1963-66)

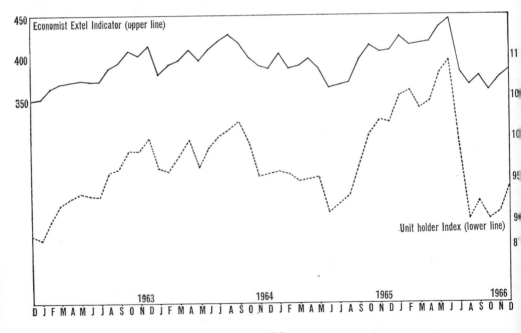

ance of the other industry groups in the generated portfolios. Allowance was made for dividends; and the comparisons were then made.

It should be emphasised that the random portfolios consist of unmanaged investments. The industry weightings were chosen as at 1 January 1964 and were not altered over the period. Managers of the unit trusts had the opportunity to change their investments over the period, as economic conditions dictated. So, if anything, there is a bias in favour of the unit trusts; they should have performed better than the random investments.

Another method of calculating capital growth was to compare the 'mid price' during 1963 with the mid price during 1966, the mid price being the median of the highest and lowest of the offer prices for the respective year. This method smooths out the short-term fluctuations, and gives a possibly more representative indication of the performance of the prices over time. It is not possible to compare such a measure of growth with a market average however, as such mid-point indices do not exist and would be difficult to interpret if they did exist.

Dividends are calculated net of the standard rate of income tax applicable to the particular year. Capital gains tax was not allowed for, as it only became operative during the later part of the period being studied, and the tax rates to be applied would depend on such factors as whether the gain was on a short- or long-term investment.

The second part of the study, which exam-ines the performance of unit trusts over a ten-year period, was felt to be necessary in case the results from the three-year period were not representative. For each of the ten years from 1957 to 1966, the performance of a sample of trusts, ranging from 11 in 1957 to 36 in 1966, was examined. The performance being examined was the change in price from 1 January to 31 December in the particular year plus the dividend received net of the standard rate of tax.

It would have been difficult to generate random portfolios in each of the ten years with similar industry weightings to the trusts, so in the ten-year part of the study the comparison is with the *Economist* Extel Index of share prices. The change in this index of prices from 1 January to 31 December is calculated, and the average dividend yield for each year is added on net of tax.

THREE-YEAR COMPARISON

The findings of the study were that over the recent three years unit trusts on average performed no better than a portfolio of random investments in the same industries in which the trusts themselves invested.

Table 4 shows the performance of the sample of unit trusts, and Table 5 the performance of the random sample. As can be seen, the change in market price plus the accumulation of dividends produced for the random portfolios a loss of 1·42 per cent and for the sample of unit trusts a loss of 1·20 per cent. However, *the difference between these two sets of results is insignificant.*[2] The main results showing the percentage gain or loss on the investments are summarised in Table 1.

None of the individual differences for any year shown in Table 1 is significant, and no significance can be attached to the fact that in two of the three years the unit trusts had the better performance.[2]

While the main purpose of this article is to show that unit trusts on average performed no better than a random portfolio of investments

Table 1 Unit Trust v. Random Portfolio[1] Performance (price changes plus dividends[2]) [%]

	Unit trusts	Random portfolios
1964[3]	−3·80	−4·62
1965[3]	+7·40	+9·77
1966[3]	−5·15	−6·58
1964-1966[4]:		
—earnings reinvested at 4½%	−1·20	−1·42
—earnings reinvested at 8%	−0·87	−1·06

[1] See text, pp 195-6 .
[2] *Dividends net of tax at the standard rate, but no allowance for Capital Gains Tax.*
[3] *1 January to 31 December.*
[4] *1 January 1964 to 31 December 1966.*

[2] Throughout this paper the level of significance is at the 95 per cent confidence level (i.e., there is only a 5 per cent chance, statistically, that there could be an undetected *significant* difference between two compared sets of performance figures).

in the same industry, it is also clear that in two of the three years examined the unit trusts on average did not perform well in absolute terms, showing losses on their investment. However, this does not reflect on investments in unit trusts in any special way, as, over these two periods the stock market as a whole performed badly. The FTA index shows a performance over the three years of —6 per cent + 5 per cent and —11 per cent.[3] So the poor performance of unit trusts over the two periods is just a reflection of general stock market behaviour.

This might suggest that the managers of the unit trusts select the right industries in which to invest, but then having done this the companies they select perform no better than the average in these industries. There is an additional fact adding support to this hypothesis. As has already been explained, no switching was allowed for in the random portfolios, the weighting as at 1 January 1964 being maintained throughout the three-year period. The managers of unit trusts had the opportunity over the period not only to switch companies within an industry so as to find those that performed better than average, but also the opportunity to switch their investments between industries. Despite this opportunity to manage their funds they performed no better than random.

The conclusions so far have related to the average performance of the sample of unit

trusts. Certain trusts, of course, performed much better than the market average or the random portfolios; and in the sample of 36, six performed better in all three years. Only two trusts performed worse than average in all three years, although a further nine performed worse than average in two of the three years.

The range of performance is perhaps surprising. Over the three-year period, the leading unit trusts were showing an overall gain including reinvestment of dividends of around 11 per cent, whereas the worst performers were showing a loss of 12 per cent to 13 per cent. This is calculated on price changes from 1 January 1964 to 31 December 1966. The range of performance is even more dramatic when mid-point changes are considered. The change in the mid-point price for 1963 to the mid-point price for 1966, with reinvestment of dividends, shows leading performers with a 25 per cent growth and the worst performers with a loss of 15 per cent for one trust and 8 per cent for another. For mid-point prices yearly comparisons are not very meaningful, as the mid-point price in one calendar year might be only a short distance away from the mid-point price for the next calendar year.

From the data available a further comparison can be made between trusts specialising in capital growth and trusts promising high income. A few years ago income trusts were doing surprisingly better in terms of capital appreciation than were capital trusts; now, however, the capital growth trusts are showing the better performances. It would be interesting to know what the overall performance of these two types of trust was like, allowing for capital growth and dividends. In the sample investigated, ten trusts placed emphasis on capital growth and three on high income. The results of this very small sample are shown in Table 2.

Statistically none of the differences in Table 2 is significant[4]. On year-end prices, the capital-growth trusts show a better performance in two of the three years, while with changes between mid-point prices the high-income trusts show the better performance in two of the three years.

Table 2 Capital Growth *v.* High Income Unit Trusts' Performance (price changes plus dividends[1]) [%]

| | Capital growth | | Unit trust type High income | |
	Mean (%)	Standard deviation	Mean (%)	Standard deviation
1964[2]	−2·44	6·77	− 4·74	3·04
1965[2]	+7·41	4·93	+ 8·90	1·26
1966[2]	−4·57	1·83	− 7·58	3·18
1963–64[3]	+8·86	3·48	+10·17	2·39
1964–65[3]	+0·13	2·79	+ 0·83	0·87
1965–66[3]	+3·04	2·78	+ 1·23	2·88

[1] *Dividends net of tax at the standard rate but no allowance for Capital Gains Tax.*
[2] *1 January to 31 December.*
[3] *'Mid points' of share prices, i.e., the median of the highest and lowest of the offer prices for the respective year.*

[3] Allowance has to be made to the FTA index for the addition of dividends.

[4] Refer to footnote 2.

Table 3 Unit Trust v. Market, 10-year Performance (price changes plus dividends[1]) [%]

	Number of trusts	Unit trusts	Stock market[2]
1957	11	+ 2·76	− 3·96
1958	11	+37·14	+44·92
1959	12	+50·69	+54·01
1960	14	− 2·83	− 1·91
1961	17	+ 8·85	+ 4·33
1962	17	+ 6·28	− 1·30
1963	17	+24·62	+21·68
1964	31	− 3·80	− 3·72
1965	31	+ 7·40	+ 8·67
1966	31	− 5·15	− 7·02

[1] Dividends net of tax at the standard rate.
[2] Basis: Economist *Extel Index*, plus year-end dividend yields.

TEN-YEAR COMPARISON

It was intended at the outset of the study to compare the performance of unit trusts over a ten-year period with the behaviour of random portfolios over the period. This was not found to be possible because over the ten years there was a great deal of switching of funds in the unit trusts between one industry and another. If the random portfolios were based in holdings in January 1957 this switching would not be allowed for, and the results of the random portfolios would not therefore be really comparable to the performance of the unit trusts.

A sample of unit trusts were examined and their performance for each of the ten years from 1 January 1957 to 31 December 1966 compared with an index of stock market prices. The gains or losses were calculated for each year on year-end prices. The *Economist* Extel Index was used to calculate the changes in the market average, and dividends were allowed for, calculated on the basis of year-end dividend yields.

Not many unit trusts were in existence at the beginning of the period, and it was not always possible to obtain a complete set of financial data of those that did. Consequently the sample size in the early years is small.

The results are given in Table 3.

As can be seen the unit trusts once again on average perform no better than an index of average market performance. In 5 of the 10 years, 1957, 1961, 1962, 1963 and 1966 the unit trusts performed better than the market average. But this is not significant since by pure chance one would expect the unit trust figure to be better than the market figure five times out of the ten. The conclusion is that over the ten-year period the unit trusts on average perform no better than the general market average.

Looking at each of the ten years, and taking into account the variance about the means, only one of the ten years shows a significant difference between the two sets of performance, namely 1962, when statistically the trusts showed a level of performance better than market average.

CONCLUSIONS

It has been shown that during 1964–66 the average unit trust performed no better than random portfolios selected from the same industries in which the trusts themselves invested. The unit trust managers may have selected the correct industries in which to invest but it does not appear that they have been able to choose the best performers within the industry.

On the brief evidence in this study it appears that in good years the unit trusts do worse than the random investments, but in bad years they perform better. This is what

Table 4 Unit Trust Performance (price changes plus dividends[1]) [%]

	Average gain	Standard deviation	Best performance	Worst performance
1964[2]	−3·80	5·64	+ 5·73	−17·07
1965[2]	+7·40	5·18	+14·47	− 6·88
1966[2]	−5·15	2·98	+ 0·79	−12·21
1963–64[3]	+7·24	5·60	+20·70	− 5·57
1964–65[3]	−0·38	3·30	+ 5·08	−11·98
1965–66[3]	+3·53	2·71	+ 7·64	− 1·82
1964–66[4,5]	−1·20	6·45	+16·47	−17·87
1963–66[3,5]	+10·87	8·95	+25·83	−14·63

[1] Dividends net of tax at the standard rate but no allowance for Capital Gains Tax.
[2] 1 January to 31 December.
[3] Mid-points of share prices, i.e., the median of the highest and lowest of the offer prices for the respective year
[4] 1 January 1964 to 31 December 1966.
[5] Plus reinvested earnings.

Table 5 Random Sample[1] Performance

Port-folio	1964	1965	1966	Capital gain	1964 to 1966 Divi-dends	Total[2]
1	− 5·79	+12·15	−6·42	−10·57	+10·36	− 0·21
2	− 3·21	+10·07	−8·89	− 9·77	+ 8·96	− 0·81
3	− 3·64	+ 9·60	−2·63	− 8·06	+11·33	+ 3·27
4	− 7·92	+ 7·65	−6·05	−16·37	+ 9·44	− 6·93
5	+ 1·52	+ 9·93	−9·59	− 6·66	+ 8·66	+ 2·00
6	− 3·25	+ 9·57	−6·89	− 9·92	+ 9·17	− 0·75
7	− 6·46	+10·86	−5·17	−10·98	+ 9·95	− 1·03
8	− 2·01	+10·48	−7·09	− 8·22	+ 9·61	+ 1·39
9	− 5·17	+ 8·52	−4·42	−11·66	+10·59	− 1·07
10	−10·31	+ 8·82	−8·62	−18·54	+ 8·42	−10·11
Mean	− 4·62	+ 9·77	−6·58	−11·07	+ 9·65	− 1·42
Stand-ard de-viation	3·35	1·27	2·15	—	—	3·98

[1] See text, pp 195-6 .
[2] Capital gain plus dividends.

one might expect as unit trusts are to some extent conservative investments, the risks being spread over a number of stocks. With the diversification that unit trusts undertake it could be argued that they provide lower risks, even though their performance is no better than average; but it is not possible to draw any conclusions on this point from the findings of this paper.

No attempt has been made to analyse the unit trusts by size to see if the majority of the investors' funds are in the safer trusts, *i.e.*, those with smaller fluctuations. The performance of the average unit trust has been found to be not very dramatic despite the claims of some prospectuses. While it is perhaps true that trusts provide a safer form of investment, it should be realised that their returns are no better than average.

DO NEW UNIT TRUSTS PERFORM BETTER THAN OLD ONES?

T. E. CRANSHAW

Introduction

During the last few years, the opinion has gained ground that new unit trusts perform better than old ones[1], and in the national press, investment advice has been based on it[2]. The two main reasons for holding this opinion are clear. First, one can see why one should expect it. New trusts have small sums to invest, which can easily be placed in the shares of the management's choice. Size, it has been said, is on their side. Moreover, new trusts do not have the burden of "dead wood", of shares which may have served their purpose, but which are difficult to shed without involving a loss. Second, the lists of "top twenty" trusts which are published annually, or even twice annually, seem to have contained a disproportionately large number of new unit trusts. For example, in 1969, out of 174 trusts, 29 were new. Thus if they performed the same as old trusts one might have expected one-sixth of the top twenty trusts, i.e. about 3, to be new ones. In fact, we find six of the top twenty trusts were new, in apparent confirmation of the expectation that new trusts should have better performance.

The first reason above gives the question a wider significance than that purely of advantageous investment. For if it were found that new trusts only perform the same as old ones, the question would be forced on us "where has our argument gone wrong?" It is therefore a matter of importance to investment analysts to know whether or not new trusts perform convincingly better than old ones.

It is the object of this paper to subject the question to an elementary statistical scrutiny, using data prepared by the Unitholder. "New trusts" are defined as those making their first appearance in the tables, i.e. for each year from January 1st to December 31st, new trusts are those formed more recently than the preceding January 1st. "Old trusts" comprise the remainder in the tables. No attempt has been made to correct the tables for those trusts which have been closed or amalgamated with others during the period under consideration, which is January 1st 1962 to December 31st 1969. They are in any case, quite a small number. Eight trusts which enjoy special tax advantages have been excluded. The performance figure taken is the capital gain+dividend, and for 1969, allowance has been made for capital gains tax paid by the management.

Results

The results of the investigation are given in the accompanying table. Along the top are the dates for the period concerned. Line 1 gives the total number of trusts, and line 2 gives the number of new trusts. Line 3 gives the number of new trusts to be expected in the top twenty on the assumption that their performance is in all ways the same as that of old trusts, and line 4 gives the numbers actually observed. In column 10 is shown the totals of lines 3 and 4. It will be seen that in 5 out of the 8 years the number of new trusts in the top twenty did exceed the expected number, and that the total for all 8 years, 33, is decidedly larger than the expectation, 23.3. The difference is probably not as great as expected by those whose memories go back only a year or two, but it is at least statistically significant at the 5 per cent level, and the belief that new trusts are represented more frequently in the top twenty than their numbers would lead one to expect seems to be confirmed. However, in lines 5 and 6 we record the average performance for each year of all trusts and new trusts only. Here it will be seen that new trusts sometimes perform better than all trusts, and sometimes worse. In column 10 we show the total gains scored by all trusts and by new trusts. From this we see that a man who invested in all trusts would have seen his money grow at a rate of 8.8 per cent per year, whereas a man who each year cashed all his units and invested in the year's new trusts would, neglecting management charges, etc., have seen his money grow at a rate of 9.2 per cent. The difference, 0.4 per cent is much less than the management charges, and bearing in mind that we are here concerned with an average of about 130 figures which themselves fluctuate by about 5–6 per cent (see later) it is hardly significant, and surely too small to be of consequence to the average unit trust investor. How is this conclusion to be reconciled with the earlier statement that new trusts score more top-twenty successes ?

The simplest explanation of this apparent paradox is that the results of new trusts are more widely dispersed than those of old trusts, and the simplest way of testing this explanation is to compute some measure of the dispersion of the two sets of results. The usual statistical quantity for this measure is the root mean square dispersion,

$$r = \sqrt{\sum \left(x_i - \bar{x}\right)^2 / N}$$

where x_i, $i = 1, 2, 3 \ldots$ N are the individual results, and $\bar{x}$ is their average. In lines 7 and 8 we show r calculated for old and new trusts for each year. It will be seen that with the exception of 1962 and 1963 when the numbers of new trusts were too small to give a reliable measure, the dispersion for new trusts is always considerably greater than for all trusts. To this extent, the simple explanation remains tenable.

It would, of course, be an inevitable corollary of this explanation that new trusts would also be over-represented in lists of bottom twenty trusts. Accordingly in line 9, we have counted this number, and in column 10 we record the total for the 8 years. It will be seen that the total is almost the same as the number in the top twenty, providing further confirmation of this explanation of the paradox. At the least, we may say that the fact that new trusts get more results in the top twenty can hardly provide an investment guide, since they get an almost equally large number in the bottom twenty.

It may be thought that the R.M.S. dispersion is rather too abstract a concept to form a convincing basis for investment decisions. In this case, the findings of this section can be demonstrated in another way. Let us divide the total number of trusts in each year into four equal quarters, in order of performance. Then, if new trusts performed the

same in all respects as old trusts, we would find equal numbers of new trusts in all four quarters. If they performed better than old trusts, there would be more new trusts in the upper quarters, and if worse, there would be more in the lower quarters. If their average performance were the same as old trusts, but with a different chance of very good or very bad performance, then we would find the same number of new trusts in the upper half as in the lower half, but different numbers in the inner and outer quarters. In lines 10–13, we have recorded these numbers for each year, and again the totals are given in column 10. It will be seen that the numbers in the upper and lower halves are substantially the same. However the number in the outer quarters is 80 compared with 52 for the inner quarters. Again we see that the expectation performance, i.e. the average performance of new trusts is indistinguishable from that of old trusts, but the chance of very good or very bad performances are much greater. As investments, their expectation is the same as old ones, but they are decidedly riskier.

Discussion

We have now to consider how the results given above might come about. That new trusts are riskier investments than old may be easily explained by the suggestion that they are not yet invested in so many shares, and so their risk is not so widely spread. Since the spread of risk is the strongest argument in support of investment in unit trusts, to this extent new trusts are contra-indicated. From the fact that their average performance is the same as that of old trusts we must conclude either that investing small sums is not easier than investing large sums, and that old purchases which " have served their purpose " are in fact as good as any new purchases that are made, or that managers do not possess the skill to take advantage of the easier situation presented by new trusts. The first alternative seems contrary to reason, and forces us to entertain the possibility that the second is the correct explanation. In this connection, we must point out that it is entirely consistent with the observation that the performance of unit trusts in one year is very little correlated with past performance[3], and with the demonstration that unit trust performance differs very little from the performance of randomly selected portfolios[4].

	Year	1962	1963	1964	1965	1966	1967	1968	1969	Totals
1	No. of trusts	50	54	65	92	111	125	145	174	
2	No. of new trusts	3	4	11	27	19	14	20	29	127
3	Expected no. in top 20	1.2	1.5	3.3	5.8	3.4	2.2	2.6	3.3	23.3
4	Actual no. in top 20	2	1	6	7	3	2	6	6	33
5	Average of all trusts	4.3	19.0	—3.7	9.1	—5.4	30.2	37.7	—13.3	96.4
6	Average of new trusts	5.3	21.8	—2.0	8.4	—6.9	28.5	41.2	—11.3	103.1
7	r all trusts	4.2	6.8	5.1	3.8	3.9	8.2	7.6	7.1	
8	r new trusts	4.1	3.8	7.2	5.2	5.6	8.6	10.3	8.5	
9	New trusts in bottom 20	1	1	3	8	7	1	4	4	29
10	1st quarter	2	1	6	8	3	2	6	11	39
11	2nd quarter	0	2	2	3	2	4	4	9	26
12	3rd quarter	0	0	1	7	5	2	5	4	24
13	4th quarter	1	1	2	9	9	6	5	5	38

REFERENCES

[1] J. A. Aczel, " Unit Trusts, their Growth and Performance ". E.A.C. Jun. Chamber of Commerce for London, 1970.

[2] J. Davis, *The Observer*, January 11 1970, M. Stone, *The Times*, February 21 1970.

[3] R. W. Rutherford, *Investment Analyst*, December 1969.

[4] J. M. Samuels, *The Bankers Magazine*, 1493, 80, 1968.

Composite Measures of Performance

J Dixon

In the following study the measures of portfolio performance developed by Sharpe, Jensen and Treynor are each applied to British unit trust data. The measures are related. Both Sharpe's and Treynor's measure excess return per unit of risk, but Sharpe's measure uses *total* risk and Treynor's uses *systematic* risk, where systematic risk is defined as the non-diversifiable risk of a stock or portfolio. In theory Sharpe's measure should only be used for efficient portfolios and so Treynor's measure is preferable when it is unknown whether the portfolio is efficient or not. Both Jensen's and Treynor's measures use systematic risk and are hence closely related. Jensen's is simpler and it is convenient that the usual regression tests can be applied although great care should be taken in doing so because there is a substantial amount of evidence that the underlying population is not normally distributed but has a stable distribution with characteristic exponent $\neq 2$.

If the measures are to be used to rank portfolios with different levels of systematic risk, Treynor's measure is preferable as it adjusts for the systematic risk of the particular portfolio. If on the other hand the portfolio is being compared with the performance of the market, there is nothing to choose between the two measures.

The Measures

(i) Jensen's measure, J, is simply the regression estimate $\hat{\alpha}$; from the simple regression of the trust's performance on the market's performance.

(ii) Treynor's measure, T, is defined as:

$$T = \frac{\bar{R}_i - R_f}{\beta_i}$$

where β_i is the regression estimate of the slope coefficient in the regression of the fund's performance on the market's performance.

- $\bar{R}_i$ is the average return of the ith fund and
- R_f is a risk-free rate of interest

(iii) Sharpe's measure, S, is defined as:

$$S = \frac{R_i - R_f}{\sigma(R_i)}$$

where $\bar{R}_i$ is the average return of the ith fund and

$\sigma(R_i)$ is the variability (standard deviation) of that return.

(iv) A further measure, M, was developed which is an extension of Sharpe's measure but which uses the mean absolute deviation instead of the standard deviation to measure variability. This is done because the underlying population may be stable rather than normally distributed.

The Data

The data consist of weekly price observations for the period January 1966 through December 1971 on 50 unit trusts, the names of which are given in the annex. The offer price was used in all cases as these prices directly relate to the underlying value of the portfolio. The management has some discretion in relating the price of units to the value of the fund, but it is not in their interest consistently to set the price either as high or as low as the values allow. There is therefore no consistent bias in using these price data as a measure of the asset value of the portfolio. The rate of return on the portfolio also has to take into account its earnings. All the trusts in the sample announce their earnings half-yearly, and these data were collected from the Unit Trust Year Book. A slight problem arises over how to allocate them on a straight line basis over the whole year. Also collected were weekly data on 3 stock market indices: the *Financial Times* industrial ordinary index, which consists of 30 shares, the *Financial Times* actuaries all-share index and the *Financial Times* 500 index which is identical to the all-share index except that it excludes the financial sector. Dividend yields are calculated for each of these indices and these were also collected weekly. Arbitrarily the day chosen in the week was Wednesday.

Some measure of the 'riskless' rate of interest is also needed before any empirical results can be computed. Weekly treasury bill rates were collected. These are not strictly comparable with the weekly price and index data because they were the Friday rate for the beginning part of the period and the Thursday rate for the latter part. In fact in all the empirical work that follows this weekly rate is not used in the regressions and instead we simply assume that the rate is constant and take the constant rate as 5 per cent which is very close to the average rate for the period. (This treatment is not satisfactory but the alternatives are not apparent at the moment.)

Empirical Results

(a) Agreement of measures

The trusts were then ranked by the performance measures for each market index. In each case the ranking of the trusts was almost exactly the same with Jensen's measure being slightly more sensitive than Treynor's to the choice of index. The absolute values of the measures rather than the ranking of the trusts are however affected by the choice of index. Jensen's measure is designed to give us a cardinal measure of the reward for bearing risk, and the dimension of this measure is a rate of return. A comparison of the average values of the three Jensen measures shows that they are 0.0005, −0.0001 and −0.0003 for the regression on the FT industrial ordinary index, the FTA all-share index and the FTA 500 share index respectively. The approximate annual equivalents of these are 2.6 per cent, −0.5 per cent and −1.6 per cent; not a large absolute difference but fairly crucial. If however the measures are only being used to rank funds then the choice between index is not important, and we are given some confidence in the use of a market index in a proxy for the 'market portfolio' because the measures are stable over different proxies. In what follows only results based on the regressions using the FTA all-share index will be presented as this most nearly matches the concept of the market portfolio.

The measure of agreement between the rankings of the trusts by the various measures is given by the following rank correlation matrix overleaf.

These rank correlations are not as high as those found by Smith[1]. However these performance measures are meant to do more than give the relative performance of the trusts; they are meant to be an absolute measure of performance, in which case it is the product

Table 1	S	M	J	T
S	1.0000	0.9673	0.8155	0.8384
M		1.0000	0.8318	0.8579
J			1.0000	0.9249
T				1.0000

moment correlations that are of importance. The product moment correlation matrix is present in the following table:

Table 2	S	M	J	T
S	1.0000	0.9928	0.8967	0.7213
M		1.0000	0.8605	0.7863
J			1.0000	0.5250
T				1.0000

The surprising feature of this table is how poor the agreement is between Jensen's and Treynor's measures. As was to be expected there is very close agreement between S and M, and the level of agreement between Jensen's measure and these two is quite high, but Treynor's measure is rather on its own, which is surprising given its great similarities with Jensen's measure.

(b) The Performance of the Trusts

To compare the performance of trusts with each other one needs to take into account the management charges which differ to a certain extent between funds. However, we are more interested in comparing the performance of this sample of funds with the simple investment strategy of buying a stake in the market at the beginning of the period and holding it until the end. If managers cannot do better than this with their funds, then they are not earning their keep, and certainly not justifying their management expenses as the portfolios could be picked in a much cheaper way (by a pin).

Histogram 1 shows the distribution of reward to variability ratios and the corresponding measures for buying a stake in each of the market indices and holding it until the end of the period are also marked. It is seen that just over half the trusts perform better than a holding in the FT industrial ordinary index, but that well under half perform less well than a holding in either of the other two indices. The corresponding histogram for the distribution of the reward to mean absolute deviation ratio shows an exactly similar picture. This evidence is quite encouraging from the trust manager's point of view because it can be argued that the industrial ordinary index represents a real alternative holding for an investor as it consists of only 30 shares, whereas the other indices are not possible holdings. But later evidence will suggest that these two measures are less satisfactory than the ones based on systematic risk.

Histograms 2 and 3 present the distribution of Jensen's measure based on regressions on the FT industrial ordinary index and on the FT all-share index respectively. The distribution of this measure based on regressions on the 500 share index is almost identical with the latter. It is seen that more than half the trusts performed less well than a holding in the all-share index, ie that for more than half the trusts the measure is negative. But when the comparison is made with a holding in the industrial ordinary index, then more than half did better, but very few of either the positive or negative coefficients are significant.

The general conclusion from these measures must be that the trusts on average do not do any better than a naive investment policy of buying a random portfolio and holding, and that they therefore do not justify their research expenditures. There are also only three significant positive values using a T-test which suggests that there is very little evidence of trusts performing better than a naive investment policy.

Histogram 1: Unit Trust Performance v Market Indices 1966-71 (Sharpe's Measure)

FTIOI: Financial Times industrial ordinary index
FTAAI: Financial Times actuaries all-share index
FTA 500 I: Financial Times actuaries 500 share index

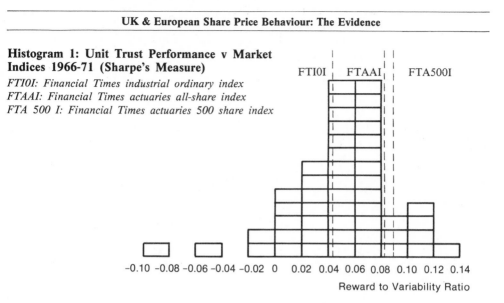

Reward to Variability Ratio

Histogram 2: Unit Trust Performance as Measured by Jensen's Measure 1966 - 1971

Regressions based on Financial Times industrial ordinary index

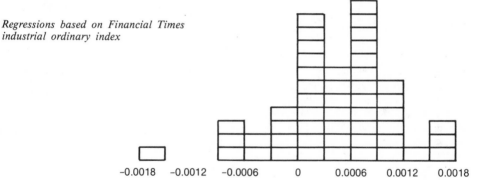

Histogram 3: Unit Trust Performance as Measured by Jensen's Measure 1966 - 1971

Regressions based on Financial Times actuaries all-share index

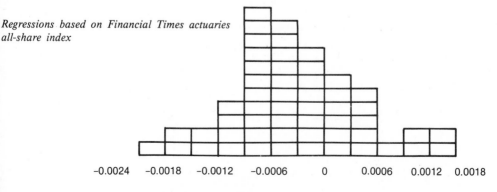

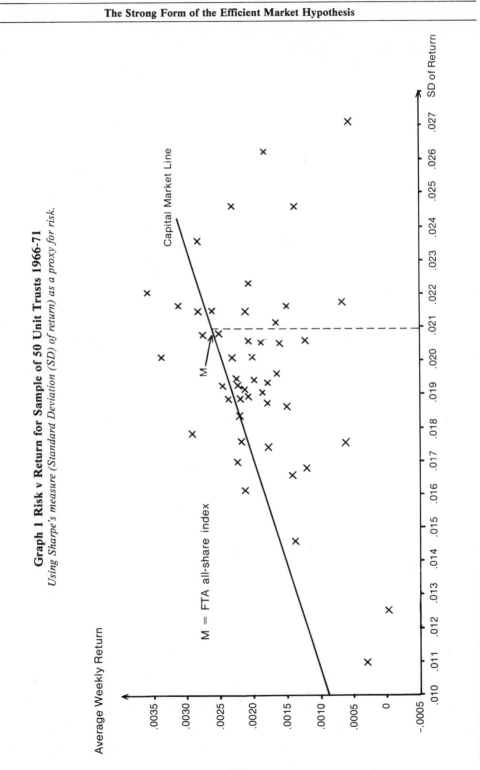

Graph 1 Risk v Return for Sample of 50 Unit Trusts 1966-71
Using Sharpe's measure (Standard Deviation (SD) of return) as a proxy for risk.

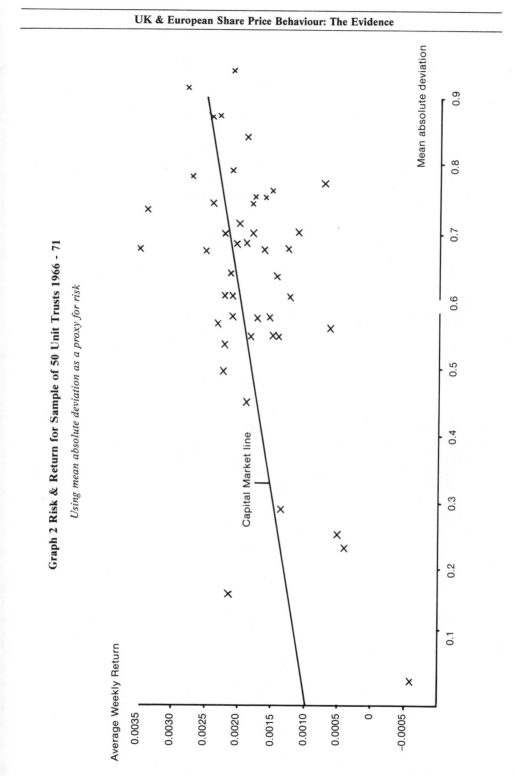

Graph 2 Risk & Return for Sample of 50 Unit Trusts 1966 - 71

Using mean absolute deviation as a proxy for risk

(c) The Fit of the Model

(i) The theory would lead us to expect that there is a positive straight line relationship between risk and return. Investors are averse to a risk and so demand a premium in the form of higher return for accepting risk. If this is true and if the expectations turn out to be realised on average, then the relationship will be observed in past data.

Graph 1 shows average weekly returns for the 50 trusts plotted against the risk measure favoured by Sharpe, the standard deviation. There is a pronounced positive relationship which is as expected but the points do not lie very close to any straight line indicating that either the risk measure is not very satisfactory, or that the ex-post realisations were very different from the expectations. The capital market line is also drawn in on this graph. This is the line which represents all combinations of holdings in the riskless asset and in the market portfolio. As can be seen, a substantial number of funds performed less well than this over the period.

Graph 2 shows the same as Graph 1, except that mean absolute deviation is used as a measure of risk instead of standard deviation. The points more nearly fall on a straight line suggesting that this is a slightly better measure of risk.

(ii) For both Jensen's and Treynor's measures it is necessary to run regressions of trust return on market index return and something should be said about how well determined these relationships are. In general the regressions are satisfactory as judged by the normal criteria. The average coefficients of determination for the three sets of regressions are:

0.41 (FT ordinary index)
0.44 (FT all share index)
0.46 (FT 500 index)

and these averages are slightly distorted by two trusts, Target Preference and Target Income. It is possible that these should be excluded from the sample, as they behave atypically in almost every respect; and while awkward data points cannot just be discarded these two trusts underwent radical reorganisation within the sample period and it is arguable that they are not the same entity throughout. This is especially true of Target Preference.

The pattern of the least square residuals also gives confidence in the regressions. They conform closely to the usual assumptions. There is no evidence of any auto-correlation; the Durbin-Watson statistic being very close to 2 for all the regressions. This also gives confidence in the linear hypothesis. The model suggests that there is a linear relationship between these rates of return and if a quadratic relationship was in fact a better fit then this would show up in the pattern of the residuals.

---

1 K V Smith, *Portfolio Management,* Holt, Rinehart and Winston, 1971

Name of Trust	Average Weekly Return 1966-71	Standard Deviation of Weekly Return
1 Abacus Grants	0.00208	0.0224
2 Allied First	0.00182	0.0192
3 Allied Growth and Income	0.00210	0.0189
4 Electrical and Industrial	0.00178	0.0187
5 Metals and Minerals	0.00112	0.0006
6 Allied Capital	0.00220	0.0187
7 Allied High Income	0.00224	0.0170
8 North American	0.00055	0.0271
9 Unicorn Income	0.00229	0.0187
10 Unicorn Trustee	0.00240	0.0215
11 Ebor Capital Accumulator	0.00274	0.0209
12 Ebor Commodity Share	0.00180	0.0191
13 Ebor Property and Building	0.00223	0.0177
14 Ebor General	0.00297	0.0178
15 First Provincial High Distribution	0.00152	0.0186
16 'Reserves'	0.00150	0.0217
17 Hill Samuel British	0.00213	0.0215
18 Hill Samuel Capital	0.00288	0.0215
19 City of London	0.00276	0.0236
20 Gold and General	0.00142	0.0246
21 Jessel Income	0.00222	0.0182
22 Jessel New Issues	0.00234	0.0201
23 Capital Priority	0.00309	0.0216
24 Financial Priority	0.00344	0.0201
25 High Income Priority	0.00217	0.0190
26 M & G General	0.00211	0.0187
27 M & G Dividend	0.00178	0.0174
28 Mutual Security Plus	0.00207	0.0206
29 Mutual Income	0.00250	0.0208
30 National Scotunits	0.00144	0.0166
31 Security First	0.00144	0.0148
32 Oceanic Progressive	0.00060	0.0178
33 Oceanic High Income	0.00120	0.0206
34 Oceanic General	0.00074	0.0218
35 Practical	0.00220	0.0161
36 S & P Capital	0.00175	0.0195
37 S & P European Growth	0.00133	0.0212
38 S & P High Yield	0.00205	0.0191
39 Scotbits	0.00233	0.0247
40 Scotyields	0.00241	0.0194
41 Target Consumer	0.00203	0.0201
42 Target Financial	0.00354	0.0220
43 Target Growth	0.00162	0.0205
44 Target Income	0.00039	0.0110
45 Target Preference	- 0.00017	0.0125
46 Vavasseur Capital	0.00189	0.0261
47 Commonwealth	0.00177	0.0194
48 High Income	0.00189	0.0205
49 Leisure	0.00160	0.0211
50 Orthodox	0.00126	0.0167

U.K. UNIT TRUST PERFORMANCE 1964–74

C.W.R. WARD AND A. SAUNDERS*

INTRODUCTION

There have been a number of empirical studies[1] of U.K. Unit Trusts based on fairly general assumptions about the nature of capital markets. As far as we are aware, only two studies, Dixon's (7) and Briscoe, Samuels, and Smyth's (4), have directly attempted to employ a composite test of performance based on the measurement of returns and the associated riskiness obtained by investors holding units. Most investors would agree that the relevant measure of return would include both capital gains and dividends, although they might not accept any one definition of risk. Specifically, in the context of the Sharpe (18) – Lintner (11) Capital Market theory a case could be established for using two different definitions of risk involving either total or its systematic component. However it might be argued that this Capital Market theory has only been developed to analyse United States Stock Exchange data and Mutual Fund performance, and that the performance of U.K. Unit Trusts cannot satisfactorily be explained in the context of these models. Although the central aim of this paper is to evaluate the performance of Unit Trusts, a large part of our investigation necessarily concerns the applicability of the model to the U.K. Stock Market.

The first section of the paper is a discussion of the theoretical framework of Capital Market theory and its implications for Unit Trust investors. The second section deals with our empirical results. In particular we (a) compare Unit Trusts using the composite return/risk measures suggested by Sharpe (19), Treynor (22) and Jensen (9) in their analyses of Mutual Fund performance, (b) discuss the consistency of Unit Trust with Mutual Fund results and (c) discuss the implications of the results for Unit Trust investors.

THEORETICAL FRAMEWORK

The Capital Market theory on which this study is based asserts that the expected return on any asset traded in the Capital Market is directly related to the expected risk from holding that asset in an efficiently diversified portfolio. Since it is assumed that all the "price-making" investors are holding well diversified portfolios, it follows that the price of each security in the market will be adjusted until the relationship between expected return and risk is consistent with the price-makers return/risk attitudes.

The authors are Lecturers in Monetary Economics and Finance at the City of London Polytechnic. (Paper received August 1975)

An important result of this argument is that in determining whether a security should be held by an investor, the total risk of a security is less important than the effect its purchase has on the investor's portfolio. This argument implies that some shares, for example, commodity shares, which may be intrinsically risky, will still be bought, even with the expectation of a relatively low return, since, if these returns have low correlations with the returns from holding other equities, portfolio risk will be reduced. For example Sarnat points out[2] that in the period 1963–70, "The impact of commodity shares on the portfolio is particularly noteworthy: the inclusion of these shares in the opportunity set materially improves the risk return position of investors in the United Kingdom".

In the models developed by Sharpe (18) and Lintner (11) (hereafter referred to as S–L) it is assumed that investors can borrow or lend at a given "riskless" rate of interest. Consequently the expected return on any security is given by the following equation,

$$E(R_i) = R_F + \frac{Cov(R_i, R_m)}{\sigma^2(R_m)} \; (E(R_m) - R_F) \tag{1}$$

where $E(R_i)$ = expected return of the security i, where i = 1 ... n

$\qquad R_F$ = the return from lending or the cost of borrowing at the "riskless" rate.

$Cov(R_i, R_m)$ = The covariance of returns from holding the security i and the returns from the "market" portfolio. This is the contribution to portfolio risk caused by the holding of the security i.

$\qquad E(R_m)$ = the expected return from holding the "market" portfolio.[3]

In testing whether the model holds, two possible assumptions can be made. The first and most simple is that on average the expectations of investors are correct, thus over a given period the actual realised returns reflect the expected values. The second, made by Jensen (10) is that a linear relationship exists between the ex post returns on any security and a general market factor. An expression for the expected return on any security, conditional on the market factor can be derived from the following assumed relationship;

$$E(R_i \; R_m, \beta_i) = R_F(1 - \beta_i) + R_m\beta_i \tag{2}$$

here β_i = the estimated $\dfrac{Cov(R_i, R_m)}{\sigma^2(R_m)}$

However, it is important to point out that from exhaustive testing on U.S. data by Fama and McBeth (8) amongst others[4], there appears to be some doubt whether the returns of securities are sufficiently determined by specifying R_F, R_m and β_i. In particular Black, Jensen and Scholes (3) found that a more appropriate ex ante model might be defined in terms of $E(R_z)$, $E(R_m)$ and β, where $E(R_z)$ was the expected return from a portfolio which has a β of zero. The effect of this modification is that the expected returns from portfolios with a β of less than 1 are higher than those expected with the S–L model, and, the expected returns of high β portfolios are lower than in the S–L model. However we are not aware of any empirical study on U.K. data, using the methods of Black, Jensen and Scholes (3) or Fama and MacBeth (8).

If the model does hold then one would expect that a random portfolio of securities would have returns not significantly different from those conditionally expected. Hence, the difference between the observed return and the conditional expected return J in Equation (3) below may be used as a measure of Trust Management efficiency (as used by Jensen (10) for Mutual Funds in the United States)

$$J = R_i - E(R_i | R_m, \beta_i) \tag{3}$$

which by substitution into Equation (2) gives,

$$J = R_i - R_F - \beta_i(R_m - R_F) \tag{4}$$

Treynor (22) independently developed an alternative measure of investment management performance which implicitly used the same model, and suggested that the relevant measure T was the "excess" return per unit of systematic risk, i.e.,

$$T = \frac{R_i - R_F}{\beta_i} \tag{5}$$

A third measure proposed by Sharpe (19) reflects the observation that most Unit Trust (or Mutual Fund) portfolios are highly diversified, and that the returns from holding units are closely related to the return from holding the market portfolio. This implies that β_i can be written as,

$$\frac{\text{Côv}(R_i \, R_m)}{\hat{\sigma}^2(R_m)} \simeq \frac{\hat{\sigma}(R_i)}{\hat{\sigma}(R_m)} \tag{6}$$

Consequently Sharpe (19) has proposed the measure S, as the appropriate measure of performance, where

$$S = \frac{R_i - R_F}{\sigma(R_i)} \tag{7}$$

(This can be seen to be $\simeq T \div \sigma(Rm)$ provided that the portfolio returns are closely correlated with the market.)

Of the three, the Jensen measure appears to be the most elegant since it lends itself to statistical testing more readily than the others. Nevertheless for the purposes of ranking, Treynor's (22) measure is slightly more attractive as it measures the marginal "excess" return per unit of expected risk. Both the Treynor (22) and Jensen (10) measures will compare diversified or undiversified Trusts, but there is an implicit assumption made in comparing the performance of undiversified Trusts that the investor will diversify. In other words, even if it could be established that the investment performance of a Unit Trust was consistent from one period to the next it could not be inferred that the investor should place all his funds in a Trust ranked "best" by the Jensen or Treynor measure. The reason for this is that the risk factor taken into account is market risk rather than total risk. Hence a Trust ranked "best" by Jensen's or Treynor's tests might have a very high individual risk factor (e.g. a Commodity Unit Trust) and should therefore constitute only a part of the investor's portfolio.

From the investor's point of view, if Unit Trust performance ranking was established to be consistent ex post, and he wished to make only one investment, it might be more appropriate to use Sharpe's measure since it takes into account the total riskiness of the investment rather than the contribution to portfolio risk. But if it is not established that fund investment performance is consistently better than expected (and most of the studies on Mutual Fund data suggest that it is not)[5] then the implication is that investors have a number of choices open to them. Firstly they can invest and diversify on their own account by choosing a number of shares at random and "gear" their portfolios up or down by borrowing on the strength of their investments or by placing some cash on deposit. However this might be construed as being a time-consuming and even a complex task. Secondly they can cut out the task of selection by buying two or three well diversified Unit Trust units and gearing up or down. The difference between these two alternatives will depend on the transaction costs involved and on the charges levied by the Unit Trust managements.[6] A third, and slightly less efficient method, is to invest in two or three Unit Trusts which appear to have a stable market risk-factor policy which is consistent with the investor's own preferences. The fourth and final method would be to choose one (well diversified) Unit Trust with a stable individual risk-factor. These alternative investment policies all assume that the expected return from holding a portfolio will depend upon its market risk. This raises a question relating to the stability of the market risk factors exhibited by Unit Trusts. For, whilst Jensen (10) found that the β coefficients were relatively stable over a 20 year period, Campanella (5) discovered some tendency for Mutual Fund β's to change, primarily because of movements into and out of cash. This is a particularly important factor in examining U.K. Unit Trust performance over the past three years, since many Trusts have held an unprecedentedly large proportion of their assets in the form of cash or short term deposits. This has had the effect of decreasing the β factor of the portfolio — the β of a portfolio being closely approximated by a weighted average of the constituent β's. Since the covariance of returns between deposits and the market portfolio is very low, the β factor of the proportion on deposit will similarly be very small.

The only possible justification (given the implications of the model) for Unit Trusts to change their β factors radically is if Unit Trust managers could forecast the return on the market portfolio significantly more accurately than the rest of the market. Whilst no empirical work has been published in the U.K. on this question, most of the U.S. empirical studies, for example Jensen (10), Treynor (22), Campanella (5), suggest that as a group, fund managers are no better than average in their forecasting ability and that movements into and out of cash may only affect the stability of β rather than gain super-normal profits.

EMPIRICAL RESULTS

We first calculated the continuously compounded annual rates of return for forty nine Unit Trusts over the nine year period 1 January 1964 to 31 December 1972. Then using the twelve month deposit rate (Local Authority) as an appropriate measure of the Risk Free Return (R_F) and the F.T. 650 index (R_{mt}), two sets of regression results were derived: the first set were based on the annual rate of return from holding the 'Index' (R_{mt}), the second, on the "excess" returns, i.e. ($Ru_{it} - R_{F_t}$) and ($R_{mt} - R_{F_t}$).

Our justification for using two methods for estimating β_i is based on the possible criticism of Jensen's assumption of a constant Risk Free rate. Smith and Tito[7] estimated β_i using both methods for Mutual Funds and found close agreement between the two sets of estimates. We calculated, using Smith and Tito's data, that the R^2 was 0.9997. Using our own data the R^2 was 0.9969. The conclusion appears to be that either method can be used without fear of introducing significant bias.[8]

Consequently, although each set provided us with three statistics for each Unit Trust, the regression coefficient $\hat{\beta}_i$, the correlation coefficient $\hat{\rho}$ (Ru_i, R_m) and the variance of returns $\hat{\sigma}^2$ (Ru_i), only one set of statistics (in which R_F was allowed to vary) was employed to derive all three performance measures: S, T and J 1. The second set was only used to devise one alternative measure J 2.

The Unit Trusts were then ranked using each measure (See Appendix I) and the

·rankings were compared for consistency by calculating the rank correlation coefficients between the different measures (see Table 1 below).

TABLE 1
RANK CORRELATION FOR THE PERFORMANCE MEASURES FOR THE UNIT TRUSTS 1964–1972

	J1	J2	T	S
J1		.9836	.9825	.9692
J2	.9836		.9869	.9865
T	.9825	.9869		.9699
S	.9692	.9685	.9699	

Our correlations were very similar to those found by Smith and Tito (21) but higher than those found by Dixon (7). Any differences probably reflect the investment horizon chosen, a characteristic noted and discussed by Russell (14) (15) as the 'Granger' effect. This result implies that any of three methods will provide approximately the same ranking of Unit Trust performances.

Having ranked the performances, the question still remains whether the rankings reflect significant management superiority or inferiority. This may be examined by testing the Jensen performance measure (J 1) for statistical significance. Since the value of the Jensen estimate is given by the intercept term in the regression equations, and where returns are assumed to be normally distributed, a t-test of significance can be used on the estimates. The t-values calculated and shown in Appendix II reveal that no Unit Trust achieved a significantly superior rate of return over the period. On the other hand nearly a quarter (21%) of the sample performed significantly worse than expected. This can be compared with Jensen's (9) study of Mutual Funds which showed that over the period 1945–64 just over 12% of the sample performed significantly worse than expected. A number of possible explanations for these results can be advanced:

(a) The Capital Asset Pricing Model does not satisfactorily explain the price structure of the U.K. Stock Market, (b) the selection of the Index to represent the Market portfolio is incorrect, (c) British Unit Trusts managers generate greater management or trading expenses than their American counterparts.

Whilst the three hypotheses are not mutually exclusive, some light can be thrown on the relative importance of each by looking at the relationship between rates of return and risk outside the sample period.

Since the Pricing Model postulates a linear relationship between the risk and return, one would expect that in a period in which the market index fell (e.g. 1973, 1974) those Unit Trusts with the greatest systematic risk would perform significantly worse than those with less systematic risk. As can be seen from Diagram I the ex post Security Market Line divides the 49 Unit Trusts in the risk-return space into two segments, with 28 trusts performing better and 21 worse than expected.

There is also a clear and significant relationship between the ex post returns and the β coefficient. As Jensen has argued,[9] one would not necessarily expect the ex post values to be symmetrically distributed around the Market Return — Riskless Rate Line. In particular, during a period when the ex post market line has a negative slope (see Diagram I), inefficiently diversified Trusts may out-perform an efficient portfolio with the same level of systematic risk. Such a result, Jensen argues, should be attributed to good luck rather than superior trust management. As most of the Unit Trusts in the sample appear to be well diversified this argument does not appear to impose a significant bias. One could indeed argue, on the basis of the 1973 results, that Unit Trusts performed as predicted by the Capital Market Model and that the investor was only marginally gaining[10] by investing through the medium.

Looking at the 1974 results (Diagram 2) it appears that the majority of the Trusts out performed the market line. One explanation for this, is that during both 1973 and 1974 most Unit Trusts revised the composition of their portfolios, holding a greater proportion of short term assets, as shown in Table 2 below.

TABLE 2
COMPOSITION OF HOLDINGS (MARKET VALUE)

	Total holdings at Market Value	Short Term Assets Net		Company Securities	
		value	%	value	%
1972	2553	229	9.0	2321	90.9
1973	2097	333	15.9	1756	83.7
1974	1400	391	27.9	981	70.1

Source, *Financial Statistics,* May 1975

218

DIAGRAM 1
SCATTER DIAGRAM OF RISK (β) AND RETURN FOR
49 UNIT TRUSTS IN 1973

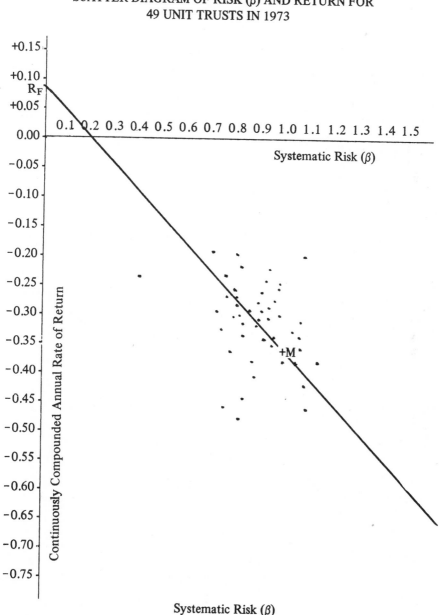

DIAGRAM 2
SCATTER DIAGRAM OF RISK (β) AND RETURN FOR
49 UNIT TRUSTS IN 1974

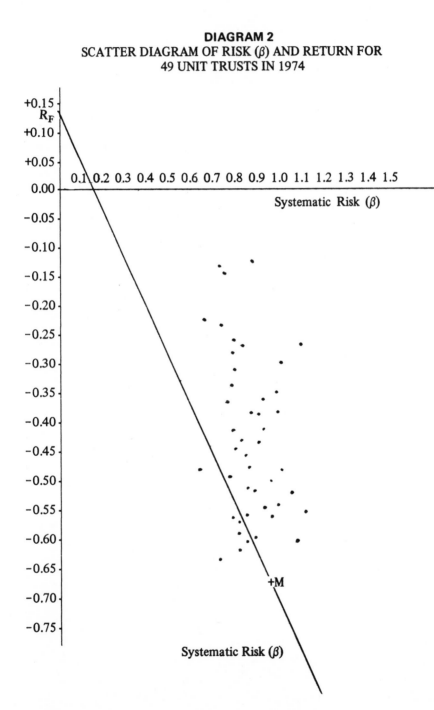

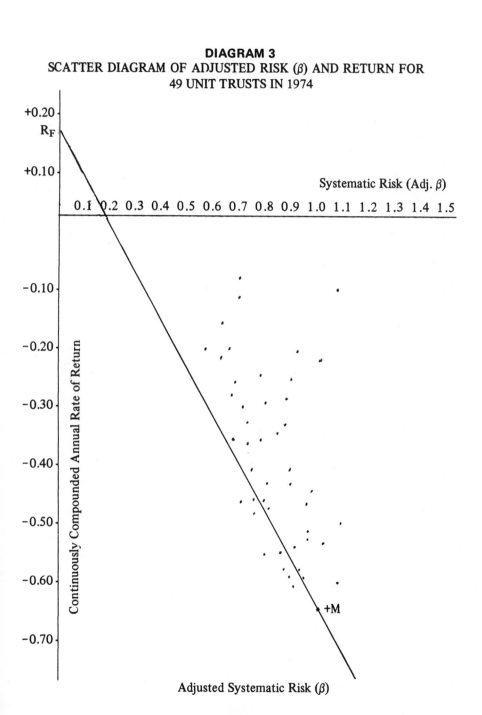

DIAGRAM 3
SCATTER DIAGRAM OF ADJUSTED RISK (β) AND RETURN FOR
49 UNIT TRUSTS IN 1974

221

Whilst part of this change is obviously due to the fall in Stock Market Prices during this period, there still appears to have been an active switching policy from long term to short term assets.

In the United States, Campanella (5) found similar adjustments taking place in Mutual Fund Portfolios from year to year and concluded that the movement into and out of short term assets was more significant in explaining changes in the Funds' β characteristics than the composition of the security portfolio. Consequently we feel that in analysing 1974 results, it is important to take into account the change in the β characteristics of each trust due to the proportionately larger holdings of short term assets.[11]

The actual returns for 1974 are plotted against the adjusted β's in Diagram 3. It appears that despite the β adjustment there are still a large number of Trusts (40) performing better than expected. But the inference that should be drawn from this is not that the selection of securities during this period was especially efficient, but rather that the β characteristics of the Trusts were changing too fast for our adjustment procedure. Consequently our adjusted β values are probably too high and the Trusts appear to have performed better than they actually did.[12]

The second possible explanation was that the selection of the index to represent the Market Portfolio was incorrect. The issue in dispute here is the identification of the Market Portfolio. Dixon (7) found that the choice of Index[13] for the purpose of ranking Unit Trust performance was arbitrary, although from the point of view of Capital Market Theory the differences may be crucial. We therefore used the widest possible definition of Market Index, the "650", since it incorporates both financial and industrial sectors.

The final explanation is that British Unit Trusts generate greater management/ trading expenses than their American counterparts. One complication in quantifying the importance of this factor is that whilst transaction costs are reflected in Unit Trust returns, no such allowance is made in calculating Market Portfolio performance. However, Corner and Burton (6) found that U.K. trust management expenses were considerably higher[14] than those of U.S. Mutual Funds, which suggests that high expenses may be a significant factor in explaining the differences between U.K. and U.S. open-ended fund performance.

A further aspect which affects the "usefulness" of the model is the matching of the model "riskiness" with investors' expectations. In particular the question should be raised whether model classifies as "high risk" those Trusts which investors would classify as being "high risk". This has been discussed by Jensen (10) and McDonald (12) with respect to Mutual Fund data, both of whom found that high risk (β)' funds were similarly classified by investors.

In the U.K. investors might find it difficult to agree on risk — classification, although the Unit Trust Year Book (23) provides some information on which to base such a classification. We classified on the basis of two criteria, first the name of the Trust, and second the brief description of the Trust portfolio appearing in the Unit Trust Year Directories/Books 1964–74 (23) (see Table 4 below).[15]

TABLE 4
GROUPED UNIT TRUSTS 1964–74

	Income	Inter-national	Balanced	Specialist	Capital
Number	5	9	25	5	5
Mean $\hat{\beta}$	0.783	0.849	0.898	0.915	0.959
Mean $\hat{R}$	0.073	0.091	0.098	0.114	0.096
Mean $\hat{\sigma}^2$	0.030	0.038	0.037	0.047	0.052

Five categories were chosen: Income, International, Balanced, Specialist and Capital. A priori one would expect that these Trusts aiming for long term capital growth would have a high β because of the greater systematic variability in their short term returns, whereas at the other end of the scale, Income Trusts would be expected to have low systematic risk. As can be seen from Table 4, the Capital Trusts had a higher mean β (and σ^2) than the Income Trusts as predicted by Capital Market Theory. Additionally, as one would expect, the International, Balanced and Specialist groups had greater systematic risk than the Income Trusts but less than the Capital Trusts. These results suggest that investors in Unit Trusts could use the β coefficient as a consistent measure of risk on which to base their portfolio policy.

CONCLUSION

We have argued that the measurement and inclusion of risk is useful in assessing Unit Trust performance. It has been shown, using annual data, that the precise way in which risk is incorporated is not crucial since the three methods of performance ranking produced very similar results.

We also showed the definition of risk (β) which was a priori most acceptable, was consistent with investors expectations even though from year to year the Trust managers adjusted their portfolios and in the process of so doing, altered the risk factor of their Fund(s).

If Unit Trust Managers maintained the level of risk (β) then investors might reasonably use Unit Trusts as a mechanism for buying into an efficiently diversified portfolio. If, as we found during 1973 and 1974, the risk characteristics were changing, then the "usefulness" of the Trusts would be diminished, unless of course managers have a more accurate forecasting ability than the market price makers. In the light of the 1964—72 empirical results this view appears insupportable.

The major implications that can be drawn from this paper are (1) that the U.K. Stock Market is efficient in the sense that high risk (β) portfolios can expect to earn higher returns than lower risk (β) portfolios, and (2) that the sample of Unit Trusts examined over this period performed relatively poorly compared to the market.

NOTES

[1] Corner and Burton (6), Briscoe, Samuels and Smyth (4), Samuels (16) and Dixon (7).

[2] Sarnat (17) p.62.

[3] The market portfolio is defined as the portfolio containing all securities in the market in proportion to their market value.

[4] See Black, Jensen and Scholes (3), Miller and Scholes (13).

[5] Jensen (10), Campanella (5), McDonald (12).

[6] For further discussion of this point see Black and Scholes (2).

[7] Smith and Tito (21) page 338.

[8] The means and standard deviation of the βs were co-incident (to two places of decimals) being 0.88 and 0.12 respectively.

[9] Jensen (10) pp.196—199.

[10] Since 28 of the 49 Unit Trusts outperformed the Market Line.

[11] In adjusting the β for use in the 1974 analysis we restricted the adjustment procedure by using information available for the period up to the end of 1973. Whilst this probably implies that our adjustment is biased in favour of the trusts, it is still a test of the predictive power of the model.

[12] Since the β characteristics of Trusts have been reduced over the 1973–74 period because of the switch into short term assets, on average the Trusts might be expected to perform significantly worse than the Market Index in a "bull market" e.g. January–March 1975 (M. Bayliss (1) pointed out that in the first six months of 1975 the average Unit Trust rose by only 53.9% compared with a rise of 105.7% in the F.T. All Share Index).

[13] Indices compared by Dixon (7) F.T. Industrial Ordinary, F.T. Actuaries All Share Index (650) and the F.T. Actuaries (500) Index.

[14] Corner and Burton (6) found the ratio of expenses to net assets was for the U.K. 1.68% (median) and for the U.S. 0.79%.

[15] For details of classification see Appendix II.

REFERENCES

(1) Bayliss M., "Not a Performance to be ashamed of", THE TIMES 28/6/75.

(2) Black F. and Scholes M., "From Theory to a New Financial Product" JOURNAL OF FINANCE, 1974, pp.399–438.

(3) Black F., Jensen M. and Scholes M., "The Capital Asset Pricing Model: Some Empirical Tests", in STUDIES IN THE THEORY OF CAPITAL MARKETS, edited by Jensen M.C., New York, Praeger, 1972.

(4) Briscoe G., Samuels J.M. and Smyth D.J. "The treatment of risk in the Stock Market" JOURNAL OF FINANCE, September 1969, pp.707–714.

(5) Campanella F.B. THE MEASUREMENT OF PORTFOLIO RISK EXPOSURE, THE USE OF THE BETA COEFFICIENT. Heath, 1972.

(6) Corner D.C. and Burton H. INVESTMENT AND UNIT TRUSTS IN BRITAIN AND AMERICA, Elek, 1968.

(7) Dixon H.D., "Composite measures of performance": Unpublished working paper, University of Exeter, Department of Economics, 1973.

(8) Fama E.F. and MacBeth J.D. "Risk, Return and Equilibrium: Empirical Tests" JOURNAL OF POLITICAL ECONOMY, 1973, pp.607–635.

(9) Jensen M.C., "The Performance of Mutual Funds in the period 1945–64" JOURNAL OF FINANCE, May 1968, pp.389–416.

(10) Jensen M.C., "Risk, the Pricing of Capital Assets and the Evaluation of investment Portfolios", JOURNAL OF BUSINESS, April 1969, pp.167–247.

(11) Lintner J. "Security Prices, Risk and Maximal Gains from Diversification", JOURNAL OF FINANCE, December 1965, pp.587–615.

(12) McDonald J.G. "Objectives and Performance of Mutual Funds 1960–69", JOURNAL OF FINANCIAL AND QUANTITATIVE ANALYSIS, June 1974, pp.311–333.

(13) Miller M.H. and Scholes M. "Rates of Return in Relation to Risk: a Re-examination of some Recent Findings", in STUDIES IN THE THEORY OF CAPITAL MARKETS, edited by Jensen M.C., New York, Praeger, 1972.

(14) Russell A.H. "The City University F.T. Actuaries, Data Bank of Daily Share Prices" in MATHEMATICAL METHODS IN INVESTMENT AND FINANCE, edited by Shell K. and Szegö G.P., North Holland, 1972, pp. 638–654.

(15) Russell A.H., "Estimation of β in the Sharpe/Tobin Capital Asset Evaluation Model", THE STATISTICIAN, Vol.XXIII No.1, March, 1974.

(16) Samuels J.M. "The Performance of Unit Trusts", BANKERS MAGAZINE, August 1968, pp.80–87.

(17) Sarnat M. "The Gains from Risk Diversification on the London Stock Exchange", JOURNAL OF BUSINESS FINANCE, Autumn 1972, pp.54–64.

(18) Sharpe W.F. "Capital Asset Prices: A Theory of Market Equilibrium under Conditions of Risk", JOURNAL OF FINANCE, 1964, vol.19, pp.425–442.

(19) Sharpe W.F., "Mutual Fund Performance", JOURNAL OF BUSINESS January 1966, pp.119–138.

(20) Sharpe W.F., PORTFOLIO THEORY AND CAPITAL MARKETS, McGraw-Hill, 1970.

(21) Smith K.V. and Tito D.A., "Risk – Return Measures of Ex-Post Portfolio Performance" in INVESTMENT PORTFOLIO DECISION-MAKING edited by Bicksler J.L. and Samuelson P.A., Heath, 1974.

(22) Treynor J.L. "How to Rate Management of Investment Funds" HARVARD BUSINESS REVIEW, Jan.–Feb. 1965, pp.63–75.

(23) Unit Trust Year Directories/Books 1964, 1965, ... 1975, Fundex.

APPENDIX I

RANKING OF UNIT TRUSTS' PERFORMANCES

	J1	J2	T	S
Allied Capital	12	11	12	11
Allied First	23	23	23	21
Allied G. Inc.	9	9	9	8
B.I.F.	7	7	7	4
B. Life	39	37	40	38
Crescent High	26	28	29	24
Crescent Reserves	40	39	39	39
Discretionary	6	6	6	5
Elec. & Ind.	18	19	17	17
Hill Sam. Brit.	36	35	35	34
Hill Sam. Cap.	11	13	11	14
Hill Sam. Inc.	37	36	38	36
Hill Sam. Int.	32	25	33	35
J.–L. Cons.	49	49	48	47
Jessel Global	35	38	31	33
Jessel New Iss.	30	34	24	30
M. & G. General	13	12	13	12
M. & G. Midland	8	8	8	9
M. & G. 2nd Gen.	2	2	2	2
M. & G. Trustees	5	5	5	6
Metals, Min. & Com.	33	31	37	37
Mutual Sec.	22	22	21	15
Nat. Bif.	20	21	18	20
Nat. Dom.	17	15	20	13
Nat. Scot.	34	33	36	32
Nat. Sec. 1st	41	41	42	42
Nat. Shield	31	27	34	31
Ocean Gen.	47	46	47	46
Practical	10	10	10	10
S. & P. Cap.	28	26	30	29
S. & P. Fin.	4	4	4	1
S. & P. Inc.	44	43	45	48
S. & P. I.T.	38	40	32	40
Scot. Bits.	19	18	19	25
Scot. Shares	25	29	26	23
Stockholders	3	3	3	3
Target Cons.	45	45	41	41
Target Fin.	1	1	1	7
Target Prof.	48	47	49	49
Trade Union	21	17	25	16
Tyndall Cap.	15	14	14	22
Tyndall Inc.	27	30	28	26
Unicon Cap.	29	32	27	27
Unicorn Gen.	16	16	16	19
Unicorn Trust	14	20	15	18
Vav. Cap.	46	48	46	45
Vav. Int.	24	24	22	28
Vav. Inc. & Ass.	43	44	44	44
Ulster	42	42	43	43

APPENDIX II

	$\alpha_1 = J_1$	t_{J1}	Average Annual Return	β	Durbin Watson Stat.	Variance Trust σ^2(Ru)	Classifi- cation
All. Cap.	−0.009	−.76	.111	.94	2.65	.039	Capital
All. 1st	−0.016	−1.41	.10	.89	2.2	.035	Balanced
All G. & I.	−0.004	−.35	.114	.912	3.43	.038	Balanced
B.I.F.	−0.012	−.16	.114	.862	3.33	.033	Balanced
B. Life	−0.031	−2.61	.082	.80	1.97	.029	Balanced
Cres. High	−0.019	−1.64	.096	.858	1.47	.041	Income
Cres. Reserves	−0.033	−2.58	.038	.874	1.69	.035	Balanced
Discret.	0.001	0.66	.120	.929	2.11	.038	Balanced
Elec. & Ind.	−0.014	−1.16	.103	.90	1.57	.036	Balanced
Hill. Sam. Brit.	−0.027	−1.94	.09	.886	1.02	.036	Balanced
Hill. Sam. Cap.	−0.009	−.51	.113	.987	1.16	.046	Capital
Hill. Sam. Inc.	−0.028	−2.46	.086	.848	2.74	.033	Income
Hill. Sam. Int.	−0.022	−.88	.09	.79	1.13	.038	Internat.
J−L Cons.	−0.077	−2.45	.028	.668	1.28	.037	Internat.
Jessel Global	−0.026	−1.8	.101	1.09	2.08	.055	Internat.
Jess New Iss.	−0.021	−1.22	.107	1.09	2.29	.059	Specialist
M & G General	−0.01•	−.75	.110	.938	2.66	.039	Balanced
M & G Midland	−0.002	−.154	.121	1.008	1.74	.047	Balanced
M & G 2nd Gen.	0.011	.85	.13	.93	1.89	.039	Internat.
M & G Trustee	0.002	.14	.123	.969	1.97	.042	Balanced
Met. Min. & Comm.	−0.025	−.91	.086	.78	1.1	.041	Specialist
Mutual Sec.	−0.016	−1.61	.101	.883	3.0	.034	Balanced
Nat. Bif.	−0.014	−1.06	.1	.826	3.57	.031	Capital
Nat. Domestic	−0.015	−1.1	.103	.905	2.34	.037	Balanced
Nat. Scot.	−0.025	−1.9	.087	.799	2.32	.029	Balanced
Nat. Sec. First	−0.037	−1.86	.073	.769	2.85	.031	Balanced
Nat. Shield	−0.022	−1.08	.088	.752	1.35	.029	Internat.
Ocean General	−0.063	−3.77	.053	.873	1.52	.036	Balanced
Practical	−0.008	−.49	.109	.88	2.26	.037	Specialist
S & P Capital	−0.02	−1.08	.094	.845	1.09	.036	Internat.
S & P Financial	0.006	.356	.119	.805	2.16	.031	Specialist
S & P Income	−0.044	−2.73	.068	.796	2.06	.030	Income
S & P Inc. Trust	−0.029	−.97	.097	1.074	3.25	.097	Capital
Scot Bits.	−0.014	−.73	.101	.866	2.77	.04	Balanced
Scot Shares	−0.019	−1.83	.1	.921	1.83	.036	Balanced
Stockholders	0.007	−.35	.121	.821	1.11	.035	Internat.
Target Cons.	−0.045	−3.26	.085	1.14	2.63	.06	Balanced
Target Financial	0.023	−.979	.147	1.021	3.57	.067	Specialist
Target Pref.	−0.072	−2.46	.018	.373	1.58	.009	Income
Trade Union	−0.016	−1.31	.096	.785	3.38	.028	Balanced
Tyndall Cap.	−0.013	−.59	.109	.945	1.39	.045	Balanced
Tyndall Income	−0.02	−1.36	.097	.892	2.3	.036	Income
Unicorn Cap.	−0.02	−1.6	.098	.992	2.22	.039	Balanced
Unicorn General	−0.013	−.87	.104	.893	3.41	.038	Balanced
Unicorn Trustee	−0.012	−.99	.109	.968	3.21	.043	Balanced
Vav. Cap.	−0.061	−3.46	.06	.969	2.5	.047	Capital
Vav. Int.	−0.017	−.91	.102	.943	1.87	.044	Balanced
Vav. Inc. Assets	−0.044	−2.54	.069	.806	2.04	.032	Internat.
Ulster	−0.038	−3.67	.071	.737	2.72	.023	Balanced

UNIT TRUST RISK-RETURN PERFORMANCE
1966-1975

Peter Moles and Basil Taylor

Introduction

There have been a number of studies in this journal dealing with the performance of unit trusts. The study of which this article is a summary is an elaboration and up-dating of the first part of the Russell and Taylor paper[1]. It concerns the application of risk-return analysis to 86 unit trusts for the 20 half-year returns‡ December 31st, 1965 to December 31st, 1975 and its use, along with other measures, in the assessment and prediction of performance and risk. The 86 trust funds constituted 70% of all trusts in December 1965; the excluded trusts included all tax exempt funds and all funds for which the data base was somehow suspect. The remaining 70% may be considered a fairly representative sample of the whole. The extent of sample bias is, however, hard to determine.

The concept of a portfolio or a security's response to the market—the risk-return approach—has already been written about in these pages, notably by Brealey[2], Ellis[3], and Henfrey[4]. At present there is continuing debate over the appropriateness of this relatively new analytical technique which has uses in assessing performance, the setting of investment goals, and estimating risk. The basic philosophy behind the model is that the responsiveness of a portfolio or a security can be measured against that of a suitable market index, the resultant least-squares, best fit estimate being its "Characteristic Line". The slope of this is its "beta-coefficient", better described by the term systematic risk. "Beta" can also be regarded as that portion of risk in a portfolio which cannot be diversified away. It measures the variability of the portfolio relative to the variability of the market. Thus a beta of 0.5 means the portfolio's return fluctuations are dampened by half, relative to the market fluctuations.

A beta of 1.5 implies that the portfolio accentuates market fluctuations by half. Low beta portfolios are considered defensive, high beta portfolios aggressive. Consequently, in theory, the beta of a portfolio can be considered a good estimate of the likely exposure to market fluctuations and allows the choice amongst portfolios by their betas.

It was expected that unit trusts would have

---

‡The return for each period on the jth fund was calculated as:

$$R_{j,t} = \log_e(P_{j,t+1} + (D_{j,t}T_t)) - \log_e(P_{j,t})$$

where $P_{j,t}$ was the offer price of the fund at the beginning of the tth period, D_j was the dividend for the fund for the period, T_t was (1 − prevailing tax rate), $D_{j,t}T_t$ being the net dividend. The market portfolio return was calculated as in reference 1, page 17, b footnote.

The risk-free account was the rate on deposits in building societies adjusted for a six monthly basis from annual returns

$$R_{f,t} = \tfrac{1}{2} \log_e(1 + r_B)$$

where r_B is the annual rate of interest for building societies adjusted for tax at their preferential rate. Fund returns are, in effect, as after deducting the semi-annual management charge, which is usually less than ¼% of the asset value per unit.

Figure 1

Histogram of Half-Year Returns Trust No. 2

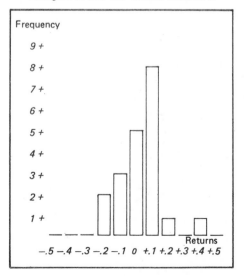

Figure 2

RISK-RETURN PLANE 1966 - 1975

Log_e Terminal Wealth Ratio

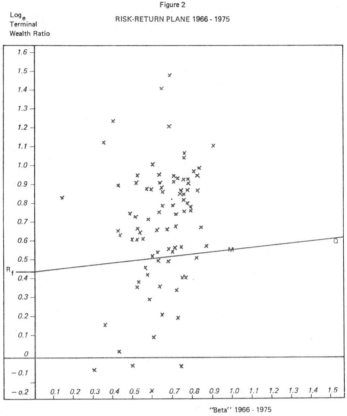

"Beta" 1966 - 1975
(Systematic Risk)

betas according to their advertised designation:—"income funds" concerned with a steady flow of dividends to be low risk, and therefore, low beta type; "balanced funds" to be of medium risk, and of average beta—and "growth funds" aiming at maximising long term growth to have a high risk, reflected in high betas. From the background of theory, the specialized trusts were expected to be a problem in that their fluctuations would have a low correlation with the market due to overseas elements and this would render their betas of minimal value as a guide to the investor. (The value of beta as a criterion depends upon the Characteristic Line having a "good fit" to the data—i.e. a high correlation—see Russell and Taylor[1], Figures 1 and 2.)

The Risk-Return Model

Two measures of risk were calculated: the standard deviation of returns from the average return, and beta (the systematic risk element). Table 1 gives details of the variability of fund returns. The rate of return on the trusts had varied on average by 18.4% over the ten years of six-month periods. There was consequently a considerable chance of making a loss over a six-month period, as Figure 1 indicates. This is the histogram of returns for trust No. 2 over the ten years, and is typical of a sample of 86 trusts. On two occasions this fund had negative returns (losses) of −20%, on three occasions of below −10%, and in 8 half-years had returns of 10% plus, with one occasion of an above-40% return.

TABLE 1
Variability of Returns for Unit Trusts 1966-1975

Trusts	Standard Deviation*
All	.18389
Income	.18500
Balanced	.18717
Growth	.18400
Specialised	.17857
Index (F.T. Actuaries All-Share)	.24398
Range:—	
low	.10737
high	.25992

$$*\text{Standard Deviation} = \sqrt{\frac{1}{N\text{-}1}\left(\sum_{t=1}^{N} R_{j't} - \bar{R}_j\right)^2}$$
for jth fund

TABLE 2
Regression Statistics 1966-1975

Trusts	Number	Intercept (Alpha)	Beta	Correlation
All	86	.0153	.67398	.88945
Income	18	.0220	.70900	.93000
Balanced	32	.0143	.71656	.93506
Growth	10	.0220	.68800	.89900
Specialised	26	.0091	.59165	.80159
F.T. Actuaries				
All Share Index		0.0	1.0	1.0

$$R_{j,t} = A_j + \beta_j R_{M,t} + e_j$$

$$\beta_j = \frac{\text{Covariance of Trust with Market}}{\text{Variance of the Market}}$$

Figure 3

Stability of Beta Coefficient 1966 - 1970/1971 - 1975

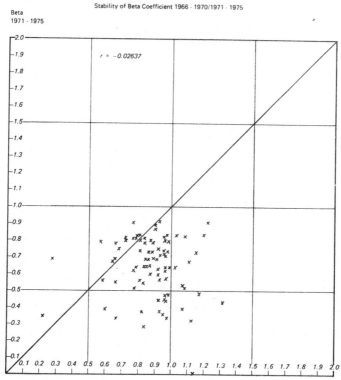

Beta 1971 - 1975

r = −0.02637

Beta 1966 - 1970

231

The risk-return results as set out in Table 2 proved disappointing. There was no real relationship of beta and type of fund as expected. This is a staggering finding! Indeed on grouping these results (Figure 2) of return against systematic risk there appeared to be no systematic relationship of beta to return: the trusts lie scattered haphazardly across the risk-return space. Worse still, on dividing the 10-year period and recalculating the betas for these two sub-periods, the constancy of the coefficients was found to be negligible. This is shown in Figure 3. The correlation of beta period 1 (1966-1970) to beta period 2 (1971-1975) was −0.02637, a result not significantly different from zero. (The pilot study carried out by Russell and Taylor[1] foreshowed these results and contrasted the emerging British scene with that of America in Figures 5 and 6.)

Testing the value of beta in one time period to the return in the next period, the correlation of beta in period 1 to return in period 2 was calculated and was found to be significantly negative, −0.31291. In retrospect, it would appear to have been better to have chosen a low beta in the earlier period in order to obtain above average returns in the next period! It thus makes a mockery of any attempts at using beta as a convenient criterion on which investor preferences can be based. The behaviour of the estimates seems to be hopelessly random, both on the risk-return plane and through time.

Measuring Performance

Arising from the new received theory of capital asset prices there is a framework for measuring fund performance widely applied in American studies which we have applied here. The principle is to compare a trust's performance as to return over a number of years with that of a notional portfolio specially calculated to have the same variability or beta. The contents of that portfolio is, in effect, the market index adjusted with varied quantities of a risk-free security. Thus such a yardstick portfolio could be invested in either the market index, or a risk-free account, or some combination of both, or even the market index geared up by borrowed money at the risk-free rate.

This alternative, risk-adjusted, index strategy is summarised by the line R_fMQ in Figure 2; all funds above the line beat this notional portfolio (sometimes in the research literature called a *naive portfolio*). A vertical line from the fund to line R_fMQ represents the additional return generated by "good management", the point of intersection of both lines representing the "naive portfolio" at an equal systematic risk level to the managed fund.

TABLE 3

Performance Appraisal

Trusts	Fund Return	Naive Fund	Excess Return
	(1)	(2)	(1)-(2)
All	.67076	.56526	.10550
Income	.83000	.56900	.26100
Balanced	.67193	.56988	.10205
Growth	.87600	.56700	.30900
Specialised	.48013	.55640	−.07627

Table 3 exhibits the second remarkable result of these researches, sharply contrasting, it would seem, the British scene from the American experience—viz. the average of all funds and the average fund by categories (except the specialised group) actually *beat* this "naive portfolio". Twenty-one funds were below the line, 65 above. All the funds appeared to have a lower risk than the market and thus would be considered conservative. The mean excess return for all trusts was .1055 which implies that unit trust managers were generating about 1.1% per annum excess return on average above the risk-adjusted market alternative. The picture is intriguing in that this excess return is not spread evenly among the categories of trusts. The growth funds, a small group with ten trusts, generated about 3.1% more, income funds 2.6% more, balanced funds about average, but specialised trusts had negative management ability of −0.8%. This may be in part due to the abysmal performance of one particular specialised international trust in the sample. However, it may also indicate something about the U.K. market versus sector and overseas opportunities. Table 4 shows the breakdown of management ability according to type for the specialised funds. Here apart from the commodity trusts, the international and U.K. specialists were unable to exploit their sectional or overseas advantages. In fact specialisation proved a liability.

TABLE 4

Breakdown of Specialised Trusts by Categories

	Return	Beta	Correlation	Excess Return
COMMODITY TRUSTS				
4 trusts	.7817	.46514	.68149	.23900
Range: high	1.2210	.74989	.92433	.68300
low	.3358	.15417	.19340	−.23800
INTERNATIONAL TRUSTS				
8 trusts	.4357	.47235	.69256	−.10800
Range: high	1.1094	.59524	.87183	.57700
low	−.4968	.36893	.47677	−1.03900
UK SPECIALIST TRUSTS				
14 trusts	.4222	.69594	.89820	−.10800
Range: high	.94400	.81046	.98437	.37100
low	−.0616	.31928	.72842	−.62400

Fund Performance

In Table 5 the wealth ratio, or relative, can be seen as the amount the investment of £1 would have grown if invested in any of the fund averages over the 10 year period—£100 invested in the average of the 10 growth funds, including reinvested net dividends, would be worth £240.12 at December 31st, 1975.

TABLE 5

Returns 1965-1975

Fund Type	Number	Wealth Ratio	Log_eTerminal Wealth Ratio
All	86	1.9557	.67076
Income	18	2.2933	.83000
Balanced	32	1.9580	.67193
Growth	10	2.4012	.87600
Specialised	26	1.6162	.48013
Index	1	1.7118	.53760
R_t	1	1.6349	.49160
Range: high		4.6954	1.54660
low		.6084	−.49680

The natural logarithm of the terminal wealth ratio is the continuously compounded rate which would obtain the wealth relative at the end of the period. By displacing the decimal point one place to the right one obtains the average annual rate of return for the various classes of investments: for the growth funds this was about 8.76% per annum.

Figure 4 shows the performance of some of the trusts of the principal management groups used in the study. It is worth noting that the trusts of each group seem to perform together—not altogether unexpectedly. Compare the performance of group "d" to group "e". All group e's trusts are below the line R_tMQ, all group d's trusts are above the line.

Components of Performance

An attempt was made to assess the predictability of performance through the use of two multiple regression models. The following variables thought to account for performance were imputed into a step-wise regression package for both models:—

(1) Standard deviation of returns—a risk measure or surrogate, measuring the total risk of the portfolio.

(2) The beta coefficient, or systematic risk, that proportion of risk due to the market.

(3) The correlation coefficient, this measures the goodness-of-fit of the regression line, or beta, to the market.

(4) Price, December 1965 (Model 1) and December 1970 (Model 2), because there is evidence that price has some function as a risk and performance surrogate—despite the fact that this goes against all received theory.

(5) Three dummy variables, one each for income, growth and specialised categories, to explain the funds' objectives and capture effects not represented by other variables.

For *Model 1* the following four were also included.

(a) Durbin-Watson statistic, to capture the non-market residual effects of performance. It is a measure of the auto-correlation of the regression residuals;

(b) the number of shares (December 1975) to test whether the number of shares had an important effect on performance, but note its ex-post nature;

(c) size (December 1975) because there is considerable controversy as to whether small or large trusts are to be preferred. This variable, despite its ex-post effect, was used to capture the size effect on performance;

233

Figure 4

RISK-RETURN PLANE 1966 - 1975

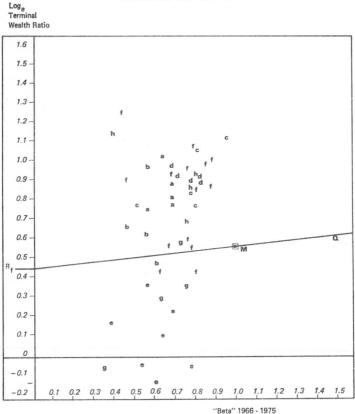

"Beta" 1966 - 1975
(systematic Risk)

(d) yield (December 1975) to test whether yield explained anything of performance, but like size and the number of shares there could be a serious degree of ex-post effect in its inclusion.

For *Model 2* a number of measures of performance commonly found in the literature were calculated to ascertain their predictive ability.

(a) Alpha, which is a measure of management's ability to generate above average returns;

(b) the same measure but adjusted for systematic risk levels (Alpha/Beta);

(c) fund return minus the risk free rate adjusted for systematic risk (Excess Return/ Beta) a systematic risk-adjusted return measure of ranking portfolios and performance;

(d) (Excess Return/Standard Deviation of Return) is as in (c), except that total risk, not merely systematic risk, is used;

(e) selectivity is the excess return above the naive portfolio, alternative strategy;

(f) also included is the regression intercept and the logarithm of the Terminal Wealth Ratio for return in the previous period. If performance is not random then high return should persist from period to period.

The two models were tested: *Model 1* using the entire 10 year estimates for the inputs, because it was an ex-post model; and *Model 2* using the five year estimates for the period 1966-1970 to predict the returns for the period 1971-1975, it being an ex-ante model.

Model 1 investigated some alleged new wisdom concerning unit trusts. The order in which the variables entered the regression model was indicative of their explanatory power in predicting performance. The totality of variables accounted for a mere 21.15% of performance, or to put it another way 78.85% was unexplained. However the model made some interesting findings, the sign for the specialised trusts' dummy variable was negative, confirming what has already been said about the specialised trust group in the period 1966-1975. Yield was also negative in sign which may be explainable by the fact of dividend restraint and its effect upon growth, where a rapid rise in price will reduce the running yield, but also since growth stocks performed well and they had a low yield. It is interesting to note that beta only enters the model in seventh place, two dummies, price, size, yield and the number of shares are all more significant. In the final formulation of the model, neither beta nor the standard deviation of returns (the two risk surrogates), have significant regression coefficients. The most significant variable appears to be price. The model was not very predictive, nor successful in uncovering identifiable characteristics for the successful performers in the period 1966 to 1975.

Model 2 was an ex-ante model in which the previous period set of performance measures and risk-return estimates were used to predict performance in the subsequent period. The model, as laid out at its most predictive, explained 47.2% of return in the next period. Two dummy variables, the regression intercept, the standard deviation of returns, the correlation coefficient, alpha and price were the explanatory variables. One must wonder about the real as opposed to the statistical significance of these variables, there is certainly a modicum of accident in the inclusion of at least one variable. For instance, the dummy variable concerning income trusts was included because in the period 1971-1975 there happened to be an emphasis on income stocks and consequently income trusts did relatively well. Whether this would be true, say, from 1976-1980 is very much in doubt.

Conclusions

One must consider the attempts at trust assessment using the multiple regression models something of a failure. Certainly the performance variables from period 1 were insufficient to predict performance in period 2. However there is just a hint that performance is, for some trusts at least, carried over from one period to the next. The correlation between performance in period 1 and performance in period 2 was 0.23274 which is significant at the 0.05 level, i.e. there was a 19 in 20 chance that the observed behaviour was significant and not accidental.

One must be wary of a blind application of modern investment techniques without a proper analysis of their validity. The results shown here highlight the inherent dangers in such an attitude. *Beta (or systematic risk) gave a poor showing, appearing totally unstructured and apparently completely random in its behaviour.*

The results concerning performance appraisal and predictability have certain implications for investors. (i) Investors might do better to seek diversification among trusts, not merely within a specific management group as these tended to perform together but by diversifying between management groups. (ii) Both beta and the standard deviation of returns are useless in assessing the likely risk to be borne or the likely return. This negates the use of systematic risk as a convenient label on which investor preferences can be based. (iii) There appears to be little differentiation of trusts by objective, the only group which could be said to be significantly different were the specialised trusts. (iv) Investors would be well advised to avoid the specialised trusts as a long term investment unless performance through the use of two multiple regression models were not very successful.

To summarise, it appears that unit trusts as a whole were a desirable investment medium, with many funds being able to generate higher than average returns.

This study is now being extended: To all 118 unit trusts available for the period; using other surrogates for the "risk-free rate of return", especially the Treasury bill rate; using quarterly returns; using gross as well as net of Tax returns; applying further measures of significance.

there were exceptional reasons; their performance potential was not borne out in the decade 1966-1975. In this they are contrasted with the other categories which did relatively well against the benchmark measure. (v) There was considerable reward in choosing the right trust or bunch of trusts. This choice factor would have made the most difference in terms of return over the period, a good choice in any of the categories would have outperformed an average choice in any of the others since the ex-post performances were so varied. Unfortunately the attempts at finding variables explaining future

REFERENCES

1. Russell, A. and Taylor, B., *"Investment Uncertainties and British Equities"*, Investment Analyst, December 1968.

2. Brealey, R. A., *"The Impact of the Market on British Share Prices"*, Investment Analyst, October 1969.

3. Ellis, P. J., *"Beta Coefficients for Investment Trusts"*, Investment Analyst, December 1974.

4. Henfrey, Dr. A., *"Risk Factors for Individual Securities in Three European Stockmarkets"*, Investment Analyst, May 1975.

APPENDIX—REGRESSION MODELS

Model 1

Log_eTWR 1966/75 $= a_0 + a_1 \text{(Dumy 3)} + a_2 \text{(Price)} + a_3 \text{(Size)} + a_4 \text{(Dummy 1)} + a_5 \text{(Yield)}$

a_0 −1.1167	a_1 −.16500 (−1.502)	a_2 .00221 (2.565)	a_3 .00127 (0.680)	a_4 .24795 (2.201)	a_5 −.03573 (−1.325)
	$+ a_6$ (No Shares) .00085 (1.186)	$+ a_7$ (Beta) −2.17566 (−0.649)	$+ a_8$ (Durbin) −.03574 (−0.352)	$+ a_9$ (Dummy 2) .07029 (0.531)	$+ a_{10}$ (Stan. Dev.) 8.93277 (0.755)
	$+ a_{11}$ (Correlation) 1.87608 (0.689)	Multiple R^2, adjusted, $= .215$			

Model 2

Log_eTWR 1971/75 $= a_0 + a_1 \text{(Dummy 1)} + a_2 \text{(Intercept)} + a_3 \text{(Stan. Dev.)} + a_4 \text{(Correlation)}$

a_0 −.89303	a_1 .19897 (3.941)	a_2 37.58879 (1.331)	a_3 .51880 (0.1530)	a_4 1.06624 (1.905)
	$+ a_5$ (Dummy 2) .09680 (1.539)	$+ a_6$ (Alpha) −32.26783 (−1.129)	$+ a_7$ (Price Dec 1970) .00059 (1.081)	Multiple R^2, adjusted, $= .472$

a_8 . . . Log_eTWR 1966–1970
a_9 . . . Beta Coefficient
a_{10} . . . Alpha/Beta
a_{11} . . . Return 1966–1970/Beta
a_{12} . . . Return 1966–1970/Standard Deviation of Return
a_{13} . . . Dummy 3
a_{14} . . . Selectivity

SHARPE PERFORMANCE AMONG PENSION FUNDS?
by P. H. Richards*

The recent work of Roll[1] has virtually undermined the validity of the Jensen[2] and Treynor[3] performance tests. The main reason for this is that where these tests identified "good" or "bad" performance, the only valid conclusion that should be drawn is that the proxy for the market (for example, the F.T. all-share index) used in each case is inappropriate. In other words the Jensen and Treynor tests will tell us something about the market proxy but nothing about portfolio performance.

This study applies the Sharpe[4] performance measure (which is not affected by Roll's work) to the U.K. equity portfolios of a number of pension funds.

Methodology

Sharpe's model specifies the riskiness of a portfolio as the variability of returns as measured by the standard deviation of returns. Thus each portfolio can be described by its rate of return and its risk. To choose between two portfolios involves a trade-off between risk and return and this can be accomplished by applying Sharpe's test. Historic data are used to calculate rates of return and standard deviations of return. A risk-free asset is also included (treasury bill rate is used in this study). Here risk-free means having standard deviation of return of zero. These data can then be plotted graphically.

I represents the risk-free asset and i is the risk-free rate of return. Each portfolio can then be ranked in terms of the slope of the line IP —this is the Sharpe measure of performance. In this way, portfolios having different risk characteristics can be compared. For example, portfolio P^1 is less risky than portfolio P but, as it lies on the line IP, it has the same Sharpe coefficient and therefore has achieved the same performance as portfolio P. It is easy to see that a portfolio identical to P^1 in terms of risk and return could be constructed by an appropriate combination of portfolio P and the risk-free asset I. Hence it is appropriate that P and P^1 have the same Sharpe coefficient. Portfolio P and P^1 can be regarded as superior to portfolio Q since they lie to the north-west (the direction of increasing return but decreasing risk) of Q. In terms of the Sharpe test, the line IP has greater slope than the line IQ.

As a yardstick for measuring absolute rather than comparative performance, it is easy to include the F.T. all-share index as an additional portfolio. Performance can then be compared to the index.

Data

Unlike unit trusts, pension funds do not lend themselves readily to performance testing. The chief problem is calculating rates of return in the absence of regular valuations. The data used here are quarterly rates of return for the U.K. equity portfolios of funds participating in the Bacon & Woodrow performance measurement service, over the period 1st January, 1970 to 31st December, 1977. The rates of return are based on quarterly valuations of the portfolios subject to adjustment to take account of positive cash flow into the fund. Where there is a cash inflow into the fund on a day for which no valuation exists, a distortion in the calculated rate of return can arise. The adjustment used

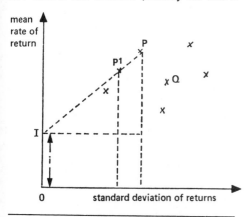

* I should like to thank Messrs. Bacon & Woodrow for the use of their data, Mr. Sidney Benjamin and Mr. Colin Lever, two of the partners, for helpful suggestions and Miss Daphne Webb for computing assistance.

here is to calculate the DCF internal rate of return using valuations at the beginning and end of each quarter and allowing for the size and timing of the cash in-flows during the quarter. Most pension funds are expanding to varying extents so all are affected by this adjustment. Consider an example. The mean rate of return of the F.T. all-share index over the period was 3.777% per quarter and an average for cash in-flow can be taken as 4% per quarter. Suppose the cash in-flow occurs in the middle of the quarter and suppose further that the return on the index is earned either (a) in the first half of each quarter; or (b) in the second half. Then the above method of adjustment will provide two different answers:—

Alternative (a) 3.856%⎰
Alternative (b) 3.693%⎱ average rate = 3.779%

Thus it can be seen that this method of adjustment can give a small upward bias to the rates of return. However, there is a further source of error. The cash in-flow is invested at offer prices but valued at bid pices. Transaction costs will also have an impact on the new money. This factor will therefore bias downwards the estimated returns earned by the pension funds. To compensate for this, the returns on the F.T. all-share index are adjusted on the basis of a 4% cash in-flow each quarter which suffers transaction costs and bid/offer valuation change totalling 4.5%. Of course, if individual funds have lesser rates of cash in-flow, the comparison will become biased against the index and vice versa. However, it could be argued that the more cash there is to invest, the greater is the fund manager's opportunity to restructure the portfolio without incurring additional costs.

Results

The results of the Sharpe test for 17 pension funds and the F.T. all-share index are set out in the graph below. In summary form, they are:—

Period 1970-1977	Sharpe coefficient
Best performing fund	0.60
Worst performing fund	0.25
Average for 17 funds	0.39
F.T. all-share index	0.50
F.T. all-share index (after adjustment for new money)	0.45
Number of funds beating the index	5
Number of funds beating the adjusted index	8

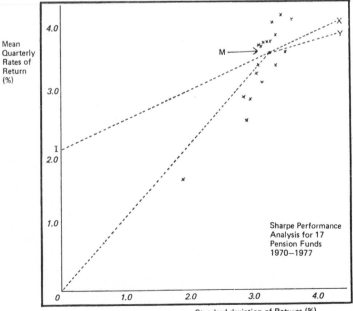

Sharpe Performance Analysis for 17 Pension Funds 1970–1977

"M" represents the F.T. all-share index (adjusted for new money)

"I" represents the risk-free asset (average treasury bill rate)

The average Sharpe coefficient is well below that for the all-share index even after adjustment of the latter for new money. This difference can be expressed in terms of a rates of return by applying the average Sharpe coefficient to the two indices.

Quarterly rates of return	Mean rate of return	Return implied by average Sharpe coefficient
F.T. all-share index	3.78%	3.41%
Adjusted all-share index	3.59%	3.41%

Although in aggregate the funds do little worse than the index, it is clear that 5 funds beat the market index even before any allowance is made for new money. This can therefore be regarded as evidence of superior performance subject only to the caveat that the method of adjustment for cash in-flow may be partly responsible.

Over a full year, the two rates of return for the index generate a difference of 0.85%. Clearly this adjustment could have a substantial impact on performance measurement especially for those funds growing rapidly. This argues for better data collection.

A number of points emerge from the diagram. The plots, with one exception, are clustered around the plot for the adjusted index. In terms of risk, the plots are particularly close although this might be expected as within a portfolio of U.K. equities there is only limited opportunity to vary risk significantly. The general shape of the plots indicates, as would be expected, a positive relationship between risk and return. However, the slope of a line drawn through these plots would appear to be steeper than that (IMX) which would be expected under Sharpe's model. This effect may be exaggerated by the poor performers—those plots below the line IMX. This poor performance could be due to poor diversification leading to above average risk, or, heavy transaction costs.

The funds exhibiting superior performance are represented by those points lying above the line IMX.

The line IMX represents those portfolios which could be constructed by a combination of the F.T. all-share index (M) and treasury bills (I). That part of the line to the right of M, (i.e. MX), represents portfolios which could be achieved by borrowing at treasury bill rate and investing in the index. In practice, few borrowers would pay only treasury bill rate. The line MY represents a cost of borrowing of 2% p.a. over treasury bill rate, a more realistic cost of borrowing. In fact for this particular group of funds, this adjustment of the cost of borrowing does not alter the results as no plots lie between MX and MY.

The use of treasury bills as the risk-free asset poses one problem. It is implicit in this assumption that the standard deviation of returns is zero. Obviously it is zero for any one quarter, but over the 8 years considered was not zero—in fact, the standard deviation was 0.11%. A number of alternatives arise. The point I could be plotted on the line of standard deviation $= 0.11\%$. This would move the line IMX only slightly and would not affect the performance rankings. The problem which then arises is that a combination of treasury bills and the market would not lie on a straight line but on a curve lying above IM. However, it would lie very close to the line.

Sharpe used a U.S. government security having a maturity exactly matching the period covered by his data. Here, an 8-year gilt could have been used. There are several drawbacks. Returns in each quarter vary. Thus the standard deviation is only zero over the whole 8-year period. Also, performance should be looked at on a continuous basis rather than over just 8 years. As a last resort, an investment in cash could be considered. A zero rate of return would have zero standard deviation. This suggestion is represented by the line OM. In fact only one of the poor performers becomes a good performer when the line OM is substituted for IM.

Trends

The above test was repeated on a larger group of data for the periods 1970–1973 (24 funds) and 1974–1977 (67 funds). The results were:—

	Sharpe Coefficient	
	1970–1973	1974–1977
Best performing fund	0.12	0.65
Worst performing fund	−0.33	−0.63
Average of all funds in sample	−0.07	0.36
F.T. all-share index	−0.09	0.57
Adjusted all-share index	−0.16	0.54
Number of funds beating the index	14 (58%)	9 (13%)
Number of funds beating the adjusted index	17 (71%)	12 (18%)
Number of funds in sample	24	67

	Sharpe Coefficient			
	1970/71	1972/73	1974/75	1976/77
Best performing fund	1.30	0.00	1.24	1.12
Worst performing fund	0.67	−1.31	−1.05	0.15
Average of all funds	1.04	−0.95	0.10	0.71
F.T. all-share index	0.89	−0.92	0.28	0.81
Adjusted all-share index	0.84	−0.97	0.27	0.77
Number of funds beating the index	16 (67%)	20 (39%)	10 (12%)	23 (25%)
Number of funds beating the adjusted index	19 (79%)	25 (49%)	14 (71%)	30 (33%)
Number of funds in sample	24	51	83	91

The period 1970–1973 was characterised by a rapid fall in the market from a peak in 1972. As a result, the values of the Sharpe coefficient are predominantly negative. This is undoubtedly an exceptional situation. A negative value corresponds to the situation where higher risk is rewarded by a lower return. This may invalidate the method of measurement of the Sharpe coefficient. When trying to measure the mean of a distribution by sampling from the distribution, it is important to get as many data items as possible. However, there is always the possibility that each item is drawn from just one side of the distribution with obvious consequences for the mean. Suppose we toss a coin 10 times, and, heads appears 9 times. Should we conclude that heads are 9 times more likely to appear than tails? Of course, the answer is No, as there is always a small chance that 9 heads will appear in 10 throws. Here we have the situation of a succession of negative rates of return. In the long run, rates of return are positive so the results for this period may be subject to error.

Having said that the two periods provide a great contrast the earlier period is characterised by superior performance while the later period by inferior performance. This pattern is repeated when the data is split down into 2-year periods. The main drawback of the shorter timescale is that the smaller quantity of data will produce a more inaccurate measure of mean rates of return and standard deviation. This will be mitigated by the increase in the number of funds included, but may distort the measurement of the Sharpe coefficient for the F.T. all-share index.

Subject to any measurement problems associated with the returns on the index, it is clear from the above that it is either becoming increasingly more difficult to generate good performance, or those funds joining the service towards the end of the period are poor performers. The trend could also be explained by a combination of these factors.

This breakdown also clarifies the earlier finding of significant superior performance in the period 1970–73. Instead of this being due to measurement error brought about by negative rates of return, it is now clear that this good performance occurs particularly in the first 2-year period, when returns were positive.

The fact that poor performance is prevalent in the later periods may be due to improved efficiency in the stock market brought about by tougher rules of disclosure and an outlawing of insider dealing.

Ranking

To examine the consistency of performance, the original sample of 17 funds is split into two smaller time periods: 1970–73 and 1974–77. The funds are then ranked according to the value of the Sharpe coefficient. Thus each fund will have a ranking for each period. These can be represented graphically.

It can be seen that there is a positive relationship between the rankings. For example, 6 of

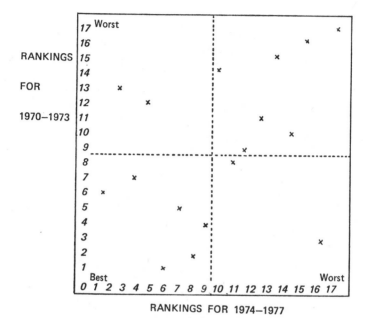

RANKINGS FOR 1974–1977

the top 8 in the earlier period maintain their position in the second period. Likewise, 7 of the worst 9 in the earlier period stay in the bottom 9 in the later period.

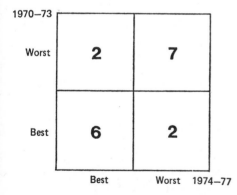

Put rather crudely, the above table shows that an investor selecting one of the 8 best performers in the first period would have a 6:2 chance (75%) of holding one of the 8 best in the second period. Conversely, if he had chosen one of the 9 worst performers then the chance of holding one of the worst in the second period would have been 7:2 (78%).

The Spearman correlation coefficient which is a mathematical measure of correlation was calculated for these rankings to be $+0.377$ confirming that good (bad) performance tends to be followed by good (bad) performance.

These results suggest that performance can be predicted albeit imperfectly.

Conclusion

Looking at the performance of the portfolios in aggregate, over the longer period no superior performance was observed. However on an individual basis, at least five funds out of a sample of 17 beat the market index. Looking at these superior performers over the shorter 2-year periods, they did not always beat the market. However this latter result may be due to the small data base for the 2-year periods. Obviously, the quality of the results could be improved with more data and by more accurate estimation of rates of return.

The results do not support the Efficient Market Hypothesis since evidence of superior per-

241

formance has been discovered. However, the evidence also confirms that it is extremely difficult to beat the market and therefore the appropriateness of the Hypothesis is probably more a question of degree. The market can be regarded as highly efficient but not fully efficient. But for the majority of fund managers who did not beat the market, their performance would not be impaired if they did assume the market to be fully efficient. Indeed there could be scope for an improvement in performance.

References:

1. A Roll:
   (a) "A Critique of the Asset Pricing Theory's Tests: Part 1", *Journal of Financial Economics*, 4, 1977, pages 129–176.
   (b) "How the Securities Market Line Cannot Distinguish Superior Assets (or portfolios) from Inferior Assets (or portfolios) Ex-post or Ex-ante", *Working Paper UCLA*, March 1977.
   (c) "Testing a Portfolio for Ex-ante Mean/Variance Efficiency", *Working Paper UCLA*, March 1977.

2. M. C. Jensen: "Risk, the Pricing of Market Assets and the Evaluation of Investment Portfolios", *Journal of Business*, April 1969.

3. J. Treynor "How to Rate Management of Investment Funds", *Harvard Business Review*, January/February, 1965.

4. W. F. Sharpe: "Mutual Fund Performance", *Journal of Business*, January 1966.

CHAPTER 5

Efficiency in the European
Stockmarkets

The concept of diversification is fundamental to portfolio management and a statistical model describing the trade-off between risk and return was developed in Chapter 2. Once full diversification has been reached within the UK market, the next logical step is international diversification. Inevitably, there is some inter-relation between different economies and hence capital markets: for example the 1973 oil price rise affected world trade and every domestic economy. In most cases the effect was detrimental (although in Arab stock markets it was doubtless the opposite). However, there is a sufficient degree of divergence in the behaviour of different stock markets for international diversification to be attractive. The degree of divergence is best expressed as a correlation coefficient of the returns of the various markets. A coefficient of one would indicate perfect correlation, zero would indicate no correlation while minus one would indicate perfect negative correlation. Lessard [55] calculated these for world markets for the period 1959-73. These are summarised in the table below. Note that the coefficients are all positive but generally quite small. Where particular economies are related, the coefficient is quite high: Canada and the US for example where the coefficient is 0.793.

The benefits of international diversification are best illustrated by a chart produced by

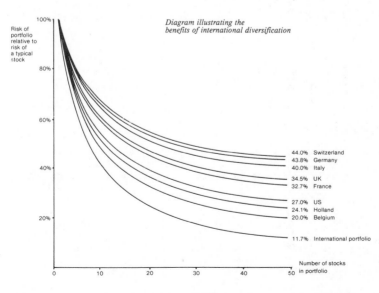

Diagram illustrating the benefits of international diversification

Risk of portfolio relative to risk of a typical stock

44.0% Switzerland
43.8% Germany
40.0% Italy
34.5% UK
32.7% France
27.0% US
24.1% Holland
20.0% Belgium

11.7% International portfolio

Number of stocks in portfolio

243

Correlations of monthly price relatives for 16 national stock market indices: January 1959–October 1973

	Australia	Belgium	Switzerland	Denmark	Spain	France	Germany	Netherlands
Australia	1.000	0.178[c]	0.210[b]	0.171[c]	0.089	0.123	0.186[c]	0.243[b]
Belgium	0.178[c]	1.000	0.528[a]	0.207[b]	0.174[c]	0.556[a]	0.465[a]	0.574[a]
Switzerland	0.210[b]	0.528[a]	1.000	0.113	0.040	0.533[a]	0.600[a]	0.624[a]
Denmark	0.171[c]	0.207[b]	0.113	1.000	0.225[b]	0.112	0.072	0.32
Spain	0.089	0.174[c]	0.040	0.225[b]	1.000	0.292[a]	0.080	0.057
France	0.123	0.556[a]	0.533[a]	0.112	0.292[a]	1.000	0.423[a]	0.455[a]
Germany	0.186[c]	0.465[a]	0.600[a]	0.072	0.080	0.423[a]	1.000	0.520[a]
Netherlands	0.243[b]	0.574[a]	0.624[a]	0.132	0.057	0.455[a]	0.520[a]	1.000
Italy	0.100	0.293[a]	0.372[a]	0.127	0.039	0.284[a]	0.360[a]	0.231[b]
Japan	0.190[c]	0.114	0.199[b]	0.222[b]	0.028	0.126	0.188[c]	0.200[b]
Norway	0.135	0.446[a]	0.231[b]	0.244[b]	0.203[b]	0.313[a]	0.215[b]	0.227[b]
Austria	0.007	0.243[b]	0.307[a]	0.204[b]	0.047	0.263[a]	0.432[a]	0.237[b]
Sweden	0.326[a]	0.411[a]	0.308[a]	0.161[c]	0.180[c]	0.271[a]	0.316[a]	0.274[a]
UK	0.353[a]	0.275[a]	0.260[a]	0.022	0.050	0.223[b]	0.248[a]	0.375[a]
USA	0.225[b]	0.339[a]	0.431[a]	0.010	0.004	0.173[c]	0.335[c]	0.568[a]
Canada	0.261[a]	0.377[a]	0.431[a]	0.087	0.081	0.258[a]	0.357[a]	0.536[a]

Correlations of monthly price relatives for 16 national stock market indices: January 1959-October 1973.

	Italy	Japan	Norway	Austria	Sweden	UK	USA	Canada
Australia	0.100	0.190[c]	0.135	0.007	0.326	0.353[a]	0.225[b]	0.261[a]
Belgium	0.293[a]	0.114	0.446[a]	0.243[b]	0.411[a]	0.275[a]	0.339[a]	0.377[a]
Switzerland	0.372[a]	0.199[b]	0.231[b]	0.307[a]	0.308[a]	0.260[a]	0.431[a]	0.431[a]
Denmark	0.127	0.222[b]	0.244[b]	0.204[b]	0.161[c]	0.022	0.010	0.087
Spain	0.039	0.028	0.203[b]	0.047	0.180[c]	0.050	0.004	0.081
France	0.284[a]	0.126	0.313[a]	0.263[a]	0.271[a]	0.223[b]	0.173[c]	0.258[a]
Germany	0.360[a]	0.188[c]	0.215[b]	0.432[a]	0.316[a]	0.248[a]	0.335[a]	0.357[a]
Netherlands	0.231[b]	0.200[b]	0.227[b]	0.237[b]	0.274[a]	0.375[a]	0.568[a]	0.536[a]
Italy	1.000	0.087	0.164[c]	0.228[b]	0.166[c]	0.195[b]	0.128	0.142
Japan	0.087	1.000	0.057	0.143	0.086	0.103	0.149[c]	0.220[b]
Norway	0.164[c]	0.057	1.000	0.256[a]	0.289[a]	0.129	0.035	0.135
Austria	0.228[b]	0.143	0.256[a]	1.000	0.099	0.023	0.092	0.172[c]
Sweden	0.166[c]	0.086	0.289[a]	0.099	1.000	0.274[a]	0.289[a]	0.347[a]
UK	0.195[b]	0.103	0.129	0.023	0.274[a]	1.000	0.276[a]	0.265[a]
USA	0.128	0.149[c]	0.035	0.092	0.289[a]	0.276[a]	1.000	0.793[a]
Canada	0.142	0.220[b]	0.135	0.172[c]	0.347[a]	0.265[a]	0.793[a]	1.000

[a] Significance under 0.001 [b] Significance under 0.01 [c] Significance under 0.05

Solnik [56] of the reduction in risk which can follow from such diversification. Weekly price data for over 300 European stocks over the period 1966-71 were used.

The chart shows how risk can be reduced by increasing the number of stocks in portfolios invested in each of 7 European stock markets and in the US. Risk is measured by the variance (the square of the standard deviation) of portfolio returns expressed as a percentage of the variance of the return of a typical share of that country. Thus for most countries, the benefits of diversification are substantially achieved once the number of stocks has reached 20. The benefits of international diversification are achieved in a similar way as the bottom curve above shows. The international portfolio is based on equally weighted investments in each country. By its position in the chart, the international portfolio shows how much further risk can be reduced by an international spread.

In practice exchange controls, or the threat of the imposition of exchange controls, complicate and make riskier the achievement of successful international diversification. Both France and the UK have introduced additional exchange control restrictions during times of monetary crisis. However, the EEC countries are committed to dismantling any such restrictions between member countries and this problem may therefore disappear within the EEC.

This chapter is concerned with the efficiency of the stock markets of continental Europe. Not every country is covered and the review of literature is not necessarily comprehensive. However the research is of high quality and includes both weak, semi-strong and strong form tests although not every stock market is tested for all three forms.

The Americans have sometimes referred, somewhat disparagingly, to the 'Mickey Mouse' stock markets of continental Europe. The main reason for this is probably the comparatively small size of the markets. But in theory, the size of the market is not necessarily an inhibitor to efficiency. The conditions for efficiency might well prevail regardless of the size of the market. A fund manager will of course be interested to know whether a particular market is efficient. If it is not efficient then he should move research resources into that market to try and obtain superior rates of return.

Weak Form Tests

Solnik [17]

Solnik estimated serial correlation coefficients of returns for European and US stocks over the period 1966-71. Comparing the results with the US, Solnik observed that European coefficients were more apparent and generally positive, suggesting perhaps a slight degree of inefficiency although the coefficients were still small. They were largest for daily returns but declining as longer intervals were used (weekly, fortnightly and monthly). No attempt was made to estimate whether sufficient profits could be made to cover transaction costs. Solnik pointed out that positive serial correlation could be created by a slow adjustment of prices to new information. This would explain why serial correlation was less noticeable for longer time intervals. Alternatively, it could be due to the nature of the data — for example the non-trading effect could produce such distortions, especially over shorter time periods. However, the stocks chosen were frequently traded, usually at least daily, so this is a less likely cause. The most likely explanation is that the serial correlation is not sufficiently pronounced to cover the necessary transaction costs which would be incurred in taking advantage of this phenomenon. This point is basica ...ᴄ difference between a perfect market and an efficient market, explained in Chapter 1.

France

Semah, Serres and Tessier [57] analysed 58 shares over the period January 1964-February 1969 using a filter test with different sizes of filter. They concluded that for 70 per cent of their sample, there was at least one filter which after allowing for transaction costs still produced more profit than a buy and hold strategy. This result is not convincing evidence of inefficiency since, as was seen in Chapter 1, if the search is extensive, one profitable system can always be found and may be due entirely to chance.

Galesne's [58] study made allowance for the possibility that the discovery of a successful filter could be due to chance. His method was to examine whether the filter was consistently successful over time. Using a long time period (1957-71) and 99 French stocks, Galesne first confirmed the above result, finding at least one successful filter for each stock. It was noted that profitability or success of the filter was very sensitive to small changes in the filter size. The data were than split into two consecutive time periods in two different ways:

(i)   1957-63, 1964-71;   and
(ii) 1957-68, 1969-71.

split (i): the successful filter, established from the earlier interval data, was used on the later interval. Only 15 stocks showed true stability (ie the filter was successful in the later interval) while over two-thirds of the stocks were outside the tolerance range of profitable filters.

split (ii): similar results were obtained. Only 12 stocks demonstrated true stability.

Galesne concluded that although filters could generate spectacular profits, to be exploitable, the filter size must be consistent. No such consistency was observed and the market can be regarded as efficient in the weak sense.

Germany

Conrad and Jüttner [59] have tested the weak form hypothesis for 54 shares quoted on the German stock market during the period 1968-71 (daily prices were used). Two types of test were employed — an analysis of runs, and calculation of the serial correlation coefficient. A 'run' is a series of '+++' where each '+' implies an increase in share price over the day, '−' indicates a decrease and 'o' represents no change.

The runs test indicated a tendency for a particular sign to persist. In other words the symbols +, −, o tended to cluster together into runs more frequently than would be expected if the underlying series were truly random. This would be consistent with positive serial correlation between successive daily rates of return and this the second test sought to discover. The correlation coefficients are set out below.

The correlation coefficients are not close to zero but neither are they predominantly positive or predominantly negative. No test was made to exploit this. Conrad and Jüttner were forced to the conclusion that the German market was not efficient.

Runs and Serial Correlation Tests

Stocks	Serial correlation coefficients for daily changes and lag one	Stocks	Serial correlation coefficients for daily changes and lag one
RWE	−0.4790[1]	Daimler Benz	+0.0616[1]
Veba	+0.0277	NSU	−0.4691[1]
Gelsenk.Bergw	+0.0086	Volkswagen	−0.4383[1]
Hamborner Bgw	+0.0671	AEG	−0.4884[1]
Harpener Bergb	+0.1498[1]	Brown Boveri	−0.5021[1]
Preussag	+0.0626[1]	Seimens	+0.0504
Wintershall	+0.0017	Zellstoff.Waldh	+0.1156[1]
Hoesch	−0.4815[1]	Salamander	−0.2981[1]
Ilseder Hütte	+0.1476[1]	Dortmd.Aktien Br	+0.0652
Klöckner Bergb	+0.1714[1]	Dortmd.Union Br	+0.1456[1]
Klöckner Werke	+0.1025[1]	Löwenbräu	−0.4994[1]
Mannesmann	+0.0809[1]	Schultheis Br	−0.4856[1]
Rhein Stahlwerke	+0.0031	Süddt.Zucker	−0.3528[1]
Thyssen-Hütte	+0.0369	Grün-u.Bilfinger	−0.4922[1]
BASF	−0.5010[1]	Holzmann, Philipp	−0.4704[1]
Farbenf.Bayer	+0.0848[1]	Karstadt	−0.4964[1]
Höchster Farbw	+0.1188[1]	Kaufhof	−0.3655[1]
Chemieverwaltg	+0.0886[1]	Neckermann	−0.4457[1]
Degussa	−0.1393[1]	Hapag	−0.0404
Rütgerswerke	+0.0029	Bayer Hyp. u. Wechs	−0.2683[1]
Schering	+0.0746[1]	Bayer. Vereinsb	−0.3276[1]
Phönix-Gummi	−0.0121	Berliner Handelsg	−0.2576[1]
Dyckerhoff-Zement	+0.1293[1]	Commerzbk	−0.3902[1]
Heidelbrg.Zement	−0.1036[1]	Dt.Bank	−0.3491[1]
Demag	+0.1221[1]	Dresdner Bk	−0.2719[1]
Klöckner-Humbold	−0.2168[1]		
Linde	−0.0097		
MAN,Augsbg	−0.0690		
BMW	+0.0945[1]		

1. The coefficients of these stocks exceed 2σ, where $2\sigma = \sqrt{1/N-1} = 0.06974$

Guy [60] has also looked at serial correlation coefficients of German equity securities. His data base was more extensive covering the period 1960-71. A total of ninety shares were studied, fifty of which were those German companies with the largest market capitalisations (as at 31st December, 1970) and the remainder were chosen at random from all the other listed shares. Serial correlation coefficients were calculated for each group using monthly rates of return. The data were also split into two consecutive periods and the test performed on each sub-period in exactly similar fashion to Solnik [17]. The results are set out below with those of Solnik for comparison:

Average Serial Correlation Coefficients	50 Major	40 Random	Total (90)	Index
Sub-period 1: 1960-65	.104	.024	.068	.207
Sub-period 2: 1965-71	.098	.048	.076	.217
Total period: 1960-71	.102	.031	.071	.211
Solnik (1966-71, 35 shares)			.058	

The index used is published by the Stat Budesamtes.

The coefficients are all positive and in the majority of cases quite small. Sub-period 2 coincides almost exactly with that used by Solnik and the coefficients are quite close. In fact, Solnik's sample contained a large proportion of the largest companies. However his result (0.058) is more in line with Guy's '40 Random' sample (where the coefficient was 0.048) than either the '50 Major' (coefficient 0.098) or the total sample (coefficient 0.076).

The most interesting feature of Guy's results is that the coefficients for the larger companies were in all cases greater than those for the random companies (and hence greater than those for the total) but less than the coefficients for the index. Problems with data (non-trading etc) have already been suggested as an explanation for serial correlation in indices. But for large well-researched companies, it is more likely to be the other way round. However, no attempt was made in the study to construct any trading rule to take advantage of this phenomenon. Thus this does not necessarily imply that the German market is inefficient. This evidence is consistent with that of Conrad and Jüttner. However, no tests were made for efficiency. Given the low levels of correlation observed, it would appear unlikely that much profit would be generated.

Holland

Theil and Leenders [61] adopted an approach similar to that of Dryden [10, 12]. They looked at the proportions, in a sample of shares, showing either rises, falls or no change at all. An information theory approach was used to measure the accuracy of various proposed methods for predicting the proportions of the above prevailing on any one day. Using this technique, the most successful (or least unsuccessful) method of forecasting was as follows:

Forecast proportion of shares showing rises = Simple average of
[yesterday's proportion plus
the long run average proportion]

and likewise for the proportions of shares showing falls and shares recording no change. The actual overall averages were:

Proportion showing rises   40%
Proportion recording no change 20%
Proportion showing falls   40%
                                          100%

The data comprised daily price movements for 450 shares quoted on the Amsterdam stock exchange between November 1959 and October 1963.

The main conclusion to be drawn from this study is that today's proportions depend on yesterday's to some extent. There is therefore some serial dependence although whether this phenomenon could be profitably exploited remains to be seen.

Norway/Sweden

Jennergren and Korsvold [62] have performed a number of tests of the weak form hypothesis on 45 of the most frequently traded shares listed on the Oslo (15) and Stockholm (30) stock exchanges. The data consisted of daily prices over the period 1967-71 except that prices were taken only where at least one transaction in that stock had occurred. Thus effects of non-trading are removed. Three types of test were applied to the data:

(i) Serial correlation coefficients of daily share price differences were calculated for each share using a range of lags from one day to thirty days. For a lag of one day, the coefficients are mostly positive and not very close to zero indicating a degree of serial correlation. For lags longer than one day, the serial correlation coefficients are generally quite small and of differing signs.

		Serial Correlation Coefficient (lag of one day)
Norway:	Highest (Borregaard)	0.215*
	Lowest (Bergens Privatbank)	−0.095
	Mean absolute value	0.083
Sweden:	Highest (Skandia)	0.192*
	Lowest (Monark)	−0.118*
	Mean absolute value	0.109

* All these coefficients are statistically significant

Borregaard, which exhibited the greatest degree of correlaton was also the share for which the most data items were available. To the extent that there were more days on which at least one transaction occurred, Borregaard can be regarded as one of the most frequently traded shares of the sample (which in any event was chosen because of the frequency of transactions).

(ii) A runs test was performed to compare the total number of runs of all types with the number which would be expected if share prices were random. Looking at daily price changes, in every case the number of runs actually observed fell below that predicted. This confirms that runs tend to persist for longer than would be expected.

(iii) Jennergren and Korsvold also looked at the distribution of rates of return and concluded, as did Brealey, that there were differences between the observed distribution and that predicted by a normal distribution.

Finally, it was noted that the smaller stock market, Norway, coincided with the lower mean absolute serial correlation coefficient. It has been suggested in the UK evidence that larger companies attract more research interest and are therefore more likely to be efficiently priced. It is thus surprising that Norway, in serial correlation terms is more efficient than Sweden. There are several possible explanations: the 15 Norwegian stocks may, on average, be larger than the 30 Swedish; the result may be due entirely to chance; or it may be that Norwegian transaction costs are lower than Swedish and that therefore there is more scope for dealing against any inefficiency. Transaction costs were not mentioned so no firm conclusion about efficiency can be drawn.

It was left to Jennergren [63] to include transaction costs in a separate study of weak form efficiency on the Swedish share price data only. A filter test, which was a modification of that employed by Dryden [11], was applied to the data. The modifications to the system were designed to accommodate features of the stock exchange trading mechanics peculiar to Sweden. Two main alterations were incorporated: (i) short sales were not permitted since no such facility exists on the Stockholm exchange; and (ii) transactions precipitated by the operation of the filter were assumed to be effected on the next following day on which a transaction in that stock occurred. This is simply to allow for the longer communication period in the market and for the comparative lack of frequency of transactions. Any surplus cash was assumed to earn bank deposit interest.

One interesting innovation was that while transaction costs were fully taken into account, so also was the tax rate of the investor. Tax plays a very important part in the mechanics of price making. Consider for example the predilection of high marginal rate tax payers for low coupon gilts where the objective is to ensure that the return on the investment is subject to capital gains tax, the rate of which is lower than income tax rates. Jennergren thus went a step further in constructing a realistic method of testing a filter system. Taking a marginal tax rate of 75 per cent which Jennergren argues is typical for most private individuals, the filter systems tested (ranging from 1 per cent to 20 per cent) were considerably less profitable than a policy of buy-and-hold.

However, for institutions, the situation is different. Corporation tax is levied at the same rate on income as on capital gains. Thus some of the tax advantages (low rates of capital gains tax) of a buy-and-hold policy which accrue to an individual, do not arise in the case of a corporation. Since the tax system does not discriminate between capital gain and income, it was sufficient to examine the filters on a pre-tax basis. Only the filters in the range 10-20 per cent managed to beat the buy-and-hold portfolio. The table below sets out Jennergren's results for this range of filters. Each result represents the average final value of an initial investment of SwK 10,000 in each of the 30 shares. Cases 1 and 2 indicate that the system begins by a holding of cash (ie deposited in the bank account) and a holding of shares respectively.

Filter Size	10%	12.5%	15%	17.5%	20%
	SwK	SwK	SwK	SwK	SwK
Average Results:					
Case 1	15,500	16,400	16,800	16,600	15,700
Case 2	15,500	16,600	17,300	17,500	16,800

A buy-and-hold policy produced a final value of SwK 15,800, while an investment in the bank account produced only SwK 12,500. It is clear that three filters on a Case 1 basis and 4 filters on a Case 2 basis, beat the buy-and-hold policy. However, this result is not entirely conclusive. The data base is short and the above result may be entirely due to chance — a peculiarity of this particular set of data. For example, the differences between the results for Cases 1 and 2 will be due entirely to the characteristics of the data at the beginning of the period. Eventually each case will fall into line, both showing investments in the bank or in the share simultaneously. Thus the two cases differ only in respect of the period before they fall into line and no significance should be read into any differences in the results of each case.

The only sure way of knowing whether these results are significant is to repeat the test on separate data. Otherwise, the above can only be regarded as tentative evidence.

Jennergren in his study made two other points not hitherto discussed in relation to the weak form hypothesis. Firstly, risk is not explicitly taken into account. The buy-and-hold policy used as a yardstick does not necessarily have the same risk characteristics as the filter system being studied. Obviously the most meaningful comparison can be made when the risk levels match. In this instance the filter system will imply an investment alternating between the bank account and a particular share. As such it involves a lesser degree of risk than a policy of continuously holding that share. Thus if additional risk is rewarded with additional return, the buy-and-hold policy would be expected to beat the filter systems. This therefore adds weight to the findings of inefficiency.

Secondly, Jennergren discussed the possibility that transactions precipitated by a filter rule could alter the price. Any unusual buying or selling activity might well affect a share price since other market operators could interpret the activity as conveying information, good or bad, about that company. On the other hand, the rest of the market might attach no significance whatsoever. Jennergren assumed that the share price might be biased by SwK2 up or down depending on the nature of the transaction. He then re-tested each of the filter rules for only some of the stocks. Profitability was of course reduced but no firm conclusion could be reached.

The Semi-Strong Hypothesis

Forsgårdh and Hertzen [64]

Forsgårdh and Hertzen performed a test of the semi-strong hypothesis on the Swedish stock market. The particular event studied was the announcement of earnings and the technique employed was a novel adaptation of residuals analysis. The diagonal model was used to produce forecasts of 24 share prices around the time of the announcement of preliminary results during 1969 and 1970. At the same time, estimates of the earnings figures to be announced were obtained from a representative cross-section of analysts and investors. These estimates were then compared with the actual announced earnings. The novelty of the methodology lay in the next step which compared two ratios:

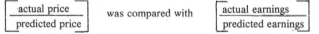

A positive relationship was observed. Thus where actual earnings exceeded predictions, the actual share price also exceeded the predicted price. More importantly, the observed relationship was able to show that the price movement was entirely explained by the earnings announcements and that the bulk of this price movement occurred in the announcement week. The conclusion reached was that the 'results lend support to the hypothesis that the Swedish stock market is efficient in the semi-strong sense'.

Strong Form Hypothesis

Spain: Palacios [65]

Palacios analysed the performance of 15 Spanish mutual funds in the period 1966-71 (although not all the funds were in existence for the whole of the period). A number of tests were used including the Sharpe reward/variability test. Only 3 funds managed to beat the market. Even when heavy management expenses (0.5-2 per cent pa) were added back, only 4 of the portfolios managed to beat the market — convincing evidence of efficiency.

Palacios also looked at performance within the period to determine if there was any variation.

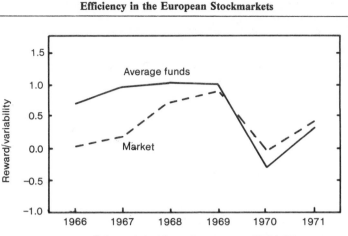

Mutual fund performance: 1966-71

The chart sets out the Sharpe performance test for each of the 6 years. The subject of the comparison is an 'average' portfolio consisting of those mutual funds in existence in each year. Superior performance at the beginning of the period was succeeded by inferior performance at the end. Palacios attributes this improvement in efficiency to the increasing significance of the mutual funds during the period. The first funds were introduced in 1966 and rapid expansion then took place. Thus by the end of 1971, there were sufficient analysts for the Spanish market to be efficient.

France: McDonald [66]

A Sharpe performance test was included in McDonald's study of French mutual funds. Over the period August 1967 to November 1969, the Sharpe test produced the following rankings:

Sharpe test:	Best performing	Soginter	
		Sogevar	
		Optima	
		Epargne Mobilière	
		France Placement	
		Slivam	} equal ranking
		French market portfolio	
	Worst performing	France Investissement	} equal ranking
		Sliva France	

It is apparent that 5 of the 8 funds beat the market portfolio, a result which could be explained by chance. However, it is perhaps more likely, in view of the extent of the 'superior' performance, that the results are not due entirely to chance. McDonald concluded that superior performance was demonstrated although this was also based on additional tests, the validity of which has since been questioned.

The data took account of management charges and brokerage but did not allow for the ability of each fund (with the exception of Sliva France, which failed to beat the market in any case) to invest abroad. To the extent that the funds availed themselves of this opportunity, performance superior to a naive investment in the French market would be expected. In fact Soginter, which topped the performance table, held more than half of its portfolio in foreign stocks over much of the period. The results of the test are therefore inconclusive, serving only to illustrate the benefits of international diversification.

McDonald discussed a number of factors peculiar to the French market and which might give rise to inefficiency. In particular he identified the meagre (by US standards) flow of information on companies as providing an opportunity for those analysts employed by the banks managing the funds to use banking relationships to obtain information and improve their forecasts. This could then lead to superior performance. Whether such performance has been achieved in practice is a question which can only be answered by a study which excludes the foreign part of a French mutual fund portfolio.

NOTE ON THE VALIDITY OF THE RANDOM WALK FOR EUROPEAN STOCK PRICES

BRUNO H. SOLNIK*

I. INTRODUCTION

The purpose of this note is to test whether European stock prices follow a random walk. A sample of 234 securities from 8 major European stock markets is used in this study. Some of the standard serial correlation tests which have been traditionally performed on the New York Stock Exchange are being applied to this body of data.

The development of the random walk concept originated in some empirical findings that successive price variations were uncorrelated (Kendall [6], Osborne [10], etc.). It is now widely believed that the New York Stock Exchange is an efficient market and that U.S. security price behavior is quite consistent with a random walk concept. The most comprehensive work in this area is the study by Fama [4] on 30 Dow Jones Industrial stocks for a five-year period (1956-1961); for all differentiating intervals (from daily to monthly), the serial correlation coefficients were small and generally not significantly different from zero. However some authors (see Cheng and Deets [1], Jenning [5]) have recently suggested that a rebalancing strategy of portfolio investment will work better than a Buy and Hold strategy because of the existence of negative serial correlation of security prices. While this time dependence is only one of the arguments advanced in favor of the rebalancing strategy, it would certainly work in favor of the strategy.

Reviewing the literature, it appears that Cootner [2], Moore [8], and Cheng and Deets [1] found a preponderance of negative signs for weekly changes, as did King [7] for monthly price relatives. Although Fama [4] reached the same conclusions for four- and nine-trading day changes, he found opposite results (i.e., positive serial correlation) for daily or sixteen-day returns. So did Kendall [6] for weekly returns.

Few serious tests of the random walk have been performed on European data. This was probably due to the lack of systematic computerized data bases. In 1953 Kendall [6] did not find any evidence of systematic price patterns for British securities. However some evidence of positive serial correlation has been found more recently on the Dutch market (Theil and Leenders [11]) and the British Stock Exchange (e.g., Dryden [3]).

The first goal of this note is to study the distribution of serial correlation coefficients of common stocks for each European market and draw comparison with the results found by Fama [4] on a comparable sample of American stocks. No important deviations from the random walk are found. Then the stationarity over time of serial correlation coefficients for individual securities

* Assistant Professor of Finance, Graduate School of Business, Stanford University. I am greatly indebted to Franco Modigliani, Jerry Pogue, Stewart Myers, Myron Scholes and William Bradford.

TABLE 1

NUMBER OF STOCKS FOR EACH NATIONAL STOCK MARKET

France	65 stocks
UK	40 stocks
Germany	35 stocks
Italy	30 stocks
The Netherlands	24 stocks
Belgium	17 stocks
Switzerland	17 stocks
Sweden	6 stocks

is investigated. The results are quite different from those found for the U.S. and would indicate a lesser efficiency of most European stock markets.

II. THE DATA USED

The data base consists of daily prices and dividend data for 234 common stocks of eight European countries.[1] The time period covered is from March 1966 to April 1971.

The distribution of the sample by country is shown in Table 1. Within each European country, the companies in the sample tend to be the largest in terms of market value of shares outstanding. The 30 Italian stocks, for example, comprise about three-fourths of the market value of all listed Italian shares. For the United Kingdom, France and Germany, the number is not as high but still in excess of 50 per cent in each case.

Security returns were computed on a daily, weekly, bi-weekly and monthly basis. Returns were computed as follows.

$$r_t = \frac{P_t + d_t - P_{t-1}}{P_{t-1}}$$

where

r_t = the return during interval t,
P_t = the stock price at the end of period t,
P_{t-1} = the stock price at the end of the previous period,
d_t = dividends paid during the interval (assuming payments on ex-dividend dates).

The data were corrected for all capital adjustments (splits, rights, etc.). This feature can be very important in countries where payments to stockholders take the form of capital adjustments rather than dividends (e.g., Italy). Dividend data were not readily available for three of the countries, the Netherlands, Sweden and Switzerland; thus return is measured in these cases by the percentage of change in stock prices.

---

1. The data base was generously provided by Eurofinance, a prominent European investment house.

III. THE RESULTS

1. Serial Correlation Coefficients

The period covered consists of 1310 daily observations. Serial correlation for weekly, bi-weekly and monthly returns were also computed for the 5-year period.

Confidence limits for the sample correlation coefficient, ρ, have been computed, given the true population correlation coefficient (here $k = 0$) and the number of observations N (62 for monthly returns). With serial correlation coefficients computed on monthly returns, the 95% confidence limit would be 0.24, −0.24. If the sample correlation coefficient of a given stock is larger than 0.24 (or smaller than −0.24), we can reject the hypothesis that the true correlation is zero (random walk) at the 95% confidence level. These 95% confidence limits have been estimated for all the time intervals used in this study. It has been shown that these limits around zero are approximately equal to twice the standard error σ (up to the 3rd decimal for $N > 50$). Therefore in the tables we will generally refer to 2σ rather than the 95% confidence limits keeping in mind that they are equal.[2]

This test could be applied to each individual stock. However since information exists for several stocks in the same market, there is a more efficient way to analyze the degree of efficiency of each national market. Thin markets, poor disclosure of information, or discontinuity in trading could create systematic deviations from the random walk. Therefore, following Fama [4], a sample distribution of correlation coefficients was derived crosssectionally over all stocks of a national stock market. In other words one serial correlation coefficient per firm is computed over the whole period and we look at their distribution for each country.

The results are similar for all European countries, therefore the analysis will be conducted using the French market as an example.[3]

In Figure 1, the distribution found by Fama [4] for daily U.S. returns for a comparable period is adjacent to the one which was found for France; the dashed line represents two standard errors from zero. It can be noticed that the French distribution for *daily* changes (like those for all European countries) is much flatter than that for America without any mode around zero, while the random walk would predict a bell shaped distribution more tightly grouped around zero. As in the case of the American data, the sample distribution has a fatter tail than was expected. While only 5% of the coefficients should be larger than 0.07 (2 Standard errors), this is true for 37% of the

---

2. Were the distribution normal, this equality would be always exact. However the density function for correlation coefficients is much more complex. When the returns have finite variance, the standard error σ of the serial correlation coefficients for a large number of observations is given by the Anderson formula.

$$\sigma = \frac{1}{\sqrt{N-1}}$$

For more details see Kendall [6].

3. The sample of French securities was the largest with 65 stocks.

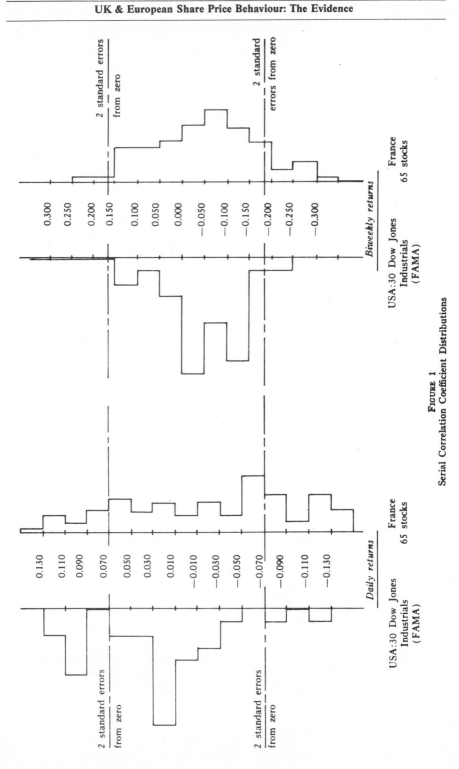

FIGURE 1
Serial Correlation Coefficient Distributions

U.S. stocks and over 50% of the French stocks.[4] Similarly the sample dispersion, SD, is much larger than the standard error σ predicted by the random walk theory.

It appears that the deviation from the random walk gets less significant for longer time intervals. The second plot of Figure 1 compares, for example, the distributions for bi-weekly returns; the distribution of correlation coefficients assumes a shape more in line with the random walk theory and the percentage of stocks having a coefficient larger than two standard errors (dashed line) gets very small. The dispersion around zero is still larger than in the American case and than its predicted value σ.[5]

The same conclusions can be reached for all European stock markets by looking at Table 2. For each time interval this table gives the mean serial correlation coefficient in each country, the sample dispersion (standard deviation), the ratio of this sample dispersion to the computed standard error, the number of stocks with a correlation coefficient greater than twice its standard error and the number of positive coefficients.[6]

Again, all the sample serial correlation coefficients are quite small although slightly larger, on the average, than their U.S. equivalent; for all intervals, the distribution of coefficients for European stock markets are a little less tightly grouped around zero than for the N.Y.S.E. For *daily* returns, violations of the random walk are more apparent than on Wall Street. This could be due to the thinness of the market and the discontinuity in trading. The slow diffusion of relevant information among investors may be important. It would imply that it takes more time for prices to adjust to new information. These irregularities should disappear when biweekly or monthly returns are used and in fact departures from the random walk get less significant with increasing time intervals. This can be seen by the reduction in the number of statistically significant coefficients.[7] Besides, the sample distribution conforms very closely with the curve predicted by the theory when monthly returns are used. The sample dispersion, SD, is almost equal to its predicted value σ and the fat tails have disappeared.

No evidence can be found in those European results for the predominance of negative serial correlation. In the case of biweekly returns, for example, only two countries exhibit a tendency towards negative time dependence: France and Switzerland are the only countries to have a larger proportion of stocks with negative serial correlation during the recent years. However, this pattern changes completely for other differencing intervals and no general conclusions can be drawn.

Little evidence has therefore been found which would support the claim

4. Although coefficients greater than two standard deviations are statistically significant at the 95% level of confidence, the real magnitude of their effect is still very small.

5. The scale has been changed to allow for a better test of significance. In both cases the unit of the scale can be taken as the standard error.

6. Since only 6 stocks are included in the Swedish sample, the results for the Stockholm stock exchange are not very meaningful.

7. However, since increasing the interval reduces the number of observations N, the standard error σ increases and so does the average absolute size of the coefficients (but less than σ).

TABLE 2

SUMMARY STATISTICS OF SERIAL CORRELATION COEFFICIENTS DISTRIBUTION FOR 8 EUROPEAN COUNTRIES AND THE USA

Daily Returns

Country	Serial Corr. Average	Dispersion of Sample Distribution S.D.	S.D./σ	Number of Terms ≥ 2σ	Number of Positive Terms
France	−0.019	0.082	2.5	41/65	33/65
Italy	−0.023	0.069	2.1	9/30	14/30
U.K.	0.072	0.066	2.0	21/40	34/40
Germany	0.078	0.075	2.2	23/35	28/35
Nederlands	0.031	0.060	1.8	9/24	17/24
Belgium	−0.018	0.066	2.0	5/17	7/17
Switzerland	0.012	0.073	2.2	4/17	11/17
Sweden	0.056	0.049	1.5	1/6	3/6
USA	0.026	0.057	1.7	11/30	22/30

σ = 0.033

Weekly Returns

Country	Serial Corr. Average	Dispersion of Sample Distribution S.D.	S.D./σ	Number of Terms ≥ 2σ	Number of Positive Terms
France	−0.049	0.095	1.6	17/65	21/65
Italy	0.001	0.086	1.4	5/30	14/30
U.K.	−0.055	0.068	1.1	7/40	8/40
Germany	0.056	0.072	1.2	8/35	27/35
Nederlands	0.002	0.074	1.2	3/24	14/24
Belgium	−0.088	0.067	1.1	5/17	1/17
Switzerland	−0.022	0.066	1.1	1/17	6/17
Sweden	0.024	0.040	0.7	1/6	4/6
USA	−0.038	0.075	1.2	5/30	9/30

σ = 0.06

Biweekly Returns

Country	Serial Corr. Average	Dispersion of Sample Distribution S.D.	S.D./σ	Number of Terms ≥ 2σ	Number of Positive Terms
France	−0.050	0.115	1.3	6/65	21/65
Italy	0.050	0.100	1.1	3/30	21/30
U.K.	0.005	0.098	1.1	3/40	20/40
Germany	0.038	0.103	1.1	4/35	17/35
Nederlands	0.052	0.104	1.1	3/24	16/24
Belgium	0.019	0.116	1.3	1/17	10/17
Switzerland	−0.063	0.097	1.1	1/17	3/17
Sweden	0.070	0.030	0.3	0/6	6/6
USA	−0.053	0.084	0.9	2/30	6/30

σ = 0.09

Monthly Returns

Country	Serial Corr. Average	Dispersion of Sample Distribution S.D.	S.D./σ	Number of Terms ≥ 2σ	Number of Positive Terms
France	0.012	0.104	0.9	1/65	38/65
Italy	−0.027	0.110	0.9	1/30	7/30
U.K.	0.020	0.108	0.9	1/40	19/40
Germany	0.058	0.099	0.8	2/35	23/35
Nederlands	−0.011	0.134	1.1	2/24	9/24
Belgium	−0.022	0.133	1.1	1/17	5/17
Switzerland	−0.017	0.150	1.3	1/17	7/17
Sweden	0.140	0.138	1.2	1/6	6/6
USA	0.009	0.099	0.8	1/30	17/30

σ = 0.12

TABLE 3
CORRELATION BETWEEN ESTIMATES OF THE TWO PERIODS

Country	SC_1/SC_2 Daily	SC_1/SC_2 Biweekly
France	0.48	0.27
Italy	0.31	0.34
U.K.	0.14	0
Germany	0.58	0.37
Netherlands	0.08	0.18
Belgium	0.32	0.42
Switzerland	0.36	0.38
Sweden	0.88	−0.48

that some European markets are, *ex-post*, more efficient than others. Efficiency, however, may have dimensions in addition to serial correlations.

Let us now look at the stability of the time dependence relationship of returns on stocks.

2. Stability of the Estimates

For serial correlation to be used in a meaningful way it should be stable over time. In the random walk framework, observed time dependence is purely accidental. A stock exhibiting more serial correlation than another in one period would not be expected (50% chance) to do so in the next period. In this section we look for the predictability of those serial correlation coefficients on an individual basis.

In order to do this, the total period has been split into two subperiods:

Period 1: March 1966-November 1968
Period 2: December 1968-April 1971

The coefficients were first computed separately for those two periods. Then cross-section (product moment) correlations of serial correlation coefficients between the two periods were computed and are shown in Table 3.

Surprisingly enough, there is some evidence of stability of serial correlation coefficients for individual stocks. Thus a stock which tends to exhibit positive (or negative) serial correlation in one period keeps this characteristic in the following periods. Only in the case of Great Britain is this property not displayed.[8] This could be expected since the London market is by far the largest stock market after Wall Street and generally considered as fairly efficient.[9]

The evidence presented above suggests that the European stocks may be classified into two categories:

a) stocks with long period fluctuations around the mean (low frequency) or varying mean—positive correlation;

8. Again the case of Sweden is more special since the sample consists of only 6 stocks.

9. The total market value of outstanding shares was close to $200 billion in 1970 which is more than all other European markets put together. Besides, the large volume of transactions and the jobber create a deeper market.

b) stocks with short period fluctuations around the mean (high frequency) —negative correlation.

Some specific characteristics of European stock markets might explain these departures from the random walk. Although the data were not available to study their impact, some tentative explanations can be advanced.

Positive serial correlation could be created by a slow adjustment to new information. Because of the generally poor information diffusion process on European stock markets and the existence of privileged channels (inside information), it will take some time for all information to be fully reflected in the price (distributed lag model?). Although securities included in this study are the most extensively traded stocks in their respective countries,[10] their market is still very thin compared to a typical U.S. stock. Characteristics of thin markets and discontinuity in trading could explain the existence of stable negative correlation.[11] As a matter of fact, some limited information on the volumes of transaction for French, Belgian, Italian and German stocks would indicate that less traded shares tend to exhibit stable negative serial correlation. The data are too fragmentary to allow for any strong test of this aspect.

IV. CONCLUSIONS

This note tests the adequacy of the random walk hypothesis for European stock prices by studying serial correlation coefficients and their stability. Deviations from the random walk seem slightly more apparent in the European stock price behavior than in the American price behavior. However, the serial correlation coefficients are still quite small (R square of less than 4%) and probably negligible from an investor point of view. While those deviations appear more significant for daily price changes, any investment strategy which would attempt to use them would involve prohibitive daily transaction costs.

Finally the serial correlation coefficients for individual stocks were found to be fairly stable over time. Since no systematic patterns have been found for the coefficients signs, any investment strategy which attempts to profit from existing time dependences should work selectively on a stock by stock basis rather than on the market as a whole.

Explanations for these departures from the random walk can probably be found in some of the technical and institutional characteristics of European capital markets: loose requirements for disclosure of information, no control on insiders' trading, thin markets, discontinuity in trading. With the exception of the British market where prices seem to behave much like U.S. stock prices, all other markets tend to exhibit quite unexpectedly similar behavior.

One might expect the market inefficiencies described above to have a greater impact on the behavior of European stock prices than has been presented here. The conclusions must therefore be regarded as tentative. We have dealt with a preselected sample of the most traded stocks on each exchange; the results

10. Most of them are the object of daily transactions.

11. Niederhoffer and Osborne [9] have shown that the difference between the bid and ask price would create negative correlation. In thin markets the spread will be larger resulting in systematic time dependence.

might be quite different with a more representative sample of shares. More definitive conclusions must await more extensive and statistically powerful tests of the random walk for European stock prices.

Finally, other dimensions of market efficiency should be looked at before any general conclusion can be drawn about European markets.[12]

REFERENCES

1. P. L. Cheng and M. K. Deets. "Portfolio Returns and the Random Walk Theory," *Journal of Finance*, March 1971, pp. 11-30.
2. P. H. Cootner. "Stock Prices: Random vs. Systematic Changes," *Industrial Management Review*, Spring 1962, Vol. 3, No. 2, pp. 24-45.
3. M. Dryden. "Share Price Movements: A Markovian Approach," *Journal of Finance*, March 1969, pp. 49-61.
4. E. Fama. "The Behavior of Stock Market Prices," *Journal of Business*, January 1965, pp. 34-104.
5. E. H. Jennings. "An Empirical Analysis of Some Aspects of Common Stock Diversification," *Journal of Financial & Quantitative Analysis*, March 1971, pp. 797-813.
6. M. G. Kendall. "The Analysis of Economic Time Series: Part I; Prices," *Journal of the Royal Statistical Society*, March-April 1953, Vol. 7, pp. 145-173.
7. B. F. King. "Market and Industry Factors in Stock Price Behavior," *Journal of Business*, January 1966, pp. 139-190.
8. A. B. Moore. "Some Characteristics of Changes in Common Stock Prices," in *The Random Character of Stock Prices*, Cootner (ed.), (The M.I.T. Press—1964), pp. 139-161.
9. V. Niederhoffer and M. F. M. Osborne. "Market Making and Reversals on the Stock Exchange," *Journal of the American Statistical Association*, December 1966, pp. 897-916.
10. M. F. Osborne. "Periodic Structure in the Brownian Motion of Stock Market Prices," *Operations Research*, Vol. 10, May 1962, pp. 345-375.
11. H. Theil and C. T. Leenders. "Tomorrow on the Amsterdam Stock Exchange," *Journal of Business*, July 1965, pp. 277-284.

12. That is, even if prices follow a random walk, it does not imply that the markets are fully efficient. Tests of the market model and others would provide additional insights on European capital markets.

FRENCH MUTUAL FUND PERFORMANCE: EVALUATION OF INTERNATIONALLY-DIVERSIFIED PORTFOLIOS

John G. McDonald[*]

I. Introduction

THE PURPOSE of this study is to measure the investment performance of French mutual funds, as examples of internationally-diversified portfolios. French mutual funds or SICAV differ from mutual funds in the United States in two important respects.[1] First, the great majority of SICAV hold both domestic and foreign securities, with the largest foreign positions in stocks and bonds listed on the New York Stock Exchange. Second, most SICAV have been established, marketed and managed by French banks, which may have both investment banking and commercial lending operations, a practice forbidden in the U.S. under the Glass-Steagall Banking Act of 1933.[2] Relative to other investors in that domestic environment, many French banks enjoy substantial advantages in financial-analysis resources and access to current information on French firms. Measurement of the investment performance of the French-securities portion of these portfolios constitutes a "strong-form" test of capital market efficiency in France.[3]

The potential advantages of international diversification in common stock portfolios have received considerable attention in the mean-variance framework of Markowitz and Tobin.[4] Papers by Grubel and by Levy and Sarnat demonstrated that efficient internationally-diversified portfolios, constructed from *ex post* returns and standard deviations of return on market indices, generally dominate the results for single nation market portfolios.[5] In the

* Associate Professor of Finance, Graduate School of Business, Stanford University. I am indebted to Patrice Mignon and Gilles Cahen-Salvadore for helping to gather and process the data. Thanks are due to Alan Kraus, Robert H. Litzenberger, William F. Sharpe, Bruno H. Solnik, Jacques-Henri Gougenheim and Richard A. Cohn for their comments and suggestions. Support for this research was provided by a Dean Witter Foundation grant to Stanford University. Assistance in Paris was graciously provided by faculty members of the Centre d'Enseignement Supérieur des Affaires and the University of Paris.

1. French mutual funds, *Sociétés d'Investissement à Capital Variable,* are commonly called SICAV.

2. In 1971, the U.S. Supreme Court reaffirmed this important institutional difference in the two countries in the case of *Investment Company Institute vs. The Comptroller of the Currency.* The majority opinion stated that U.S. banks may not operate investment funds for certain pooled accounts in direct competition with the mutual fund industry, reasoning that it would involve the banks in issuing and distributing "securities" in violation of the Glass-Steagall Act. See (27).

3. In Fama's (6) framework, one strong-form test of capital market efficiency examines the investment performance of individuals or institutions that may have privileged access to investment information.

4. The normative framework formulated by Markowitz (17) and Tobin (25) provided the point of departure for the well-known theory of capital market equilibrium of Sharpe (21) and Lintner (16), used in this study.

5. Grubel (10) used monthly returns on market indices, converted to dollars at the current

context of portfolio choice these results must be interpreted with caution, as one cannot demonstrate with *ex post* returns on market indices alone the extent to which international diversification is desirable. The important question is whether efficient (*ex ante*) multinational portfolios of individual securities dominate efficient portfolios constructed from stocks in a single country, and on this issue the evidence is limited.[6]

In part the issue rests on the effective degree of integration of the world's equity markets. Given the prevailing impediments to international diversification (special taxes, exchange controls, etc.), it seems clear that reality lies somewhere between two hypotheses: the fully-integrated one-market hypothesis, where in the Sharpe-Lintner model of capital market equilibrium one would expect efficient portfolios of domestic common stocks from a number of nations to lie along a common capital market line;[7] and the fully-segmented market hypothesis, where one would expect a unique capital market line in each national market.[8] In fully-integrated markets, a portfolio which purchased common stocks in a second country would gain only the "pure diversification" advantage of access to a larger part of the total universe of securities.[9] The segmented-market hypothesis implies potential advantages from international investment beyond those associated with pure diversification, as more favorable ratios of expected return to non-diversifiable risk may be available in foreign markets. In weakly-segmented capital markets, where fund managers view foreign securities as price-takers, one would expect both pure diversification and perceived return-risk advantages to motivate foreign holdings. Under either integrated or segmented market hypotheses, if fund managers felt they could make superior forecasts of foreign market returns or of non-market components of expected returns on individual foreign stocks, they would be further motivated to invest outside the domestic market.

This paper presents a model to evaluate the performance of funds holding securities in two countries. The measurement of returns on fund and market portfolios and on a risk-free asset is explored in the French environment, and

exchange rate, in 11 countries in 1959-67. Levy and Sarnat (15) used annual changes in market indices in 28 countries in 1951-67. Miller and Whitman (19) and Lee (13) have applied the mean-variance framework to the analysis of aggregate bond holdings and capital movements.

6. For example, Lessard (14) demonstrated with individual securities in Argentina, Brazil, Chile, and Columbia in 1959-68 that *ex ante* efficient portfolios of 30 stocks from the four countries dominated, in subsequently observed mean and standard deviation, *ex ante* efficient portfolios of 30 stocks from a single country. Efficient portfolios have maximum expected return at a given level of risk.

7. See Sharpe (21), (23) and Lintner (16). The capital market line, which in mean-variance portfolio theory represents the linear trade-off between expected return and standard deviation of efficient portfolios, would be identical in all nations under perfect integration.

8. Cohn and Pringle (4) discuss the potential effect of removal of existing capital-flow restrictions on the capital market line.

9. "Pure diversification" implies a decrease in total variance of expected portfolio return as a security is added to the investment universe which is less than perfectly positively correlated with the market return as described in Section II. Thus, the ratio of expected return to total risk as measured by variance could be increased by international diversification, whereas the ratio of expected return to non-diversifiable risk could not be increased by investing in more than one of these fully-integrated markets. Some evidence in support of the integrated-market hypothesis is presented by Agmon (1).

a sample of funds is evaluated using monthly data in the 1964-69 period. The findings suggest "superior analysis," relative to a naive investment strategy, by most of the funds on the French-securities portion of the portfolios. This evidence of market inefficiency in the strong-form sense is consistent with advantages in access to current information on domestic firms which French banks and their mutual fund managers appeared to have in this period.

II. Measuring Performance of a Multi-national Portfolio

Under the specific assumptions of the Sharpe-Lintner capital asset pricing model, the expected one-period return $E(R_i)$ on an asset or portfolio i can be represented as follows:

$$E(R_i) = R_f + B_i(E(R_m) - R_f) \tag{1}$$

where R_f is the risk-free return over the period, $E(R_m)$ is the expected return on the market (the portfolio of all securities), and B_i is a measure of non-diversifiable risk. In a fully-integrated, one-market world, "the market" may be defined as the aggregate portfolio of all assets with uncertain return in all nations, weighted by their market value in a common currency and adjusted for all double-counting associated with inter-company holdings and companies listed on exchanges in more than one country.[10] In a world of segmented markets, R_m and B_i may be defined relative to the domestic market alone.

In applying the asset pricing model in (1) to the task of portfolio performance measurements, Jensen demonstrated using a market model and some reasonable approximations that portfolio return may be expressed in terms of realized, rather than expected, market returns.[11] In this framework a measure of performance d_{ij} may be defined for any well-diversified portfolio i in market j as follows:

$$d_{ij} = R_{ij} - E(R_{ij})$$
$$= R_{ij} - [R_f + B_{ij}(R_{mj} - R_f)]. \tag{2}$$

In a multiperiod context, the excess return on portfolio i over the risk-free rate R_f may be expressed as a function of the performance measure d_{ij}, non-diversifiable risk B_{ij}, and the return R_{mj} in market j for each period t:

$$R_{ijt} - R_{ft} = d_{ij} + B_{ij}(R_{mjt} - R_{ft}). \tag{3}$$

If the fully-integrated market hypothesis obtains, d_{ij} and B_{ij} may be estimated for an internationally-diversified portfolio by least-squares regression in Equation (3) of excess portfolio returns on the "world market" portfolio.[12] Under

---

10. The total market value of common stocks on nine major stock exchanges was distributed as follows (in billions of dollars): U.S.—New York Stock Exchange, 742; London, 254; Tokyo, 58; U.S.—American Exchange, 50; Germany (seven cities), 29; Paris, 25; Amsterdam, 14; Milan, 13; Brussels, 7. These figures reflect the arithmetic mean of market values and exchange rates at the beginning and end of the year 1971. The total of $1,192 billion, with two-thirds in the U.S., reflects some double counting of foreign listings on the New York, American and London exchanges. See (5).

11. See Jensen (12).

12. Time series of returns on such an aggregate portfolio were developed subsequent to this study by Solnik (24).

the fully-segmented markets hypothesis, in its extreme form, internationally diversified portfolios are presumed not to exist. If the hypothesis is recast to admit a small number of portfolios with access as price takers to two markets, then characterized as weakly-segmented, the return on portfolio i depends on the fractions x_1 and x_2 invested in markets 1 and 2 and on the market returns R_{m1} and R_{m2}.[13]

$$R_{it} - R_{ft} = x_1(d_{i1} + B_{i1}(R_{m1t} - R_{ft})) + x_2(d_{i2} + B_{i2}(R_{m2t} - R_{ft}))$$

$$= \phi_i + B^*_{i1}(R_{m1t} - R_{ft}) + B^*_{i2}(R_{m2t} - R_{ft}) \tag{4}$$

where
$$\phi_i = x_1 d_{i1} + x_2 d_{i2} \tag{4a}$$

$$B^*_{i1} = x_1 B_{i1} \qquad \text{and} \tag{4b}$$

$$B^*_{i2} = x_2 B_{i2}. \tag{4c}$$

The new measure of portfolio performance ϕ_i may be estimated in equation (4) using ordinary least squares provided the market returns R_{m1} and R_{m2} are independent, an assumption shown in Section III to be satisfactory in the case of the Paris and New York Stock Exchanges.[14]

III. Data on Returns in the French Environment

A. *The French Fund Sample*

In March 1964, forty years after the establishment of the first American mutual fund, SICAV were allowed to sell fund shares to French investors. The industry grew from seven funds in 1964 to 28 funds with assets of approximately $2 billion in 1969, including 17 "diversified" funds holding domestic and foreign stocks and bonds securities and 11 "income" funds holding only debt securities. Regardless of investment objectives, all funds are required to invest at least 30 per cent of assets in bank deposits or marketable debt denominated in French francs.[15] Unlike American funds, SICAV may distribute realized capital gains to investors only after retained earnings equal to one-half the fund's capital have been accumulated, where minimum initial capital was $4 million; dividends and interest are distributed. The sample in this study comprises the portfolios of eight of the oldest French funds, all "diversified" funds of which seven may hold foreign stocks and one (Sliva France) may invest only in French securities. Three of the sample funds began public sale in the first month permitted under the law, hence the data

13. The same risk free rate R_{ft} is assumed to exist in the two markets. The fractions x_1 and x_2 may vary in each period. In this study they are assumed to be parameters, measured mid-way in the 28-month internal shown in Tables 4 and 5 and discussed in Sections IV and V.

14. If effectively a one-market rather than segmented-market world exists, estimation of (4) is tantamount to using a multiple-index model in the face of the lack of data on "world market" portfolio returns. Equation (4) could be expanded to include three or more markets or nations, however coefficients could be estimated under the usual ordinary least squares assumptions only so long as the various market returns could reasonably be assumed to be independent.

15. Other restrictions provide that no more than 5 per cent of fund assets can be invested in securities of a single issuer, except the State; no more than 5 per cent of the common stock of one company can be purchased by a fund. Most funds are sold with an initial sales charge or "load" of 4.75 per cent.

begin in April 1964; the five other sample funds were introduced between June 1964 and March 1966.

Monthly data were gathered on each of the sample funds from the first full month after public offering to November, 1969. A fund's monthly return is defined as the change in net asset value (*la valeur liquidative*) from beginning to end of month plus all cash distributions paid during the month, divided by beginning net asset value.[16] Net asset value implies total current market value per fund share.

B. *The Risk-Free Rate in France*

The yield to maturity on government securities is usually used as the risk-free lending alternative for institutional investors over the holding period in question, one month in the present study.[17] Three times a month the Treasury in France auctions 360-day bills (*bons du tresor*). Once issued, the bills are not traded publicly as are their counterparts in the U.S. Holders can demand premature reimbursement by the Treasury after three months or may sell to the Banque de France after nine months. Bills may be traded among financial institutions, but transactions in bills with one month to maturity are not common, and quotes on one-month yields to maturity on treasury bills are not published. One-year risk-free rates may be estimated from data on yields to maturity in each treasury bill auction; these data have been published since 1967, when auctions replaced almost entirely the negotiated sales of bills.

A viable one-month investment alternative, a holding which is effectively risk-free, is a time-deposit in a "blocked account" (*compte bloqué*) in a French bank.[18] Such deposits in excess of $20,000 are subject to negotiated interest rates, which are not publicly available. Rate of return data on one-month blocked accounts were gathered with the cooperation of a Paris bank, through review of records showing rates on which blocked-account negotiations

---

16. Fund returns on American stock holdings were affected for many months prior to August 1969 by anticipations of a devaluation of the French franc against the dollar, so that the eventual 12 per cent devaluation in that month brought about in some cases a *loss* rather than a windfall gain on U.S. stock holdings. If in March 1969, for example, a fund wished to buy 1000 shares of Syntex at $30, a stock not traded in Paris, exchange controls under the *par contre* system suggested that shares listed on the NYSE stock exchange be mailed to New York and sold in dollars with the proceeds used to buy Syntex shares. One fund, for example, used holdings of Royal Dutch shares, originally purchased in Amsterdam. If a fund did not wish to sell existing holdings in NYSE listed stocks, it might have purchased IBM in francs on the Paris Bourse and resold these shares in dollars in New York. As an example, assume that IBM, quoted at $300 a share in New York, was trading at 1725 rather than 1500 francs a share in Paris, representing an expected devaluation of 15 per cent away from an official exchange rate of 5 to 1. Thus, an investment of 172,500 francs in April might have enabled a fund to purchase 100 shares of IBM in Paris, resell them in New York, and purchase 1000 shares of Syntex gross of commissions. If at the time of the 12 per cent devaluation in August Syntex shares were still traded at $30 in New York, their value to the fund would have dropped to 168,000 francs as the uncertainty as to the magnitude of the exchange-rate adjustment was resolved. Under these rules purchase of shares on foreign exchanges cost three commissions plus mailing and insurance costs and had no effect on the French balance of payments. Following devaluation of the franc in 1969, this system of controls was replaced by the *devise titre* system.

17. See Sharpe (22) and Jensen (12), for example.

18. Deposits in nationalized French banks are, of course, effectively guaranteed by the Government.

were based in each month of this study. Thus, monthly risk-free rate R_f used in all subsequent estimation is this blocked-account rate available to large investors in France.[19]

C. The Market Return

Observations of the French market return are based on the index of the Compagnie des Agents de Change (C.A.C.), a daily market-value-weighted index of 430 French stocks listed on the Paris Bourse.[20] The market-return is the percentage change in the C.A.C. index, from the first trading day to the last of each month, plus an estimate of percentage dividend yield on the index over the month. Observations of the United States market return are based on Standard and Poor's 500 index, where return is the sum of the percentage change in the index from beginning to end of the month, plus estimated dividend yield.[21]

D. Relationship of French and U.S. Market Returns

Monthly returns on the French market index were only slightly positively correlated with monthly returns on the U.S. market index, as indicated by a bivariate correlation coefficient of 0.043 for the 68-month period 1964-69.[22] Many institutional investors and government officials share the impression that the underlying distributions of market returns are independent in these two countries.[23] For the period 1966–71 Solnik found correlation coefficients of 0.050 and 0.056 for bi-weekly and monthly observations of French and U.S. market returns.[24] Grubel and Fadner have demonstrated that correlation between inter-country pairs of stocks is an increasing function of holding

19. The findings reported in Tables 1-5 were obtained using the one-month blocked-account rate to large depositors as a measure of R_f. Substantially similar regression results were obtained using one rough surrogate for R_f which may be calculated from data which are more readily available than blocked-account rates through the Treasury Division of the Ministry of Finance. It was assumed in each month that a portfolio of 360-day bills had been purchased over the previous twelve months and that a measure of current month's yield was the arithmetic mean of yields-to-maturity at issue of this series of bills. Note that current market yields subsequent to the issue of such bills are not published and that the latter surrogate for one-month bill yields ignores certain term structure of interest rate considerations.

20. Composition of the important market indices in ten major nations is described by Montier (19).

21. Dividend yield is reported weekly by Standard and Poor. Each month's yield is the arithmetic mean of four weeks' figures, stated in units of per cent per month. Ideally, U.S. market returns should be adjusted in each month for average changes in exchange rates implicit in the prices of American stocks listed in New York and Paris, as discussed in footnote 16. Two crude approximations were used: equations were estimated with the entire 12 per cent devaluation of the franc assumed to affect the August 1969 Standard and Poor's 500 return, viewed from France, and with no adjustment to the Standard and Poor's 500 returns in 1969. The results reported in Tables 1-5 reflect the latter assumption.

22. Regression of monthly returns on the French Market index (R_{m1}) on monthly returns on the U.S. Standard and Poor's 500 index (R_{m2}) in the period 1964-69 reveals no significant relationship:

$$R_{m1} = 0.0054 + 0.0598\ R_{m2} + u.\ (R^2 = 0.0018)$$
$$(t\ 0.97)\ \ (t\ 0.35)$$

23. See, for example, Rendu (20).

24. See Solnik (24).

period, as longer-run factors such as economic growth rate and general price stability exert a greater common influence among nations.[25] Thus, if quarterly or annual holding-period returns were used, higher positive correlation between French and U.S. indices would be expected.

IV. PERFORMANCE OF FRENCH FUNDS, 1964-69

Regression results for the estimation of equations (3) and (4) are shown in Tables 1 through 4. Table 5 presents a summary of performance measures. Returns on each of the funds, from first month following introduction to November 1969, are significantly related to the French market return, with correlation coefficients between 0.41 and 0.89, as given in Table 1.[26] Sliva France, which is in its by-laws restricted to French securities, exhibits the highest degree of domestic diversification with 79 per cent of the variance in fund return (R^2) explained by the French market return, somewhat higher than the mean figure for U.S. mutual funds.[27] At the other extreme, the French market explained only 17 per cent of Soginter's return, as the fund held more than one-half of its portfolio in foreign stocks over much of the period. Non-diversifiable risk B_1 with respect to the French market ranged from 0.25 to 0.55 for the eight funds, reflecting both the requirement that 30 per cent of assets be held in deposits and bonds and the prevalence of holdings in foreign securities whose returns were not significantly correlated with the French stock market return.

Jensen's performance measure d reflects return in excess of the *ex post* return from a "naive-strategy portfolio" of equivalent risk B_1, implemented by dividing the portfolio between the French market portfolio and the risk-free alternative in bank deposits or treasury bills. All eight funds had an estimated d greater than zero, whereas only 43 of 115 U.S. funds in Jensen's sample for 1955-64 exhibited a positive d.[28] However, the all-French fund, Sliva France, exhibited the smallest value of d, approximately one per cent per year.

In the two-market model of equation (4) excess returns on the fund are regressed on excess returns on French and U.S. market indices, as shown in Table 2. The independence of the two markets over this period is reflected in the estimates of fund B's with respect to the French market, as estimates of

25. See Grubel and Fadner (11). This finding is consistent with the higher correlation coefficient (0.34) between U.S. and French indices found by Levy and Sarnat (13) based on annual returns, 1951-67. Note, however, that tests with annual data often have problems of small-sample bias, as relatively few observations are used in estimating correlation coefficients.

26. Each fund's B_1 estimate is significantly positive at the 0.95 level. R^2 is the square of the correlation coefficient, adjusted for degrees of freedom in Tables 2-4.

27. Jensen (12) found a mean R^2 of 85 per cent for a sample of 115 American mutual funds based on *annual* returns in 1955-64. The mean R^2 for American mutual funds using *monthly* returns was approximately 60 per cent in the period 1960-69.

28. Only the estimate of d for Soginter was significantly greater than zero at the 0.95 level. The reader is cautioned in comparing estimates across funds in Tables 1 to 3, as the observation period for French fund depends on its introduction date. Performance comparisons for a common time period follow in Tables 4 and 5. Only funds which invested in American securities prior to the period of market anticipation of the devaluation of August 1969 profited from this exchange rate change, as discussed in footnote 16.

TABLE 1

Estimates of Fund Performance (d) and Systematic Risk (B_1) Relative to French Market

Fund	Measurement Period (Month-Year)	$\bar{R}$(a)	σ(b)	d	t-d	B_1	t-B_1	R^2
A. Epargne Mobiliere	(4-64 to 11-69)	.00611	.0222	.00137	.82	.394	10.49	.62
B. France Investissement	(4-66 to 11-69)	.01101	.0302	.00224	.61	.476	6.07	.51
C. France Placement	(7-64 to 11-69)	.00705	.0269	.00171	.63	.364	5.99	.36
D. Optima	(5-64 to 11-69)	.00720	.0221	.00267	1.19	.285	5.75	.34
E. Sliva France(c)	(4-65 to 11-69)	.00650	.0263	.00095	.58	.546	14.31	.79
F. Slivam	(4-64 to 11-69)	.00676	.0244	.00203	.96	.391	8.29	.51
G. Sogevar	(4-64 to 11-69)	.00725	.0229	.00252	1.38	.392	9.63	.58
H. Soginter	(12-64 to 11-69)	.01124	.0253	.00668	2.21	.249	3.47	.17
France: C.A.C. index	(4-64 to 11-69)	.00584	.0369					
U.S.A.: S&P 500 index	(4-64 to 11-69)	.00624	.0267					

Model, Equation (3):

$$R_i - R_f = d_i + B_{i1}(R_{m1} - R_f) + e_i,$$

with monthly observations of fund return R_1, risk free rate R_f and French market return R_{m1} (Compagnie des Agents de Change index).

(a) Arithmetic mean of monthly returns.
(b) Standard deviation of monthly returns.
(c) Investments limited to French securities.

271

TABLE 2

ESTIMATES OF FUND PERFORMANCE (ϕ) AND SYSTEMATIC RISK (B^*_1 AND B^*_2) RELATIVE TO FRENCH AND U.S. MARKETS

Fund	$\overline{R}^{(a)}$	ϕ	$t - \phi$	B^*_1	$t - B^*_1$	B^*_2	$t - B^*_2$	R^2
A. Epargne Mobiliere	.00611	.00108	.67	.389	10.84	.133	2.70	.66
B. France Investissement	.01101	.00121	.36	.469	6.54	.261	2.94	.60
C. France Placement	.00705	.00104	.47	.346	7.04	.386	5.88	.58
D. Optima	.00729	.00218	1.06	.277	6.12	.229	3.68	.44
E. Sliva France(b)	.00650	.00091	.55	.544	14.14	.036	.77	.79
F. Slivam	.00676	.00152	.80	.383	8.98	.233	3.98	.60
G. Sogevar	.00725	.00223	1.27	.388	9.87	.132	2.46	.61
H. Soginter	.01124	.00619	2.35	.231	3.68	.335	4.35	.37

Model, Equation (4):

$$R_i - R_f = \phi_i + B^*_{i1}(R_{m1} - R_f) + B^*_{i2}(R_{m2} - R_f) + e_i$$

with monthly observations of fund return R_i, risk free rate R_f, French market return R_{m1} (Compagnie des Agents de Change index) and United States market return R_{m2} (Standard and Poor's 500 index).

(a) Arithmetic mean of monthly fund returns.
(b) Investments limited to French securities.

TABLE 3

ESTIMATES OF FUND PERFORMANCE (ϕ) AND RISK: DOWN-MARKET PERIOD IN FRANCE. 1964-67

Fund	Measurement Period (Month-Year)[a]	$\bar{R}$[b]	σ[c]	ϕ	$t - \phi$	B^*_1	$t - B^*_1$	B^*_2	$t - B^*_2$	R^2
A. Epargne Mobiliere	(4-64 to 7-67)	.00135	.0183	-.00031	-.17	.363	8.44	.163	2.78	.66
B. France Investissement	(4-66 to 7-67)	.00055	.0126	-.00350	-.84	.330	2.37	.158	1.06	.45
C. France Placement	(7-64 to 7-67)	.00108	.0203	-.00226	-1.03	.318	5.96	.350	4.99	.60
D. Optima	(5-64 to 7-67)	.00257	.0157	-.00007	-.04	.250	5.85	.228	3.91	.54
E. Sliva France[d]	(4-65 to 7-67)	.00013	.0228	.00159	.66	.569	8.45	.070	1.03	.73
F. Slivam	(4-64 to 7-67)	.00224	.0211	.00069	.35	.418	8.90	.228	3.56	.69
G. Sogevar	(4-64 to 7-67)	.00270	.0195	.00133	.71	.392	8.77	.144	2.35	.67
H. Soginter	(12-64 to 7-67)	.00476	.0165	.00151	.65	.151	2.26	.332	4.77	.46
France: C.A.C. index	(4-64 to 7-67)	-.00343	.0411							
U.S.A.: S&P 500 index	(4-64 to 7-67)	.00736	.0300							
France: Risk free rate	(4-64 to 7-67)	.00350								

Model: Equation (4), as in Table 2.

(a) From time of fund introduction to end of July 1967.
(b) Arithmetic mean of monthly returns.
(c) Standard deviation of monthly returns.
(d) Investments limited to French securities.

TABLE 4

ESTIMATES OF FUND PERFORMANCE (ϕ) AND RISK: UP-MARKET PERIOD IN FRANCE, 1967-69

	Fund	Measurement Period (Month-Year)	$\bar{R}$[a]	σ[b]	ϕ	$t - \phi$	B^*_1	$t - B^*_1$	B^*_2	$t - B^*_2$	R^2
A.	Epargne Mobiliere	(8-67 to 11-69)	.01290	.0253	.00223	.69	.416	6.08	.093	1.04	.63
B.	France Investissement	(8-67 to 11-69)	.01437	.0332	.00319	.73	.458	4.94	.292	2.41	.60
C.	France Placement	(8-67 to 11-69)	.01494	.0320	.00580	1.32	.322	3.46	.440	3.63	.57
D.	Optima	(8-67 to 11-69)	.01365	.0275	.00503	1.11	.278	2.87	.235	1.87	.37
E.	Sliva France [c]	(8-67 to 11-69)	.01287	.0280	.00030	.12	.545	1.09	.005	.07	.81
F.	Slivam	(8-67 to 11-69)	.01322	.0273	.00402	1.00	.319	3.74	.273	2.45	.50
G.	Sogevar	(8-67 to 11-69)	.01375	.0256	.00375	1.02	.371	4.74	.132	1.29	.53
H.	Soginter	(8-67 to 11-69)	.01865	.0309	.01076	2.04	.231	2.05	.340	2.31	.32
	France: C.A.C. index	(8-67 to 11-69)	.01908	.0463							
	U.S.A.: S&P 500 index	(8-67 to 11-69)	.00425	.0355							
	France: Risk free rate	(8-67 to 11-69)	.00475								

Model: Equation (4), as in Table 2.

(a) Arithmetic mean of monthly returns.
(b) Standard deviation of monthly returns.
(c) Investments limited to French securities.

TABLE 5

COMPARISON OF PERFORMANCE MEASURES, 1967-69

Fund	Sharpe[a] Measure $(\bar{R} - \bar{R}_f)/\sigma$	Treynor[b] Measure $(\bar{R} - \bar{R}_f)/B_1$	Jensen[c] Measure d	Two-market[d] Measure ϕ	Return to Non-Diversifiable[e] Risk in France $(\bar{R} - \bar{R}_f)/\sigma r$	Estimate of d_1 ϕ/x_1
A. Epargne Mobiliere	.322 (4)[f]	.0187 (6)	.00190 (7)	.00223 (7)	.403 (6)	.00316
B. France Investissement	.290 (7)	.0185 (7)	.00215 (6)	.00319 (6)	.398 (7)	.00556
C. France Placement	.319 (5)	.0245 (3)	.00421 (2)	.00580 (2)	.529 (3)	.01073
D. Optima	.324 (3)	.0271 (2)	.00419 (3)	.00503 (3)	.584 (2)	.00906
E. Sliva France	.290 (7)	.0150 (8)	.00028 (8)	.00030 (8)	.323 (8)	.00030
F. Slivam	.310 (6)	.0224 (5)	.00305 (5)	.00402 (4)	.485 (5)	.00577
G. Sogevar	.351 (2)	.0226 (4)	.00327 (4)	.00375 (5)	.487 (4)	.00562
H. Soginter	.450 (1)	.0602 (1)	.00955 (1)	.01076 (1)	1.297 (1)	.02375
French market portfolio	.310	.0143	0	0	.310	

Period: Monthly returns, August 1967 to November 1969.

(a) See reward-to-variability ratio in Sharpe (23).
(b) See Treynor (12). B_1 was estimated in equation 3 using the French market index and data for 1967-69.
(c) See Jensen (12). d was estimated in equation 3 using the French market index and data for 1967-69.
(d) See Table 4.
(e) The correlation coefficient between fund return and French market return is r.
(f) Fund rankings are in parentheses.

B*$_1$ in Table 2 with the U.S. market return added as an independent variable are only slightly different from B$_1$ in Table 1. The estimate of sensitivity to the U.S. market B*$_2$ is significantly positive, at the 0.95 level, in all seven funds permitting foreign holdings.

The new performance measure ϕ reflects the return in excess of that obtainable by partitioning the portfolio into two parts: fraction x$_1$ in a French naive-strategy portfolio with risk B$_1$ = B*$_1$/x$_1$ as defined in equation (4b); fraction x$_2$ = 1—x$_1$ in a U.S. naive-strategy portfolio such that B$_2$ = B*$_2$/x$_2$.[29] The estimate of ϕ is positive for all eight funds, but not significantly different in magnitude from d in any case. Addition of the U.S. market return adds zero (in the case of the all-French-securities fund, Sliva France) to 20 per cent to the percentage of variance explained in fund returns; in the portfolios of Soginter and Optima, less than one-half of total variance of fund returns is explained by French and U.S. market indices, indicative of diversification in stocks of more than a dozen countries.[30]

How is the estimate of ϕ affected by omitted market return variables in equation (4), for funds which held securities from Britain, Japan, and other nations? If the omitted market return were perfectly positively correlated with French or U.S. market returns over the period, its entire effect would be reflected in the estimate of B*$_1$ or B*$_2$; if it were perfectly independent of the market returns in France and the U.S., the omitted market's effect would be reflected in ϕ. Available evidence indicates that London and Tokyo market returns, using monthly data, were positively correlated with U.S. market returns coefficients in the range 0.19 to 0.35.[31] In the period 1967-69, for example, the mean monthly return on the London index (Financial Times Industrial) approximately equalled that on the U.S. index reported in Tables 4 and 5, whereas the return on the Tokyo index (Dow Jones) had the same order of magnitude as the French market's mean monthly return, reflecting significant increases in market value in that period. Thus, French funds' investments in Japanese stocks in particular may be reflected in estimates of both B*$_2$ and ϕ, and the interpretation of ϕ that follows is subject to this qualification as to the potential effect of omitted markets, a caveat which the author wishes to stress.

A. Performance in Up-Market and Down-Market Periods in France

The data series for each fund was split into two parts on August 1967, so that performance could be compared during the 1964-67 bear market and the

29. As an example in this two-market problem, assume that a portfolio has been divided x$_1$ = x$_2$ = 0.5 during the period, and that we have estimated B*$_1$ = 0.3 and B*$_2$ = 0.5. It follows that B$_1$ = 0.6 and B$_2$ = 1.0, so that the "naive strategy" portfolio would have been divided in half, with 60 per cent of the first half invested in the French market portfolio at R$_{m1}$ and 40 per cent in bank deposits or treasury bills at R$_f$, and the second half invested entirely in the U.S. market portfolio at R$_{m2}$. An estimate of ϕ equal to 0.01 would indicate returns of one per cent per month greater than would have been realized in the above strategy, where one cannot assess from estimated ϕ alone the relative magnitudes of d$_1$ and d$_2$ attributable to each market in equation (4a).

30. At the end of 1968, for example, Soginter held 50 stocks from 14 countries and Optima had 156 company names from 11 nations in their stock portfolios. Each held approximately two-thirds of its portfolio in French and American securities.

31. See, for example, Agmon (1) for the period 1961-65 and Solnik (24) for the period 1966-71.

1967-69 bull market in France, and so that the second segment could provide a consistent time period for comparison of various performance measures in Table 5. The down-market period results in Table 3 indicate that while all eight funds had positive absolute returns over the period, only four of eight had positive ϕ; none had ϕ significantly greater than zero, that is, there was no excess return significantly better than the two-country, naive strategy described above producing the same $B*_1$ and $B*_2$. In four funds (C, D, E and G) one cannot reject the hypothesis that the estimate of down-market risk $B*_1$ in Table 3 equaled the up-market estimate in Table 4; only three funds (A, B and H) had significantly lower French-market $B*_1$ in the bear market, indicating an attempt on the part of fund managers to reduce the non-diversifiable risk of the French portion of the portfolio in the down-market.[32] As the percentage of variance explained by the French market return alone was higher in the down-market than in the up-market in six of eight cases, it appears that the funds were not generally able to shift their portfolios to foreign markets in anticipation of the French market decline.[33]

B. *Comparison of Performance Measures, 1967-69*

Tables 4 and 5 present performance comparisons over 28 months, 1967-69. Measures of total risk σ of each of eight French funds fell in a relatively narrow band (0.0256 to 0.0332), and all funds had returns which were less variable than market returns in France or the U.S. All funds had mean returns less than the mean French market return in this period.

Sharpe's reward-to-variability ratio, mean excess return on the fund divided by standard deviation of fund returns, provides a good measure of performance for a French investor with a relatively large amount of his wealth invested in one of these funds, where total fund risk rather than its non-diversifiable component is relevant. The ranking of funds by this ratio in the first column of Table 5 roughly parallels the ranking by degree of diversification in the French market, as the "all-domestic" fund Sliva France ranks last and the "international" fund Soginter ranks first. Sharpe (23) found values for the reward-to-variability ratio for 34 American funds which are larger than those of all French funds in this sample except Soginter. These findings are consistent with the longer-run evidence that U.S. market returns have been higher and less variable than the French market returns,[34] so that *ceteris paribus* French funds investing in the U.S. market would be expected to have had better investment performance than wholly-domestic French funds. As discussed in Section I, investment in securities outside France has two positive effects on the reward-

32. A lower $B*_1$ in the down-market period need not imply, of course, that fund managers were able to forecast market returns, as managers may have responded after the fact to falling market prices, and the $B*_1$ of an unmanaged portfolio would be expected to decline with volatile stocks falling in value more than less-volatile stocks, altering the weights of securities in the portfolio. Campanella (3) concluded that mutual funds in the U.S. were not generally able to forecast American market movements in the period 1960-68.

33. Percentage of variance explained by the French market return alone may be viewed as a measure of degree of diversification in French securities.

34. See Table 1 and also Levy and Sarnat (13).

to-variability ratio, $(\overline{R} - \overline{R}_t)/\sigma$: the "pure diversification" effect which would obtain even in fully-integrated capital markets; and the more favorable return-risk ratio in the U.S., which would be expected to persist in a fully-integrated capital market if the French market had greater total risk and smaller non-diversifiable risk than the U.S. segment of the world market.

A measure of the non-diversifiable portion of total risk is relevant for well-diversified fund portfolios or for a French investor who holds only a part of his wealth in a mutual fund so as to diversify at the individual level. Two ratios of reward to non-diversifiable risk are presented in Table 5. Treynor's measure produces a ranking of French funds by ratio of mean excess return to B_1 which roughly parallels the ranking by Sharpe's return-to-total-variability ratio. A similar measure appropriate for cross-country comparisons of mutual fund performance is the ratio of excess return to total non-diversifiable risk, $(\overline{R} - \overline{R}_t)/\sigma r$, which is obtained in dividing the Sharpe measure by the correlation coefficient r between fund and French market return, or in dividing Treynor's ratio by σ_{m1}.[35] As demonstrated in the fifth column in Table 5, this measure simply yields the Treynor rankings, but in addition reflects the overall variability of the market. The striking result is that the top-ranking fund had a ratio of return to non-diversifiable standard deviation which was four times as high as the eighth ranking fund.

The estimates of Jensen's measure d and our two-market measure were positive for all eight funds in this period. For example, with Silva-France, a fund restricted to French securities, an estimate of d near zero indicates that the same total return could have been produced, holding management costs constant, by dividing the portfolio with 55 per cent (B_1) in a French market portfolio and 45 per cent in bank deposits or treasury bills; as this naive strategy presumably could have been implemented at a minimal management cost, the naive-strategy results may be considered as good or better than the actual results in the period. The findings in Tables 2, 3 and 4 suggest that the one-market model in which d was estimated, summarized in equation (3), is not well specified in the case of 7 of 8 funds for which the estimate of B^*_2 for the U.S. market return was generally significant. The comparable measure ϕ in the two-market equation produced a fund performance ranking very similar to the ranking of d. While ϕ appears to be greater than d for each fund, one cannot reject the hypothesis that the two estimates are equal in each case, given their standard errors.

The last line in Table 5, the "French market portfolio," represents a hypothetical fund with portfolio composition identical to the French market-value-weighted index, ignoring any transaction costs needed to maintain that portfolio composition over time. If performance is measured by return to total variability, seven of eight funds did as well or better than this hypothetical fund in 1967-69. Thus, for an investor desiring less total variance than the French market return and having a large part of his wealth invested in one of these funds so that total variance is the relevant risk measure, per-

35. Recall that for fund i, $B_1 = (\sigma_i r)/\sigma_{m1}$, where σ_{m1} is the standard deviation of the French market return.

formance of these seven funds may be judged satisfactory. For a French investor with a small part of his wealth committed to a fund, i.e., with home-made diversification in his portfolio of wealth, the measures of return adjusted for non-diversifiable risk (columns two and five of Table 5) for all eight funds indicate superior performance relative to this hypothetical French market portfolio.

V. ARE FUND MANAGERS "SUPERIOR ANALYSTS" OF FRENCH SECURITIES?

A number of factors might favor French banks, as mutual fund managers, in their effort to perform "superior analysis" in forecasting returns on French stocks. Unlike American brokerage firms, French brokers (*agents de change*) did not actively distribute investment research to institutional and individual investors.[36] The absence of an organized security-analysis industry as it is known in the U.S. in part reflects the comparative advantage of French banks in doing in-depth analysis of companies, and banks as the largest institutional users of investment research have developed substantial internal analytical staffs. Under French law, commercial lending and investment banking relation-ships may have been of considerable advantage to banks in their role as port-folio managers, whereas similar intra-bank use of information not available to the general public would have been prohibited in the U.S. under the Glass-Steagall Act, the Securities Exchange Act of 1934, and subsequent court rulings. France first established a commission to regulate financial information and security markets, the C.O.B., in 1967.[37] The major securities law of December 1970 spelled out initial restrictions on the use of non-public information—restrictions which were not in force in the 1964-69 sample period. In this environment, evaluation of mutual fund returns may be viewed as a strong-form test of capital market efficiency.

One cannot measure directly whether mutual funds were superior analysts of French stocks, i.e., determine if d_1 is positive in equation (4a), as returns on the domestic-securities portion of internationally-diversified fund portfolios are not available. To approximate the contribution to the performance measure ϕ made by French stock selection, we assumed in equation (4a) that d_2 is zero and that similar contributions from holdings in other markets outside France (the extension of (4a) with further terms of d_3, d_4, etc.) are zero as well. Mutual fund studies by Sharpe (23), Jensen (12), and Friend, Blume and Crockett (7) suggest that American funds are unable consistently to produce superior returns relative to realized market returns and systematic portfolio risk. The largest foreign positions of French funds have been in U.S. stocks, and it is plausible to assume that French funds are no better able than Ameri-

36. A number of institutional investors support common investment research in organizations such as Eurofinance. Annual balance sheet and income statement data on French firms are widely disseminated; however, few companies listed on the Paris exchange issued consolidated statements in the 1964-69 period and few reported earnings per share more frequently than once a year. Invest-ment research by member-firms of the Paris Bourse increased somewhat subsequent to the period of this study.

37. The Commission des Operations de Bourse (C.O.B.) parallels the Securities and Exchange Commission of the U.S.

can funds to forecast individual stock returns in the U.S. Thus, $d_1 = \phi/x_1$ in equation (4a). Estimates of ϕ were taken from Tables 4 for 1967-69, and the fraction of fund portfolios invested in French stocks and debt x_1 was observed for each fund as of December 31, 1968.[38] The range of values of x_1 indicates holdings of 45 to 100 per cent of fund assets in French securities, a proportion assumed here to be a parameter for each fund in the 1967-69 period.[39] The resulting estimates of d_1 are shown in the last column of Table 5. Three of eight funds (C, D and H) had a "superior" return d_1 on French securities of one per cent a month or better, with more than two per cent a month for the highest fund, Soginter. Three other funds (B, F and G) had d_1 estimates greater than one-half of one per cent a month. In sum, 6 of 8 funds appear to have d_1 on the French portion of their portfolios of 6 to 28 per cent annual rate of return in excess of that expected given the systematic risk of domestic security holdings; the remaining two funds show d_1 estimates only slightly greater than zero.

All fund returns were measured net of total management expenses and brokerage costs. With average commissions of 1.2 per cent and average annual portfolio turnover of 15 per cent, adding back total brokerage fees would increase returns by 0.0036 a year or .0003 a month.[40] Annual management fees varied from 0.21 to 0.50 per cent of assets, with an average of 0.32 per cent for the sample. The combined effect of transaction and management costs was to lower estimates of return, d and ϕ, by an average of 0.00057 per month or two-thirds of one per cent a year. These findings support the conclusion that fund managers in general were superior analysts in terms of forecasting returns on French securities, and that three funds, Soginter, France Placement and Optima, achieved striking results in 1967-69.

To attempt to assess fund managers' views as to superior analysis in their organizations, the author interviewed representatives of the managing banks of all funds in the sample. Opinion varied widely as to the use and relative importance of insider or privileged information on companies. Only one fund indicated that banking relationships with companies reduced their flexibility in buying and selling stocks of these companies in the mutual fund. Several funds suggested that privileged information was sometimes available on clients of the bank and on other companies, but that the relatively long time horizon on equity investments in most funds and the lack of liquidity in many French stocks made short-term trading operations impractical.[41] Few French com-

38. The values of x_1 were obtained from the fund association A.S.F.I. in Paris: Epargne Mobiliere, 0.706; France Investissement, 0.574; France Placement, 0.540; Optima, 0.555; Sliva France, 1.00; Slivam, 0.699; Sogevar, 0.668; Soginter, 0.453.

39. The portfolio composition of all mutual funds in France which were classified as "diversified" comprised 34 per cent French stocks, 25 per cent French bonds and 9 per cent cash and short term debt, for an aggregate x_1 of 0.68 at the end of 1968.

40. The commission expense of 1.2 per cent—including 0.4 per cent to the broker, 0.3 per cent tax, and a 0.5 per cent clearing charge—was not subject to a volume discount during the study period.

41. Without the block-trading capability present in New York, French fund managers usually limited transactions to 20 per cent participation in the regular daily trading volume of a French stock. Only a dozen most-active French stocks had average daily volumes exceeding $200,000 on

panies release quarterly earnings statements, so that individual investors generally have difficulty in up-dating expectations of many financial variables related to market value. The mutual funds' advantage would seem to be less a matter of companies revealing dramatic items of "insider information" to the banks, but more importantly a question of continuing contacts inside companies whereby analysts with banking affiliations may monitor developments on a more current basis than individual investors.

The results of this study suggest that, through mutual funds, small investors in France profited in 1964-69 from the comparative advantage of banks in security analysis; prior to 1964 only owners of large portfolios profited from this expertise as clients on bank trust departments. At present only 3 per cent of the French population are shareholders in common stocks and mutual funds, compared to 15 per cent in the U.S., and this difference is even larger if claims on equity holdings of pension funds are added. Given current financial reporting practice, the "superiority" of performance of mutual funds in choice of French stocks implies that portfolio profits attributable to banks' investment research skills and access to timely and accurate information were passed on in part to fund shareholders, principally small investors.

As the chief regulating agency, the C.O.B. is conscious of the necessity of speeding the information flow from companies to the general public.[42] The securities law of 1970 states that no insider, analyst, professional investor or banker can use material non-public information for his personal profit. Interpretation of the law with respect to mutual funds and fiduciary account management remains to be done. It seems unlikely that statutory and regulatory constraints on fund managers will change abruptly in the next few years, as the initial thrust of regulatory concern seems properly to be directly at corporate insiders.

VI. CONCLUSIONS

This study investigated the investment performance of eight of the oldest French mutual funds, from month of introduction to 1969. The findings suggest that the funds generally produced superior risk-adjusted returns. As an initial strong-form test of market efficiency outside the U.S., the study supports the impression widely held by French investors that their market was inefficient with respect to the completeness and speed of dissemination of information germane to investment decisions. Similar measures applied to American funds in past studies have found less than one half of sample funds "superior" with respect to naive portfolio strategies in the U.S. market. Funds which invested in the U.S. market in 1964-69 generally profited from a higher return at a given level of variance than that reflected in French market returns. Ex-post, the higher U.S. returns more than compensated for the added transaction costs associated with investing in foreign-currency securities. No

the Paris exchange, so that to accumulate a $1 million position in a stock often required a month or more. Block transactions have been negotiated somewhat more frequently since the period of this study.

42. See Burgard (2) and the Annual Reports of the C.O.B. (5).

evidence was found as to fund managers' ability to forecast general market trends so as to effect major shifts in the proportions of a portfolio invested in each country. More importantly, the findings indicate that the funds were generally able to attain "superior" returns relative to naive portfolio strategy of equal risk on the French securities in their portfolios, indicating superior skills in analyzing domestic securities and the generally advantageous position of French banks, as fund managers, in access to current information on French companies.

The findings indicate that the sample of funds offered investors a relatively limited spectrum of investment objectives, measured with respect to total or non-diversifiable risk. No fund's portfolio had greater total risk or produced greater returns than the French market portfolio in the period 1964-69. It is desirable in an efficient financial market that institutional portfolios be as unconstrained as possible in formulating investment objectives and portfolio policy, including target risk levels, and that each investor be free to choose from a large menu of funds a portfolio suitable for his own preferences. Accordingly, it would seem unwise and unnecessary for the French government to maintain the requirement that 30 per cent of fund assets be held in cash or French debt securities, so that some funds may define and pursue higher risk-return objectives at the level of "aggressive growth" funds in the U.S. It follows that funds which maintain existing levels of total and non-diversifiable risk could choose portfolios in the absence of the 30 per cent constraint which would produce expected returns as great or greater than expected returns under the existing constraint.

In the period of this study, the internationally-diversified fund's trade-off was between a comparative advantage in superior information on French stocks, on one hand, and the diversification benefits and higher expected returns in American stocks than in French stocks at a given level of variance, on the other. As French funds grow in size, their ability to profit from superior information in French stocks, thinly traded in terms of daily volumes by institutional investors' standards, will diminish. Therefore, advantages in execution and liquidity afforded by block-trading capabilities in foreign securities in the U.S. and Great Britain, together with perceived advantages in expected return relative to risk in foreign stocks, may induce French mutual funds to invest more and more abroad, reducing percentage holdings in French stocks. The desire of concerned French officials to channel savings of small investors into domestic equity investments is reflected in the exchange control systems for securities under which the SICAV have operated. It is possible both that French investors would face a more desirable investment opportunity set (in expected return-risk terms) and that capital costs would be lower for French firms if government controls on securities were removed. These and other important policy questions provide opportunities for future research.

REFERENCES

1. Tamir Agmon. "The Relations between Equity Markets—A Study of Share Price Co-movements in the U.S., U.K., Germany and Japan," *Journal of Finance*, XXVII (September, 1972), pp. 839-855.

2. J. J. Burgard. "Comment Ameliorer l'Information sur les Societes," *Analyse Financière*, No. 5 (Second Quarter, 1971), pp. 1-7.

3. Frank B. Campanella *The Measurement of Portfolio Risk Exposure*. Lexington, Mass.: Lexington Books, 1972.

4. Richard A. Cohn and John J. Pringle. "Imperfections in International Financial Markets: Implication for Risk Premia and the Cost of Capital to Firms," *Journal of Finance*, XXVIII (March 1973) pp. 59-66.

5. Commission des Operations de Bourse. *Rapport au Président de la Republique*. France, 1971.

6. Eugene Fama. "Efficient Capital Markets: A Review of Theory and Empirical Work," *Journal of Finance*, XV (May 1970), pp. 383-423.

7. Irvin Friend, Marshall Blume, and Jean Crockett. *Mutual Funds and Other Institutional Investors: A New Perspective*. New York: McGraw-Hill, 1970.

8. Georges Gallais-Hamonno. *Les Sociétés d'Investissement a Capital Variable (SICAV)*. Paris: Presses Universitaires de France, 1970.

9. ————. "La Supériorité de la Gestion Collective de l'Epargne Mobilière: Analyse Methodologique et Application aux SICAV," *Consommation*, No. 1 (1970).

10. Herbert G. Grubel. "Internationally Diversified Portfolios: Welfare Gains and Capital Flows," *American Economic Review*, LVII (December 1968), pp. 1299-1314.

11. Herbert G. Grubel and Kenneth Fadner. "The Interdependence of International Equity Markets," *Journal of Finance*, XXVI (March 1971), pp. 89-94.

12. Michael C. Jensen. "Risk, the Pricing of Capital Assets, and the Evaluation of Investment Portfolios," Journal of Business, XLII (April, 1969), pp. 167-247.

13. C. H. Lee. "A Stock-Adjustment Analysis of Capital Movements: The U.S.-Canadian Case," *Journal of Political Economy*, LXXVII (July-August, 1969), pp. 512-523.

14. Donald R. Lessard. "Multinational Portfolio Diversification for Developing Countries," (Unpublished doctoral dissertation, Stanford University, 1970).

15. Haim Levy and Marshall Sarnat. "International Diversification of Investment Portfolios," *American Economic Review*, LX (September 1970), pp. 668-675.

16. John Lintner. "The Valuation of Risk Assets and the Selection of Risky Investments in Stock Portfolios and Capital Budgets," *Review of Economics and Statistics*, III (February 1970), pp. 87-99.

17. Harry Markowitz. "Portfolio Selection," *Journal of Finance*, VII (March 1952), pp. 77-91.

18. Norman C. Miller and Marina v. N. Whitman. "A Mean-Variance Analysis of United States Long-Term Portfolio Foreign Investment," *The Quarterly Journal of Economics*, LXXXIV (May 1970), pp. 175-192.

19. Bruno Montier. "Les Indices Boursiers dans le Monde," *Analyse Financiére*, No. 1 (Fourth Quarter, 1969), pp. 11-26.

20. Gabriel Rendu. "Evolution Comparée des Bourses de Paris et de New York." *Banque*, CCXCIV (March 1971), pp. 256-266.

21. William F. Sharpe. "Capital Asset Prices: A Theory of Market Equilibrium under Conditions of Risk," *Journal of Finance*, XIX (September, 1964), pp. 425-442.

22. ————. "Mutual Fund Performance," *Journal of Business*, XXXIX, Part 2 (January, 1966), pp. 119-138.

23. ————. *Portfolio Theory and Capital Markets*. New York: McGraw-Hill, 1970.

24. Bruno H. Solnik. "European Capital Markets: Towards a Theory of an International Capital Market," Unpublished Ph.D. Thesis, M.I.T., August, 1972.

25. James Tobin. "Liquidity Preference as Behavior Towards Risk," *Review of Economic Studies*, XXV (February, 1958), pp. 65-86.

26. Jack L. Treynor. "How to Rate Management of Investment Funds," *Harvard Business Review*, XLIII (January-February 1965), pp. 63-75.

27. *United States Law Week*, 39 (April, 1971), pp. 4406-4414.

Conclusion

The remarks which follow relate mainly to the UK market. However, they are relevant to European markets and indeed any type of market to the extent that efficiency prevails.

Clearly there are many areas requiring further and better research. Conditions in the market place change over time. It would be informative to repeat some of the early work on more recent data. Also, great improvements in technique have been made, for example, the testing of a filter system has been refined to quite a sophisticated degree. Nevertheless there is still scope for greater accuracy and realism. For instance, in the evidence presented, no allowance was made for account trading. This possibility has consequences for transaction costs and for the cost of financing transactions since settlement is automatically delayed. Likewise with the databanks used in the various studies, improvements could be made. Longer time periods, more stocks, the identification of non-trading days and so forth can all help to remove error and raise the quality of the results. Steps in this direction have been taken with the establishment of a number of computerised databanks which doubtless will produce more accurate results.

The direction of the research should also be considered. More evidence of the strong form hypothesis would be desirable, particularly of performance of institutions other than unit trusts and pension funds. If the market is efficient as per the strong form hypothesis then the semi-strong form hypothesis and the weak form hypothesis also hold. Also, it is only the strong form hypothesis where the evidence has pointed to any doubt about efficiency. Hence more research could be enlightening.

The question which remains is whether the efficient market hypothesis is a satisfactory explanation of share price behaviour? For the weak form and semi-strong form, the weight of the evidence is overwhelmingly in favour of efficiency. That is to say, the evidence suggests that the stockmarket rapidly and accurately discounts new information into share prices. This implies that any system based on historical share price data (eg chartism) is futile, and further, that no use can profitably be made of publicly available information. Hence, subject to a number of caveats mentioned below, investment analysis is likewise largely futile.

However, for the strong form hypothesis, the evidence is not quite so powerful. At an aggregate level, efficiency is demonstrated. But as individual cases of superior portfolio performance have been observed, the market cannot be said to be fully efficient. It is perhaps a question of degree. The market may be said to be highly efficient. But this does not imply that the hypothesis should be abandoned. The most important discovery is that the majority of funds fail to match the performance of the market index. In other words, professionally managed funds do not even match the performance of a naîve index portfolio. This single fact must argue for a reassessment and reorganisation of the investment process. For those funds exhibiting poor performance, a number of factors may be at work. Firstly, poor diversification can produce a high risk factor for a given level of return. Secondly, if a portfolio is turned over once each year, transaction costs of the order of four and a half per cent of the gross fund could be incurred. Thirdly there are the investment management costs — sometimes of the order of one per cent. Finally, there is the possibility of a tax liability, for example in respect of capital gains. These expenses could all be reduced and performance thereby improved if the fund manager were to formulate his strategy on the basis of the market being virtually 100 per cent efficient. This means that a policy of buying a core portfolio and holding that portfolio should be pursued. No attempt at research or analysis should be made and no transaction costs should be incurred. In this way, performance for the majority of funds could be significantly improved. The fund manager's main task would obviously be to choose the core portfolio at the outset and arrange for the investment of new cash inflows. Thus the act of management would be concentrated at the point of investment of new cash.

However, before developing this concept of efficient investment, it is worth remembering that traditional investment management techniques may still have some part to play. That superior investment portfolio is possible, although rare, implies that there is some market inefficiency which might be exploitable. Inside information is one possible but unlikely explanation and, in view of pending legislation, will be ignored. Two alternatives remain. Firstly, some analysts may have superior forecasting or analytical ability. Their judgement may be superior to that of the market as a whole and therefore their estimate of what the share price should be may be more accurate than the actual market price. That such people exist would not necessarily be revealed by the work reviewed here which employs large samples. The task then is to determine which analysts if any can provide information or advice which has some economic value: that is, information which is not already discounted in the share price. A number of appropriate techniques have been discussed in the earlier part of the book. However, the cost of identifying and monitoring analysts would have to be taken into account. They would obviously have to earn their keep. After all, the occasional good buy may not cover the cost of their employment.

Secondly, it may be that while there is a great weight of analytical resources focused on the stock market, this may not be directed equally at every company. Those shares with small capitalisations do not usually interest institutions overmuch. It may just be that traditional investment analysis could be profitably employed here. This would also have to take account of the costs of research. As small companies by definition offer only a limited opportunity to invest, it is possible that the cost of identifying inefficiently priced shares is not covered by the profits generated. However, it would not be difficult to research this and indeed some of the evidence has touched briefly on this point.

The testing of shares for efficient pricing also applies to other stockmarkets where efficiency has not yet been established. In the pursuit of more effective diversification, overseas stockmarkets will have to be considered. Thus the method of investment management will depend on how efficiently the market place makes prices.

The Role of Investment Management

But even if every stockmarket were efficient, this would not mean that the investment manager would become otiose. His role should comprise two activities. Firstly, he must act as a counsel to the investor in respect of the choice of risk strategy to adopt. The choice of desired risk level is the most important investment decision from which all other decisions follow. But it may well be that the specification of desired risk is not a complex decision. Indeed it might be an obvious choice and not actually require any input from the fund manager: for instance, the trustees of a pension fund may be solely responsible for the choice of risk. Alternatively, the manager could offer the investor the risk choice by organising unit trusts with different risk characteristics, low risk and high risk. In any case the risk decision is not a permanent choice and can always be reassessed and such reassessment may require the advice of a fund manager. Risk relative to the market can be easily specified — it can be determined in terms of beta. Beta factors of 1.5 and 0.5 would signify high and low risk portfolios respectively. However, in absolute terms, the risk of the market can vary. Thus a high risk portfolio (beta of 1.5) when in absolute terms the market is low risk, could be less risky than a low risk portfolio (beta of 0.5) at a time when the market is high risk. Obviously the fund manager's assessment of the absolute level of risk (and return) offered by the market will be vital advice to the investor, especially when he is considering the risks of alternative investment media. Clearly the role of the fund manager at this stage need not be trivial and would in fact be highly skilled.

The second activity is the implementation of the adopted risk strategy. This involves the construction of the optimum portfolio — that portfolio which offers the best return for the given level of risk. Obviously this has to take account of opportunities for investment overseas which can reduce risk. Indeed, extensive diversification, expecially overseas, is the principal economic benefit which fund managers can offer investors.

Where shares are efficiently priced, the manager would buy a core portfolio which would remain unchanged, subject only to changes in market efficiency or the target risk level. Where shares are not efficiently priced, traditional investment analysis techniques could be employed to generate superior profits. There would also be administrative tasks, tax, accounting etc, which the fund manager would be expected to undertake.

The Role of the Analyst

If the discovery of efficiency has reduced the job of the fund manager then it has virtually removed the *raison d'être* for the investment analyst. Obviously it could not disappear completely since it is the concerted actions of analysts which create an efficient market place. In any event, to the extent that some inefficiency remains, then as outlined above, a job for the analyst remains. But what must be in doubt is whether the present research effort in aggregate terms is a sensible use of resources. The question which must be asked is whether research resources are squandered on the analysis of companies which are efficiently priced? To answer this question, the analyst, research manager or fund manager should assess the analyst's recommendations to test that the value of his output is exceeding his cost. This is something which should become included in the new role of the investment manager as outlined above.

The new role of the analyst, if indeed he is to enjoy an existence separate to that of an investment manager, should be directed at the assessment of risk. After all, the job of the investment manager has been defined to include the construction of a portfolio with specified risk characteristics. Such a task clearly involves the measurement of risk on an individual stock basis and on a portfolio. This is not easily achieved. The difficulties have been fairly fully described earlier in this book. This is perhaps one area where analysis might usefully make a contribution.

Factors Affecting Efficiency

Market efficiency is a highly desirable economic objective ensuring optimum allocation of resources to the good of all. Thus an obvious avenue of extension of this concept is to other commodity markets. Such markets should be tested for efficiency: if efficiency is proved then there could be some economic benefits to be gained by a rationalisation of the market process analogous to that described above for the stockmarket. If the market is found to be inefficient then steps can be taken to create the conditions for efficiency to prevail. This might be achieved by improving information flows both in terms of the quantity provided and the speed and extent of dissemination.

It is also worth considering the effect of the level of disclosure of information on the market mechanism. For example, the information provided by companies is quickly reflected in share prices. In other words, companies are allocated the correct share price on the basis of the information provided. Clearly if more information is provided then such information would be discounted by the share price and uncertainty would be reduced. Thus, subject to such further information not compromising the company by, for example, assisting competitors, a higher level of disclosure would be beneficial for share prices and hence for the allocation of capital resources within the economy. The responsibility for setting higher levels of disclosure rests ultimately with government but there are the stock exchange authorities, accounting institutes and the companies themselves which can, and do, take the initiative.

Finally, it is worth considering one other important determinant of market efficiency — transaction costs. Some small degree of inefficiency — in the shape of serial correlation — was observed although no advantage could be taken because transaction costs would more than absorb any profits. Therefore the larger transaction costs are, then the greater will be the degree of inefficiency which will prevail. The abolition of two per cent stamp duty would therefore help improve the level of market efficiency.

Brokerage is the other major transaction costs. It is somewhat ironic that the stock exchange, whose function is to create a free market place, should resort to fixed prices (minimum levels of commission) and not freely-determined market prices when it comes to charging for a broker's services. There are signs that this may change and perhaps follow the example set by Wall Street. Efficiency can only be improved by lower transaction costs.

Bibliography

1. P A Samuelson   'Proof that properly anticipated prices fluctuate randomly', *Industrial Management Review,* Vol 6, spring 1965

2. M G Kendall   'The analysis of economic time series, Part 2: Prices', *Journal of the Royal Statistical Society,* Vol 116 (A), 1953

3. L Bachélier   *Théorie de la speculation,* Paris, Gauthier-Villars, 1900

4. H V Roberts   'Stock market "patterns" and financial analysis: methodological suggestions', *The Journal of Finance,* Vol XIV, No 1, March 1959

5. M F M Osborne   'Brownian motion in the stock market', *Operations Research,* Vol 7, March/April 1959

6. H Working   'Note on the correlation of first differences of averages in a random chain', *Econometrica,* Vol 28, 1960

7. R A Brealey   'The distribution and independence of successive rates of return from the British equity market' *Journal of Business Finance,* Vol 2, 1970

8. S W Cunningham   'The predictability of British stock market prices', *Applied Statistics,* Vol 22, 1973

9. M M Dryden   'Share price movements: a Markovian approach', *The Journal of Finance,* Vol XXIV, March 1969

10. M M Dryden   'Short-term forecasting of share prices: an information theory approach', *Scottish Journal of Political Economy,* November 1968

11. M M Dryden   'Filter tests of UK share prices', *Applied Economics,* Vol 1, 1970

12. M M Dryden   'A statistical study of UK share prices', *Scottish Journal of Political Economy,* Vol 17, 1970

13. A G Kemp and G C Reid   'The random walk hypothesis and the recent behaviour of equity prices in Britain', *Economica,* Vol 38, 1971

14. B Mandelbrot   'The variation of certain speculative prices', *The Journal of Business,* Vol 36, 1963

15. D H Girmes and A E Benjamin — 'Random walk hypothesis for 543 stocks and shares registered on the London stock exchange', *Journal of Business Finance and Accounting,* spring 1975

16. R J Griffiths — *'Relative strength - an indicator for investment in the equity market,'* unpublished MSc thesis, Department of Statistics, Cranfield College, 1970

17. B H Solnik — 'Note on the validity of the random walk for European stock prices', *Journal of Finance,* Vol XXVIII, 1973

18. J R F Guy — 'The stock exchange London: an empirical analysis of monthly data from 1960 to 1970', *European Finance Association 1975 Proceedings,* North Holland, 1976

19. D H Girmes and D C Damant — 'Charts and the random walk', *The Investment Analyst,* No 41, 1975

20. J M Brew — 'The trustees' meeting - a City daydream', *The Investment Analyst,* No 28, 1970

21. H M Markowitz — 'Portfolio selection', *Journal of Finance,* Vol VII, 1952

22. P H Richards and A Contesse — 'Risk analysis in the North Sea', *The Investment Analyst,* No 41, 1975

23. R A Brealey — 'The impact of the market on British share prices', *The Investment Analyst,* No 24, 1969

24. S D Hodges and R A Brealey — 'Using the Sharpe model', *The Investment Analyst,* No 27, 1970

25. P H Richards — 'Dividend controls: fact or fancy?', *The Investment Analyst,* No 44, 1976

26. M A Firth — 'The incidence and impact of capitalisation issues', *Institute of Chartered Accountants in England and Wales Research Committee Occasional Paper,* No 3, 1974

27. M A Firth — 'An empirical investigation of the impact of the announcement of capitalisation issues on share prices', *Journal of Business Finance and Accounting,* Vol 4/1, 1977

28. R C Morris — 'Evidence of the impact of inflation accounting on share prices', *Accounting and Business Research,* spring 1975

29. M A Firth — 'The performance of share recommendations made by investment analysts and the effects on market efficiency', *Journal of Business Finance,* Vol 4, 1972

30. M A Firth — 'The information content of large investment holdings', *The Journal of Finance,* Vol XXX, 1975

31. M A Firth — 'The impact of earnings announcements on the share price behaviour of similar type firms', *The Economic Journal,* Vol 86, 1976

32. A Saunders and R S Woodward — 'Money supply and share prices: the evidence for the UK in the post-EEC period', *The Investment Analyst,* No 46, 1976

33. J R Franks, J E Broyles and M J Hecht — 'An industry study of the profitability of mergers in the United Kingdom', *The Journal of Finance,* Vol XXXII, 1977

34. M A Firth — *Share Prices and Mergers,* Saxon House, 1976

35. A J Merrett, M Howe and G D Newbould — *Equity Issues and the London Capital Market,* Longmans, 1967

36. P R Marsh — *An Analysis of Equity Rights Issues on the London Stock Exchange,* unpublished PhD thesis, London Business School, April 1977

37. M D Fitzgerald — 'A proposed characterisation of UK brokerage firms and their effects on market prices and returns', *European Finance Association 1974 Proceedings,* North Holland, 1975

38. Money Which? — Survey of unit trust performance in *Money Which?,* June 1974

39. J M Samuels — 'The performance of unit trusts', *The Bankers Magazine,* 1493, BPC (Bankers Magazine) Ltd, 1968

40. R W Rutherford — 'Ranking correlation of unit trust performance 1963-8', *The Investment Analyst,* No 25, 1969

41. T E Cranshaw — 'Do new unit trusts perform better than old ones?', *The Investment Analyst,* No 26, 1970

42. A Russell and B Taylor — 'Investment uncertainty and British equities', *The Investment Analyst,* No 22, 1968

43. G Briscoe, J M Samuels and D J Smythe — 'The treatment of risk in the stock market', *The Journal of Finance,* Vol XXIV 1969

44. M C Jensen — 'The performance of mutual funds in the period 1945-1964', *The Journal of Finance,* Vol XXIII 1968

45. J L Treynor — 'How to rate management of investment funds', *Harvard Business Review,* Vol 43, No 1, 1965

46. W F Sharpe — 'Mutual fund performance', *The Journal of Business,* Vol 39, 1966

47. R Roll — 'A critique of asset pricing theory's tests: part 1', *Journal of Financial Economics,* 4, 1977 pp129-176
'How the securities market line cannot distinguish superior assets (or portfolios) from inferior assets (or portfolios) ex-post or ex-ante', *Working Paper UCLA,* March 1977

'Testing a portfolio for ex-ante mean/variance efficiency', *Working Paper UCLA,* March 1977

48. J Dixon — *Composite Measures of Performance,* unpublished working paper, University of Exeter, Department of Economics, 1973

49. C Ward and A Saunders — 'UK unit trust performance 1964-74', *Journal of Business Finance and Accounting,* Vol 3/4, 1976

50. M A Firth — 'The investment performance of unit trusts in the period 1965-75', *Journal of Money, Credit and Banking,* November 1977

51. P Moles and B Taylor — 'Unit trust risk-return performance, 1966-75', *The Investment Analyst,* No 47, 1977

52. J P Holbrook — 'Investment performance of pension funds', *Journal of the Institute of Actuaries,* Vol 104 (Part 1), No 425, June 1977

53. Bacon and Woodrow — *Measurement of Investment Performance,* Reports for 1975 and 1976 and retrospective analysis, August 1976 and May 1977 respectively

54. P H Richards — 'Sharpe performance among pension funds?', *The Investment Analyst,* No 51, 1978

55. D Lessard — 'World, country and industrial relationships in equity returns', in *International Capital Markets,* edited by E J Elton and M J Gruber, North Holland, 1975

56. B H Solnik — 'Why not diversify internationally rather than domestically?' *Financial Analysts Journal,* July-August 1974

57. J Semah, C Serres and B Tessier — *L'ordinateur speculateur,* Dunod, 1970

58. A Galesne — 'Performances and validity of a filter strategy on the French stock market 1957-1971', *European Finance Association 1974 Proceedings,* North Holland 1975

59. K Conrad and D J Jüttner — 'Recent behaviour of stock market prices in Germany and the random walk hypothesis', *Kyklos,* No 3, 1973

60. J R F Guy — 'The behaviour of equity securities on the German stock exchange', *Journal of Banking and Finance,* 1, 1977

61. H Theil and C T Leenders — 'Tomorrow on the Amsterdam stock exchange', *Journal of Business,* July 1965

62. P Jennergren and P E Korsvold — 'The non-random character of Norwegian and Swedish stock market prices', in *International Capital Markets,* edited by E J Elton and M J Gruber, North Holland, 1975

63. P Jennergren — 'Filter tests of Swedish share prices', in *International*

	Capital Markets, edited by E J Elton and M J Gruber, North Holland, 1975
54. L Forsgårdh and K Hertzen	'The adjustment of stock prices to new earnings information' in *International Capital Markets,* edited by E J Elton and M J Gruber, North Holland, 1975
55. J A Palacios	'The stock market in Spain: tests of efficiency and capital market theory', in *International Capital Markets,* edited by E J Elton and M J Gruber, North Holland, 1975
56. J G McDonald	'French mutual fund performance: evaluation of internationally diversified portfolios', *The Journal of Finance,* Vol XXVIII, 1973

Author Index